LANDSLIDE

LANDSLIDE

*LBJ and Ronald Reagan at the
Dawn of a New America*

★ ★ ★

JONATHAN
DARMAN

RANDOM HOUSE

NEW YORK

Published in the United States by Random House, an imprint and
division of Random House LLC, a Penguin Random House Company, New York.

RANDOM HOUSE and the HOUSE colophon are registered
trademarks of Random House LLC.

LIBRARY OF CONGRESS CATALOGING-IN-PUBLICATION DATA
Darman, Jonathan.
Landslide : LBJ and Ronald Reagan at the dawn of a new America / Jonathan Darman.
pages   cm
Includes bibliographical references and index.
ISBN 978-1-4000-6708-4
eBook ISBN 978-0-8129-9469-8
1. Johnson, Lyndon B. (Lyndon Baines), 1908–1973—Political and social views.   2. Reagan,
Ronald—Political and social views.   3. United States—Politics and
government—1963–1969.   4. Liberalism—United States—History—20th
century.   5. Conservatism—United States—History—20th century.   6. Politics, Practical—
United States—History—20th century.   7. Political culture—United States—History—20th
century.   8. Social change—United States—History—20th century.   I. Title.
E846.D37 2014
320.097309'046—dc23
2013047619

Printed in the United States of America on acid-free paper

www.atrandom.com

2 4 6 8 9 7 5 3 1

First Edition

Book design by Victoria Wong

For Julie Granum

Contents

Prologue

Men on Horseback

There is but one way to get the cattle out of the swamp.
And that is for the man on the horse to take the lead.
—LYNDON JOHNSON

When he woke to great glory, he wanted even more. Midmorning on Wednesday, November 4, 1964, Lyndon Baines Johnson arose from his bed in the familiar surroundings of the LBJ Ranch. He had been president for eleven months. In that time, he had made frequent trips from Washington back to his home in the Texas Hill Country. The ranch offered familiar comforts he could not find in the White House: the live oaks that lined the verdant banks of the Pedernales River, the sprawling Hill Country vistas, and his herd of prized cattle that, as his Texas forebears had done, he would corral from on top of a horse.

And this particular trip home brought the greatest pleasure of all: a chance to vote for himself as president of the United States. It was a pleasure he had not known before. He had assumed the presidency on November 22, 1963, in an awful, frenzied moment: his Secret Service agent's knee in his back, his face pressed to the floor of a limousine speeding through the Dallas streets. It was surely the

© Bettmann/CORBIS

© Murray Garrett/
Getty Images

most ignominious ascent in the history of the office. After Kennedy's death, Johnson would later recall, the American people were "like a bunch of cattle caught in the swamp." He came from a line of ranchers; he knew what he had to do. "There is but one way to get the cattle out of the swamp," he said, "and that is for the man on the horse to take the lead."

He had led by example, executing his office with force and resolve and such unstoppable energy that no one would ever doubt that he was the president. But all along, he knew the difference. He had never *won* the presidency.

Until now. The previous day—Election Day—he had risen with the sun. With his wife, Lady Bird, he was third in line at the polling booth in Johnson City, Texas, casting a ballot for himself and his running mate, Hubert Humphrey. He'd spent the rest of the day nervously quizzing aides for any and all news from the various states. Then, just before seven o'clock that night, NBC News called it—it would be a Johnson victory over the Republican candidate, Barry Goldwater. The margin, the network predicted, would be astounding—something greater than 20 percent. Johnson did not yet know the exact tally, which would turn out to be 43,129,566 votes, 61 percent of the American electorate. And he had not yet heard all the columnists and commentators proclaiming the start of a long liberal era to come. But he knew the most important thing: he had won the White House with the largest portion of the popular vote of any president in American history.

A landslide. For a man like Lyndon Johnson—a man who had lived and breathed politics since childhood, a man whose greatest ambition was to earn approval from millions of people he would never meet—there was no greater triumph. Years later he would recall the sensation: "For the first time in all my life, I truly felt loved by the American people."

He spent that night toasting the returns with family, friends, and supporters at Austin's Driskill Hotel. As Tuesday night turned to Wednesday morning, he lingered with the well-wishers, drinking in their praise. When at last he closed his eyes back home at the ranch, it was nearly dawn.

Yet he woke up only a few hours later that Wednesday morning still unsatisfied. Through the night, he had nursed his private resentments. Goldwater, or "that son of a bitch," as Johnson referred to him that day, had never called to concede. Somehow it was fitting that the Arizona senator would bungle the most important custom in American democracy. He had bungled every other rule of modern presidential campaigns. He hadn't shown any interest in moderating his hard-line conservative stances after securing his party's nomination. He hadn't spent the fall campaign trying to win the favor of the voters in the American middle, the ones who decided elections. He hadn't shown much interest in winning the favor of any voters at all.

And at the end, when it was clear to everyone that he was finished, he hadn't picked up the phone to call Johnson. As the hour grew late on Election Day, long after it became obvious that the Goldwater campaign was over, the candidate's staff sent word that he was analyzing results and would have no further comment that night. In truth, he had simply gone to bed.

Therefore, despite the landslide of Tuesday night, it was not until Wednesday morning that Johnson's victory became official. He watched from his bedroom at the ranch as "that son of a bitch" read a telegram of concession on TV. And so, the morning after the election, Johnson was still hungry for the outpouring of praise and affection he believed he was due. To find it, he turned to another familiar comfort: the phone. In the days after the election, he reveled in the customary calls of congratulation from elected officials around the country. Chicago's mayor, Richard J. Daley, knew that Johnson would want to hear numbers. "By God, we said we would get you seven-fifty in Chicago, and it will be closer to eight fifty or nine hundred thousand." Daley, perhaps the most powerful and effective boss in the Democratic Party, was no bosom friend of LBJ's. Earlier that year, Johnson had obsessed over rumors that Daley was aiding a plot to steal the party's nomination from him and give it to

Johnson's nemesis, Bobby Kennedy, instead. But Daley knew what power looked like. On the phone with Johnson, he offered praise: "May the lord shower his blessings upon you and your family."

For some politicians, these ritualistic exchanges are exhausting and irritating. The endless, empty praise; the "send my love to your wife and give her a kiss for me"; the inflated flattery from "good friends" who would put a knife in your back if the circumstances required. For Johnson, the ritual was the whole point. He had spent his life in a business filled with champion fawners. Now it was time for them to fawn over him.

"Mr. President?" asked California governor Edmund "Pat" Brown, on the phone from the Golden State, ready to fawn away.

Johnson greeted him: "Well, you oughtta be a banker, Pat."

"A banker?" asked Brown. "Why?"

"Well," the president answered, "you're so damn conservative, you told me we'd carry it by over a million." He was talking about California, the largest state in the nation. "I think you beat it, didn't you?"

Like Daley, Brown had his numbers ready to go: "About a million four," the governor cooed.

"Well, why don't you go in the banking business?" said the president. "Go to lending money, a fellow that conservative . . ."

"You were great," Brown sputtered, "my God!"

Johnson had stepped on Brown's headline—the better-than-expected margin—leaving him stumbling for other morsels to present. So the governor dived into a more detailed report. He told Johnson that he had failed to carry only three California counties. He'd lost San Diego, the die-hard conservative stronghold, but that was no surprise. He'd lost Sutter County, but that was the smallest county in the state. And he'd lost Orange County, the mass of middle-class suburbs to the south of Los Angeles.

Brown knew that this last one was strange. Johnson had carried many heavily *Republican* counties across the country in the election. Yet in Orange County, registered Democrats and Republicans made up roughly equal portions of the electorate. Its voters were solid white-collar professionals, up-and-coming Americans who'd headed to the suburbs to live the good life. On paper, they looked exactly like all the other reasonable-minded middle-class Americans who had recoiled from Goldwater and given Johnson his landslide. "I'm already going to work," Brown assured the president. "I've got the Orange County publishers here for lunch, I'm going to find out what the hell's wrong. And I'll make a report to you the first time I see you."

But Johnson wasn't interested in hearing about Orange County. He wasn't interested in any of the counties he'd *lost*. "How many counties you got?" he asked.

"We've got fifty-eight counties and you won fifty-five."

That was more like it. "Oh," said Johnson. "That's wonderful."

Then he steered the conversation back to the pleasant interplay of solicitation and praise. They talked of a happy future, of the big things Johnson wanted to do with his huge majority in Congress. Already, Johnson's staff was developing plans for a great legislative push in the first hundred days of his new term. The president wanted bills providing massive funding for education, a health insurance program for the aged, and programs that would end poverty in America once and for all.

And that was just the beginning. In Congress, he had the most formidable progressive majority of any president in modern American history, and he intended to use it. By the end of his term, he wanted to fulfill the sweeping promises of the Great Society, his domestic program, securing a record that would make him as significant a progressive president as his personal hero, Franklin D. Roosevelt, and earn him a place of immortal greatness in American history.

He was ready to get to work. "You've got to help a lot," he told Brown, generously. "We'll do some plotting and planning as soon as we can get recuperated and get our marbles back."

Brown agreed. And he wanted to talk about his own future, too.

That future, everyone in politics seemed sure, was bright. He was about to start his seventh year as governor. He'd been a national star ever since his last race in 1962, when he'd defeated Richard Nixon, the former vice president of the United States. As governor of the nation's largest state, he had spearheaded projects in housing, education, and infrastructure that were of a piece with Johnson's grand ambitions for the country.

Already, he was on a short list of Democratic politicians who might succeed Johnson in the White House in the long liberal era to come. He wasn't particularly telegenic, he wasn't a naturally likable guy, but, well, neither was Lyndon Johnson, and look what the party and the people had given him. Brown could go far. To prove it, he was contemplating a run for the governorship in two years' time. It would be a historic achievement—no Democrat had ever won the California governor's mansion for three consecutive terms—but Brown was a heavy favorite. "We ought to talk about keeping this governorship," he told Johnson that day, "which I think is going to be key."

"I've already told you what I'm going to do about that," said Johnson. "My whole stack is in—money, marbles and chalk—with Brown."

Johnson was sincere that day when he promised Brown he would do whatever he could to help in the next election. But he didn't know, couldn't know, that day in November, just how much his world would change in two years' time. And he could never have imagined how much of his own legacy to the country would be shaped by the winner of Brown's governor's race.

One week before Brown and Johnson spoke on the phone, the week before the election, the actor Ronald Reagan appeared in a special prime-time broadcast on NBC. Reagan's was a well-known face. Older Americans remembered his brief career as a Hollywood heartthrob in the early 1940s, and millions of younger viewers knew him as the longtime host of the popular evening television program

General Electric Theater. In his eight years on the broadcast, he'd rested secure in the knowledge that he had the thing he wanted most: millions of eyes looking at his handsome face.

By the autumn of 1964, however, those eyes had moved on to someone else. *GE Theater* had been canceled two years earlier, a victim of shifting public taste. Since then Reagan had struggled to find work. He'd tried to make another run in films, but the jobs were few and far between. "You've been around this business long enough," the studio boss, Lew Wasserman, told him, "to know that I can't force someone on a producer if he doesn't want to use him."

The only place he was still reliably treated like a star was in the country's marginalized conservative movement. Politics had been a passion for Reagan since his youth. In the 1930s, he, too, had idolized FDR, listening closely and imitating the president as he delivered his Fireside Chats. But in the past decade, his passionate anticommunism had drawn him toward right-wing politics, where campaigns were happy to use a handsome movie actor as a public surrogate. In the last weeks of the Goldwater campaign, a group of wealthy California businessmen purchased national airtime to broadcast Reagan making the case for Goldwater in a speech.

He made for great TV, and his half-hour pitch probably did more for Goldwater than the GOP's entire yearlong campaign. Still, the title given to the speech—"A Time for Choosing"—was odd and even a little pathetic. No one thought Barry Goldwater had a chance of winning. For most voters that year, the time for choosing had long since passed. They were not going to choose Goldwater. If conservative politics was Reagan's path to stardom, it seemed he had better get used to a life of obscurity.

Reagan, too, spent time in that late fall of 1964 on his own ranch in the Santa Monica mountains, Yearling Row, where he raised thoroughbred horses, dashing hunters and jumpers with shiny coats and long sinewy legs. Leaning his flat back forward as he rode his mare over a jump, the handsome actor looked like a noble general or a hero of the Old West, the kind of parts he liked to play. But he was alone in the mountains and there was no one around to watch.

Soon, though, the title of Reagan's Goldwater speech would prove apt. For America in the mid-1960s, the time for choosing had only just begun. Only two years after his landslide, Johnson's dreams of immortal greatness would vanish for good. In the midterm election of 1966, American voters would deliver a powerful rebuke to Johnson at the ballot box. That year, Democrats lost a staggering forty-seven House seats. The Republicans, so recently written off for dead, won nine new governorships, three new Senate seats, and 557 seats in state legislatures nationwide.

Johnson's era of progressive reform was over, his power forever diminished. "In the space of a single Autumn day," *Newsweek* would write, "the 1,000 day reign of Lyndon I came to an end: The Emperor of American politics became just a president again."

And from California, there were signs of even greater troubles to come. Pat Brown had been right to dwell on those voters in Orange County. They, along with millions of white middle-class suburbanites like them across the country, would fuel a powerful national backlash against Johnson's party and policies. The mysterious citizens of Orange County voted for Brown's Republican opponent for governor by a three-to-one margin. And they worked, passionately, for that Republican candidate across the state that year, helping him to defeat Brown by nearly a million votes. Now this new Republican governor had a landslide of his own.

That new governor was Ronald Reagan, the man from B movies and *GE Theater*.

He had campaigned that year as a Western white knight, a "citizen-politician" riding down from his mountain retreat to save his state from the encroaching government and the corrupt men who ran it. He'd won the race not just by attacking Brown, but by attacking Johnson, too, detailing all the ways that the president's promises of liberal utopia had failed to come to pass. The movie star governor, with his movie star looks, had become a sensation in the national press. It was clear his rise was only beginning. As Reagan basked in his victory that November, some in the press wondered if he might just be the next president of the United States.

In just over a thousand days—the time between Johnson's ascent to the presidency in the wake of Kennedy's death and Reagan's election as governor of California—both men's lives were transformed. A president who had tried for immortality as a latter-day Franklin Roosevelt had watched his liberal majority collapse. An underemployed middle-aged actor with radical conservative views had become his party's future and the most exciting political story in the United States. Prophecies of a long liberal era in American politics had been cast aside. Now, instead, came the first signs of modern conservatism's rise to dominance in the decades to come. In those thousand days, Johnson and his party had learned a painful truth: the man who takes the highest spot after a landslide is not standing on solid ground.

What had really happened to America in those thousand days was bigger than any election—bigger than a party's legislative majority or a president's program or a charismatic conservative's rise to the top, bigger even than the formidable personalities of Reagan and Johnson and the surprising story of their reversal in fortunes.

In the course of those thousand days, America itself changed forever. In some important ways, it became a better version of itself. During those years, the nonviolent civil rights movement saw its greatest achievements. Its brave campaigns in the Deep South, along with the deaths of movement martyrs in Neshoba County, Mississippi, and Selma, Alabama, forced the country to face what for a hundred years it had ignored: the systematic use of violence to oppress and disenfranchise Southern blacks. In the Civil Rights Act of 1964 and the Voting Rights Act of 1965, Johnson broke the back of the Southern segregationist caucus on Capitol Hill once and for all and ensured the constitutional rights of all Americans, regardless of race. In March 1965, Johnson, the first president elected from the

South since the Civil War, spoke three words in the House chamber and changed the course of history: "We shall overcome."

With his mastery of the Congress, Johnson also managed to bring home the great progressive achievements a generation of Democrats had failed to deliver. He created programs to provide for the health of the elderly and the poor, and he secured massive federal funding for education of the nation's young. He had declared war on poverty and for a time convinced his country that that war could actually be won.

But there were darker changes, too. For most Americans at the beginning of the thousand days, Vietnam was a little-known country in a faraway corner of the world. A thousand days later, Vietnam was an American war with nearly four hundred thousand American troops on the ground and more soon to go. In the course of the thousand days, the Johnson administration made the fateful decision to "Americanize" the Vietnam conflict, despite Johnson's own doubts about whether the war could be won, locking in a policy that would end up costing fifty-eight thousand American lives.

At the beginning of the thousand days, intellectuals and urban planners had imagined utopian cities of the future in America where, with the help of good government, all citizens would share in productive, fulfilling lives. By the end, the cities Americans saw on their television screens were terrifying places—ghettos roiled by fire and looting, lawless deserts filled with people leading lives of despair.

Politics changed, too. Politicians discovered the political power of white rage and white racism, beyond the Democratic Party and beyond the Deep South. At the beginning of the thousand days, the party of Lincoln was an active partner with Northern liberals in legislative efforts to enhance civil rights. By the end of the thousand days, the Republican Party had begun to assemble a new coalition built in part on the resentment white voters felt toward African Americans and other minorities. That coalition would rule the country for several decades to come.

At the beginning of the thousand days, Americans had heralded the rapid changes coming to the world and looked toward the future with interest, excitement, and desire. But hope and fear are always closer than we think: both concern themselves with a world that is changing, a future that is unknown. After a thousand days and a series of traumas, a sense of foreboding and danger that had long lurked under the comfortable optimism of affluence emerged to dominate the national mood.

And perhaps the most enduring change was the one that was hardest to see until long after the thousand days had come and gone: how in that moment of taut anxiety, fantasy took hold of American political life. When the thousand days began, America was still ruled by the same consensus politics that both parties had used to govern since the time of Franklin Roosevelt and the New Deal. That consensus was optimistic in intent. The parties' leaders agreed that the complexities of modern life required an active federal government that provided its citizens with protection from the ruthlessness of the free market; an enlightened government that sought to improve the quality of American life. But the consensus was also deeply realistic; even presidents like Roosevelt and John F. Kennedy, who had great ambitions for government, took for granted that change was slow and that the future was impossible to predict.

By the end of the thousand days, the consensus was forever fractured and the tradition of realism and humility in mainstream politics was gone.

In its place was a new kind of politics in which voters chose between two fantasies of the American future, two myths in which the federal government could only be America's salvation or America's ruin. These two myths were born from opposite ideologies, but they promised the same thing: an America where all problems could be conquered and *would* be conquered soon. Both visions would inspire millions of Americans in the 1960s and in generations to come. But they would also divide and coarsen the country. Over time, the gap between fantasy and reality would grow and grow, leaving government in a state of dysfunction and paralysis.

The myths endured long past the anxious aftermath of the Kennedy assassination, long past the 1960s, in large part thanks to the two ambitious men who shaped them: Johnson and Reagan. In the course of the thousand days, Johnson and Reagan each captured the nation's attention by confidently offering a story of America and the path it needed to follow. The stories they told were powerful and compelling ones, and Johnson and Reagan each used his story to accomplish big things. They were inspired to make these myths for the nation by the same force: their shared need to be the hero, the man who led the way.

Their fantastic visions have outlived them both, shaping our politics to this day. And over time these visions have made it harder for Johnson's and Reagan's heirs in government to see the world as it really is, harder for us to see what is real. Today, their lingering myths make the country hard to govern at all. This is the story of the thousand frenzied days in which American politics began its lurch toward fantasy, leaving reality behind. It is the story of a brief, defining moment when the modern era's iconic liberal and conservative presidents shared the national spotlight, when these two men seized the opportunity to resurrect their careers and play the part of hero. And it is the story of how, in a moment of profound uncertainty, America's politics began to fracture.

LOOKING BACK ON the twentieth century, Lyndon Johnson and Ronald Reagan appear as citizens of two distinct ages, men of destiny for two very different times.

Johnson took the oath of office inside a cramped, sweltering airplane cabin at Dallas's Love Field on November 22, 1963. His most pressing task was to calm and reassure a nation reeling after the sudden death of its president—and to take charge with a new story of American renewal.

Grabbing hold of the optimistic, utopian spirit of his age, Johnson spoke of a future of unlimited possibility in which government would solve the great problems of American life—poverty and discrimination, hunger and disease. Not only that, he promised that if the country adopted his Great Society domestic program, this near-perfect future would be at hand. "It's the time of peace on Earth and good will among men," he declared in a speech a few days before his landslide election in 1964. "The place is here and the time is now!"

Johnson's confident promises echoed the utopian visions of progressive intellectuals in the early sixties. To them, the nation's unprecedented economic affluence, combined with breakthroughs in medical and social science, meant that no problem was beyond the capabilities of rational, competent government.

Johnson's countrymen thrilled to this fantastic vision and believed it would soon come to pass. After all, they thought, why shouldn't it? People living in postwar America were experiencing prosperity previously unknown by citizens of any country in the history of the world. In the last three decades, their government had brought its people back from the ravages of economic depression, reorganized the nation's economy three times, transformed its infrastructure with new highways, bridges, tunnels, and dams, and defeated the greatest force of tyranny the world had ever known. After the Second World War, the country had assumed a position of global preeminence from which it guaranteed the security of nearly half the world. Why shouldn't such a great nation be able to ensure prosperity for its citizens for all time? As many as 1.2 million people—a record—stood on the National Mall to watch Johnson take the oath of office after his landslide victory. "Is our world gone?" Johnson asked in his inaugural address. "We say 'Farewell.' Is a new world coming? We welcome it—and we will bend it to the hopes of man."

That was January 20, 1965—the midway point of the 1960s, that electric and anguished decade. The organizers of the festivities recorded Johnson's optimism on the front of the inauguration program: "All that has happened in our historic past is but a prelude to the Great Society." What they did not know was that Lyndon Johnson's brightest promises usually hinted at a lifelong split within him, his tendency to see only two possibilities in any endeavor: total, transformative victory or utter, disastrous defeat. He made his promises all the more extravagant when trying to will away his fears of catastrophe. And Americans listening to Johnson speak that day had not yet learned the central lesson of the sixties: history never turns out exactly the way we think it's going to.

For indeed, when Reagan took the oath of office at his own inauguration sixteen years later, the mood of the country had sharply changed. The intervening years had been a time of war, division, disappointment, and fear. Americans had witnessed some of the lasting social progress Johnson promised—the great legislative achievements of the civil rights movement and the end of racial apartheid in the South along with the rise of the women's movement and the sexual revolution—but they had also lived through hard years marked by crisis, scandal, and decline. Overseas, they had seen their country's image of invincibility marred forever—many could still recall the image of an American helicopter hurtling desperately away from the U.S. embassy in Saigon. At home, they had seen the decay of American cities, the gloomy end of the postwar boom, and the rise of economic stagnation and inflation. Their faith in democratic institutions had been shaken by a series of political assassinations and assassination attempts. Their faith in democratic leaders had been damaged by the lies of Vietnam and Watergate. Those sixteen years had been long ones—years that changed America and diminished Americans' expectations of what their government could do.

And so when Reagan took the oath that day in 1981 after winning the presidency in a landslide of his own, the country thrilled to his vision, too, a vision that was essentially the opposite of the one Johnson had offered two decades before. Reagan, too, offered an idealized image of America's future—one in which the nation's problems could at last be solved and its promise could be renewed. "We have every right," Reagan said in his inaugural address, "to dream heroic dreams." But the way to achieve those dreams was the opposite of the path Johnson imagined: limit the power of government so that the creative potential of American individuals could be unleashed. "In this present crisis, government is not the solution to our problem," he said. "Government *is* the problem."

Through the long telescope of history, then, the ground between Reagan and Johnson appears vast, the distance between two opposite visions from two opposite moments in time. And it is the distance, as well, between two opposite types of men. It is hard to think of two presidents in modern history, after all, who approached the office more differently than Reagan and Johnson. Johnson was among the most hyperactive executives the White House had ever seen, always seeking to put his fingerprints on every last scrap of administration business no matter how large or small. Early in the Johnson presidency, James B. Reston, the Washington correspondent for *The New York Times,* worried over the punishing regime the president was observing in the White House. Johnson, wrote the columnist, "has three telephones in his car, with five circuits, and the amazing thing about it is that he seems able to talk on all five at once, carry on a conversation in the back seat, and direct traffic on the side." In his short time as president, Reston wrote, Johnson "had done everything but cut the White House lawn."

This was hyperbole, but not by much. Like both John F. Kennedy and Richard M. Nixon, his predecessor and his successor, Johnson secretly recorded many of his White House telephone conversations. (The recordings of Johnson's conversations were released to the public in the 1990s and are a key source for this narrative.) His conversations reveal a president who insisted on personally selecting and approving everything—the locations of bombing targets in Vietnam, the line items in billion-dollar spending bills, the hairstyles of the secretaries sitting outside his door. He wanted to be involved in all of it. Learning that a White House aide failed to wake him in the night to inform him of an administration defeat on Capitol Hill, Johnson was upset. "When you're bleeding up on that Hill," the president explained, "I want to bleed with you."

That would never be Reagan—an actor learns early the benefits of a good night's sleep. From his earliest days in politics, Reagan was supremely confident in his own abilities as an executive. He had come to prominence in a career in which he constantly had to *give up* control—to producers and directors and studio bosses, to makeup designers and camera operators and press agents, to critics and millions of anonymous strangers who would form consequential opinions of him as they watched on distant screens. When he began his political career in the mid-1960s, he took to the disaggregated life of a political candidate quickly. Most first-time candidates struggle to adapt to an existence in which they must surrender control of their lives to other people. Reagan had been doing it for years. He understood an important distinction that Johnson never grasped: being in control and being successful aren't always the same thing.

And so, as president, Reagan often seemed only vaguely aware of the pressing business of his own administration. Americans grew accustomed to a leader who liked naps and long vacations and days spent ambling on horseback on his mountain ranch above the Pacific. His aides worried at times over the cumulative effect in the press that he appeared too detached from decision making, too much a figurehead. They wondered if they ought to brief reporters on the more punishing aspects of the president's working regime. Reagan advised them to keep quiet; in the long run, it was always better to appear above it all. Like Johnson, he was a rancher, but he stayed out of the swampy muck.

Each was a gifted performer and raconteur who could captivate an audience. But they excelled in different settings. Johnson was best in person. He was overwhelming, always, and his conversations hummed with transactional momentum. He told involved and engaging Texas tall tales, but he usually told them in order to drive home a pertinent point. He made use of his large girth and six-foot-three-inch frame. All the clichéd metaphors of politics—glad-handing, buttonholing, back stroking, arm twisting—were things Johnson actually, physically did in order to get his way. His greatest asset was his intuitive sensitivity to human emotion, his unmatched ability to spot people's highest ambitions and their darkest fears. Even Alabama governor George Wallace, one of the twentieth century's most notorious racial demagogues, found himself mesmerized by an impassioned Oval Office conference with Johnson in the midst of a tense 1965 standoff over racial protests in Wallace's home state. "Hell," said Wallace afterward, "if I'd stayed in there much longer, he'd have had me coming out for civil rights."

A conversation with Reagan, on the other hand, was usually pleasant and entirely superficial. In his early days as a politician, supporters would often walk away from first encounters with candidate Reagan disappointed. He'd told funny jokes, they'd laughed heartily, they'd had a ball. But they couldn't remember much if any *substance* to what he'd said. The problem wasn't that Reagan was an empty suit; rather, he struggled to connect with people when they came too close. Even his own children encountered a fog in their father's eyes when they greeted him in a room. He was friendly, but he gave the impression that he was meeting them for the first time.

He was better with an audience watching him. Better still if they were watching him on a television screen from the comfort of their own homes. In these moments, he was great. He launched his 1966 campaign for governor with a thirty-minute television advertisement in which he pensively strolled around a comfortable living room. It was all so wonderfully familiar and authentic. There were pictures on the wall and a fire in the fireplace; Reagan's sharp, pithy summation of California's and the nation's problems seemed to come to him spontaneously, a kindly father figure opining on issues of the day. None of it was real—the sentences were scripted and the living room was a studio set. But Californians didn't mind; they were starting to expect their politicians to be great performers on TV.

Television was taking over politics in the midsixties. Anyone who'd lived through the Kennedy years could see that. Johnson could see it, and he worked tirelessly to adapt, but never with much success. As president, he obsessed over his televised press conferences, bringing in a shifting cast of experts for coaching on his diction, his posture, his eyewear. But his problem was fundamental: performing for a TV camera, he could never do what he did in person, he couldn't see his audience and adapt his personality accordingly. And that introduced a terrifying possibility: that the people watching would see him as himself.

Johnson and Reagan, then, were both stars, but stars of different eras. It is difficult to fit them inside a single picture—when the mind focuses on one of them, the other becomes a blur. Even in the lore of practical politics, where both have assumed vaunted status in recent years, they inhabit separate realms. Reagan is the president that politicians from both parties publicly say they admire—principled, noble, and strong. But Johnson is the president they secretly long to be—ruthless, effective, a man who got big things done.

Yet when we look at Reagan and Johnson as actual human beings, we are left with an odd set of facts. These two heroes of opposite eras were born less than three years apart. They both came of age in the early decades of the twentieth century and were shaped by the same events. Both lived through the Great Depression and served in World War II; both saw the rise of the Cold War and shrewdly maneuvered in their respective fields through the havoc of the McCarthy era. The Reagan who took the oath of office in 1981 was not a young man; he was two weeks shy of his seventieth birthday. And he was not new to presidential politics—he had been running for the office for the better part of two decades. In fact, he'd had his eye on the White House ever since the midsixties, when he'd dreamed of dislodging its occupant: Lyndon Johnson.

And the vision Reagan articulated in his inaugural address was, in fact, a vision born in the midsixties, a vision made possible by the Johnson years. The ideas he articulated—virulent anticommunism abroad, freeing the individual from the shackles of the state at home—were not new. They had been guiding principles of the right since the Roosevelt administration; they were the ideas Goldwater ran on in 1964. But for a long time, those ideas had been too fantastic and ridiculous for the mainstream. To most Americans, it was self-evident that a modern state facing the complex problems of the modern world needed a robust national government to guide it through.

But as Johnson's promises for America's utopian future moved into the realm of fantasy, the fantasies of limited government on the radical right suddenly became legitimate, too. Reagan, whose career had given him a healthy respect for the mercurial nature of public mood, waited for the right moment—when public trust in Johnson's promises first began to falter—to unleash his own competing myth. Johnson promised that his government would soon deliver the nation from all troubles, but the nation grew more troubled by the day. Only then did the conservative case against government begin to seem not so crazy after all. Or, at least, no more crazy than the other side. Once the formerly reasonable people took their rhetoric into a new realm of fantasy, politics became about choosing: which fantasy sounded best?

Is a new world coming? We welcome it and we will bend it to the hopes of man.

Government is not the solution to our problem. Government is the problem.

Reagan and Johnson were speaking in different eras. But they were speaking to each other.

Both were telling stories of America and its future. In these stories, the country was facing a historic moment of choice, the consequences of which would be felt for generations. The stakes were high: "Abundance or annihilation," said Johnson at the dedication of the 1964 World's Fair, "development or desolation, that is in your hands." Later that same year, Reagan gave his "Time for Choosing" speech: "We'll preserve for our children this, the last best hope of man on earth, or we'll sentence them to take the last step into a thousand years of darkness."

Yet while the consequences of making the wrong choice were severe, to Johnson and Reagan, the right and wrong paths were clear.

And each man assured Americans that all they had to do was choose the right path—his path—and they would be delivered from harm, ready for their future of ecstatic possibility. They were confident that the country would make the right choice. After all, there would be someone there to guide them.

That was what drove them to tell their stories in the first place; each man needed a story in which he could play the hero's part. For despite all their differences, Reagan and Johnson were at heart driven by the same fundamental need: to be the hero and receive the world's admiration and acclaim. One was a rancher down in the muck, the other was a cowboy riding along the ridge. But at the end of the day, each of them was a man on horseback, commanding the attention of the world.

That driving need shaped both of their lives. It propelled them up from lonely childhoods in obscure regions of the country and compelled them to work harder than all their peers. In both of them, it was a need born early, nursed by the love of ambitious, adoring mothers. As they grew older, it was shaped by the cautionary example of their fathers, Jack Reagan and Sam Ealey Johnson, Jr., two men who had also had dreams of being a hero but who had instead chosen paths that led to ruin and disgrace.

As young adults, their shared need brought them both acclaim and attention. "Heady wine," Reagan called it, and Johnson would have known exactly what he meant—it tasted so sweet. Each found successively larger stages so that by their late twenties, Johnson and Reagan had become, respectively, a United States congressman and a Hollywood actor with a million-dollar studio contract. Settled in their businesses' respective capitals on opposite coasts, each spent much of the next two decades in his rightful place, as one of the most recognizable men in town.

Then, sometime in middle age, the wine dried up and the eyes of the world drifted away, leaving Reagan and Johnson each to contemplate the same future, one in which his purpose for living was gone.

That was the future that lay ahead of both of them the day that

John F. Kennedy went to Dallas. On November 22, 1963, when the story of their thousand days begins, Reagan and Johnson were both well into middle age and far from the limelight. Reagan was working on a troubled movie set, playing the part of a cuckolded gangster in a dark, violent drama—the kind of work he hated but the only work he could get. Johnson was wasting away in the miserable obscurity of the vice presidency. Excluded from the circles of influence, a figure of ridicule in the capital he had once ruled, he had descended into deep depression, convinced he would never hold real power again.

Then shots rang out from the Texas School Book Depository in Dallas's Dealey Plaza and everything changed. The sudden, shocking death of President Kennedy left the nation stunned and uncertain how to go on. Americans needed a story to believe in. In the thousand days that followed, Johnson and Reagan would each seize the chance to offer a new way forward. It was a risky proposition—in mythology, a hero who seeks greatness must tempt fate and the wrath of the gods. For Johnson, the bill would come due even before the thousand days were up. Still, it was an opportunity each of them would die to take. For each of them it was one last chance at greatness. One last chance to be the man on the horse.

PART I

★ ★ ★

Shadows

"A sad time for all people": Lyndon B. Johnson addresses
the nation from Andrews Air Force Base while his wife,
Lady Bird, looks on, November 22, 1963.
© AP Photo

CHAPTER ONE

Stories

November 23, 1963

At the beginning, the worst part is the uncertainty. Later, after the mourning dignitaries have come and gone, after the black crape has been taken down from the chandeliers and the funeral geldings have been put out to pasture, people will remember this weekend as a time of great sadness. For years and then decades, they'll look back and remember their sorrow. They'll say they knew, instantly, that life would never be the same again. But that will be memory doing memory's ruthless work, obliterating any discordant details, imposing order where once there was none. In these first hours, there is sadness, but mostly there is chaos and the dreadful unknown: What has happened to America? And what is going to happen next?

So everyone turns on their television sets, hoping to find out. On NBC's *Today* show, the clocks on a wall are comfortingly definitive. On the East Coast, it is just after seven o'clock in the morning. The date is November 23, 1963. Millions of Americans are waking up after a night of troubled sleep. Watching the program, they see the host's face contort in sudden pain as he speaks the words:

"The president of the United States is dead."

Ah, yes, that is certain, too.

By now there are agreed-upon facts: At lunchtime the previous day, President John F. Kennedy, on a political trip to Texas, rode in an open limousine toward the center of Dallas. At 12:30 Central Time, shots struck his motorcade as it moved through the city's Dealey Plaza. By 12:45 P.M., CBS, NBC, and ABC had interrupted their programming to bring word of the shooting. At 1:35 P.M., the network Teletypes carried a wire from UPI: "Flash: President Kennedy Dead." Now, nearly eighteen hours after the shooting, it is impossible to find an American who does not already know the news the host has just delivered—that the president of the United States is dead.

Still, he says it. It is the first line in a script he must read, timed to a movie montage with carefully selected background music. It is the starting point of an elaborate story he is about to tell, the summary of what is known.

He goes on:

"The body of John Fitzgerald Kennedy is at this moment in the White House. And it is a much saddened nation and world that greets this day . . ."

The screen switches to scenes from the day. There is the dead president at Dallas's Love Field, very much alive, gracefully descending from Air Force One. And there is his beautiful wife, Jacqueline, wearing a pink suit and a pillbox hat, brushing the hair out of her face. He smiles and nods at local dignitaries on the tarmac. She clutches a bouquet of red roses to her breast. They climb into an open-topped limousine.

"At about 12:30 the motorcade turned the corner and approached the triple underpass feeding the Stemons expressway . . ."

The smiling Kennedys turn a corner and disappear from view.

". . . and then three shots rang out in quick succession and the pleasant day turned into a nightmare of confusion and horror."

The camera jolts and drops to the ground. The narration goes silent and the music is gone.

"The president died at about one P.M. . . . Meanwhile Dallas police had captured twenty-four-year-old Lee Oswald, an acknowledged left-wing supporter of Fidel Castro . . ."

*"He was later charged with the murder of the president . . . he
has thus far admitted nothing."*

Then a quick cut. Now, onscreen, we see a blurry shot of two
large airplane tails, parked on a runway, behind a high fence.

*"Vice President Lyndon Johnson recited the oath of office and
assumed the presidency . . ."*

But we do not see the oath taking. We do not see any pictures of
Johnson. All we see is more of the airplane tails and the fence.

*"At 6:05 Eastern Time, the presidential plane landed at Andrews
Air Force Base in Washington. The bronze coffin carrying the thirty-
fifth president was taken from it and loaded into a Navy ambulance."*

Onscreen it is now nighttime on another tarmac. From the back
of the airplane, Air Force One, we see men emerge, carrying a coffin.

*"Then, a still blood-spattered Mrs. Kennedy was taken down.
She seemed still in a state of shock as she was taken to the ambulance."*

A solid mass of men in uniforms and dark suits parts for Jacqueline Kennedy. She does look dazed, but also regal and poised.
The shot lingers on her, beautiful and tragic, as she waits to get
into the ambulance. The narration has stopped again, as if out of
respect.

Then there is a quick, disorienting cut to a far less pretty picture.
On a nondescript slab of concrete, Kennedy's vice president stands
with his wife. He looks tired and old.

*"A few minutes later, the waiting crowd and the nation at large
heard their new president, Lyndon Johnson."*

Johnson seems confused. Before speaking he looks to both sides
and then down at his notes, exposing a balding head. He is speaking
but we can't hear him, there is too much background noise. We hear
principally the roar of airplane engines. Only when they deign to
pause can we catch Johnson, midsentence—

". . . time for all people."

The shot switches to a wider camera angle. At the greater distance, he is hard to make out—there is a glare off his glasses, and the camera picks up only dark circles where his eyes should be.

"For me it is a deep personal tragedy . . ."

An anonymous figure walks into the shot just behind Johnson, as though unaware he is even there.

"I will do my best. It is all I can do. I ask for your help. And God's."

Finally, the roaring airplanes have their way and the camera cuts away from this lonely old man.

Then the narration picks up again:

"It was about 4:30 this morning when President John Fitzgerald Kennedy was returned to the White House."

Now words and image and music are once again aligned. In place of the unsettled tarmac scene, we have a splendid tableau—a hearse approaching the north entrance of the White House, led by an honor guard, the great house lit up with lanterns, the president coming home.

It is a short but compelling montage, and Americans will watch it again and again this day. Broadcasters have suspended regular programming and advertising. Every second of airtime across three networks belongs to the news divisions.

This is how it works in America this weekend—the normal rituals and routines have been thrown out. Outside the NBC studios, midtown Manhattan, America's mass media capital, has been transformed by the events of the past twenty-four hours. The department stores have taken down their Christmas decorations and replaced them with black mourning scenes. From St. Patrick's Cathedral, the sound of an organ playing "The Star-Spangled Banner" slips out onto the street. Most theaters, movie houses, and restaurants in the city have closed their doors. The Stork Club, a hub of café society, stays open but is mostly empty. "The people here . . . are like the people out on Christmas Eve," the headwaiter explains. "They have no home."

The balance between cause and effect seems off, reason itself suspended. Kennedy had led the West and harnessed the most terrible arsenal of weapons ever known to man. Now he has been shot down by an anonymous madman who stored his rifle in a suburban garage. Kennedy had invited the nation to join him on a thrilling journey toward the future. Now he has become the past.

No one seems to be in charge. The president is dead. His successor is out of sight. Only a single White House photographer, snapping pictures in a hurry, has captured his swearing in. For a while, the phones in Washington don't even work.

Americans need to look for authority somewhere new. They know where to find it. Most turned on the television the moment they heard what happened in Dallas and they haven't turned it off since. On average this weekend, American households will watch 8.5 hours of television each day. Everyone is looking to the people on their screen for answers. NBC's David Brinkley calls the White House to see if staffers there have any news. "No," comes the reply, "we were watching you to see if you had any."

For the networks, this new authority is a daunting challenge. There are still few hard facts from Dallas, a meager diet for so many hours of airtime. TV programmers experiment with other ways to fill the time—broadcasts of memorial concerts or prayer vigils—but viewers at home aren't interested. They prefer news, even the same, sad facts, even if they've heard them before. The repetition is comforting. TV anchors that weekend, one viewer will later write to NBC's Chet Huntley, are like "old friends . . . telling us about the tragedy until we could absorb it."

So that's what the anchors do: tell the country what they know, over and over again. This morning, NBC will replay the same montage, with the same background music, the same pictures, and roughly the same script, at least once every half hour.

This Saturday morning, when everything is uncertain, this is one thing Americans have. They do not have their president, they do not have normal life, they do not have faith that everything will be okay. All they have for certain is a story:

The president went to Dallas on a bright autumn day.

There, a madman shot and killed him.

He returned to his capital in a coffin.

In her agony, his widow has shown unimaginable strength.

The vice president has recited the oath of office and assumed the
    presidency.

But that isn't the point of the story. The point of the story is the
first thing the news host told them, the one thing everyone knows for
sure: the president of the United States is dead.

AT 8:40 THAT Saturday morning, two iron gates opened outside an
imposing gray mansion in the Spring Valley section of Washington.
A black limousine slid down a driveway scattered with dead leaves.
Under police escort, the car turned south and sped swiftly through
the capital's near-deserted streets. Lyndon Baines Johnson, the living president of the United States, was en route to the White House.

Most Americans did not witness this procession. The networks
had sent crews to stand outside the Johnson family home, where
Johnson had spent the night after returning from Dallas. Earlier in
the hour, a host had promised *Today*'s viewers that the program
would show the new president leaving his home for the White House.
But when the gates opened, NBC was in the midst of its montage,
and the program's producers chose to stick with their scripted story.
By the time it was over, Johnson's car had disappeared.

A day earlier, the man inside the limousine had been the vice
president, touring his home state of Texas with Kennedy. He and his
wife, Lady Bird, had planned to host the Kennedys at their ranch in
the Hill Country, west of Austin, that Saturday morning. To think of
the things they'd been worried about just a day earlier—which cham-
pagne and cigarettes to procure for Mrs. Kennedy; how to accommodate the special plywood and horsehair mattress favored by the
commander in chief.

How quickly it had all changed. The Johnsons had been riding several cars behind the Kennedys as the presidential motorcade made its way through Dallas. They were waving at the crowds when they heard a loud explosion. As the smell of gunpowder filled the air, Johnson looked up and saw a body hurtling toward him. It was Rufus Youngblood, the Secret Service agent charged with protecting the vice president's life. Youngblood ordered Johnson to get down and the vice president obeyed, pressing his face to the floor. Another shot echoed through Dealey Plaza. Johnson wouldn't know it for another hour, but in that moment, John Fitzgerald Kennedy's life ended. As he stared at the floor of the limousine and felt the weight of Youngblood digging into his back, Lyndon Johnson became the thirty-sixth president of the United States.

For a moment, all was silent, and then a ghostly voice came over the Secret Service radio: "Let's get out of here." The limousines careened through the streets of Dallas until at last they reached Parkland Hospital. There, doctors worked over Kennedy's body, still trying to save his life, but Jacqueline Kennedy, looking on, knew that these efforts were in vain. Her pink suit was covered in her husband's blood and brain tissue, and she had held a piece of his skull in her hand. "They've killed him," she had repeated over and over again.

At the instruction of his security detail, Johnson took shelter in a warren of inner offices away from the operating table, where he and Lady Bird huddled and waited for news. Johnson stood six feet three inches, weighed more than two hundred pounds, and was, by long reputation, one of the most willful and powerful men Washington had ever seen. But under Parkland's harsh lights, he was strangely passive, almost childlike, complying with Secret Service orders, refusing to make any decisions, asking repeatedly for direction from Kennedy's staff. Finally came Kennedy's stricken assistant, Kenneth O'Donnell, with the news: "He's gone."

He was President Johnson now. All his adult life, Johnson had striven for the presidency—worked for it, obsessed over it, longed for it above all else. He had sought his party's nomination twice—unofficially but aggressively in 1956, officially and even more aggressively in 1960—but never managed to win it. The failure was the great disappointment of his life. Now, at last, it had happened—he had secured the office, but in a manner such as this.

The Secret Service was anxious to get him out of Texas, unsure what danger remained. Johnson needed little convincing. He worried that Kennedy's assassination might be the first step in a Communist plot that could also include his own murder and possibly even nuclear war. Hunkered down in the security of Air Force One, he waited at Love Field long enough to collect Kennedy's widow and to see the dead president's coffin loaded into the rear of the plane. And, at his insistence, he recited the oath of office before the five-hour flight back to Washington. But no sooner had he spoken the words "so help me God" than he ordered the plane into the sky.

Greeted at Andrews Air Force Base outside Washington by Defense Secretary Robert McNamara and National Security Advisor McGeorge Bundy, he'd asked for any news of further crisis in the world. There was none, no wider threat. Still, when, well after midnight, he finally climbed into his own bed, he asked several aides to stay with him. In the darkness, he made sure they understood: They were not to leave him alone.

Now, though, it was morning, and the fear was beginning to pass. He'd seen what they were broadcasting on television and sensed the crisis of authority. Americans, he would later say, "were all spinning around and around, trying to come to grips with what had happened . . . like a bunch of cattle caught in the swamp." He knew what was required: "There is but one way to get the cattle out of the swamp. . . . And that is for the man on the horse to take the lead, to assume command, to provide direction."

He knew he could provide it. For things to feel certain again, America needed a different story. Not the story of John F. Kennedy's life or the story of his death. It needed a new story with a new hero. And he was the one to give that story to the country. That was what he'd always wanted, to be the nation's hero. He knew this was his best chance, and his last.

ALL HIS LIFE, Johnson had longed to be the central figure in a great drama. He came from a line of men who were expected to make their mark, and did. Lyndon Baines Johnson was born in 1908 in a remote farmhouse on the Pedernales River, not far from the town of Johnson City, named for his frontier forebears. Family lore had it that these forebears had settled that part of the Texas Hill Country through great feats of courage—fighting off hostile Indians, starving through droughts, stamping out prairie fires. Through the generations, their offspring gained a strong dose of self-assurance. "Hell," said a contemporary of Sam Ealy Johnson, Lyndon's father, "the Johnsons could strut sitting down."

From his earliest days, young Lyndon was encouraged to think of himself as the natural heir to these men. In 1965, his mother, Rebekah Baines Johnson, published *A Family Album,* a history of the Baines and Johnson families. Her description of her son's birth went as follows: "Now the light came in from the East, bringing a stillness so profound and so pervasive that it seemed as if the earth itself were listening. And then there came a sharp, compelling cry—the most awesome, happiest sound known to human ears—the cry of a newborn baby; the first child of Sam Ealy and Rebekah Baines Johnson was 'discovering America.'"

A child raised by such a mother was clearly also discovering what the warm glow of adoring eyes upon him felt like; by the time he could walk and talk, he was determined to get as much of that feeling as he could. And from the men in his family, he saw how. Both of his grandfathers were Texas politicians—one was a state legislator and a Texas secretary of state. His father, Sam Jr., served in the Texas legislature, where he passionately fought for policies to improve and transform the life of the forgotten little people in the isolated backcountry. In his early years, Lyndon would watch with wonder as his father, the politician, would enter and conquer a room, turning every eye toward him. Politics, young Lyndon understood, was power, and with power came respect, admiration, even love. He knew it could all be his. On the day of his birth, the family story had it, his grandfather had ridden a horse through the Hill Country, shouting: "A United States Senator was born today!"

Soon, the future senator was demanding the world's attention wherever he went. As a boy of only five or six years, at the Hill Country's Junction School, Johnson refused to read unless he was at the very front of the room, sitting in his teacher's lap, with all of his classmates looking on. In *The Path to Power*, the first of his definitive volumes on the life of Lyndon Johnson, the historian Robert Caro describes that young student in "Miss Kate" Deadrich's Junction School class: "When Miss Kate excused one of her students to use the privy out back, the student had to write his name on one of the two blackboards that flanked the back door. The other students wrote their names small; whenever Lyndon left the room, he would reach up as high as he could and scrawl his name in capital letters so huge that they took up not one but both blackboards. His schoolmates can remember today—seventy years later—that huge LYNDON B. on the left blackboard and JOHNSON on the right."

He did not grow subtler with age. In August 1934, just shy of his twenty-sixth birthday, Johnson met a recent graduate of the University of Texas, Claudia Alta "Lady Bird" Taylor, and was certain he had found his future wife. On their first official date, Lady Bird would later say, "he told me all sorts of things that I thought were extraordinarily direct for a first conversation . . . about how many years he had been teaching, his salary as a secretary to a Congressman, his ambitions, even about all the members of his family, and how much insurance he carried." The date turned into a four-day visit to the Johnson family ranch, an interview with his mother, even a trip to the Johnson family cemetery. The goal, Johnson later said, was "to keep her mind completely on me." It paid off. In two months' time, Lyndon and Lady Bird Taylor were married.

And it paid off in Washington, where Johnson labored hard—as hard as the old-timers had ever seen a man work—to keep *every-one's* mind completely on him. Even in a town of strivers, Johnson's string of prodigious successes was legendary: as a twenty-three-year-old clerk to a Texas congressman, he joined the fraternity of congressional aides known as the "Little Congress" and quickly became the group's "boss." Then he himself was elected to the real Congress from Texas's Tenth District at the age of twenty-eight. He was such an audibly enthusiastic New Dealer, he earned the favor of President Franklin D. Roosevelt, who let a thirty-two-year-old Johnson announce his campaign for a Texas Senate seat from the White House lawn. He lost that race, but he won seven years later in 1948, when he beat a beloved former governor, Coke Stevenson, by a margin of 87 votes in the Democratic primary. (This victory earned him the nickname "Landslide Lyndon.") And then, incredibly, just four years later, his colleagues voted him in to the position that would define his life: Democratic leader in the United States Senate.

The Senate was not, by most lights, the right place for a young man who longed to make his name quickly. By custom, senators shunned the use of first and last names in favor of "the senator from Texas" or, better yet, "the distinguished junior senator from Texas." But the upper chamber of Congress was the perfect setting for the grand story of Lyndon Johnson. It was, Johnson said on arrival, "the right size"—small enough, with only a hundred members, for Johnson to know each member personally, to watch a man at close enough range to see the opportunities he presented—and the dangers. Johnson triumphed in the Senate, Caro writes in his third volume, *Master of the Senate*, by practicing his "genius for studying a man and learning his strengths and weaknesses and hopes and fears . . . what it was that the man wanted—not what he said he wanted but what he *really* wanted—and what it was that the man feared, *really* feared."

He took a calcified, cautious Senate and made it into a pulsating power center, with Lyndon Johnson as its heart. Other senators observed the way the majority leader moved down the Capitol's corridors, the way he communicated disapproval with a single drop of his pen, the way he could turn a simple handshake into a full-body massage for a senator who had something he wanted, or turn a pat on the shoulder into a choking death grip. It had a name: "the Johnson treatment"—Lyndon's stamp, pressed hard on the greatest deliberative body known to man. When the old bulls of the Senate saw him in the hallways they genuflected and called him by his honorific title: *Mr. Leader!*

A leader he was—perhaps the most effective party boss in the Senate's history and, after President Eisenhower, the most powerful man in Washington at the time. For Johnson, though, the point of power was not just having it, but making sure the world knew you had it. He quickly discovered that the reporters who covered the Senate struggled to find ways to make the byzantine legislative process accessible to their readers. But give them a good story—with good human details and a compelling character at the center—and they'd write what you wanted, even if nine times out of ten, the compelling character was you. As a consequence, he was not only the most effective majority leader of the modern era, but the most famous, too.

His ultimate ambition, though, remained as big as the letters he had scrawled across Miss Kate's blackboards at the Junction School. As a young congressman, Johnson instructed aide Horace Busby to refer to him by his initials in press releases. "FDR-LBJ, FDR-LBJ—do you get it? What I want is for them to start thinking of me in terms of initials."

Now, as his car sped forward, he could see the White House. FDR, his idol, had lived in that house for twelve years, longer than any man before him, and now, thanks to the Twenty-second Amendment limiting presidents to two elected terms, longer than any president ever would again. Under the provisions of that amendment, a vice president who succeeded to the presidency of another person with less than two years left in that president's term could run for up to two additional terms of his own. Kennedy's term had only fourteen months left. Altogether, Johnson's presidency could last nine years, longer than anyone's but Roosevelt's.

It was enough time to be as great as Roosevelt, too. Enough time to get great things done, to do what Johnson men were supposed to do—make life better for the common man. Then, in glory, he could go back to Texas and die.

First, though, he had to do what he had always done—make the story about *him*. He had to take the White House and make it *his* White House so that even a child passing by on Pennsylvania Avenue would see the great white columns and remember who lived inside: not "the president," but *"LBJ."*

As the new president's car pulled through the gates of the White House complex that morning, his small coterie of aides and assistants were already hard at work. On any given day, Johnson expected his staffers to be present and ready to execute his orders the moment he walked through the door. Today of all days, they knew Johnson would want everything to go exactly as he wished.

So Mildred Stegall, a veteran Johnson aide, had been in the Vice President's Office, suite 272-76 of the Executive Office Building, when the National Security Advisor, McGeorge Bundy, came by earlier that morning. Greeting Johnson at Andrews the night before, Bundy had urged him to send strong signals to the world that the work of the government continued. To that end, he felt that Johnson should move into the Oval Office as soon as the next morning. Now, though, he had a different message for the new president, which he asked Stegall to relay: "When you and I talked last night about when the President's office in the West Wing would be ready, I thought possibly it would be immediately. However, I find they are working on President Kennedy's papers and his personal belongings and my suggestion would be that—if you could work here in the Executive Office Building today and tomorrow, everything will be ready and clear by tomorrow."

Leaving these instructions, Bundy returned to the West Wing himself. Johnson's aides proceeded with their work. The Vice President's Office was lovely, with high ceilings and sweeping vistas of the National Mall. But for most of the Johnson staff, it was unknown territory. Almost all of them worked out of another office Johnson kept in the Capitol, the office where he spent nearly all his time. His young secretary, Marie Fehmer, had been to the White House campus—which included the Executive Office Building on the other side of West Executive Avenue from the West Wing—only a handful of times. The night before, after getting off the helicopter from Andrews, Fehmer had gotten separated from Johnson's other aides. She stumbled around the basement of the West Wing, lost in a strange new place.

Johnson's staff was hardly more familiar with the people who worked in the West Wing. Had they been they might have known how to interpret Bundy's polite Yankee understatement—that beneath his "my suggestion" and "if you could" lay a simple message: It's a bad idea for you to go into the Oval Office. They might have thought to relay this message to Johnson, at the time still at home.

But Johnson's staff was not accustomed to close communication with Bundy or any of the other Kennedy aides. Johnson's office had a special phone line for calls from the White House, but in his nearly three years as vice president, it almost never had rung. No one from the Kennedy White House was calling Lyndon Johnson. No one from the Kennedy White House was thinking about Lyndon Johnson much at all.

Johnson's decision to accept Kennedy's offer of the vice presidency had shocked Washington. After defeating Johnson for the Democratic nomination in 1960, Kennedy offered Johnson the bottom half of the ticket out of courtesy. Like everyone else, Kennedy assumed that Johnson would turn it down. Johnson had made no secret of the fact he considered Kennedy a lightweight, almost a nonentity in the caucus he controlled. It was hard to imagine Johnson playing second fiddle to anyone, let alone a young upstart.

And yet when Kennedy made the offer, Johnson said yes. He had several good reasons for doing so. He knew that with a president from his own party, his power as majority leader of the Senate would be dramatically curtailed. He also harbored hopes that he could make the vice president's ceremonial powers as president of the Senate more than ceremonial—remaining the leader of the Democratic caucus, a kind of prime minister to Kennedy's head of state. (These hopes were quickly quashed.) And he had been in the Congress at the time of Harry Truman's ascension to the presidency after the death of FDR. Though he would never say it after Dallas, he knew that the vice presidency was not a job without the possibility of promotion.

Still, considering Johnson's lifelong desire to be at the center of things, it is hard not to see his acceptance of Kennedy's offer as an act of willful self-harm. If there is one thing the vice president is not supposed to do, after all, it is to keep everyone's eyes on him. In losing the nomination to Kennedy in 1960, he was losing his best shot at ever being president, the defining goal of his life. When Johnson looked to the future, he tended to see two possibilities: the grandest of glory, or catastrophe on an unimaginable scale. Robbed of his chance at glory, he said yes to Kennedy, and brought the catastrophe on.

For, whatever his reasons for taking the job, the effect was utter misery. Worried that Johnson would use his deep ties to conservative Southern senators and form an independent power base, Kennedy's aides excluded him from all decisions of any consequence. President Kennedy himself warned his staff not to antagonize Johnson. "You are dealing with a very insecure, sensitive man with a huge ego," he told them. "I want you literally to kiss his fanny from one end of Washington to the other." But in his new position, Johnson seemed to have transformed into a different person: quiet in meetings, fawning to the president, "a spectral presence," in the words of one Kennedy lieutenant. The Kennedy aides, at first puzzled by the transformation, eventually delighted in it. When they spoke of Johnson at all, it was usually to make an unflattering joke.

The wounds to Johnson's ego were small but constant. Embracing the vice president's traditional role as a stand-in host for the president, the Johnsons bought a grand mansion, The Elms, to live in, hoping it would be a second social center of Kennedy-era Washington. But the parties everyone in Washington really wanted to be invited to were on the other side of the Potomac River, at Hickory Hill, the home of Robert and Ethel Kennedy. On the rare occasions when the Johnsons were invited to Hickory Hill parties, Ethel seated them at the "losers' table."

Swiftly, devastatingly, Johnson's carefully cultivated image as a man of action disappeared. Most difficult for him to bear was his altered status on Capitol Hill. Johnson's former Senate colleagues—the men who had praised him and pleaded with him and revered him for the better part of a decade—quickly made it clear that he no longer had the power to make them do what he wanted. Harry McPherson, a Democratic Senate aide who would work in the Johnson White House, recalled watching Johnson enter the Senate Democratic cloakroom about a month after he assumed the vice presidency. The cloakroom had once been the very epicenter of Johnson's power, the place where it was easiest to keep everyone's eyes on him. As majority leader, Johnson would walk in and "it was like the teacher walks into the room and says 'Now, we're going to teach the class. You kids have had a nice social hour here, but we're going to start learning some history.'" But when he walked in that day as the new vice president, the senators barely turned their heads. The change was final and total. "It was a very subtle thing," said McPherson, "but you could feel it."

As the vice presidential years wore on, Johnson would spend more and more days lying in bed, just looking at the ceiling. He drank heavily. He had suffered a serious heart attack at the age of forty-six and had tried since then to stick to a careful diet. But as vice president, he gave up, and his weight ballooned. A few months before the Kennedy assassination, McPherson visited Johnson at The Elms. "He looked absolutely gross," McPherson would later say. "His belly was enormous and his face looked bad, flushed, maybe he had been drinking a good deal. But he looked like a man who was not trimmed down for anything. His life was not causing him to come together physically, morally, intellectually, any way." In the last months of Kennedy's presidency, as corruption charges swirled around an old Johnson lieutenant, Senate aide Bobby Baker, Johnson fretted over rumors that Kennedy planned to dump him from the ticket when he ran for reelection in 1964. The people close to Johnson, meanwhile, worried that he would not even live to see that year out.

And so the confidence with which *President* Lyndon Johnson was now walking from his limousine into the west entrance of the White House had a double significance. Taking command, he was starting a new story not just for the country, but for himself. Walking into the White House, *his* White House, he was bringing himself back to life. He could be the hero, calming the country as it faced the crushing anxiety of its suddenly uncertain future. For the first time in a very long time, his own future held the possibility of something other than decline.

BUT IT WAS not his White House, as he was about to discover in the most public fashion. His assistants had not relayed Mac Bundy's urgent subtext—*stay out of the Oval Office*. Walking into the Executive Mansion that morning, Johnson was entering a building full of Kennedy staffers who had gathered there that morning, if they'd left at all the night before. There was nowhere else for them to go. None of them had slept much. Most of them had been drinking heavily for well over twelve hours. Now, in the sickly gray daylight, they were looking for a new release. As happens to mourners when the shock of grief starts to subside, they found themselves overtaken with anger. And the most obvious target for their rage was the large, obtrusive Texan making his way through the hallways, acting as if he owned the place.

As the Kennedy people saw it, there were many grievous offenses of which Johnson—for that was what they all still called him, or maybe "Lyndon" but never "the president"—had been guilty the previous day. He'd commandeered Air Force One after the shooting.

He'd insisted that, as president, he should take the president's plane back to Washington, not the Boeing 707 that functioned as the vice president's plane. Poor Jackie, arriving on Air Force One from the hospital, the president's blood still streaked across her skirt, had found Johnson sprawled on *her* bed. Then he'd kept her waiting, sitting on a sweltering tarmac, for some Texas crony judge of his to arrive and deliver the oath of office. And when that judge did arrive, Johnson had insisted that President Kennedy's widow stand beside him for the oath. Mrs. Kennedy had to stand and look on, silently, as that Texan assumed her dead husband's responsibilities.

Most of this talk was unfair. The Secret Service had ordered Johnson onto Air Force One. Desperate to get in touch with Washington to find out if the country was under broader attack, he had gone to the presidential bedroom in search of a working telephone. He had vacated the room in a fearsome hurry the moment that the president's widow appeared. His insistence that he take the oath before leaving Dallas was understandable, and indeed necessary, to assure the nation that the transfer of power, as provided by the Constitution, had in fact taken place. As vice president, his most important responsibility was to be prepared to assume the presidency at a moment's notice. That was all he had tried to do.

But to Kennedy's aides, every presidential act Johnson undertook was by definition reprehensible. On arrival back in Washington he'd asked for two pieces of presidential stationery. "He can't even let the body get cold before he starts using his stationery," a Kennedy aide remarked in disgust. They didn't bother to ask what he needed the stationery for: letters of condolence to President Kennedy's two small children.

The nasty account of the events in Dallas spread quickly. Soon it was the Kennedy loyalists' gospel truth. It was the beginning of a pattern that would shape Johnson's presidency: the contest between the Kennedy men's story and his own.

But Johnson couldn't yet see that. To be sure, he could sense the blazing resentment as he made his way through the West Wing that morning. He had already decided he would do everything he could to placate these people and persuade them to stay. That would be a crucial part of the story he was going to tell. If he was to appear to the world as John F. Kennedy's strong successor, he needed the support of John F. Kennedy's staff. He'd worked out a line he would use on many of them in the days ahead: *I know how you're hurting . . . I need you more than he needed you.* The Kennedy people, too, were stuck in a swamp, the toxic mud of their own grief. He would lead them out of it. So he moved through the West Wing determined to act confidently as the president.

And for that he needed a phone. For Johnson, a phone—or, really, several phones, with dozens of specially programmed buttons and at least two secretaries specially trained to work those buttons to reach anyone in the world at a moment's notice—was the essential tool of any powerful man. Truly important people, he believed, could reach anyone, at any time. Johnson aides learned to keep their phones close to their beds, ready for the inevitable postmidnight command. In the modern world, a phone determined the difference between the impotent men, who pondered, and the powerful men, who could *act*. He was the president now, he had to act, and he needed the president's phone.

But the president's phone was in the President's Office, and the President's Office was still guarded by Evelyn Lincoln. Lincoln had been Kennedy's personal secretary since he'd entered the Senate in 1953. She was fiercely protective of her boss and felt that she and she alone knew who were his real friends and who were the phony pretenders. Johnson, she told anyone who would listen in the days after the assassination, fell in the latter camp. She had clocked the amount of time Johnson spent in private consultation with Kennedy: In the year 1961, it had been ten hours and nineteen minutes. In 1963, it was down to one hour and fifty-three minutes. On the flight back from Dallas she'd led a group of female Kennedy aides as they walked by Lady Bird Johnson, refusing to offer a smile or extend a hand.

Now Johnson marched into the Oval Office, beckoning Lincoln to join him for a word. "I need you more than you need me," he said. "But . . . I also need a transition. Can I have my girls in your office by 9:30?" Tight faced, Lincoln acquiesced: "Yes, Mr. President."

Johnson pushed forward. That was all he needed. Kennedy's secretary quietly excused herself. As he entered the Oval Office, the scope of his new power must have struck him, the way it strikes so many presidents when they stand alone for the first time in the solemn majesty of that space. The story of his presidency had begun.

But it would last for only a moment. Sitting outside the office, Lincoln seethed. A day ago she'd been the eyes and ears of the most powerful man in the world. Now this crass Texan with *his girls* was throwing her out on her ear. And she, the sainted president's trusted guardian, could not do a thing about it.

There was someone else, however, who could, and as it happened, that person was walking by her desk at precisely that moment. She caught his eye, and when he entered her small office outside the Oval Office, Lincoln burst into tears. She signaled toward Johnson. "Do you know he asked me to be out by *9:30*?"

Her visitor's face filled with fury. He could not let that happen. And he wouldn't. He was Robert Kennedy, attorney general of the United States, brother of the late president. He knew how to keep Lyndon Johnson out of the Oval Office. He had been doing it for years.

Bobby Kennedy had been enjoying lunch by the pool at Hickory Hill when he learned of his brother's death. He had retreated instantly into shock and grief, pacing back and forth over the green lawns. He emerged long enough to take a call from Johnson on the tarmac in Dallas. "First he expressed his condolences," Kennedy would later say. "Then he said . . . this might be part of a worldwide plot, which I didn't understand, and he said a lot of people down here think I should be sworn in right away. Do you have any objection to it? And—well, I was sort of taken aback at the moment because it was just an hour after . . . the President had been shot and I didn't think—see what the rush was. And . . . at the time, at least, I thought it would be nice if the President came back to Washington—President Kennedy."

Bobby had waited anxiously for the flight from Dallas to arrive at Andrews. Rushing onboard, he breezed past the new president, muttering, "Where's Jackie?" He escorted the widow through the long night, riding with her and Kennedy's body in an ambulance to Bethesda Naval Hospital, where they sat vigil with friends and family members as doctors performed the autopsy. He'd stayed by her side when they returned to the White House and the coffin was laid in the East Room.

A small, slight, younger son, Bobby had struggled to distinguish himself in the crowded Kennedy family. Eventually, he'd found the role of enforcer—the fierce attack dog who barked off any threat to his older siblings. In his brother's presidency he'd played the part to perfection, ruthlessly seeking out any disloyalty or disservice to President Kennedy. Now, though, he had been shoved into a new role: the leader, the oldest surviving brother, the protector of all the Kennedys, living and dead. He knew how to play the part—he was a Kennedy, after all—and he seized it with confidence, impressing everyone with his sureness and strength. But in private, Bobby felt the weight of unspeakable pain. Just before dawn he stole away from the crowds of aides and family members and shut himself inside the quiet of the Lincoln Bedroom. Alone at last, he cried out: "Why, God?"

God wasn't there that Saturday morning, and neither was the president. Of that Bobby Kennedy was sure. He'd personally inspected his brother's corpse, taking in the distorted face, rendered clownlike by the undertaker's attempt to obscure the bullet wound with makeup. That wasn't the president. And the man calling himself the president, the man wending his way around the West Wing and throwing poor Evelyn Lincoln out of her office, the man whose portrait was already sitting outside the Oval Office waiting to be hung up—that wasn't the president either. That was Lyndon Johnson. The president was dead.

But now that man, Johnson, spotted Bobby at the edge of the Oval Office and moved toward him. He extended a strong handshake and tried to grope Bobby's back. "I want to talk to you," he said.

Kennedy bristled under Johnson's embrace. Okay, he said, but he would prefer not to speak in the Oval Office. Johnson acceded to his wish. They shuffled awkwardly into the little anteroom across from the presidential lavatory.

If Johnson sensed a coldness in Bobby, it wouldn't have been surprising. In the course of their decadelong acquaintance, coldness—if not overt hostility—from Bobby had been the norm. In the 1950s, when Johnson ruled Capitol Hill, Bobby had been a young lawyer for the Senate's Permanent Subcommittee for Investigations. Smaller, scrappier, and far less polished than his older brother Jack, Bobby was acutely sensitive to any slight or gesture that seemed to diminish his stature. Johnson, the majority leader, didn't think much about Bobby in those years, except as an extension of his older brother or his powerful father, Ambassador Joseph P. Kennedy. But he could nonetheless sense Bobby's insecurity and was not above poking at it. "Hey, Sonny," he would say as he passed Bobby in the Capitol's halls.

Officially they were friendly, in the way that a political party's power brokers always are, and in 1959, Johnson had even hosted Bobby at the LBJ Ranch. There, Bobby had given in to Johnson's entreaties to join him on a deer hunt. Raising his shotgun for a target, he pulled the trigger and was knocked over by the force of the gun. For Bobby, obsessed with displays of toughness, the fall was mortifying. Johnson saw Bobby's shame and went right for it: "Son, you've got to learn to handle a gun like a man."

He ought to have known better, for Bobby would have his payback a thousand times over. In 1960, Bobby fought hard to persuade his brother not to offer the vice presidency to Johnson. When Kennedy picked the majority leader anyway, Bobby spread the story that Johnson had only been offered the VP spot as a courtesy. In the Kennedy administration, the attorney general was a clearinghouse for stories of the pathetic vice president's crassness and vanity. Bobby made sure that all of Washington knew just how insignificant to the work of the Kennedy administration Lyndon Johnson was. Johnson suspected, with some good reason, that Bobby was the source for rumors that Kennedy planned to dump him from the presidential ticket in 1964.

Bobby became the human face of Johnson's torment in the vice presidency. He was the runt of an aide who had the king's ear. He was the old enemy whose torture Johnson had no choice but to take. But even worse, Bobby was a symbol of Johnson's failure. In Johnson's career in the capital, he'd always used the same simple formula for advancement: find the most powerful man, flatter him and ingratiate yourself, become indispensable. In the House, he'd done it with the Speaker, his fellow Texan, Sam Rayburn. In the Senate, there had been Dick Russell, the colossus from Georgia, who'd come to think of Lyndon Johnson as a son. There was no doubt that the most powerful man in the Kennedy administration, after Kennedy himself, was Bobby. But with Bobby, Johnson could never find a way in. It drove him mad. At one White House dinner dance, he'd followed Bobby into the family quarters. "Now, you don't like me, Bobby," the pitiful vice president had said. "Your brother likes me, your sister-in-law likes me, and your Daddy likes me, but you do not like me. Now why?"

Now, though, things had changed. He was the president and he could not be ignored. Johnson's new story would include an overture to his old nemesis. He started into the script he had worked out: *I need you more than he needed you . . .*

It would be a hard sell, persuading Bobby Kennedy to be a supporting character in the grand new adventure of Lyndon Johnson. The two seemed opposites in every way. Johnson, with his great, hulking physical presence, could take possession of a room just by entering it, while Bobby, small and wiry, grew up fighting for every morsel of attention he could get. And their differences went deeper. Bobby seemed to experience sorrow and joy more intensely than most people; he hated harder, loved deeper, *felt* more. Johnson could manufacture a feeling to suit his interests, could lie so easily, and so effectively, that it was often impossible to tell what his true feelings were.

But, as is often the case, similarity, not difference, was what drove these men apart. In the darker parts of their natures, Johnson and Bobby shared a great deal. Each had spent much of the time in his rise to power through service to someone else—Johnson to Rayburn and Russell, Bobby to his father and older brothers. Over time, a strong-willed man who plays this subservient role can develop the qualities of a caged animal. In each, there was something primitive—the obsession with loyalty, the carefully curated lists of enemies and friends. Each was capable of extravagant cruelty, the kind of public meanness that was embarrassing to watch and excruciating to bear. Unlike John F. Kennedy, whose great gift was to see the world as it was, each had a talent for convincing himself that what served his interest was also what was good and right, even when it wasn't. Each viewed politics as a bloody business in which opponents needed to be destroyed totally and unmercifully. Bobby was "a very, very ambitious young man," said Johnson. "It's just unbelievable how ambitious he is."

"I thought they'd get one of us," Bobby said on the phone with his aide Ed Guthman moments after learning of his brother's death, but "I thought it would be me." In the months ahead, Bobby would take on a vacant, ghostly quality, as though he felt that by simply going on living he was committing an act of betrayal. Bobby, the attack dog, had been his brother's crusader in the world's dark places—chasing down the bosses of organized crime, nurturing plots to overthrow Fidel Castro in Cuba. He'd created powerful enemies, all of whom would have been happy to see a Kennedy brother dead. "Without question," writes Bobby's biographer Evan Thomas, "he worried that his own aggressive pursuit of evil men had brought evil upon his own house."

These were deeply unsettling thoughts, and Bobby desperately needed release. He found it in Johnson. For if it was unfair that

Bobby should live when his brother had to die, it was a travesty of history that Johnson should now stand in the center of his brother's office. Johnson, whom his brother had mistrusted and kept at arm's length, who his brother had determined should never be allowed to win the presidency in his own right. *Johnson* was the guilty one.

I need you more than he needed you: Johnson was the one who spoke the words, but from Bobby's lips they would have been equally true.

Bobby didn't let Johnson finish making his case for the importance of showing unity in the transition. He didn't want to talk about any of that right now. What mattered in that instant was the Oval Office. President Kennedy's things were still inside and would require time to pack up. Could Johnson wait awhile before moving in?

Immediately, Johnson saw a warning. "Well, of course," he replied. Soon, he was back to his familiar pattern with Bobby, pleading his case: It wasn't he who'd wanted to come to the Oval Office. It was others who had said it was necessary. President Kennedy's men had said so. Mac Bundy, the national security adviser, had *insisted*. He was only doing his best to assure continuity of government.

Bobby did not respond. He looked at the large man standing in front of him with glazed uninterest. After a few more moments of Johnson's pleading, they parted ways.

Now Johnson had reason to worry. On television, the anchors and correspondents were already saying that Kennedy's decision on whether to stay on as attorney general would prove a key test for Johnson. He could not afford to alienate the Kennedy family. He needed them too much.

Johnson the heroic rancher was stuck in the mud. He was in John Kennedy's White House, surrounded by John Kennedy's people and John Kennedy's things, trying desperately to win John Kennedy's brother over to his side. He was the president now, but the story was still the same.

THE ANCHORS ON television were unaware of what had just taken place between the new president and the attorney general in the West Wing. Their focus was on the East Room, where, a few minutes after nine o'clock, the press was allowed in to view Kennedy's funeral bier. Under Jacqueline Kennedy's instruction, the catafalque had been constructed in replica of the one used after the assassination of Abraham Lincoln. Black crape covered the chandeliers.

And then, at 9:30, Johnson finally appeared before the cameras. Surrounded by men in dark suits, he emerged from the West Wing to the gray day outside. It was his first appearance on live television that morning, his first real chance to be the leader he knew the nation needed him to be. But his eyes were lowered and his shoulders were hunched. "Morning, Mr. President," the press shouted. But Johnson ignored them and did not say a word.

Flanked by advisers, Johnson crossed West Executive Avenue and headed toward the Executive Office Building. For nearly three years, the street had been the great divide in his life, the river that separated his isolated vice presidential island from the White House, the center of power, the place he longed to be. Now he was crossing back over, back to the place that had brought him low. He was giving in to Bobby's request and surrendering the Oval Office. "Mr. Johnson," said NBC's Ray Scherer diplomatically, "prefers to hold his appointments in his vice presidential office."

Inside that vice presidential office, Johnson's bewildered assistants tried to absorb what had just happened. Had the president of the United States really just been chased from the Oval Office? Johnson's military aide, Colonel William Jackson, insisted that Johnson retake the White House and continue the transition of power. "It will give the people confidence," he said. Johnson knew it was a lost cause: "Stop this. Our first concern is Mrs. Kennedy and her family." It was clear: the day, the mansion, the nation—all were still in the Kennedys' hands.

And the story was, too. All morning, the networks showed majestic shots of the White House, its white columns stark against the sky, a flag at half-mast, flapping in the bitter November wind. From time to time, the networks would attempt to show the exterior of the Executive Office Building, where Johnson was busily at work. But the cameras were not used to photographing this building, and it appeared onscreen as a nondescript mass of gray bricks. It was hard to look at, and the networks quickly moved on to other things. The eyes of the world would not rest on Lyndon Johnson. Not yet.

The work he could get: In late 1963, Ronald Reagan
was at work on the movie *The Killers,* in which he
played a conniving gangster.

© Universal Pictures/Getty Images

CHAPTER TWO

★ ★ ★

Watching

November 22–24, 1963

There was nothing to do but watch.

Workers in the East and Midwest had been on their lunch hour when news of the shooting in Dallas first broke. In the big cities, customers poured out of restaurants, leaving large sums on the table, unwilling to wait for the bill. The New York Stock Exchange suspended trading. Strangers heading home from work wept with one another on subway cars. Schools closed. The American Football League suspended play for the weekend, and the Harvard-Yale game was called off. Disneyland closed its gates that weekend. Parties, dances, even weddings were canceled. That weekend, most Americans stayed inside, watching the newscasters, horrified by what they were seeing, but still unable to turn off the TV.

In Hollywood it was the same as everywhere else. It had been morning on the West Coast when President Kennedy began his fateful car trip into Dallas. In Los Angeles, a crew was setting to work on a new Universal Pictures film, *Johnny North,* a remake of a movie from the 1940s, which was in turn an adaptation of a Hemingway short story called "The Killers." Universal's powerful studio boss, Lew Wasserman, had revived the old title to remake and sell the film to NBC. His plan was to produce *Johnny North* as the first full-length feature made specifically for TV.

Wasserman hired a respected film director, Don Siegel, to pull together a strong story and cast. Siegel threw out most of the 1946 picture's story line. His movie would instead focus on a pair of contract killers who are hired to murder a former race car driver named Johnny North. The title character would be played by John Cassavetes, a young actor who'd played dark, sexy leading roles on TV and film. The lead villain and the elder of the two killers, Charlie Strom, would be played by Lee Marvin, a talented, if difficult, old pro. Strom's coconspirator would be played by Clu Gulager, a young television actor. Angie Dickinson, the blazing sex symbol rumored to be a special friend of President Kennedy's, would play the leading lady, a femme fatale named Sheila Farr.

Only one supporting role remained unfilled: Jack Browning, an older gangster who plans the heist at the center of the film's plot. Wasserman told his director he had an actor in mind for the part: Why not Ronald Reagan?

Ronald Reagan? Siegel was skeptical. He had known and liked the old B-movie star for years. But Reagan was a squeaky-clean actor who'd had a squeaky-clean career in Hollywood playing squeaky-clean parts. Would he be willing to play a villain, a dirty gangster in a dark suit? So far he'd resisted all entreaties, Wasserman said, but the part would be good for him. Maybe Siegel could be the one to finally talk him into it.

Here the studio boss was probably stroking his director's ego. Wasserman, who'd built his career in Hollywood as a talent agent, had represented Reagan for decades and taken a special interest in his career. He knew as well as anyone that since Reagan had lost his regular gig as the host of *General Electric Theater* a year earlier, there hadn't been many parts on offer to him, villain or otherwise. Still, he gave Siegel the impression that Reagan would be a hard fish to catch. "I want you to talk him into playing that role," he instructed his director.

Siegel invited Reagan for lunch at the Universal commissary. It had been a while since the director had last seen the actor. The face was still familiar, of course—not just to Siegel, but to everyone in Hollywood. Since arriving in the film colony in the late 1930s, Reagan had been a kind of student body president for the movie business—never the most famous or the most successful, but always well liked. Arriving at the commissary, Reagan smiled and lit up the room, greeting old friends. He still looked like a movie star, he was still handsome, still broad and muscular, still somehow larger than his six feet one inch.

But he hadn't been in many movies since he'd taken the *GE Theater* job in 1954. To Siegel, this Reagan looked different, more mature. And he looked tan: in recent years, he'd been spending more and more of his time working at his ranch, where he raised thoroughbred jumpers and hunters. "Horses are like people," Reagan told Siegel that day at lunch. "Treat them with respect and love, and they'll do their best to give you what you want."

Over Cobb salad, Siegel made his pitch for *Johnny North*. Think of all the big-shot actors you know who've played villains onscreen, he told Reagan—Peter Lorre, James Cagney, Humphrey Bogart! It didn't exactly hurt their careers. This character, Browning, was "the boss . . . well educated, charming, yet rugged when necessary."

"What kind of money are they talking about?" Reagan asked Siegel. The director demurred. "That's up to you, your agent, and Lew Wasserman. But I know they want you badly. I'm certain the deal can be worked out to your satisfaction." By the time the check came, it seemed that Reagan was coming around to the idea. "Surely you have no objection to Universal paying for our lunch, do you?" Reagan smiled and said no. Siegel knew the part of Browning was filled.

The film went into production on Thursday, November 21. The next morning, Siegel went to visit his leading lady at a costume fitting. It was a happy scene. There was country music on the radio. Dickinson twirled to show her director a stunning red dress. "You'll steal the show," Siegel said. "I've ninety more dresses to show you," the actress said before turning happily back toward her dressing room. Later, she was to shoot the film's one truly romantic scene, in

which she would wear a shimmering white gown and dance with
Cassavetes to a slow, sad song called "Too Little Time."

Indeed. As she walked away, the country station, like radio sta-
tions everywhere, cut to a news bulletin. Years later, Siegel would
still recall the announcer's words—"We shockingly regret to inform
you that President John Fitzgerald Kennedy has just been assassi-
nated in Dallas, Texas . . ."—and then, from Dickinson, "a loud,
piercing scream." The actress crumpled in the director's arms.

Production on *Johnny North* came immediately to a halt. The
film was on a tight production schedule, but the movie studios were
shutting down, just like everything else. Wasserman made it known
that there would be no more work on the film that Friday, and Monday would be a day of mourning as well.

Ronald Reagan spent that evening at home. He had never been a
supporter of John F. Kennedy. He had been a staunch anticommunist and a true believer in conservative principles since the 1950s,
and in recent years he had become active in Republican politics. He
traveled the country giving speeches extolling the virtue of the free
market, warning against the Soviet threat, and worrying over a turn
toward statist policies in America. Three years earlier, in the 1960
presidential campaign, he had made numerous appearances on behalf of Kennedy's opponent, Richard Nixon, and he planned to do
the same for the conservative Arizona senator Barry Goldwater in
the 1964 presidential campaign. Kennedy, he'd once implied, was a
Marxist with a pretty face.

A day earlier, that sort of talk would have been unpopular but
acceptable. In the wake of Kennedy's death, it was tantamount to
treason. The newscasts that Friday afternoon still had little information on Oswald, the apparent shooter, or his politics. But Dallas was
a well-known hotbed of right-wing extremism. It didn't take much
imagination to see some way that leaders of the conservative movement might be culpable in Kennedy's death. Walter Cronkite didn't
help matters when he erroneously reported that Goldwater, asked
for a response to the news of Kennedy's death, had offered nothing

more than a cold "No comment." A mob was forming outside National Draft Goldwater Committee headquarters screaming "Murderers!"

In Southern California, Reagan's eleven-year-old daughter Patti watched her school's flag being lowered to half-mast that Friday. School was canceled, the principal announced, and it was time for the children to go home. Waiting for her mother, Patti was confronted by a fellow student: "Well, your parents will probably be happy!"

They weren't, but there was little use in arguing the point. Any kind of political discussion was suddenly in bad taste. For the moment, politics—Reagan's greatest passion in recent years—had become an unspeakable subject. Like everyone else in America, he spent time that weekend with his family, watching the unbelievable events on TV.

And waiting. For Reagan, the delay in filming would mean more days off camera. He had had plenty of those in recent years. And it would mean a revised schedule for shooting, stretching past Christmas. Which meant more time until this movie was over. This movie, which was beginning to look like a mistake.

The signs of trouble were obvious. Reagan had arrived the previous morning to shoot a scene at a location in the Toluca Lake neighborhood of Los Angeles. Thanks to the oddities of a studio schedule, the first scene to be shot in official production would be the last scene of the movie. The plan for the day was to shoot the exterior portions of the film's climactic confrontation in which Lee Marvin's character, Charlie Strom, tracks Reagan's Browning and Dickinson's Sheila Farr to an upscale suburban house. Despite suffering from a gunshot wound himself, Strom nonetheless manages to capture them both at gunpoint. Farr begs for mercy, but Strom won't hear it; he shoots Browning and Farr dead and then lurches outside, where he stumbles in extended agony and dies. It was mostly Marvin's scene, and mostly Marvin's day.

But when it came time to start shooting, Marvin wasn't there.

Reagan stepped in to fill the time, filming a simple exterior shot in which a nervous Browning hurries into the house, clutching a long case in which he's stored a large gun. They got it on film without incident.

The hours went by with no sign of Marvin. Morning turned to afternoon. Finally, a car came into view, careening back and forth across the street before coming to a stop on the lawn in front of the house. Out staggered Marvin, seriously drunk.

Siegel set to work, instructing the actor on the choreography of the death stumble. Marvin, clutching a 7-Up bottle filled with vodka, nodded along silently. "Lee had a theory about drinking," Siegel said later. "If you didn't talk, no one could smell you."

Then a funny thing happened. The camera started rolling and Marvin began to resemble his character. Sure, he could be difficult to work with, but it was hard to argue with his theatrical talents. And for an actor tasked with staggering around like he's bleeding to death, a 7-Up bottle's worth of vodka can come in handy.

The performance required multiple takes and reshoots. But the version that made it onscreen, cut with the interior shots to form the final scene of the film, was a tour de force. It begins with a close-up of Charlie Strom's feet. First, viewers see blood fall onto his shoes, then his gun drops into the frame. He is steps away from death, but he's determined to send Farr and Browning there first. Inside the house, he moves with agonized urgency, falling to the floor and yet, somehow, still managing to pull a gun on Farr and Browning. Each pleads for their life, but Marvin promptly shoots them both dead anyway. Next, he emerges back into the daylight, his white shirt soaked with blood. He wants to escape but as he struggles to get into his car, he sees a police cruiser pulling up. He points his finger as if to shoot at the cop in a final act of defiance. Then he falls straight backward. Dead. "An actor likes a death scene," Marvin's costar Clu Gulager would later say, and Marvin's was "the greatest death on-screen I think I've ever seen."

Indeed, Marvin's performance was so captivating to watch, it was easy to forget that the film's final sequence included two other actors' death scenes as well. Angie Dickinson didn't even get to die on camera. Reagan at least got to portray Browning's final moments of life. In a five-second shot, viewers see him clutch the gunshot wound in his abdomen, raise his head in agony, and fall dead on the floor. Altogether it was a serviceable, believable performance. And an utterly forgettable one compared with the long, engrossing struggle of Marvin's Charlie Strom, the one and only star in the scene.

So that would be the payoff for the long weeks of work ahead of him, to be a minor character in another man's death scene. For Reagan, too, this would be an agonizing part to play.

AFTER ALL, RONALD Reagan liked to be the star as well.

For Americans in the twenty-first century, who know how the story of Reagan's life turned out, the role of hero seems a natural fit. His presidency was filled with dramatic triumphs: the "morning in America" economic boom that followed years of economic hardship, the two landslide elections, the hard-line challenge to the Soviets that climaxed in America's triumph in the Cold War. And he was always careful to look as much like a hero as he could. He was more attractive than anyone else in Washington, his lighting was better, and his timing and his set pieces were superior, too. His adversaries were always appropriately evil, and he dealt with them with satisfyingly quick dispatch. And, most important, there was his remarkable journey from the B-movie ranks to the top echelon of revered presidents. The improbability of this progression suggested America was either a ridiculous country or a great one. Most Americans have chosen the latter interpretation. Only in their great country could an individual make such a lucky and heroic rise.

Over time, Reagan's admirers have created a familiar account of that rise, with mutually agreed-upon dramatic contours. In that story, a child of the small-town Midwest works his way from a local lifeguarding job to regional radio announcer to movie idol in late 1930s and '40s Hollywood. He finds early success playing wholesome characters in pleasant, if inconsequential, films. His onscreen persona matches his offscreen life; he has a beautiful movie star wife and children, and he's so well liked and respected in the film colony that, in 1947, his peers elect him president of the Screen Actors Guild.

Then, in the late 1940s, the hero meets his great obstacle: the collapse of his film career and the end of his first marriage. He struggles and suffers, emotionally and physically. But he perseveres, and in time he manages to reinvent himself. He finds a new wife and a new kind of celebrity as a television star and host on *GE Theater*. He grows in seriousness and stature, taking an interest in issues of substance, specifically the threat posed to the American way of life by the spread of Soviet Communism. He becomes a respected conservative speaker on politics and international affairs. By the mid-1960s, he has grown convinced that his country has reached a perilous position and that its very existence is threatened. With some reluctance, he yields to the entreaties of others and begins a career in public service that will inevitably lead to the White House, his destiny all along.

Much of this narrative is true. And yet when we ask the famous question of the storybook Reagan—*Where were you the day Kennedy was shot?*—we find a man caught someplace he is not supposed to be. He's not a retired movie star. He's a working actor, toiling in less than ideal conditions on a movie set. He's not the wholesome good guy. He's playing a distinctly unwholesome character in a distinctly unwholesome film. He's not a decade beyond the great career crisis of his life. His career is on the rocks once more. He is not obviously destined for greatness. He is fifty-two years old, looking toward his future anxiously, unsure if there is any more greatness to come. Indeed, after a couple days of shooting *Johnny North,* he has caught a glimpse of a different kind of future, one devoid of greatness, one in which he was on camera but mostly unseen.

For Reagan, that particular vision of the future would have been unpleasant in the extreme. For the real story of Reagan's life is not the story of a natural and inevitable hero, a man unquestionably destined for greatness. It is the story of a man who *makes* himself a hero while fulfilling a consuming need to be seen. Like Johnson, he longed to feel the eyes of the world on him as he played a heroic part in a grand performance. And throughout his life, he worked as hard as he could to make sure that part was his.

Like Johnson's, Reagan's drive to be seen was born in childhood. Not long before he shot his scenes in *Johnny North,* Reagan began work on a midlife memoir, eventually published in 1965. In it, he imagined the scene of his birth:

> The story begins with a closeup of a bottom in a small town called Tampico in Illinois, on February 6, 1911. My face was blue from screaming, my bottom was red from whacking, and my father claimed afterward that he was white when he said shakily, "For such a little bit of a fat Dutchman, he makes a hell of a lot of noise, doesn't he?"
>
> "I think he's perfectly wonderful," said my mother weakly. "Ronald Wilson Reagan."

To the family, the "fat Dutchman" image would stick—Reagan would always be known as Dutch. He grew up in Tampico and a succession of other small Midwestern towns, far from any spotlight. His father, a first-generation Irish American named Jack Reagan, worked as a shoe salesman. Handsome, friendly, and charismatic, Jack dreamed of making it big but had a penchant for heavy drinking that kept his dreams out of reach. His wife, Nelle, a devout Christian, took care of her husband, but her own ambitions for greatness were for her two sons: her eldest, Neil, and her favorite, Dutch.

When the boys were children, Neil was always the one in the limelight—the more popular brother, the better athlete, the bigger flirt. Dutch kept to himself, reading books and arranging toy figurines in elaborate fantasy scenes. But the quiet Reagan dreamed of greatness in his games. "His heroes," writes Lou Cannon, Reagan's esteemed biographer, "were always heroes: generals and presidents and captains of industry who had arisen from the ranks."

He hoped that someday the hero might be him. In his teenage years, he began to look the part. By then the Reagans had settled in Dixon, Illinois, the small community he would always consider his hometown. Tall, lanky, and muscular, with honey-brown hair and misty blue Irish eyes, he was a vision of youthful beauty. He knew it, and he made sure everyone else did, too. He passed some of the happiest years of his life working as a lifeguard at a popular local beach, basking in the warmth of admiring gazes. It was hard work—twelve-hour shifts, seven days a week, every day of the summer—but Reagan loved it, returning to his post each year for seven summers.

Later, his admirers in the conservative movement would identify the seed of Reagan's greatness in that bronzed lifeguard on the banks of the Rock River: Reagan the rescuer, coming to save the drowning swimmers as he would later come to save a nation fighting for its life. Reagan himself was less grandiose when recalling those summers. "You know why I had such fun at it?" he said. "Because I was the only one up there on the guard stand. It was like a stage. Everyone had to look at me."

Soon he went in search of other stages. At Illinois's Eureka College, where he enrolled in 1928, he quickly grasped the campus pecking order and joined the football squad. Initially, his eyesight and slight frame kept him on the bench, but he worked hard and eventually gained a respectable reputation as a solid player, if not a standout. Recognition came easier in the college drama club, where he immediately distinguished himself as a star. "All of this commenced to create in me a personality schizo-split between sports and the stage," he later wrote. "The fact was, I suppose, that I just liked showing off."

It was in college that he discovered the amazing effect this "showing off" could have on people. In his freshman year he spoke at a campus meeting to ask for a vote of protest against administrative cuts to academic programs. In his 1965 memoir, he recalled his performance. "I discovered that night," Reagan wrote, "that an audience has a feel to it and, in the parlance of the theater, that audience and I were together. When I came to actually presenting the motion there was no need for parliamentary procedure: they came to their feet with a roar. . . . It was heady wine."

And having tasted it, he craved more. Upon his graduation from Eureka in the spring of 1932—a time when people were lucky to find a job anywhere—he determined that he *had* to make his living in show business, Depression or no. Through persistence, he wangled himself a job as an announcer on Iowa radio. There, he first tasted the pleasures of celebrity. ("You were always aware when he came into a room that *someone* was in the room," recalled the program director for a Des Moines station.) Then, in the winter of 1937, he went to Hollywood. Calling on an acquaintance from his radio career, he secured, in quick succession, a screen test, an agent, and a contract with the studio Warner Bros. He proved a workhorse, appearing in eight films in the year 1938 and another eight in 1939. In 1940, after his memorable appearance as the doomed George Gipp— "the Gipper"—in *Knute Rockne All American,* he was close to the destiny he'd always imagined for himself: life as a genuine national star.

By then, Warner Bros. was lending its considerable resources to the cause. As part of an effort to erase Hollywood's Depression-era image as a sin-filled sewer, Warner's publicity promoted the clean-cut midwesterner with his apple-pie good looks as part of a new breed of all-American heroes in the film colony. Reagan happily played along. "I like to swim, hike and sleep," Reagan wrote in *Photoplay* magazine in 1942. "I'm fairly good at every sport except tennis, which I just don't like. My favorite menu is steak smothered with onions and strawberry shortcake. Mr. Norm is my alias." The homespun heartthrob in the movie magazines neatly matched Reagan's image of himself. He preferred, always, to play the good guy—just like everyone else, only better. In the early days of his political career, reporters would say he'd often played "the guy who didn't get the girl," a description that left him resentful. In an interview with Cannon in the 1960s, he was adamant: "I *always* got the girl."

He was particularly proud to "get" the up-and-coming actress Jane Wyman, who agreed to be his real-life wife in 1940, in a marriage made for public consumption. The Warner Bros. publicity department encouraged the match. So did the gossip columnist Louella Parsons, who threw a wedding reception for the couple at her home. In the press, the pair of nice-looking celebrities with a baby daughter named Maureen was a shining example of the wholesome new Hollywood. "The Reagans' home life is probably just like yours, or yours, or yours," said Reagan in a Warner Bros. release. "We do the same foolish things that other couples do, have the same scraps, about as much fun, typical problems and the most wonderful baby in the world."

It read like press agent nonsense, but Reagan, Cannon writes, "appears to have accepted the studio propaganda as literally true." Such was the pattern of his life. In high school and college, the girls he dated were widely admired beauties. Morris notes that when they were with him, some of these women sensed a feeling of pleasure in Reagan, the pleasure of being seen in a handsome couple, the attractive lovers, the handsome man and his gorgeous girl. With Wyman, he would be half of a beautiful, glamorous couple, and he was happy in part because the whole world could see how beautiful and glamorous they were.

His career was looking more and more wonderful, too. In 1942, Reagan earned genuine critical acclaim for *King's Row*—a serious drama, he would remind people years later, and one in which he believed he'd done his finest work. His industrious agent, Lew Wasserman, successfully negotiated with Warner Bros. to secure a new seven-year contract for Reagan, worth an impressive one million dollars.

Then war came, and his luck ran out. Reagan was a reserve cavalry officer in the U.S. Army, and after Pearl Harbor and the nation's entrance into World War II, he was placed on active duty. His poor vision prevented him from serving overseas. Instead, he was assigned to the Army Air Force's First Motion Picture Unit, producing military training films. The assignment meant that, unlike other actors of his generation, he would spend the war largely out of the public eye. Thanks to Wasserman, he still had a big studio contract, but after the war ended, Reagan saw the harsh new truth. Public tastes had changed. The emerging postwar movie idols conveyed a new kind of sensitive, complicated masculinity and rugged, rebellious appeal that were utterly foreign to "Mr. Norm."

Not yet forty, Reagan was a has-been. The descent left him despondent. He was still very much on the scene, fulfilling the obligations of his contract by appearing in increasingly lower-budget movies, and serving as president of the Screen Actors Guild. But he'd made the grim transition from burgeoning Hollywood star to familiar Hollywood presence. Attending a Guild meeting one night, he passed a crowd of photographers. "Well, at last," said a caustic onlooker, "Ronald Reagan is having his picture taken."

A series of personal calamities ensued. A newborn baby daughter died in infancy in 1947. Reagan himself became severely ill with viral pneumonia. He came close to death and would have succumbed, he later wrote, but for a kindly nurse watching over him, "coaxing me to take a breath."

And on top of it all, his treasured marriage was no longer camera-ready. Tensions in the Wyman-Reagan union had become all too easy to see. The problem: the female half of the Hollywood dream couple found her dashing leading man to be a terrific bore. "Don't ask Ronnie what time it is," Wyman was said to have warned the actress June Allyson, "because he will tell you how a watch is made." By 1947, she had given up on the marriage, and the next year, she filed for divorce. In her petition to the court, she complained that her husband talked about politics incessantly. Industry gossip had her complaining about Reagan's self-absorption—"*I couldn't stand to watch that damn 'King's Row' one more time . . .*"

The breakup was public and protracted, and Reagan was the obviously humiliated party. At first, Reagan refused to accept that his idyllic union could come to an end. That didn't stop Jane, whose career was faring far better than her husband's, from getting on with her life. Attending the 1948 Academy Awards, Reagan witnessed Wyman, still legally his wife, arrive on the arm of another actor, Lew Ayres. Ayres and Wyman had starred together in the film *Johnny Belinda,* where—according to the Hollywood rumor mill—they had grown particularly close. "Lew is the love of my life!" Mrs. Ronald Reagan declared at a Hollywood gathering around that time. Humiliated but still unwilling to give up, Reagan turned for solace to the place where his romance had first blossomed: the gossip pages. There he proceeded to further humiliate himself. "The trouble is she hasn't learned to separate her work from her personal life," he told Louella Parsons. "Right now Jane needs very much to have a fling and I intend to let her have it." He was sure that in time, he and Wyman would reconcile and "end our lives together." But his best hopes came to naught. In 1949 the Reagan-Wyman union was officially dissolved. Out of love, and out of the public eye, Reagan was at his lowest, alone.

And then he found someone who saw him as even more heroic than even he had dreamed he could be. As it happened, Nancy Davis, the pretty actress Reagan took as his second wife on March 4, 1952, had enormous eyes that seemed always to be fixed on her handsome husband. Years later, the press would write derisively about Nancy's hypnotized affect as she watched her husband on political stages. The critique was unfair: the frozen public stare masked one of modern politics' savviest thinkers. Still, it is true that when Nancy Reagan looked at her husband she saw, always, the greatest hero she could imagine. In their marriage, "Ronald Reagan always received top billing," said Michael Deaver, the long-serving Reagan aide who observed Ronnie and Nancy's marriage at close range. "Nancy wouldn't have it any other way." Nancy agreed. "My life," she wrote in her memoir, "didn't really begin until I met Ronnie."

Chastened by the sensational coverage of his divorce, Reagan was at pains to keep his new marriage out of the papers. His wedding to Nancy had only two witnesses—the actor Bill Holden and his wife, Ardis. Still, within their cocoon, the Reagans were happiest being stars together. For a wedding gift, they asked Nancy's parents for a camera they could use to make home movies of each other. Ronnie especially treasured a birthday gift from Nancy: framed still photos from all of his movie roles.

Nancy was determined to give Ronnie in his second marriage all the things that he had lacked in his first. "Jane had said publicly that she was bored by all of his talking," Nancy wrote. "But I *loved* to listen to him talk, and I let him know it." Edmund Morris, Reagan's perceptive biographer, asked him to recall his mindset in the painful early days after the end of his first marriage. Reagan responded with a line he used in other places over the years: "I think the thing that I missed most was not, uh, somebody loving me. I missed not having someone to love." Writing down Reagan's words, Morris followed them "with a spiral curlicue useful to biographers, meaning, *He feels the opposite of what he says.*"

Yet he did love Nancy, and he was devoted to her, in his own particular way. Ronnie and Nancy, as it happened, were exceptionally well matched. Like her husband, Nancy was the product of a troubled, transient early childhood, leaving her to long for storybook pictures of domestic bliss. Nancy's ideal marriage was one that looked idyllic almost all the time. At the house they would eventually move into in Pacific Palisades, California, Reagan drew a heart in the drying concrete. Inside was the inscription "ND and RR."

That house would be comfortably appointed by General Electric, the other great force of salvation in Ronald Reagan's life. By the early 1950s, Reagan's big-money Warner Bros. contracts were gone. Income was low, and commitments—two children from his first marriage, a new baby with Nancy, the mortgage in Pacific Palisades and a sprawling California ranch called Yearling Row—were high. He needed cash. He was reluctant to entertain offers from television—TV actors were considered the poor relations of the era's big Hollywood stars. But after a dispiriting run as a Las Vegas nightclub act, he grudgingly agreed to serve as the host for a new half-hour television program, *General Electric Theater,* a teleplay he would introduce each week and in which he would occasionally appear as a player.

Then something wonderful happened: *General Electric Theater* was an immediate standout hit. Onscreen in front of millions each week, he was a celebrity again—and he knew it. His reservations about television vanished. "I am seen by more people in one week," he said proudly, "than I am in a full year in movie theaters." These were the early days of TV, when an advertiser's evening offerings held a place of honor in the American family's routines. Many children of the baby boom, a generation with whom Reagan would have a long and complicated relationship, would first encounter him on their living room sets, a smiling man with a warm voice, introducing that evening's program. He became as big a celebrity as he'd ever dreamed he could be. By 1958, a survey would determine he was one of the most recognizable names in America.

And he had ample opportunity to be recognized. In addition to his television appearances, Reagan's GE contract required him to serve as a corporate ambassador, traveling the country speaking to the company's workers. The routine was punishing—in his first year, 1954, he traveled to some 185 facilities, meeting a hundred thousand GE employees. Sometimes he would give as many as fourteen speeches a day. To him, the people in the audience were strangers. But they all knew who *he* was. It is impressive to see your face on a screen or your name in lights. But to travel through a series of strange cities filled with strangers who recognize you—that is fame.

Fame feels different the second time around. The young man who first encounters it assumes it will be a permanent condition. The middle-aged man who has lost it once before knows that at any moment it might disappear.

And by 1963, when Reagan went to work on the set of *Johnny North,* fame had disappeared. A year earlier, General Electric had pulled the plug on Reagan's television show. Reagan always suspected that he was being punished for his politics. GE liked his free market talk well enough, he figured, but company executives worried about alienating the Kennedy administration, on which they depended for large contracts. The reality was probably more prosaic: the show was getting beaten in the ratings by *Bonanza.* Either way, the practical effect was the same: by 1962, Ronald Reagan was out of the public eye once more.

How did he handle this second eviction from the limelight? In the official narrative of Reagan's rise, he didn't mind much at all. By his own account, Reagan was happy to have more time off to spend at Yearling Row, tending to his hunters and jumpers and working the land, coming down from the mountains only to film the occasional spot on TV. The years immediately following the end of *GE Theater,* Nancy Reagan would later say, were "years . . . of relative calm" when her husband was "glad to have a full-time family life."

But this image of Reagan as the happy gentleman farmer who moonlighted as an actor, the rancher who was satisfied with life out of the public eye, begins to crack on close inspection. In the early sixties, Dean Miller traveled to Yearling Row for an episode of his celebrity profile program *Here's Hollywood* to interview the Reagans. "Ronnie Reagan," Miller told his viewers, was "an intent man, not only about his career but about life in general. In fact it has often been said that Ronald Reagan is on a constant crusade and a man on a soap box."

For his interview, Ronnie leaned against a white fence, his brown hair uncharacteristically flying free in the wind. Then it was Nancy's turn. She answered questions haltingly while, in the background but well within the camera's view, her husband paraded proudly on his horse. Finally the star rejoined his wife. "Nancy, what is he?" Miller asked. "Is he an actor/rancher or a rancher/actor?"

"Oh," said Nancy, not sure what to say. She smiled and laughed uncomfortably. "Well, I think probably rancher/actor."

"Which do you think he likes better?" Miller pressed.

Nancy was still unsure of herself. She looked to her husband.

"Go ahead!" said Ronnie. "I won't step on your foot right here."

Nancy proceeded cautiously. "Well, he's very fond of ranch-ing . . ."

Miller didn't wait for her to finish the thought. "Yeah, I think some day when you hang up the grease paint," he said, turning back to Ronnie, "you probably want to come out here and settle down with the kids and lead the life of a country gentleman and a working rancher."

"Yes," said Reagan, broadening his grin to show his impeccably white teeth. "I'd like that very much." His smile grew wider and his face tighter. Reagan was a better actor than he ever got credit for, but this particular performance was far from convincing. By the looks of him, settling down as a gentleman rancher was the last thing he wanted.

And that makes sense. The story of Reagan settling into life as the happy country squire has one big problem. It neglects the power of a central, shaping force in Reagan's life: his remarkable ambition.

At its heart, the life story of Ronald Reagan is the story of an uncommon ambition pursued. It is a rare ambition that gets a teen-age boy out of bed in the morning every day of his summer vacation so he can work twelve-hour shifts as a lifeguard. A rare ambition that convinces a boy from a forgettable Midwestern town that he can be a star, that propels him to talk his way into a career on the radio and then in the movies. A rare ambition that gets the GE spokesman onto a train into the hinterlands week after week, year after year, in search of crowds he hasn't yet met. A rare ambition that makes the second son of a failed dreamer into the most famous man of his age.

To Nancy, Reagan's ambition was essential to understanding him—the key part that everyone always missed. "Ronnie's easygoing manner is deceiving," she wrote after the Reagans left the White House. "Underneath that calm exterior is a tenacious, stubborn, and very competitive man. Just look at the record. Ronnie rarely loses."

And yet, somehow, this man with the unceasing desire to win, this man whose life had been shaped by his need to be a star, *this* man was, at the age of fifty-one, perfectly happy to settle down into a quiet life on his ranch?

The people around Reagan when he parted company with GE would remember otherwise. By the time the Reagans wrote their postpresidential memoirs, in which they professed to have been happy to have the extra time with the family in the post-GE years, Ralph Cordiner, the chairman of GE who fired Reagan, had died, as had Charles Brower, the head of BBD&O, the advertising agency that produced the program. For his biography of Reagan, Edmund Morris spoke to Brower's widow. She recalled the fired Reagan as despondent: "What can I do, Charley? I can't act anymore, I can't do anything else. How can I support my family?"

Reagan denied Mrs. Brower's account, but it's clear that his prospects were indeed bleak. He went back to his old agent, Lew Wasserman, who by then had become one of the great men of Hollywood, having merged his talent agency MCA with Universal Studios. Wasserman reluctantly agreed to send around Reagan's résumé but was not very encouraging, warning him, "You've been around this business long enough to know that I can't force someone on a producer if he doesn't want to use him."

Out of work, out of the public eye, Reagan was at a crossroads once again. "Like any actor," he told a magazine interviewer in 1961, "I keep thinking that the big part is still ahead of me." But he was fifty-one years old when *GE Theater* was canceled. His father, Jack, had not lived to see sixty. He had been given a chance at fame not once but twice. There was little reason to believe that a chance would come a third time.

So it is no surprise that when at last Wasserman had a role to offer Reagan, in *Johnny North,* Reagan agreed to take it, bad guy or no.

And it is even less of a surprise that when Reagan saw the reality of the role he had accepted, he was not pleased.

For the rest of his life, Reagan would say that agreeing to appear in *Johnny North,* later renamed *The Killers* before its theatrical release in 1964, had been a mistake. Some of his admirers expunge the movie from the record entirely, claiming his movie career ended with *Hellcats of the Navy,* a 1957 tale of heroism in World War II. For his part, Reagan would acknowledge *The Killers,* but only to disparage it.

Officially, his objection was the casting—he was simply not meant to play a villain. "A lot of people who went to see *The Killers,*" he wrote in his postpresidential memoirs, "kept waiting for me to turn out to be a good guy in the end and dispatch the villains in the last reel, because that's how they had always seen me before."

And it's true that *The Killers* was not the sort of film for him. Reagan not only preferred to be the good guy, he preferred stories that affirmed the essential goodness of the rest of his country and humankind, too. That wasn't *The Killers,* a film that depicts characters without conscience and a world without good. It delights in violence. The theme of evil is there from the very beginning of the film, when viewers see Marvin's and Gulager's characters hunting down North at a school for the blind where he works as a teacher under an assumed name. Entering the school, they approach the receptionist, a blind middle-aged woman in pearls, and ask where they might find him. When she tells them that he is not available, they brutally assault her, pouncing on her in her chair and throwing her onto the floor. Even to audiences in later generations, the brutality of the sequence is jarring. Later in the movie, viewers see a disturb-ing scene in which Dickinson's Farr receives a forceful blow to the face from her boyfriend, not quite a punch but significantly more than a slap. The actor to deliver the blow was none other than Rea-gan himself. The film takes a casual attitude toward murder—by its conclusion, all of the leading players have been killed by someone else. After the movie's release, Reagan's daughter Patti was forbid-den by her parents to see it. "Everybody dies in it," her mother ex-plained.

"Mr. Norm," in other words, was well outside his comfort zone on this particular movie set. Still, Reagan's real problem with *The Killers* may have had as much to do with the parts of the film he found familiar as with the parts that were foreign and abhorrent. For in truth, Ronald Reagan and his character, Jack Browning, had more in common than the actor would care to admit. In the film, the rela-tionship between Reagan's Browning and Dickinson's Sheila Farr is a complicated one. She is his girlfriend, he pays her bills and keeps her in fancy clothes. But she looks elsewhere for romance and doesn't mind flaunting her liaisons with other men in front of the world, even in front of Browning himself. Browning endures these exhibi-tions in silence.

Browning was a cuckold. And playing him, Reagan might have been transported back to the lowest moment of his life: *Right now Jane needs very much to have a fling and I intend to let her have it.*

Earlier that fall, Reagan had filmed his entrance in the film in preproduction. No one would ever mistake it for a hero's entry—for one thing, it comes thirty minutes into the film, in a scene at a race-track, where Cassavetes's Johnny North is about to take part in an auto race. With a large crowd seated in the stands, Farr joins North in the driver's pit. She drapes her arms over his shoulder and flirts: "Just kiss me, you fool!" He obliges, passionately.

The camera cuts to view the kiss from farther away, through two round holes surrounded by darkness. Someone is watching the lovers through a pair of binoculars. Then the camera cuts again, to reveal, for the first time, the face of Ronald Reagan. He is in the stands with everyone else. And he is the one holding the binoculars, pulling them slowly down from his eyes.

That was the future that lay ahead of Reagan that weekend in November. Someone else would get the girl. He would be the one who watched.

THROUGH THAT AWFUL weekend, people kept their televisions on. For most, the days blended together to make one long ghastly montage, the days distinguishable only by subtle shifts in color and motion.

Friday: Darkness and chaos at Andrews Air Force Base . . . the dead president coming down in his coffin . . . the shadows falling over the faces of the mourners . . . the widow in her pink suit with its awful stains.

Saturday: Gray everywhere. Gray skies over the White House where the president's body lay in state in the East Room. The gray-faced president, hurrying out of the West Wing . . . a series of gray-haired men parading into the Executive Office Building to meet with him. In the afternoon, the new president makes a brief statement, declaring Monday a national day of mourning. When he finishes speaking, the NBC correspondent offers commentary: President Johnson "has been, shall we say, a little bit in the background today . . ."

Sunday: A hint of light . . . a clearing in the skies above the Capitol dome . . . flags and crosses flicker across the television screen . . . a crowd of unfathomable magnitude gathers on the Mall, lining up to bid the fallen leader goodbye . . . the networks show Army cadets in the chapel at Valley Forge, singing aloud the Lord's Prayer as they kneel row on row.

But then there was another, even darker turn. From nearly the moment of his arrest for the president's murder, Lee Harvey Oswald had been a fixture on television sets. Mesmerized by the camera lights pointed at him, Dallas police chief Jesse Curry had given the media the run of his police department. An FBI agent, arriving to sit in on Oswald's interrogation, had been amazed to find whole offices reordered to accommodate network cables creeping in through windows from the street. When, just before noon Eastern Time that Sunday, the press got word that Oswald was about to be transferred to the county jail, the assembled correspondents and photographers scrambled to get fresh pictures of the most hated man in the country.

And so NBC was broadcasting live when a man dressed in a dark suit and hat emerged from a crowd of reporters in the basement of Dallas Police Headquarters and walked right up to the assassin. Viewers at home saw this man shout at the assassin and then shoot him in the abdomen. "He's been shot!" NBC's correspondent Tom Pettit narrated, just a few feet from Oswald's crumpled body. "There is absolute panic. . . . Pandemonium has broken loose!" And the images on the screen showed this was in fact the case. As reporters rushed for the body, the police tried to push them back. But they seemed unsure of themselves.

News anchors did not yet have the ability to interview their correspondents by satellite link, so the only choice the networks had was to let the chaotic images from Dallas roll—the police seizing Oswald's assailant, an ambulance arriving to take Oswald away, the ambulance pulling up the ramp out of the basement, headed to a hospital, probably Parkland, one of the bystanders observed. It all created the effect of watching a gruesome TV crime procedural as it played out in tight TV time. Within twenty minutes, the assailant had been identified as Jack Ruby, a Dallas nightclub owner with ties to the underworld.

By nightfall, Kennedy's assassin had died and the networks had more sordid information about Oswald and Ruby than they knew what to do with. NBC aired a special broadcast on the two killers, retracing the steps of each over the previous three days. The program reached a climax with a scene from the Texas Theater, the movie house where Oswald had been arrested on Friday afternoon. The empty theater had been turned into a crime scene and was out of reach of a cleaning crew. The camera turned askew as it surveyed the interior, revealing discarded popcorn and drink containers. It was the kind of place that nearly every American had visited but that most had never really seen, not under the glare of bright lights. The scene was horrible, the effect chilling. It made it seem as though guilt for the nation's tragedy could not be confined to Oswald or Ruby or Dallas. It extended further, to any American who'd nibbled popcorn in a movie theater. Offscreen, a correspondent's voice made the link more explicit:

> The chase ends in a theater. A movie theater: This tawdry place of escape for our century. This place of cheap glamour, of magnified unrealities, of safe darkness for the lonely. This place to run to when, outside, the sunlight and the glare of noise and the competition and the dangers are too much. He came to this pathetic hiding place.

So there was Ronald Reagan, who'd made his life in that place of cheap glamour and magnified unrealities.

Reagan, who'd just started filming his awful new movie, ninety minutes of shooting and dying paraded across the screen.

Reagan, whose passion was politics, but whose politics was suddenly taboo.

Reagan, who longed to be the hero but was stuck with the only part he could get: the sleazy gangster in the dark suit.

CHAPTER THREE

Myths

November 25–29, 1963

Monday, November 25, was the day of mourning. Virtually all businesses were closed, and those who had to work were never far from a television. The sounds and images shown that day would endure perpetually in the nation's memory: Black Jack, the riderless horse trotting fitfully through the streets of Washington; the din of fifty fighter jets—one for each state—and Air Force One flying in tribute over the caisson as it reached Arlington Cemetery, the fallen president's final resting place; harsh, haunting tones flowing from the bagpipes of the Black Watch of the Scottish Highlands; the hushed crowd of more than a million watching the cortege pass by on Pennsylvania Avenue; little John F. Kennedy, Jr., raising his three-year-old hand in salute.

A collection of world leaders gathered to pay their respects in an assemblage not seen since the funeral of Great Britain's King Edward VII in 1910. It included President Charles de Gaulle of France, Prime Minister Alec Douglas-Home of Great Britain, President Eamon de Valera of Ireland, Emperor Haile Selassie of Ethiopia, King Baudouin of Belgium, Queen Frederica of Greece, and Prince Philip, the Duke of Edinburgh and husband of Queen Elizabeth II. Former presidents Truman and Eisenhower—old enemies—shared a pew in St. Matthew's Cathedral and a bite to eat after the burial.

But the center of the story was Jacqueline Kennedy, walking se-

A new hero: Johnson in the Oval Office, November 29, 1963.

© Yoichi Okamoto/LBJ Library

rene and stoic through the cold, clear day. Every move she made that long weekend was part of an exquisite pageant of agony. Her timing was eerie. On Sunday, around 12:30 P.M., she stepped in front of the cameras with her children at the North Portico of the White House to drive to a memorial service for her husband in the Capitol Rotunda. Mere minutes earlier, the nation had witnessed the shooting of Oswald on TV. Yet so powerful was the scene of Jackie in black with her children in blue coats and white gloves that the memory of the terrible scene in Dallas simply slipped away.

The funeral and burial scenes on Monday were much the same— Jackie seemed to have the power to stop time. Partway through the funeral procession from the Capitol to her husband's funeral mass at St. Matthew's Cathedral, she emerged from her car and walked the remainder of the journey in full view of the cameras. The visiting dignitaries, accustomed to traveling in grand processions, followed as an ordinary mob behind her, transfixed. At the funeral mass, she watched with studied concentration, her black veil framing her face. At the burial, she grasped the hands of her dead husband's brothers and knelt on the Arlington sod in prayer. That evening, Nicole Alphand, wife of the French ambassador, watched Jackie conduct a reception for the visiting dignitaries at the White House. She looked, said Alphand, "like a Roman Queen, a stone statue." London's *Evening Standard* was especially generous: "Jacqueline Kennedy has given the American people from this day on one thing they have always lacked—majesty."

Lyndon and Lady Bird Johnson kept a respectful distance from Jackie as they all moved through the events of the day. They were around her always, even walking behind her in the procession to St. Matthew's, despite the objections of the Secret Service. But they were careful to allow a few feet of space between themselves and the widow, her children, and her husband's family.

Still, it was awkward at times—hovering over another family in its hour of suffering. The Johnsons had never spent much private time with Jackie despite both Lyndon's and Lady Bird's best efforts.

Johnson, who was powerfully drawn to vivacious and beautiful women, had feverishly sought the favor of the First Lady during his time as vice president. But his Texan courtship rituals sometimes didn't translate. In one extravagant gesture early in Kennedy's term, he'd presented Jackie with two Hereford heifers and a pony named Tex. Jackie accepted the gifts warmly but returned them two years later, saying she had no place to keep them. Undeterred, Johnson took back the animals, sold them at market, and used the proceeds to purchase the appointment book used by Abraham Lincoln in the White House. He donated the book to Jackie's White House restoration project. When Jackie wrote Johnson to thank him, Johnson penned a provocative response: "Never before has Texas beef found a market of such quality in winding up on Mrs. Kennedy's bookshelves between the covers of Mr. Lincoln's records. Too bad it couldn't be on Mr. Lincoln's bookshelves between the . . . well, never mind." As Lady Bird's biographer Jan Jarboe Russell notes, "the tantalizing ellipses were LBJ's." Liz Carpenter, a clear-eyed Johnson aide, quashed the letter before it could be delivered to Jackie, noting diplomatically in the margins that the letter was "too flip."

Now, though, the gap between the Johnsons and Jackie was greater than the differences of region or taste; it was the gap between the living and the dead. In the first moments of unexpected widowhood, Jackie could not imagine life without her husband, could not imagine life at all. Accepting staffers' condolences that weekend, she had a standard response: *Poor thing, what will become of you?* She might have been speaking to herself. Paying his respects the night of the assassination, Ben Bradlee found Jackie to be a "totally doomed child" who looked as though she had been "burned alive." She would write to Bradlee a few weeks later: "I consider that my life is over and I will spend the rest of it waiting for it really to be over."

When Franklin Roosevelt died in office in 1945, his successor, Harry Truman, had rushed to the White House to call upon the dead president's widow. Finding Eleanor Roosevelt in her sitting room in the residence, an emotional Truman asked if there was anything he could do for her. Mrs. Roosevelt was composed and correct. "Is there anything *we* can do for *you*?" she replied. "For you are the one in trouble now."

That was too much to expect of Jackie, the doomed child. The most she could do for Johnson, her husband's constitutional successor, was to include him, briefly, in her despair. On Sunday, riding to a memorial service for her husband in the Capitol, she turned toward Johnson, sitting beside her in the limousine. "Oh, Lyndon," she said, "what an awful way for you to come in."

Her first concern was the part she had to play. She was the president's widow, a public figure, and she was determined to execute her performance flawlessly. She had personally selected many of the details of the two-day funeral ceremonies—the arrangement of the caisson, the officiant at the low funeral mass, the Irish cadets who would perform a mourning drill. A black lace mantilla would be fine for her to wear to the ceremony at the Capitol, she told her White House staff, but for the funeral, only a regular mourning veil would do.

She knew that the nation would be watching. Bradlee that weekend noticed how Jackie grew distracted by the television, the images "of the country grieving, of people, including herself and her children and the other Kennedys, filing silently, prayerfully past the presidential casket on view in the halls of Congress."

Not only did she see the nation's grief, she intuited its power. The tragic spectacle she created offered catharsis to the grieving nation— and made a resounding case for her husband's greatness. It was Jackie who insisted that, to the extent good taste allowed, President Kennedy's caisson should be fashioned in the form of President Lincoln's; Jackie who took a special interest in the account of Lincoln's funeral procession; Jackie who gave America majesty because she understood majesty's special value to history. She made her husband's greatness self-evident: Only a great president could provoke such a reaction from his people. Only a figure destined for history could earn such a day.

And this case for Kennedy was, inevitably, made at the expense of his successor. What made her spectacle tragic was the unspoken belief that Kennedy's kind of grace and greatness would not, could not, be seen again. However unconsciously, the story Kennedy's widow told that day directly refuted the story Johnson was trying to tell. He believed the country desperately needed a new leader to follow, a man on a horse to guide everyone out of the mud. She gave the country Black Jack, the willful steed with empty boots reversed in its stirrups and no rider at all.

And so as the hours passed, Johnson's aides and advisers worried more and more about how he could possibly start his new story for the country. They suspected Kennedy loyalists when rumors spread through the press corps that Johnson had been afraid to walk in the procession behind Mrs. Kennedy on account of security threats. On Sunday afternoon, Johnson spoke with Jack Brooks, a Texas congressman and a close friend. "We've got to start being—not to be cold-blooded, but I mean, to be realistic," said Brooks. "We ought to be pointing out that we've got a fine president that can do the job and *is* because it's good for the . . . continuity of the country."

But Johnson did not take the bait. He simply changed the subject: "Where are you eating dinner?"

His voice was calm and measured for a man who had endured three days of strain. By then, he had stopped trying to make the cameras turn toward him. Patience and restraint had never been Johnson virtues—"Lyndon wants it yesterday" was the saying among his staff—but there was one circumstance in which he was capable of not just patience but monkish discipline and self-denial, when he was capable of putting off all pleasure and gratification, of turning away from even the things he wanted most. He could deny himself anything when he had set his mind on a plan.

And that was how he kept himself contained as the Kennedys had their days—Saturday, Sunday, and Monday. In those days they took the nation's story further and further from him, into the realm of timeless drama, the realm of myth. He did not object; he mostly stood by and watched.

In public, he would say nothing, because in private, he had come up with a strategy. He had a plan to take the emerging myth of John F. Kennedy and make it work for him.

ON SATURDAY AFTERNOON, there'd been another unfortunate scene with Bobby Kennedy at the first cabinet meeting of Johnson's presidency. After the various department heads had gathered in the Cabinet Room, Johnson, sitting in the president's place at the table, started the meeting, taking the lead in the most formal setting he'd yet attempted. But something wasn't right. The attorney general's chair was conspicuously empty.

Its occupant was no farther away than the hallway. Tending a growing crop of resentment toward Johnson, Bobby Kennedy had thought about skipping the meeting, and entered only after some strong pleading from Mac Bundy. The other cabinet members, seeing the fallen president's brother walk in, rose in respect. Johnson made a point of staying seated. Bobby looked at him in stunned disbelief. "It was quite clear," Orville Freeman, the agriculture secretary, later said, "that he could hardly countenance Lyndon Johnson sitting in his brother's seat."

What followed seemed like a scene out of *Hamlet*. The new president, in the old president's place, spoke coldly of the constitutional succession. Then Adlai Stevenson, the UN ambassador, rose to read a lengthy statement he had prepared ahead of time, praising Johnson's performance since the shooting. Stevenson, twice the Democratic Party's nominee for the presidency, had long been disdained by the Kennedys, who saw him as weak—the most unpardonable sin. To Bobby, Adlai's words were "a few paragraphs on how nice Lyndon Johnson was," he would later say. "I felt it was fine. It just struck me that he had to read the damn thing."

Then Secretary of State Dean Rusk, the senior cabinet member and another old target of Bobby's disdain, stood to offer tribute and support. "A nice little statement," Bobby would later say. "Afterwards, somebody told me how impressed Lyndon was with Dean Rusk because he's the only one who spoke up at the Cabinet meeting. So I thought . . . what he wanted is declarations of loyalty, fidelity from all of us."

Given the circumstances, loyalty and fidelity were hardly unreasonable requests. But Bobby—sleep-deprived, transformed by grief—was not inclined to be reasonable. As the meeting progressed, he said nary a word, and his silent, sullen presence took hold of the president. Johnson's own words grew uncertain and hollow. After twenty or so minutes the meeting broke up and the cabinet officers departed, unsettled.

Johnson walked out of the meeting enraged, convinced that Bobby had deliberately come in late in order to humiliate him and thwart his efforts to take control. After the meeting, Johnson called House Speaker John McCormack. "I can't sit still. I've got to keep the government going," he told the Speaker. "But I don't want the family to feel that I am having any lack of respect, so I have a very delicate wire to walk there."

And it wasn't just the Kennedy family working against him—it was almost every member of the Kennedy court. By midday on Saturday, he had announced his intention to keep all of President Kennedy's cabinet. Nor would letters of resignation, he made it known, be accepted from any of the Kennedy White House staff. To a succession of bleary-eyed Kennedy men (for they were almost exclusively men) he'd offered the same "I need you more than he needed you" line. Sometimes he would add a hopeful corollary: "I consider you one of *my* men now."

A few of them were happy to become his men. McGeorge Bundy immediately attached himself to Johnson's side, offering crisp tutorials on world affairs and confident advice on how to handle the extraordinary assemblage of foreign dignitaries descending on Washington for the funeral. Bundy had been a loyal aide and admirer of President Kennedy. The assassination, he told the columnist Joseph Alsop, had struck him harder than the death of his own father. But as a buttoned-up son of Brahmin Boston, he was out of place in the wistful Irish wake scene playing out in the White House. To serve the president, to remember that "the show must go on," to *work*—that was the best way Bundy knew to cope.

Others found this comforting as well. Robert McNamara, the dashing defense secretary whom Kennedy had lured away from the presidency of the Ford Motor Company, was known in the press for his superhuman work habits. Now was no exception. He was everywhere that first weekend, shuttling back and forth over the Kennedy-Johnson divide. One moment he was consoling Bobby and Jackie in the White House and trudging up a sodden hill at Arlington Cemetery in the pouring rain to select the Kennedy grave site. The next he was sitting attentively at a Johnson cabinet meeting, with no hint, save the water dripping from his suit, that he had anything on his mind beyond his ongoing responsibilities as secretary of defense.

Dean Rusk quickly made himself available as well. The secretary of state had been a marginal figure under Kennedy, a president who had preferred to run his own foreign policy. But Rusk's stiff propriety and bureaucratspeak—qualities that had bored the Kennedys to death—were a comfort to Johnson. And it was a comfort and a happy coincidence that these three men—Rusk, McNamara, and Bundy—who were so ready to offer their allegiance happened to be the administration's three senior civilian national security officials.

Meeting with these men, Johnson began to look like a president. On Sunday, they joined him to hear a report from Ambassador Lodge on the situation in South Vietnam. Few Americans were thinking much about Vietnam in November 1963, but Johnson was more than familiar with the dire situation there. It had been American policy since the Truman administration to oppose Communist-influenced nationalism in Indochina, a colonial holding of France. After the French were defeated by the Communist nationalist Viet Minh at the battle of Dien Bien Phu in 1954, Vietnam had been partitioned into two zones divided at the 17th Parallel with a Communist north, led by Ho Chi Minh, and a non-Communist south with a capital in Saigon. Worried that a Vietnamese peninsula united under Communist authority could lead to Communist domination of Asia and the Pacific, the United States had become the chief patron of the Saigon government, a nominally republican regime led by a devout Catholic president, Ngo Dinh Diem.

South Vietnam had been a canker throughout the Kennedy presidency. The Vietcong, a North Vietnamese–backed Communist insurgency, had waged a brutal and effective campaign against the Saigon government. They were supported by a growing number of peasants in the South Vietnamese countryside. As the situation deteriorated, the Kennedy administration bankrolled an expansion of the South Vietnamese army and sent several thousand military personnel to serve as "advisers" in South Vietnam. The administration grew exasperated with its client, Diem, whom it considered a hapless defender of the regime who had needlessly antagonized his people by oppressing the country's Buddhist majority. Three weeks before Kennedy's death, a group of South Vietnamese generals had, with tacit U.S. approval, overthrown the Diem regime and gone on to assassinate Diem and his brother. The bloody conclusion had demoralized Kennedy. By the time he'd traveled to Dallas, he was deeply pessimistic about the chances of success for his administration's policy in Indochina.

Now, though, Kennedy was gone and the policy remained. Johnson listened as his new advisers gave a grim report: the new, post-Diem regime in Saigon was incompetent, and there was little hope that *any* South Vietnamese government could withstand the Communists without direct U.S. military involvement. Johnson would have to make a decision about Vietnam policy in the not-too-distant future. None of this was startling news to him. Johnson had visited South Vietnam in 1961; he had shaken Diem's hand. And he had been watching presidents face bad news from that part of the world for a decade, first as majority leader in the Eisenhower years, then as

Kennedy's vice president. This was what American presidents did: receive grim reports about Vietnam and conclude that there was no choice, for the moment, but to stay the course. Here at last was a chance to really act like a president. With Lodge, Johnson was forceful: "I am not going to lose Vietnam."

There were other grim comforts in those first days. J. Edgar Hoover, the director of the FBI, delivered breathless updates to the new president on the investigation into the crime in Dallas. Under Kennedy, Hoover had been in an open state of war with Bobby Kennedy, his nominal superior in the Department of Justice. A Hoover friend of long standing, Johnson knew that the director had been particularly enraged by Bobby's insistence that the director's communications with the White House go through him. Shortly after his first contretemps with Bobby, outside the Oval Office, Johnson received an update from Hoover on the investigation in Dallas. When the director had finished, Johnson signaled to Hoover that things had changed: "I wonder if you will get me a little synopsis and let me have what developments come your way during the day."

In Hoover, Johnson found allegiance and validation for the fear he still felt, both of which he'd struggled to find elsewhere. In the first moments after the assassination, when an international conspiracy seemed a very real possibility, Kennedy's aides were in a state of shock, too dazed to process the potential danger. By the time they emerged from that daze, Oswald had been captured. By Saturday morning, the consensus in the press seemed to be that Kennedy's killer was a crazed lunatic, not an international saboteur, part of a larger conspiracy.

But Johnson could remember the smell of gunpowder wafting over his limousine in Dealey Plaza. He had been roused from shock sooner than the others, jolted into reality by the fear that a nuclear war was coming and that he would have to stop it. He hadn't quite let go of this fear. "What would you think of the possibility a foreign government was involved in this?" he asked Kennedy's counselor,

Ted Sorensen, on Saturday night. "Do you have any evidence?" Sorensen asked. Johnson showed him a classified memo that vaguely outlined a threat. Sorensen brushed it aside, dismissively: "Meaningless."

And as the hours rolled by, that was how most of the Kennedy men seemed to Johnson: animated only in their contempt. On Saturday, Arthur M. Schlesinger, the young historian turned Kennedy aide, quickly penned a letter of resignation to the new president, which the new president just as quickly rejected. Schlesinger begrudgingly agreed to carry on, but he wrote in his diary, "my heart is not in it." Taking a phone call from Johnson that weekend, Sorensen replied, "Yes, Mr. President," and then broke into tears. Recounting his long journey with the body of the fallen president on Friday night, Kennedy's loyal aide Dave Powers was defiant: "I carried *my* president."

When he looked at the Kennedy aides, Johnson would later say, "the impact of Kennedy's death was evident everywhere—in the looks on their faces and the sound of their voices." This made sense enough. The Washington that Johnson knew was a kingdom ruled by various tribes, a place where the fortunes of lesser men and women were tied to the destinies of the politicians they served. Allegiance was everything: you were a Kennedy person or a Johnson person. That was what the Kennedy aides were struggling with, he thought—the fall from power. "Suddenly they were outsiders," he said, "outsiders on the inside. The White House is small but if you're not at the center it seems enormous . . . So I determined to keep them informed, I determined to keep them busy."

But Kennedy's men were mourning more than just the loss of influence; they were mourning a part of themselves. Washington was "littered with male widows" after the assassination, Joe Alsop later wrote, men who knew that "nothing would quite be the same." The dead president, with his wit and his charm and his erudition and his good looks, had taken the grubby work of politics and infused it with glamour, taken the drudgery of policy work and made it into the stuff of high purpose. Working for him, his aides felt like better, brighter versions of themselves.

And they felt young. Everyone longed to be invited to the Kennedys' dinner dances, magical evenings in the East Room where the president and First Lady hosted an eclectic mix of accomplished artists and intellectuals along with glamorous jet-setters from New York and Europe. A guest at one of these occasions could see Jackie and her sister Lee cheering on Averell Harriman, the seventy-one-year-old undersecretary of state, as he enthusiastically danced the Twist. There was sumptuous French cuisine and there were easy French customs—few expressed surprise at the sight of a powerful administration official shamelessly flirting with a woman who wasn't his wife. That sort of thing was expected of Kennedy courtiers, along with a fondness for poetry and rollicking games of touch football, and a willingness to be thrown into Ethel Kennedy's pool. All together, it was another, more golden adolescence for men with gray hair.

Now it was gone. After the assassination, Mary McGrory, a reporter for *The Washington Star* and a White House favorite, mused "We'll never laugh again." From Daniel Patrick Moynihan, one of the administration's bright young intellectuals, came the instantly famous answer: "Oh, we'll laugh again, Mary, but we'll never be young again."

And when they saw Johnson asking them to work with him, *determined* to make them feel included, the Kennedy men remembered how old they really were. The new president was only eight years Kennedy's senior, but no one thought of them as peers. Johnson, said the *Times* two days after the assassination, "is of a different generation . . . from the Kennedys and their friends, although he has said privately that he admires them for being so 'hip.' " The Kennedys' friends, in turn, saw him as anything but "hip," and they loathed him for it. For when they looked at Lyndon Johnson—his hair thinning, his waist bulging, his face weathered from thirty years working the Washington system—they saw not a stranger, but themselves.

They sought escape from this sad reality in fantasies of the future. Lunching with Daniel Moynihan and John Kenneth Galbraith the day after the assassination, Schlesinger imagined a new ticket for 1964 with Bobby Kennedy as the candidate and Senator Hubert Humphrey as his running mate. The others were skeptical. For that to happen, Galbraith observed, Lyndon Johnson would have to slip up in a bad way.

So THAT WAS what he found in the White House—indifference and anger from Kennedy's family, machinations from Kennedy's men. And elsewhere in the city, there was what appeared to be the greatest threat of all: the fast-forming legend of John F. Kennedy himself. Everyone, it seemed, was reshaping the late president's life and death into a mystical tale of immortal greatness met with inevitable fate.

In Washington that weekend, otherwise rational people spoke of omens and prophecy. Everyone noted the odd collusion of the weather with the national mood. For weeks there had been unseasonably warm temperatures and hardly a cloud in the sky. And then, the morning after the assassination, came gray skies, bitter winds, and buckets and buckets of rain. Ted Sorensen recalled a conversation he'd had with Kennedy just before the president left for Dallas about the "rule of twenty." Since 1841, a president had died in office at least once every twenty years. Kennedy's death, eighteen years after Roosevelt's, continued the pattern. On Saturday afternoon, the Kennedy family announced that the president would be buried in Arlington Cemetery. As it happened, Kennedy had visited the cemetery just a few weeks earlier. A story spread that weekend of the president standing in the very spot that would become his final resting place, looking entranced. He wished, he was supposed to have said, he "could stay here forever."

Cultivating the image of urbane gentleman scholar, Kennedy and Sorensen had peppered his speeches with countless lines from poetry and scripture. Now people were poring through those lines for anything that prophesied his untimely end. A favorite poem, it was said, was Alan Seeger's "I Have a Rendezvous with Death." Everyone noted the words of the psalmist Kennedy had planned to include in the Dallas speech that he never gave: "Except the Lord keep the city, the watchman waketh but in vain."

The eager mythmakers were happy to alter Kennedy's character in order to find the haunting hand of fate. "All sorts of people are remembering all kind of things Jack Kennedy never said," his friend Charlie Bartlett grumbled. "I never heard him say he'd 'like to stay here forever.' That was not like him." (He was right—Kennedy hadn't said that about Arlington—though he had stood on the gentle slope that would become his grave site and called it "one of the really beautiful places on earth.") But no one was remembering the complete Jack Kennedy anymore—the one who loved Shakespeare and the classics but also dirty jokes and childish limericks, the man who hosted Pablo Casals at the White House but who privately preferred corny standards like "You're Part of My Heart," the one who liked poems about death but also joked about it in the easy Irish Catholic way. When Johnson worried about safety on his vice presidential trip to Vietnam in 1961, Kennedy had reassured him: "Don't worry, Lyndon. If anything happens to you, Sam Rayburn and I will give you the biggest funeral Austin, Texas, ever saw."

But that wasn't the President Kennedy people needed anymore. They needed him to be the solemn prophet of his own doom. A constellation of omens made his death somehow easier to take: he was not the victim of a freak encounter with a madman; he was a noble hero who'd met his mystically ordained fate. And as such, he would have an ancient hero's greatest reward: immortality. Soon there would be plans to rename New York's Idlewild Field as John F. Kennedy Airport, Florida's Cape Canaveral as Cape Kennedy, and New Hampshire's Mount Clay as Mount Kennedy. In the fallen president's home state of Massachusetts, the state legislature would consider embossing "Land of Kennedy" on Bay State license plates. In West Virginia, one newspaper would propose changing the name of the state to "Kennediana." Overseas, there would soon be Kennedy-

Platzes and rues J. F. Kennedy. A Bavarian mine would mint special gold and silver Kennedy medallions with the inscription WE ALL HAVE LOST HIM.

Everywhere, he was compared to another president, perhaps the greatest president, felled by an assassin's bullet nearly a hundred years before. The comparisons started mere moments after Kennedy's death. Speaking on the Senate floor on Friday afternoon, the Senate chaplain recalled words spoken after the death of Abraham Lincoln: "God lives and the government at Washington still stands." Returning to Washington from Dallas that night, Jackie sent word that a description of Lincoln's catafalque in her White House guidebook should be consulted and the structure replicated in the East Room. The next day, *The New York Times* printed Walt Whitman's elegy to the Great Emancipator, "When Lilacs Last in the Dooryard Bloom'd," on its editorial page and noted bitingly that in 1865, Dallas newspapers had cheered the president's death. To Richard Cardinal Cushing, preaching in his archdiocese of Boston that Sunday, Kennedy was "a youthful Lincoln, who in his time and in his sacrifice has made more sturdy the hopes of his nation and its people." Kennedy, said one observer, was "the second president we've lost now on the civil rights issue." That was a common impulse—to say that, like Lincoln, Kennedy had died while pursuing the highest moral calling, had worked tirelessly to transform and redeem the nation, and had paid the ultimate price. It was consolation in the face of an unspeakable loss: Kennedy was dead, but his legacy and legend would live forever.

But there was one problem with this plan: the Kennedy record. It was true that the Kennedys had brought glamour and a special grace to the capital. And it was clear that Kennedy's oratory had inspired the nation and given it a sense of renewed purpose after the dull and dowdy Eisenhower years. But his record of domestic achievements was mediocre at best. At the time of his death, Kennedy was pursuing two legislative initiatives, a civil rights bill and a tax cut intended to stimulate demand in the economy. Both were languishing on Capitol Hill, their passage far from certain despite Democratic majorities in both houses of Congress. Kennedy was a liberal who had eloquently articulated liberal ideals in his speeches, but he had done little to advance the policy aims of the left on major issues—universal health care, racial equality, and an end to poverty in the richest nation in the history of the world.

On civil rights, the signal moral issue of the day, Kennedy had been at best a reluctant leader. Kennedy always remembered that he had won the presidency in 1960 by the smallest of margins—0.1 percent of the popular vote—and that, like every Democratic president since Reconstruction, his victory had been secured with the help of a majority of states of the Old Confederacy. The Kennedy who ran in 1960, Martin Luther King, Jr., would later say, talked the right talk on civil rights, but he had been "so concerned about being President of the United States that he would compromise basic principles." Only after televised coverage of King's 1963 Birmingham campaign took hold of the nation's conscience and Northern whites (including the middle-class whites in Northern suburbs who would decide the *next* election) grew outraged at the behavior of white segregationists in the South—only then did Kennedy push for passage of an antisegregation bill.

Kennedy would never have claimed to be Lincoln, nor would he have recognized the expansive posthumous claims that were being made for his presidency. A memo that Sorensen prepared for Democratic congressmen at the beginning of 1962, touting the success to date of the Kennedy presidency, betrayed the meager policy aspirations of the New Frontier:

1. There has been no finding of communism or corruption in the government . . . 2. There has been no serious inflation, and without controls . . . 3. Budget balances (for fiscal 1963) . . . 4. No Korean-type war . . . 5. No appeasement. Increased Ike's defense budget 15% . . . 6. Religion and youth no longer issues . . . 7. Prosperity returning . . . 8. Farmers happier.

It was hardly the stuff of a transformative presidency, and Kennedy did not fool himself into thinking otherwise. A week before his death, he idly speculated about the location of his presidential library with his friend Charlie Bartlett. Then he stopped himself: "There won't be a library if we don't get a second term. No one will give a damn."

In that pithy assessment, as much as in the noble lines in the shining speeches, was a hint of what *was* special in Kennedy, what actually made him great. He had a rare ability to cut through the flattery and falsity that surround any president and to see the world as it really was. He had a higher tolerance for ambiguity, contradiction, and imperfection than many classic politicians, who tend to see things as black or white, success or failure, win or lose. He valued courage and he took informed risks, but he always understood that things might not work out the way he predicted or wished.

That was what made Kennedy a great match for his moment in history: he was a man with an exquisite sense of irony, living in a deeply ironic age. It was an age in which peace was kept by weapons that could destroy the world. An age in which a nation that fancied itself the greatest champion of individual liberty the world had ever known had concentrated in its government more power than the world had ever seen. An age in which men accepted that they would have to do bad things in order to advance a greater good.

No amount of reasoning, no clever contortion of logic could explain these contradictions. The only honest way to reconcile them was to accept that the sweep of human history is beyond human understanding, and to accept that though human beings might try, indeed *should* try, to predict the future, their predictions will ultimately fall short. Kennedy had seen his two elder siblings, destined for lives of glory, die young in tragic accidents. Twice he himself had nearly been killed by serious illness. He was a politician, a Catholic, and a Kennedy, and all of these allegiances taught him that nothing is eternal in this world. He brought to the White House an intuitive skepticism toward visions of certain victory or glory.

When, as president, he failed to heed this intuition, disaster inevitably followed. He was skeptical when, in 1961, his intelligence advisers promised that an American-backed invasion force arriving at the Bay of Pigs would prompt the Cuban people to rise and overthrow Fidel Castro. He muzzled his doubts and got the greatest fiasco of his presidency.

He swore afterward that he would not make such a mistake again, and he didn't. In October 1962, when satellite images revealed Soviet nuclear warheads in Cuba, Kennedy's military advisers counseled immediate bombing or invasion. True, such action might trigger a nuclear response from the Soviets, but in that event, they reasoned, America's superior strike force would eventually prevail. "Those brass hats have one great advantage in their favor," Kennedy mused privately at one point. "If we . . . do what they want us to do, none of us will be alive later to tell them they're wrong."

Kennedy saw the reality: there was no such thing as "winning" a nuclear war. So he found a middle path between invasion and capitulation, a path that eventually produced a safe resolution of the Cuban Missile Crisis. Under unimaginable pressure, Kennedy displayed courage reminiscent of the greatest wartime leadership of Abraham Lincoln or Franklin Roosevelt. Crucially, he was able to tolerate the anxiety of uncertainty. And he refused to relieve that anxiety with the cold certainty of doom. After his death, Kennedy's country would learn through the painful experience of Vietnam how valuable that tolerance is in a president, and how rare.

But the same qualities that made Kennedy great in moments of crisis—intuition, skepticism, realism—could often make him appear cautious and halfhearted when he turned to domestic politics. His posture on domestic issues only makes sense when considered in the context of the political forces that shaped Kennedy's day: the consensus politics that had governed America since the time of Franklin Roosevelt.

THE "NEW DEAL consensus" was born in a moment of crisis. The Great Depression of the 1930s left millions of Americans destitute. Without bold action, unrest would have threatened the survival of the republic. Responding to the turmoil, President Roosevelt offered a new covenant between the American people and their government. In exchange for expanded, centralized power, Washington would shield its citizens from the most savage effects of market capitalism with labor protections, relief for the poor, and a savings program, Social Security, for retired wage earners. This was a radical transformation for what had been an essentially conservative country, and it stoked vehement opposition from the right. But voters endorsed it, granting Roosevelt a landslide in his reelection bid of 1936, followed by two more terms in the White House in 1940 and 1944 and another for his successor, Harry Truman, in 1948.

In 1952, Dwight Eisenhower and the Republicans finally managed to recapture the presidency. Rather than rolling back the New Deal, they ratified it. In his two terms in office, Ike maintained the Democrats' tax and social welfare policies, rededicated the government's commitment to Social Security, and, through the creation of the interstate highway system and the new Department of Health, Education, and Welfare, strengthened Washington's centralized power. All the while, he maintained broad popularity. "Gradually expanding federal government," Eisenhower concluded, was "the price of rapidly expanding national growth." When Kennedy ran for the presidency in 1960, the role of government he articulated was virtually indistinguishable from that envisioned by his Republican opponent, Richard Nixon.

Yet while the New Deal consensus was broad and enduring, it was always tenuous. From the horrors of the McCarthy period, in the late 1940s and early 1950s, liberal politicians learned that they would have to be tough on Communism abroad if they wanted to pursue progressive policies at home. And even then, left-leaning Democrats were hamstrung by reactionary elements in their own coalition. In the Congress, conservative Southern Democrats held disproportionate sway, thanks to their monopoly on powerful committee chairmanships. In the Roosevelt and Truman administrations, liberals were regularly thwarted in attempts to expand labor protections, pass civil rights legislation, promote full employment, and introduce nationalized health insurance. The story of American politics in the 1930s, '40s, and '50s was that of America embracing the New Deal vision of an activist federal government protecting the common man and promoting the general welfare. But it was also the story of the failure of policymakers to bring that vision fully to pass.

Idealistic intellectuals on the left believed that the 1960s, and the Kennedy presidency, would be different. After the dull complacency and lazy materialism of the Eisenhower years, they embraced Kennedy, an attractive mainstream politician who would talk frankly about America's problems and who would urge the country to use progressive means to solve them. They saw his election as the start of a great liberal era in American politics. Through advances in technology, medicine, and the social sciences, that liberal era could produce policies that took the most difficult problems in American life—poverty, racism, disease, failures in education, housing, and urban policy—and make them obsolete. They were living in a time of unprecedented prosperity, and they believed that through enlightened economic policy, that prosperity could go on and on. With such abundance, soon every American could live a life of material comfort and spiritually fulfilling purpose. To the left's optimistic intellectuals, that glorious future was obviously near at hand.

Kennedy shared these aspirations, but not the confidence that they would soon come to pass. He saw the politics of his time with the same clear-eyed realism with which he saw everything else. And he saw that a future of liberal triumph was far from certain. He remembered the narrowness of his margin over Nixon in 1960. He saw the growing strains in the Democratic coalition, the increasing impossibility of reconciling its segregationist and civil rights wings. He wondered about the millions of middle-class Americans leaving the cities for the suburbs, leaving behind their ties to urban government programs, turning instead toward a new politics of . . . *what*? He didn't know exactly where the country was turning; more than that, he saw that the country itself didn't really know. A talented president could shape the nation's future, and he intended to try. But he would try deliberately, strategically, sometimes even cautiously. He believed that change took courage, but that it also required realism. And it needed time.

Before his death, that caution had greatly disappointed Kennedy's supporters on the left. They bemoaned the gap between his soaring liberal oratory and his paltry liberal record. They assumed he wasn't one of them—he was a conservative, like his father, or he was weak or vain. But they might have listened to his speeches more closely. Again and again, as a candidate and as president, Kennedy advised the nation that a better world was possible, but that it would not come easily and would not come soon. That was his real greatness: urging people to commit to take real risk, to work and to make sacrifices for noble goals even if they couldn't know how long it would take for those goals to be fulfilled. "All this will not be finished in the first one hundred days," he said in his inaugural address. "Nor will it be finished in the first one thousand days, nor in the life of this administration, nor even perhaps in our lifetime on this planet. But let us begin."

What, though, to make of those words now, when it had all come to an end? For the people Kennedy had left behind—his friends, his family, his followers—those were the hardest words to face. Kennedy had served as president a mere 1,036 days. The first one thousand days, the life of his administration, his lifetime on earth: all were one and the same. That couldn't be the case for his greatness—his telling them that his work was far from done.

They had to make the opposite message true: that the great struggle was over, that Kennedy's brief presidency had been a moment of unprecedented progress and achievement, that his thousand days had been time enough. Soon, they would make this their explicit message. In 1965, Schlesinger would publish the first scholarly narrative of the Kennedy presidency. In it, he made the case that Kennedy's presidency had brought transformative solutions in civil rights, nuclear arms control, the plight of the poor, relations with Latin America, and management of the economy. "He had so little time," Schlesinger wrote, but "he had accomplished so much." The author even reversed the meaning of Kennedy's inaugural message with the title of his book: *A Thousand Days*.

But in those first hours of grief, Kennedy's aides were left with a problem—how to make the case that his record of accomplishments was matchless, when his record of accomplishments was so short? How to say he changed the country when his bills for change were still languishing on Capitol Hill?

It was in that problem that Johnson saw his opening. For the Kennedys to have their myth, they needed some Kennedy accomplishments. Legislative accomplishments. And legislative accomplishments were something Lyndon Johnson knew how to deliver.

Here was his chance to change the story, subtly but unmistakably. The Monday of the funeral, he met with the nation's governors, who were assembled in the capital for the services. In tribute to the late president, he told them, he would make an all-out push for Kennedy's languishing legislative priorities: the tax cut and the civil rights bill. With these goals, it would not be disrespectful of Kennedy's memory for Johnson to seize the reins of power and lead the nation out of the swamp. It would be *honoring* Kennedy's memory. Years later, Johnson described his thinking to the historian Doris Kearns Goodwin: "Everything I had ever learned in the history books taught me that martyrs have to die for causes. John Kennedy had died but his cause was not really clear. That was my job."

The Kennedy legend, which seemed at first like a weight around Johnson's neck, would in fact be his means to rise. He would take the story that Kennedy's courtiers and family were telling and use it as his pretext for setting the country's eyes on him. The possibilities were endless. The country would watch him as he won John F. Kennedy's battle. And after a while, people would get used to watching him do great things, until *that* was the only story on everyone's mind. Carrying out the work of Kennedy's thousand days, he would earn himself an even greater thousand days of his own.

And he could see his chance to get started in the most dramatic setting possible. On Wednesday, he would address the nation at a joint session of Congress. There he would make the country watch as he grabbed hold of John F. Kennedy's myth and began to tell a new story of even more exciting possibilities to come.

JOHNSON'S UNIQUE POWERS of perception were never better than when he had a plan. When he'd set his mind on an objective, he could look at just about anyone, friend or foe, and figure out what that person needed. In their grief, it turned out, Kennedy's men were beyond decency and decorum, but not beyond vanity. On Monday, after the funeral, a bleary-eyed Ted Sorensen returned to his West Wing office, where, at the new president's request, he reviewed working drafts of Johnson's upcoming address to the nation. John Kenneth Galbraith, the liberal intellectual and Kennedy aide, had been making it known all weekend that the new president had personally requested that *he* draft the speech for the joint address. Sorensen was accustomed to having the final say on presidential speeches. Reading over the Galbraith draft that afternoon, he was unimpressed.

"So you liked Galbraith?" he asked Johnson on the phone that night.

"Yes sir, I did," the president replied.

"Well, you see, I *didn't*. So, uh—"

Johnson quickly reversed himself: "I didn't think it was any ball of fire. I thought it was something you could *improve on* . . . I read it [in] about three minutes while the economic counselors were coming in here."

He went on, puffing up Kennedy's speechwriter: "But I think a much better speech could be written. I'm expecting you to write a better one."

"All right," Sorensen said. "I'll give you another and I'll give you Galbraith at the same time and you can take a look."

Not surprisingly, poor Galbraith ended up disappointed.

But even as he genuflected, Johnson showed that he was beginning to move on. Editing Sorensen's draft, Johnson and his aides accepted deference to the old president but drew a line at deprecation of the new one. A list of Kennedy's accomplishments was shortened. The section on Johnson's agenda was lengthened. Gone altogether was Sorensen's opening line: "I who cannot fill his shoes must occupy his desk."

On the day of the joint session, Johnson asked three of the most diehard Kennedy loyalists—Ted Sorensen, Pierre Salinger, and Larry O'Brien—to ride to the Capitol with him. "This is a fine speech," Johnson said during the car ride, meaning the prepared text. "Ninety percent Sorensen, ten percent Johnson."

Sorensen was not an admirer of the Johnson changes. "No, sir, that's not accurate," he said. "Not more than fifty percent Sorensen."

"Well, anyway," said the president, "your fifty percent is the best."

"On that point, Mr. President, we agree."

Sorensen wasn't joking, but Johnson chose to laugh in response.

He laughed because he could; he knew that the speech he was about to give—100 percent of it—was going to be the start of something big. He knew it when he entered the House chamber to the booming introduction, "Ladies and Gentlemen, the President of the United States." He knew it as he reached the podium and saw the chair beside Speaker McCormick where, as vice president, he had watched Kennedy address the Congress. No more—that chair would be filled by the president pro tempore of the Senate until 1965 when, in accordance with the Constitution, a vice president would be inaugurated along with the winner of the 1964 presidential race.

And as soon as he spoke the first words of the speech, everyone in the quiet Capitol knew it too.

"All I have," he said, pausing, as if to emphasize just how much he had indeed, "I would have given gladly not to be standing here today.

"Today John Fitzgerald Kennedy lives on in the immortal words and works that he left behind. He lives on in the mind and memories of mankind. He lives on in the hearts of his countrymen."

First he echoed the sentiments that had been around the world in the past five days: "No words are sad enough to express our sense of loss."

But then he shifted that sentiment ever so slightly: "No words are strong enough to express our determination to continue the forward thrust of America that he began. . . . And now the ideas and the ideals which he so nobly represented must and will be translated into effective action."

Effective action, everyone in the chamber knew, was a Johnson specialty. And in that room, Johnson could see all of the people he would need to summon to action once more.

Here was Everett Dirksen, the Republican leader from Illinois, in love with Senate custom, more in love with his own voice. Johnson would need his tacit support to break the Southern logjam on civil rights. He would use the post-assassination distaste for extremism to pressure Dirksen to be his bipartisan partner.

Here was Harry Byrd, the patrician Virginia segregationist and ardent conservative, who railed eternally against excessive government spending and ballooning deficits. Johnson would need to find a way to appease him if he was to get the Kennedy tax cut through.

Here was Minnesota's Hubert Humphrey, the great liberal workhorse of the Senate. He was already at the top of everyone's list of possible running mates in the upcoming 1964 campaign. Johnson would have to dangle that job in front of Humphrey enough to make him *Johnson's* workhorse in the Senate now.

And here was Richard Russell, the elegant, eminent senator from Georgia, the man who had been Johnson's mentor and father figure since his early days in the Senate. Russell was perhaps the most talented legislator of the twentieth century, and unquestionably the century's most effective defender of racial segregation. The affection between Johnson and Russell was enduring. Johnson would call on the Georgian's wise counsel again and again in the days and weeks ahead. He had already determined that Russell should sit on an independent commission, headed by Supreme Court Justice Earl Warren, to investigate the Kennedy assassination. But if Johnson was going to pass the civil rights bill, he and Russell would have to go to war.

And that war, Johnson made clear, was a war he intended to win.

"No memorial oration or eulogy could more eloquently honor President Kennedy's memory than the earliest possible passage of the civil rights bill for which he fought so long. We have talked long enough in this country about equal rights. We have talked for one hundred years or more. It is time now to write the next chapter, and to write it in the books of law."

Words like these reassured many in the president's party. But Johnson was doing something more—he was recasting the country's understanding of what the grand spectacle of the past five days had been about. The moment of infinite sadness was now, in the president's words, a "moment of new resolve." The American people had become "a united people with a united purpose." By *acting,* under Johnson's sure hand, the country would "resolve that John Fitzgerald Kennedy did not live—or die—in vain." He closed the speech with lines from the hymn "America." Two days after the assassination, in the midst of that awful first weekend, he'd heard the hymn in a service at St. Mark's Episcopal Church on Capitol Hill. There the words had brought tears to his eyes. But now he read them triumphantly: *America, America, God shed his grace on thee!*

The ovation in the room was resounding, ongoing, and genuine. Members of Congress wept openly. In the press galleries, reporters' minds and pencils raced. For days, there had been only one story that mattered in Washington. Now there were new stories appearing right and left.

There was, for the first time in a long time, an exciting legislative story: a new push for action from a calcified Congress, led by the greatest legislator in a generation.

There was a story of reconciliation and redemption: the first Southern president in a century was now pledging to be the president to finally end legalized segregation in the South.

And there was a story of human will: the indomitable spirit and the restless energy of Lyndon Johnson were now married to the highest office in the land.

Johnson, of course, was at the center of all these stories, and his erstwhile adversaries were left gasping. During the speech, Schlesinger watched Bobby Kennedy "pale, somber and inscrutable . . . applauding faithfully but his face set and his lips compressed." Afterward, Joe Alsop came upon Ted Sorensen, who was still smarting over Johnson's changes to his draft. Trying to be sympathetic, Alsop said that he thought that ending with the lines from "America" had been a "corny" touch. Sorensen stared back at him blankly. Including those lines had been his idea.

But the praise for the address was otherwise unqualified, and Johnson basked in it. The crowd, he boasted afterward, had interrupted him with ovations no fewer than thirty-four times. When he'd finished speaking, he looked down at his lectern, took a sip of water, and put his glasses in his pocket. He was done for the moment, but the applause did not stop, and the camera did not cut away.

JOHNSON HAD GIVEN the country, exhausted from five emotional days of mourning, permission to get back to normal again. Television, the voice of authority in the worst moments of the assassination weekend, bolstered Johnson's message with a return to regularly scheduled programming on Tuesday afternoon. "We cannot bring him back by making sadness our national obsession," the TV host Jack Paar reminded his audience that week. "Our life goes on. Scientists, students, mothers, laborers, entertainers, all must proceed with the business of living."

And so they did, turning toward happier, lighter things. On Fifth

Avenue, the mourning crape came down and the Christmas decorations went back up. "You can't stop the living from living," said Robert Pell, chairman of the Packard Bell Corporation. "I don't know of anyone who has called off his Christmas tree." If anything, the trees would be taller and shinier this year. As the holiday approached, the nation embraced preparations for it with a manic intensity. Holiday sales in the first week of December would be up 7 percent over the same week a year earlier.

All across the country, people who had wondered how life would ever return to normal found that life picked up right where it left off. And in the West Wing of the White House, the president of the United States proceeded with the nation's business from the Oval Office. He had successfully and permanently taken possession of the space on Tuesday, November 26, when the last of Kennedy's items had been removed. Behind his desk, he placed a photograph of his late predecessor. That was his message: Johnson's toil would be blessed by Kennedy, looking on.

In this time for legends, the new president had his eyes beyond the mortal world. By turning Kennedy's work into "a martyr's cause," he would ensure that Kennedy could live forever. And that Johnson could, too.

But immortality comes at a high price. In attaching himself to the Kennedy legend, Johnson was accepting the standard of great accomplishment Kennedy had been careful not to claim for himself. By aiming for immortality, Johnson was setting out to be the hero of a myth. And in this myth, the role of hero had already been filled.

JACQUELINE KENNEDY RETREATED from public view after her husband's funeral. She did not attend Johnson's speech to the joint session. Thursday, November 28, was Thanksgiving. With her children, she spent the holiday at the Kennedy compound on Cape Cod. Everything was eerily altered. The sprawling Kennedy family was there, but they were subdued and depressed rather than boisterous and irrepressible. They were in Hyannis Port, where her husband had basked so happily in the sunshine. But now he was gone and the sunshine was, too, replaced by gray skies and a cold New England wind.

At the head of the table was her father-in-law, Ambassador Joseph P. Kennedy. Joe Kennedy was the patriarch, the one who had dreamed it all: a public life for his children, a presidency for his son, a ruling dynasty for his family someday. He was the first one to see how the Kennedys' unique mix of glamour, style, and power could be used to seduce the American public. Long before that November, before his son was turned into a martyr, he had invented a legend for the Kennedys.

The ambassador and Lyndon Johnson had never been close, but they had maintained a cordial friendship of convenience. As two powerful Democrats, each was happy to accept flattery and favors from the other, knowing fully that the time might come when one of them would have cause to put a knife to the other's throat. In the 1960 presidential campaign, when Joe Kennedy's grand ambitions for his son came up against Johnson's ambitions for himself, the knives indeed came out. As the delegates gathered at the 1960 convention to select a nominee, Johnson, still in the running, had attacked the Kennedy patriarch for his infamous tour as Roosevelt's ambassador to the Court of St. James's in the late 1930s, when he'd counseled appeasement of Hitler's Germany.

For Joe and Jack Kennedy that was politics, nothing more. But others in the Kennedy family were less forgiving. Jackie, who doted on her father-in-law, had watched in horror when, on a postconvention visit to Hyannis Port as Kennedy's newly minted running mate, Johnson had appeared before the press sitting in Ambassador Kennedy's chair. "I was just thinking," she later told Arthur Schlesinger, " 'Do you know what chair you're sitting in after the things you said about that man?' "

Now, at the forlorn Thanksgiving table, the ambassador sat in his own chair, but he seemed hardly himself. Shortly after his son became president, the elder Kennedy had suffered a massive stroke that left him paralyzed and largely unable to speak. In his house that holiday, Jackie saw a man who had lost everything. Over and over he repeated the one word he could still say: "No."

The next day, the acclaimed journalist Theodore White was in the chair at his dentist's office when he was brought an urgent message: President Kennedy's widow was trying to reach him. He rushed home and called the former First Lady, who was still at Hyannis Port. On the phone, Jackie told White she had some things she wanted to tell the nation. She hoped he would be the journalist to help her. Might he be able to come up from New York to the Cape that afternoon? She would be happy to send a Secret Service limousine.

White called the editors of *Life* magazine, where he was a contract writer. The latest edition of the magazine was already being printed—a giant commemorative issue, with page after page of vivid photographs from the funeral ceremonies—and holding open the press run into Saturday would cost the magazine $30,000 an hour. But this was an incredible story—Jackie's first interview since the assassination. The editors agreed to wait, and White hurried up to Massachusetts.

He arrived in Hyannis Port late in the evening, in a driving rainstorm. Ushered into the house, he found Jackie waiting for him in black slacks and a beige pullover sweater. She was "without tears," White would say, "drained white of face." She looked at him plaintively: "What can I do for you?" she asked softly. "What shall I say?"

It was she, however, who had summoned White to the meeting. And it was she who would control the conversation and the story. Starting in, White recalled something she'd said to him earlier on the phone, a concern she'd expressed about how history would remember her husband. He wondered if she might expand on that. Instead, she launched into something else entirely—a graphic, detailed narrative of the events in Dallas and the moments after:

Then Jack turned back so neatly, his last expression was so neat . . .

I could see a piece of his skull coming off. It was flesh-colored, not white . . .

I kept bending over him saying, Jack, can you hear me? I love you, Jack . . .

Those big Texas interns kept saying, Mrs. Kennedy, you come with us . . . but I said, I'm not leaving.

White listened in growing confusion and dread. Jackie clearly needed to get these details out of her, but they were too much for the grieving nation, too soon. Was this the reason she had summoned him? He looked at the clock. Midnight was fast approaching, and the editors of *Life* were waiting. Where was the story he was to write?

But the former First Lady knew what she was doing. "There's one thing I wanted to say," she said, shifting away from the horrid assassination scene. "I keep thinking of a line from a musical comedy. . . . At night before we'd go to sleep . . . we had an old Victrola. Jack liked to play some records and the song he loved most came at the end of this record:

'Don't let it be forgot,
That once there was a spot
For one brief shining moment
That was known as Camelot.'

That word—*Camelot*—no one had attached it to the Kennedy administration before. But how perfectly it fit. Camelot, the mythical capital of King Arthur's court, a place removed from constraints of time and geography, a place removed from the squalid ordinariness of mortal life itself. Camelot, home to the beautiful Queen Guinevere, fated to love King Arthur and to lose him and mourn him. Camelot, the poets' symbol of the ancient bond between love and predestined doom: *Oh brother, had you known our Camelot, built by old kings, age after age, so old the King himself had fears that it would fall.* Camelot, the city of lore, where knights of the Round Table dreamed of the Holy Grail and eternal life.

Camelot, not Dallas, was what Jackie wanted White to remember that night. When she'd finished talking, he stole away to a servant's room and quickly pulled together a draft that had Camelot as its central theme. It was late when he'd finished, but Jackie was still awake, waiting. He handed her a copy of his story. Then he hurried to the kitchen, where he dictated the story to his editor over the telephone.

Soon it was two in the morning. In the kitchen, White haggled with his editor, who worried that he was overplaying the Camelot theme. As they spoke, Jackie entered the room. Listening to the argument, she shook her head—Camelot *had* to stay. White continued to resist the editor's entreaties, and after a time he prevailed.

Jackie handed her draft to White. She'd marked it up heavily with her own edits and additions. After the mention of Camelot, she had amended her comments to make her meaning more explicit. Now there was an expanded quotation: "There will be other great presidents and the Johnsons have been so kind to me but there will never be a Camelot again." And at the end of the draft, White found an entirely new sentence the former First Lady had written in pencil in her own neat handwriting, her own end to the story: "And all she could think was to tell people there will never be that Camelot again!"

The careful planner: Lady Bird at The Elms, November 1963.

© Yoichi Okamoto/LBJ Library

CHAPTER FOUR

Home

December 25, 1963–January 6, 1964

Christmas Day 1963 dawned bright and clear in the Texas Hill Country. Lady Bird Johnson greeted the morning from her own bed at the LBJ Ranch. She'd had a long journey from Washington the day before and a long first month in the White House. Still, she rose early to set about her day, delivering poinsettias to Hill Country neighbors and pulling together a Christmas celebration for her family.

It had been only one month since she'd last been home. A month since she'd busily prepared for a post-Dallas visit from the Kennedys that would never come to pass. A month in which she'd seen her life altered beyond recognition. She found even the ranch transformed. Guardhouses dotted the perimeter and large searchlights surrounded the house. From now on, she supposed in her diary, "we will never be quite settled into the anonymity of darkness."

Christmas, at least, would bring some reprieve from the intrusions. The doormat at the LBJ ranch house read ALL THE WORLD IS WELCOME HERE, and over the years the Johnsons had hosted countless acquaintances from their Washington life. Christmas, though, had always been different, a retreat into another time. Typically, Lyndon and Lady Bird and their daughters would open presents and spend the day motoring through the hills of Lyndon's boyhood on the Pedernales River delivering gifts to friends and relatives—a box of candy here, a bottle of Scotch whisky there. The plan for Christmas dinner this year was much the same as it had been in years past—twenty-three family members gathered at the ranch house table.

But the old times were gone. Just as the assembled kinfolk were about to sit down to their dinner that afternoon, a large bus appeared outside the ranch house. Out poured a pack of reporters and photographers who had come for a prearranged photo opportunity of the new president celebrating his holiday.

For President Johnson, these were the most important guests of the day. He greeted them eagerly and posed happily for the photos, dressed in a green plaid jacket. The whole thing was supposed to take a moment: the press pack would get its picture and then return whence it came so that the Johnsons could celebrate the holiday in private. But after posing, the president lingered with the press, introducing his relations. The reporters dutifully wrote down the names— Uncle Huffman Baines, Cousin Oriole Bailey. Lyndon sucked in the attention. Perhaps the reporters would like a tour of the house?

Lady Bird looked on warily. Already, she'd agreed to host the press corps for a barbecue in two days' time. "Honey," she reminded her husband, "I promised to give them a wonderful tour when they come back on Friday. The turkey is ready and the dressing is not getting any better."

The president would not be deterred. "It'll only take a minute," he told her. He beamed at the reporters: "Come on in."

And so, with the dinner guests waiting, some fifty journalists trailed along behind the president as he led the way through his ranch house. He walked quickly, sharing details of the house's construction, pointing out the paintings of Texas landscapes hanging on the walls. He guided them through the collection of framed photographs, a window on Johnson family greatness. He proudly showed off a letter from Sam Houston, first president of the Republic of Texas, written to one of Lyndon's great-grandfathers.

Meanwhile, Lady Bird dashed toward the master bedroom. She

knew her husband, and she knew what was coming next. She hurried to lock the door behind her and began preparing the room for outside eyes. Sure enough, in a moment came a knock at the door and the sound of someone fiddling determinedly with the knob. Then came the raised voice of the president: "Mrs. Johnson's locked the door on me!" She opened the door and smiled as the mob barreled in.

The next stop on the tour was the outdoors, where the president held forth on the habits of the four-hundred-acre working ranch and the modern conveniences with which he had equipped it. "Lynda," he called to his elder daughter, "do you know where to turn on the Muzak?" Soon, there was dance music blasting from a speaker in a large live oak tree. He was proud of his sophisticated system: "We used to dance a lot."

Lady Bird watched as her smiling husband made his way through the pack of admiring observers. Her dinner was getting cold and her private peace had been disturbed. But here was her husband, showing off his ranch, talking of great Johnsons past and present. Watching Lyndon perform for a captive audience—this, more than anything, was what Lady Bird knew as home.

FOR A MONTH, the nation had watched with eager attention as Johnson performed an unending, fast-paced "Let Us Continue!" show. In his first weeks in office, the new president had met with the nation's governors, the Kennedy cabinet, the congressional leadership, representatives of business and labor, and leaders of the civil rights movement. He had plotted legislative strategy, consulted with his counterparts around the globe, and played host to some two hundred visitors, including much of official Washington.

It seemed he was always working, always moving. "He assumes that if there is something to be done, it must be done immediately, if not sooner," wrote James B. Reston in *The New York Times*. "He now has three telephones in his car, with five circuits, and the amazing thing about it is that he seems able to talk on all five at once, carry on a conversation in the back seat, and direct traffic on the side." Johnson, Reston wrote, "has done everything but cut the White House lawn."

Of course, this sort of showing was nothing new for Johnson. He remembered his goal: seduce the country with a fresh story of all the great things that were soon to come. And when he had his mind set on a goal, Johnson's labors knew no limit. Washington was a city that ran on the currency of ambition, a city where ostentatious displays of overwork were obligatory. And yet for the last thirty years, people who came across Lyndon Johnson had said the same thing: "I never saw a man work harder." In the 1950s, he had amassed enormous power in the Senate by making it a hub of constant activity, a study in contrast to the languid Eisenhower White House. His senators were expected to match their leader's output. One night, when Hubert Humphrey complained that he really must be getting home for dinner with his family, Johnson lost his patience. "Dammit, Hubert," the majority leader said, "you've got to make up your mind whether you're going to be a good father or a good senator." For Johnson, the answer was self-evident.

Now every waking minute was about proving he was a good president. He seemed to be everywhere. Invited for a breakfast meeting at the White House, Republican Charles Halleck, the House minority leader, accepted the president's offer of a chauffeured car to bring him to the Executive Mansion. Opening the door to the limousine, the congressman was surprised to find the president of the United States waiting for him inside. Johnson popped up constantly on Capitol Hill, dropping in at the last minute at a surprise party for the Senate majority leader one day, a Christmas party with the minority leader the next.

Arriving for a meeting with Johnson at the White House one afternoon, two Baltimore *Sun* reporters found him itching to make a jail break. Hurrying the reporters into his car, they headed for lunch with the Texas delegation on Capitol Hill. Walter Lippmann, the columnist and lion of the left, picked up the phone at his Northwest

Washington home one evening in early December and heard Johnson's voice on the other end of the line: "Could I drop by and bum a drink from you?"

He was working harder than any president Washington had seen before, and he made sure the country knew it. "Man-in-Motion Johnson," *Time* called him, "mixing solid business with image-making busy-ness." As the Johnson presidency entered its second and third weeks, his staff began feeding morsels to the press about the boss's punishing routine. Readers soon knew all about the new president's "two shift day": Up by seven with papers in bed, dictating orders to his aide, Jack Valenti. Then over to the Oval Office by nine for meetings that lasted through lunch. Next, a brief nap, followed by a swim in the White House pool, usually accompanied by a coterie of staffers who offered advice on strategy as they paddled around with their boss. (These sessions could get awkward—usually, at Johnson's insistence, no one wore clothes.) Toweled off and changed into a fresh shirt, he'd work until seven-thirty or eight, barking orders at his secretaries to get this senator or that cabinet secretary on the line. Then a late dinner with Lady Bird and their high-school-age daughter Luci (their elder daughter, Lynda, was studying at the University of Texas) and whatever pack of aides or congressmen he'd chosen to bring in for the occasion. Then more work, maybe a massage just before midnight, with three TVs blaring in the background, then reading until one or two in the morning. Then, four or five hours later, the same thing all over again.

An endless cycle of work, work, work, not just for the president, but also for his staff. The papers were full of details about the circle of able men Johnson had brought in for his White House staff—men like Valenti, the former Texas adman; Walter Jenkins, the first-among-equals aide of long standing; Bill Moyers, the polished twenty-nine-year-old Texan who, since Dallas, had never been far from Johnson's sight. These men, the press noted, had designed their lives so they could do their boss's bidding at all times. They'd learned it was best not to lunch outside the White House, lest they look up from their meals to find an alarmed maître d' rushing over to alert them to the very important person calling on the phone. They installed telephones beside their beds. In time, they would receive special cars with radio-phones so that there would never be a minute when they were out of reach. "The LBJ phone calls would catch people in the most intimate circumstances," Johnson aide Liz Carpenter would later write. "Shaving, bathing, pulling a new girdle over the knee-bones. . . . Suffice it to say that my husband more than once shouted into the night, 'I don't care if he is President of the United States! Does he have to butt into *everything?*'"

Just about. After a photo op in the White House Treaty Room, Johnson asked the assembled reporters if they'd care to walk back to the West Wing with him. Soon they found themselves on an impromptu tour of the residence, following him into the quiet splendor of the Queen's and Lincoln bedrooms. This was unknown territory. Jackie Kennedy had allowed reporters into the residence only on special occasions, during which every step had been carefully stage-managed. Now things felt considerably more ad hoc. "Isn't that bed a little short for you?" a reporter asked Johnson. "I don't know," the president replied. "I haven't slept in it."

At least not yet. If he had his way, it seemed, the new occupant of the White House would ruffle every bedspread in the residence, stamp on every piece of grass on the White House lawn, and personally inspect every piece of state silver.

And, most important, sign every bill he could get the Congress to pass. For Johnson, there was no more pressing task than proving he could get the Congress to act. Only by getting the Kennedy bills out of the Congress could his new story start to look real. The press profiles that December invariably described the new president as a master legislator, just as they invariably noted that most of the Kennedy program had been hopelessly stalled on Capitol Hill for the better part of a year. "We shall be wrong . . . if we look upon the Kennedy program as if they were an architect's plans for a building which is begun but only partly completed," Walter Lippmann wrote on December 3. "The truth is that Johnson has suddenly become president at a time of deadlock and standstill. . . ."

If Johnson didn't do something, fast, the whole mood of rapid reanimation in the country would be at risk. He spent December signing bills, puffing them up with all the drama of his office. He held grand White House signing ceremonies for billion-dollar bills subsidizing college construction, vocational training, and the fight against air pollution. He'd ostentatiously hand out pens marked "President of the United States—The White House" to grinning members of Congress. ("You're the *y* in Lyndon," he told one senator.) "Altogether," *Newsweek* noted just before Christmas, "the President used and gave away 169 pens (cost $177.45) last week and dispensed more energy than a man half his age of 55."

In exchange for those pens, he got that most valuable commodity for a president: momentum. Every new bill that Johnson signed in Kennedy's name made Johnson look like more of a winner, easing the way for an even easier victory to come. Opposition was nearly nonexistent, so determined was the country to join in the spirit of moving on. The conservative intellectual William F. Buckley was a rare voice of dismay: "Are we now being emotionally stampeded into believing that Kennedy was the incarnation . . . and that respect for him requires that we treat his program like the laws of the Medes and the Persians?"

But Johnson knew that the biggest prize—passage of Kennedy's civil rights bill—would not come nearly so easily. Over Thanksgiving, Johnson had asked Larry O'Brien, Kennedy's chief vote counter, about the prospects of the civil rights bill. O'Brien delivered a bleak report. The bill was stuck in the House Rules Committee, thanks to the committee's obstinate chairman, Howard Smith of Virginia. The White House would have to break a coalition of conservative Southern Democrats and Northern Republicans to get it out. Johnson advised a strong public campaign of moral pressure against the GOP. "Say to the Republicans, you're either the party of Lincoln or you ain't."

The message from the administration was simple: this time would be different, this civil rights bill wasn't going away. Johnson pressed the point in the most personal of ways. On December 7, he greeted Dick Russell at the White House. Throughout the difficult period of transition Johnson had leaned on his old mentor for counsel. ("Nobody ever has been more to me than you have, Dick, except my mother," he reminded the distinguished Georgian on the twenty-ninth of November.) But now, when Russell appeared at the White House, Johnson greeted him as an adversary.

"I'm not going to cavil and I'm not going to compromise," Johnson told the senator. "I'm going to pass it just as it is, Dick, and if you get in my way, I'm going to run you down. I just want you to know that, because I care about you."

"Mr. President, you may be right," Russell replied, coolly. "But if you do run over me, it will not only cost you the South, it will cost you the election."

For Johnson, though, Russell was a more potent reminder of the danger he faced if he *didn't* secure a victory on civil rights. The Georgian's devotion to segregation had come at the expense of his own ambitions for the White House. "If Dick Russell hadn't had to wear Jim Crow's collar," Johnson told an aide in the early days of his presidency, "Dick Russell would be sitting here now instead of me."

But Johnson was the one who was president. And as he looked to the new year that last week in December at the LBJ Ranch, he knew the challenge still facing him. He had to convince the country he was not just moving quickly, but moving toward great things.

As promised, two days after Christmas, the national press corps reappeared at the ranch for the barbecue with the First Family. This time, Lady Bird was ready to play the gracious hostess. After the reporters arrived, she joined them on a school bus for a guided tour of the ranch. She told the story of Lyndon's brave and illustrious forebears, the ranchers who had settled the Hill Country, how Lyndon's grandfather had settled there after the Civil War and how in time his children and grandchildren had taken over the land. She drew a link from this proud heritage straight to her husband and herself—in 1951 they had bought and renovated what became the LBJ Ranch from a Johnson aunt. "You enjoy talking about what you love," she later told her diary, "and I love this place."

Even if she hadn't enjoyed talking about it, of course, she would have done it all the same. Nearly every day in her twenty-nine years of marriage, Lady Bird had worked to understand her husband's needs and help however she could. Now was no exception: she would do her part to make sure her husband's new story took hold. She was diligent about it: "I keep reminding myself of Lyndon, for whom it is hardest of all to carry on," she told her diary in early December. "I find myself repeating that 'new resolve,' which he urged on all of us last week in his speech to Congress."

Lady Bird understood better than anyone else in the nation that whatever the people on television were saying, whatever she and her husband *wanted* them to say, the transition in the White House had in fact been far from seamless. A day after the funeral, Lady Bird had arrived at the mansion for a visit with Jackie Kennedy to discuss what life in the White House would be like. She found the widow to be "orderly, composed and radiating her particular sort of aliveness and charm and warmth." She marveled as Jackie showed her around, remarking over the trompe-l'oeils in Jackie's sitting room—"one of the most exquisite rooms I have ever seen"—and the Cézannes hanging on the wall. Still, at times the darkness crept in. Lady Bird noticed the boots that had been in the stirrups of Black Jack, the funeral procession's riderless horse, on a table in the Yellow Oval Room. "Don't be frightened of this house," Jackie told her, sounding rather like a departing mistress at the outset of a gothic tale.

That evening, Lady Bird returned to The Elms, crestfallen. Looking around at the home she had made for her family, she spoke of how much she'd miss it. It was a much more comfortable house than the White House would ever be.

In thirty years of politics, she'd endured her share of uncomfortable homes. Shortly after marrying Lyndon in 1934, she'd arrived in Washington to find that they would live in a dreary bedroom in the dingy Dodge Hotel. It was a tiny, unpleasant nest, but not so tiny as to prevent Lyndon from filling it with young congressional aides, blustering on at all hours of the day and night.

The undulations of Lyndon's advancing career would take the Johnsons to ten different homes in the next eight years of their marriage. Lady Bird suffered through the constant upheaval. Finally, in 1942, the Johnsons purchased a two-story colonial on Thirtieth Place in the sleepy outer reaches of Northwest Washington. Having at last a space of her own, she'd looked forward to taking her time decorating. But Lyndon Johnson had never taken his time with much of anything, and he quickly grew impatient with the empty rooms. Seized by impulse one day, he found a furniture auction and, all at once, bought an entire house's worth of Victorian furniture. In fact, he'd bought enough to fill a much larger home, leaving the home to sink under the weight of its own decor.

At The Elms, she finally had a chance to get it right. After Kennedy's election in 1960, the Johnsons prepared to take on the vice president's traditional role as a formal entertainer for the administration. The overstuffed house on Thirtieth Place would never be able to accommodate the large crowds the Johnsons might expect. (Congress would not designate the large Victorian house on the grounds of the U.S. Naval Observatory as the vice president's official residence until 1974.) In the spring of 1961, the Johnsons found a larger house, a three-story brick and stucco mansion in the rarefied Spring Valley section of Washington.

The house, modeled on a château in Normandy, was only thirty years old, but it aspired to ancient greatness. Named Les Ormes for the proud elm trees that dotted the property, it had been the home of the grande dame of Washington society Perle Mesta. It had a large marble foyer, sun rooms, sweeping terraces, grand chandeliers, and floors made of parquet imported from an actual Louis XV château.

Shortly after purchasing it for $160,000, the Johnsons rechristened it "The Elms." "Every time somebody calls it a château," Lyndon growled, "I lose fifty thousand votes back in Texas."

The press smirked at the Johnsons' ostentatious ambitions. ("Ormes and the Man" read the headline in *Time*.) But for Lady Bird, The Elms was a paradise. Free at last to take her time in decorating, she'd added Western accents to Mesta's French decor, covering the downstairs in satin and filling the foyer with paintings of Texas landscapes and drawings of Texas birds. In the living room, she placed a cherry-red chair "that seems to say 'Come in.' "

Her great pleasure was her garden. All her life, she had found special peace in the delicate beauty of flowers and trees. She lined the walkway to the pool with boxed English hollies. She planted zinnias, marigolds, and red, white, and pink petunias in her cutting garden. In the rich soil of Spring Valley, she had finally found a home she could love.

Now the great need of Lyndon and the nation—moving on— would require her to leave that beloved home behind. Though not right away. In her first days as a widow, Jackie had said that she intended to leave the White House quickly. But then there was Thanksgiving and the visit to Hyannis Port. November turned to December and still the old president's family remained in what was now the new president's house. Reporters and Washington gossips began to snicker, but Lady Bird silenced them with a single statement, delivered by her press secretary: "I would to God I could serve Mrs. Kennedy's comfort; I can at least serve her convenience."

Finally, on December 7, a call came from J. B. West, the head usher at the White House, informing Lady Bird that the Kennedy family had left the residence for good. Photographers snapped pictures of Jackie, dressed in black from head to toe, and the children, in their blue funeral suits, as they climbed out of a limousine in Georgetown, where Averell and Marie Harriman had made their house available for the family's use until Jackie could find a place of her own.

Meanwhile, Lady Bird and her daughter Luci were arriving at the White House with the Johnsons' two beagles, Him and Her. In her hands, the new First Lady clutched a portrait of Lyndon's first Washington mentor, the late House Speaker and eminent Texan "Mr. Sam" Rayburn. A few days later, she met with a group of female reporters in the White House library. As always, she stuck to the official message: "When I wake up in the morning," she told them, "I feel at home." But in the privacy of her diary, she noted that it would not always be easy to live life in "this glass house." In the residence, she placed her desk up against a window, looking out over Andrew Jackson's magnolias. One afternoon not long after her arrival at the White House, she stopped a maid who was drawing the curtains for the night. "Please," said Lady Bird, "don't ever close the light out until the very last ray is gone."

"I feel," Lady Bird told her diary on her first night in the White House, "like I am suddenly onstage for a part I never rehearsed." This was a common nightmare, but one that would be particularly unsettling for Lady Bird Johnson. "Practice makes perfect" was a guiding principle of her life. As a child, she would study lessons late into the night, earning nearly flawless marks in school. At the University of Texas, she majored in journalism and dreamed of an exciting life as a reporter, covering national politics. But she also took extra courses for a teaching certificate, just in case.

Assiduous preparation had been her bulwark against an unpredictable life. Claudia Alta Taylor—her lifelong nickname came from a nurse who called her "purty as a lady bird"—was born in Karnack, Texas, in 1912. Her childhood, spent in the thick forests of east Texas in a rambling white-columned mansion called the Brick House, was privileged but lonely and marred by trauma. In 1918, her mother, Minnie Pattillo Taylor, suffered a fatal injury in a fall down a circular staircase. As she lay dying in the hospital, she looked at her five-year-old daughter, Lady Bird, standing beside the bed, and wailed: "My poor little girl, her face is dirty . . . Nobody at home to take care of you but the black nurse."

But there was someone at home besides the "nurse"—the little girl's father. Thomas Jefferson "TJ" Taylor had built a great fortune as a dry goods salesman in Karnack. T.J. TAYLOR, read the sign on his store, DEALER IN EVERYTHING. Known as "Cap'n," he was a man with tremendous power and a forceful manner of exercising it. In her biography of Lady Bird, Jan Jarboe Russell quotes a Karnack neighbor: "As a child growing up, I was taught there were three things you never questioned—God, country and Mr. Cap'n."

For Lady Bird, Mr. Cap'n was an uneven presence: fawning and loving one moment, filled with fury the next, gone altogether after that. Like the man she would marry, he seemed to fill any room he entered. The Cap'n had horrible rows with any number of opponents: with Minnie's disapproving family members who would swoop in to look after her little girl; with his sons, Lady Bird's older brothers, who chafed under his rule; and with the tempestuous women he courted after his wife's death. His daughter retreated to out-of-the-way corners of the old house and quiet places in nature, seeking shelter and escape. The world around her could not be trusted. She learned to find order within herself.

It was a skill that came in handy in her first years in the nation's capital. As a young congressman's wife, she immersed herself in the byzantine regimens of protocol that governed social life in official Washington: a daily routine of afternoon visits to the homes of various dignitaries, where she'd deposit calling cards with her name and Lyndon's. The less she left to chance the better. "Usually," she would recall, "I hoped the ladies weren't in, so I wouldn't have to stay."

When her husband became a national politician, planning became more expansive and intricate. Before leaving on official trips, she would write out her outfits for each event on the schedule, planning times and location for changes of clothes. Arriving at a hotel, she would arrange her clothes in the closet in hanging bags, ordered precisely as to when she would need them.

But in adult life as in childhood, she could only impose order in her own affairs. Marrying Lyndon Johnson had taken her far from the Brick House but not out of the storm. At the house on Thirtieth Place, she would spend many a night waiting for word from her husband as to when he would be coming home. Late in the evening, she would learn, via a brusque phone call, that his arrival was imminent, that he would be bringing four, six, ten, or more guests, and that they expected supper—hot!—on arrival. A doorbell left unanswered or a drink left unserved would always prompt a familiar bellow from Lyndon: "Dammit, Bird!" Witnessing one particularly violent outburst, Speaker Sam Rayburn was stunned: "By God, he's gonna kill her!"

Sometimes, it seemed, that really was his intent. One afternoon in Washington, the couple went horseback riding in Rock Creek Park. Approaching her horse, a tempestuous stallion, Lady Bird was characteristically cautious. Her husband helped his wife gingerly onto the horse. Then, suddenly, Lyndon slapped the stallion on its rear, causing it to bolt wildly. Lady Bird, terrified, grasped at the reins as the horse nearly threw her from her mount. When the animal slowed, she returned, shaken, to her husband. "Damn you!" she said. "I could have been killed." Lyndon would not apologize. To him it was a funny joke.

More often, his attacks were psychological. Guests were constantly embarrassed by the way Lyndon tore into Lady Bird in public. He offered a running critique of his wife in which no aspect of her person was off limits. Common sources of complaint were her appearance, her clothes, and her general lack of sophistication in comparison with the well-heeled women of Washington. And when one of those women happened to catch Lyndon's fancy, he would pursue her with the same determined force he applied to the rest of his life. During their years in Washington, Lyndon had developed a reputation as one of the capital's great and shameless seducers. He had two serious extramarital affairs, one with the actress turned congresswoman Helen Gahagan Douglas, the other with the socialite Alice Glass. He made little effort to hide either relationship, squiring the women to Washington social functions, holding their hands in public, kissing them passionately in front of aides.

Lady Bird knew what was happening, and she didn't say a word. "Everyone felt sorry for her," said Virginia Durr, a friend and fellow southerner in Washington. "He yelled at her, he ordered her around. He left her alone at the most important times of her life, and made no secret of his affairs. Still, she stayed loyal." Her loyalty, it often seemed, was the most pitiful kind. To Jackie Kennedy, who knew about wayward husbands, Lady Bird gazing at Lyndon looked "sort of like a trained hunting dog."

The artful homemaker forced constantly to leave her home. The placid cultivator of order and routine married into wrathful chaos. The woman gazing lovingly at her torturer, like some kind of dog. It would seem that Lady Bird had chosen a life custom-tailored to bring her misery.

Yet there was more than that to the Johnson marriage. There were the moments of tenderness and affection. And there was the fact, obvious to anyone, that Lyndon Johnson, the most powerful man in Washington, relied on Lady Bird. He needed her more than he needed anyone else. And there was something else, something particularly important to the woman who grew up in the gothic gloom of the Brick House. During her childhood there, Lady Bird would escape to her quiet corners to read stories of ancient kings and dream of faraway lands. As a young woman, she had aspired to be a reporter in the most exotic place she could think of: Washington, D.C. She wanted to be the observer of great drama, not the center of the drama itself. But she, too, wanted to live a hero's tale.

And then she'd met Lyndon Johnson, a man who could give her exactly that life. On their first date, he told her of his work as a young congressional aide in Roosevelt's Washington. He told her of the New Deal, of the men around Roosevelt, of the busy and thrilling capital, which seemed a world away. "It was just like finding yourself in the middle of a whirlwind," she remembered years later. "I just had not met up with that kind of vitality before."

"You're seeing the best side of me," Lyndon warned her in those early days. Lady Bird was only twenty-two, but she was not naïve about human frailty. She knew that Lyndon's worst side might be very bad indeed. She also would have known the alternative available to a well-off Southern girl like herself, a future of silky drawing rooms and lamplit passages, crisp linens and climbing wisteria, a handsome husband who would never dream of being indiscreet if by chance he strayed from home. She could see it all. And she wanted more.

That was what she'd chosen in Lyndon: more. She did not regret it. "Ours was a compelling love," an octogenarian Lady Bird told Jan Jarboe Russell. "Lyndon bullied me, coaxed me, at times even ridiculed me, but he made me more than I would have been."

To wit, she was now First Lady of the United States, leading a group of reporters from that exotic city—Washington—through the hills and fields of the LBJ Ranch. And it was she who was telling *them* the origin story of Lyndon Johnson, the nation's new hero.

As the bus drove on, they spotted her husband driving through the fields with two guests—Secretary of State Rusk and Secretary of Agriculture Freeman—with the top down on his car. This was a favorite ranch pastime: Lyndon riding forward, showing off all that was his. It was this side of Lyndon that made the trade-off seem worth it. She would put up with the rages, the women, the chaos, the strangers traipsing through her house. None of that mattered as much as the way she felt when she watched Lyndon Johnson in his home country, his mind fixed on a dream.

THE JOHNSONS' VISIT to Texas was expected to last through the New Year holiday, but the "Man-in-Motion" president made clear that his week on the ranch would be no lazy idyll. The week between Christmas and New Year's Day brought a state visit by Chancellor Ludwig Erhard of Germany and large clusters of official Washington to the LBJ Ranch for meetings with the president. "It seems as if one great crescendo of activity follows another so rapidly that I wonder how Lyndon manages to shift gears," Lady Bird observed. "Rest at the Ranch is a complete misnomer to me. The airport stays busy, with planes disgorging Cabinet members with important difficult decisions, budget estimates, crises . . . I only know that somehow the Ranch manages to be restful to Lyndon."

Lady Bird was pleased, one night after dinner, to see her daughter Lynda engage with Johnson's economic adviser, Walter Heller, in a lively conversation by the fire. "Lynda Bird," the First Lady observed, "was deep in conversation with him about economics, the economy of Texas and the University of Texas . . . I could see Dr. Walter Heller responding to her, not only with interest but with respect. It was fun to watch."

The arrival in Texas of Dr. Heller, chairman of the president's Council of Economic Advisers, had not merited much attention in the press that week. Though he stood six feet four inches tall, his clunky spectacles and less-than-thrilling field of interest made him the sort of figure reporters used to fill out the lower paragraphs of their stories. No one would have guessed that the meetings he led on the ranch that week would be among the most consequential of Johnson's presidency—the setting in which the biggest dreams of the Johnson presidency would begin to form.

Heller was not the sort of man to whom Johnson was naturally drawn. A tenured faculty member at the University of Minnesota, his views on public policy had been shaped by academic textbooks, not by the rough-and-tumble of practical politics. He was exactly the sort of credentialed, liberal academic toward whom the Southwest Texas State Teachers' College graduate in the White House took a natural dislike.

But when Heller first met with President Johnson one day after Kennedy's assassination, he received a surprisingly warm welcome. He briefed Johnson on the state of the economy and the current forecasts for growth and inflation and then mentioned a plan he'd been developing for a broad "attack on poverty" under President Kennedy. Johnson lit up. He ordered the adviser to fast-track a proposal, saying, "That's my kind of program!"

My kind of program. Heller was pleased. In his years in the Kennedy administration, he had grown passionate about the issue of poverty and its root causes. He believed there was meaningful action that government could take to address the issue, but he had struggled to gain favor for his ideas in the White House. With their minds focused on the reelection in 1964, Kennedy's political aides had grown irritated by Heller's poverty talk and his pleas for action. A broad public campaign drawing attention to the poorest Americans, they believed, was the last thing a president running for reelection needed.

In truth, the issue of poverty was as vivid an illustration as any of the gap between the aims of the era's progressives and the governing philosophy of the consensus-minded President Kennedy. Ending poverty had been a nominal goal of progressives since the New Deal. For a time, it was a goal that they claimed nearly to have achieved. In 1958, the economist John Kenneth Galbraith published *The Affluent Society,* a vision of the challenges and opportunities presented by abundance. A seminal text of utopian postwar liberalism, Galbraith's book sought to reveal "the way our economic attitudes are rooted in the poverty, inequality, and economic peril of the past." Poverty in America, Galbraith said, was no longer "a massive affliction" but "nearly an afterthought." Five years later, in a classic essay in *The New Yorker,* "Our Invisible Poor," the writer Dwight Macdonald would recall Galbraith's assurance: "The interesting thing about his pronouncement, aside from the fact that it is inaccurate, is that it was generally accepted as obvious."

That attitude changed in the early 1960s, thanks to the publication of Michael Harrington's book *The Other America*. With statistics and harrowing anecdotes, the book revealed how, beneath the opulent middle-class affluence of postwar America, millions of

Americans were living in a Depression-era state of deprivation. The news was jarring to the country. How could they let so many children starve in a nation of such plenty? Scrambling to account for their previous lack of concern with the issue, liberal intellectuals responded to Harrington's revelations by claiming the book demonstrated not a failure of progressive policy, but a failure of public will. Quickly, they absorbed the Harrington critique into the optimistic spirit of the age: with the right policies, nearly all of America's poor could be lifted up into lives free of want, straightaway.

John Kennedy felt strongly about the plight of the nation's poor. As a Catholic skeptic, he was compelled to look out for the suffering of the disadvantaged, in times of abundance as much as in times of scarcity. And as a Kennedy, taught from birth of his special obligation to the least of these, he felt obliged to ease the poor's suffering, wherever he could. In the last year of his presidency, he eagerly digested Heller's alarming statistics and expressed his desire to act. Kennedy "wanted to do the right thing," writes his biographer Richard Reeves. He believed that "poverty was a problem that could be managed. He intended to do something about it—when he was sure of reelection."

But not before. Nine days before his death, Kennedy met with a group of political advisers to plan for the 1964 presidential campaign. The theme for the effort would be "Peace and Prosperity." Kennedy wondered if he might advertise his efforts to expand that prosperity to society's lower rungs by posing for photographs with poor coal miners and underprivileged blacks. "I wouldn't do that," advised Richard Scammon, his Census Bureau director. "You can't get a single vote by doing anything for poor people."

The gold mine for Kennedy, Scammon went on, was in "the new shopping centers on the highways. The voters you need, your people, men with lunch pails, are moving out to the suburbs."

Scammon had Kennedy's attention. Would his people stay *his* in their new lives? When a Democrat started to earn more money and moved his family to the suburbs, at what point did he become a Republican? While Scammon did not have precise figures, he guessed that "it might be less than $10,000 a year."

Kennedy grasped the vast implications of what he was hearing. Those criteria applied to millions upon millions of Americans. He knew what it meant: "It's going to be a new kind of politics."

It was still too early to see exactly what that new politics would be. All that was clear was that it was not the time for a broad call to action. Not with so much in flux; not in 1964. Not when the civil rights movement was poised to finally push the South from the Democrats' coalition once and for all. Not when Republicans seemed poised to break *their* pattern and nominate a red-meat conservative for the presidency, leaving the center, shrunken as it was, for the Democrats to take. Not when those men with lunch pails, *his people,* were moving out to the suburbs and moving up the income ladder. Not when his governing consensus itself was hanging by a thread.

1964 was decidedly *not* the year for an incumbent Democrat to be daring. Kennedy wanted to do something to help the poor, and he believed that he could. But he did not believe he would help them by making confident, unrealistic promises to the nation about ending the plight of poor people forever. Meeting with Heller just before he left for his ill-fated trip to Texas, Kennedy was encouraging but vague on the poverty plan: "I'm still very much in favor of doing something on the poverty theme if we can get a good program," he said, "but I also think it's important to make clear that we're doing something for the middle income man in the suburbs."

By the conventional rules of Washington, if Kennedy had kept his eye on the middle, there was every reason to believe that his successor would do the same. No one needed to explain to Lyndon Johnson how consensus politics worked. His instinctive sense for its contours had helped him pivot effortlessly back and forth across the acceptable range of political opinion for most of his adult life.

He was an ardent New Dealer when he served as Texas administrator of Roosevelt's National Youth Administration. Courting poor Hill Country voters who revered FDR, he ran for Congress from Texas's Tenth District as a New Deal evangelist. In the midterm elections of 1938, when Southern Democrats were fleeing their president in droves, Johnson made a public show of standing by him, earning lasting favor from FDR in the process. When Roosevelt died in April 1945, Johnson wept. "I thought of all the little folks," he said later, "and what they had lost. He was just like a daddy to me always."

Yet no sooner had he wiped his tears away than his New Deal passions began to cool. As soon as he was elected to the Senate in 1948, the "little folks" seemed to fade in his mind. More powerful patrons had emerged. He now had to think about pleasing a statewide electorate in increasingly reactionary Texas and pleasing the wealthy oilmen who had bankrolled his campaigns. And he had to think about pleasing the Southern legislators who, thanks to one-party rule in the old Confederacy, held seniority on every important committee in the Senate and would thus be indispensable to his rise. So the young senator Johnson quickly and enthusiastically ingratiated himself not just to the Senate's conservative budget hawks, but to its racists and Red-baiters, too. Even by the late 1950s, when his national ambitions required him to get liberal religion on civil rights, he kept his eye on his obstructionist base. "Listen," he said to Senator James Eastland, a notorious segregationist from Mississippi, in 1957, "we might as well face it. We're not gonna be able to get out of here until we've got *some* kind of nigger bill."

And from his time as majority leader of the Senate, Johnson learned just how powerful a politician who planted his feet in the center could be. His strategy as leader of Eisenhower's loyal opposition was to pay as much attention to the word "loyal" as he did to "opposition." Again and again in the Eisenhower years, Johnson and the Democrats would enthusiastically join the Republican president on major issues, skillfully separating Ike from his own party and making the GOP look outside the mainstream.

Outwardly, there was every indication in late December 1963

that the Johnson presidency would be more of the same consensus politics. After Johnson exclaimed "Let us continue!" he invited just about everyone who mattered, across the spectrum of respectable opinion, to offer counsel for the way ahead. If, by chance, these well-wishers ran into reporters on their way to and from the White House—well, there was nothing Johnson could do about that.

So the nation heard Sidney Weinberg, the managing partner of Goldman Sachs, raving about the "personal magnetism" of the new president. "If he asked you to do something—anything, you'd want to do it," Weinberg gushed. Labor was just as approving as capital. United Auto Workers president Walter Reuther, emerging from *his* tête-à-tête with Johnson, said that the president "puts the emphasis on all the right things." A Chicago public relations executive, quoted in *Time* a few weeks after the assassination, described the result: "Everyone in the country thinks he has a winner in Lyndon Johnson, the Southerners, the Negros, the budget cutters."

The *Time* article wondered who the *real* Lyndon Johnson would be. Good luck figuring that out. He sounded so sincere in his first meeting with Heller, in which he protested he was "no budget slasher" and that "John F. Kennedy was a little too conservative to suit my taste." But he sounded equally sincere when he phoned Eisenhower on Christmas Day: "What are we going to do, Mr. President?" he said, sounding exasperated. "We can't get our budget down as much as you'd like. . . . The Kennedy administration has added *one hundred thirty-three thousand employees* in three years!" (The three years, he didn't need to mention, since he and Ike had run the show.)

On the surface, there was no reason to put any stock in Johnson's professed enthusiasm for progressive ideas. No reason to think that however warm his reception—*That's my kind of program!*—Johnson would be any more inclined to pursue a broad public attack on poverty in 1964 than had been his predecessor. Heller had come to the LBJ Ranch to present plans for the program to Johnson, to see if Johnson would make the eradication of poverty a cornerstone of his presidency. If he did, he would be starting on a course far more daring than any Kennedy had ever attempted. All the rules of Washington, the rules that had governed American politics for thirty years, the rules that Johnson knew better than anyone alive, suggested that Heller would go home disappointed.

But they weren't in Washington that last week in December. They were in the Hill Country, a place where there were other rules, and other forces, that had a powerful effect on Lyndon Johnson. No one in the Hill Country would think to doubt Johnson when he proclaimed that an attack on poverty was his kind of program. He was a Johnson, and for the Johnsons, helping the little people was what politics was all about.

Lyndon had learned this politics in the cradle. His grandfather Sam Ealy Johnson was a member of the Texas People's Party. He was a gregarious, popular man who ran, unsuccessfully, for the Texas legislature in 1892 as a radical populist. The cause of his life was the sorry lot of Texas tenant farmers, alienated from the spoils of their labors by corrupt businessmen, predatory bankers, and greedy railroad barons. He taught the populist gospel to his son Sam Jr., who would in turn teach it to his son Lyndon.

The call to public life was part of their shared inheritance as well. In 1904, Sam Jr. also ran for the legislature, and this Sam Ealy Johnson won.

In office, he took up the cause of the rural poor: working to fix their rents, get them federal aid for droughts, and protect them from the conniving oil companies. He worked to build roads to reach the isolated rural poor and secured funds to help them keep their children clothed and fed.

He wanted to be their voice. It was a solitary, heroic calling, one that was his alone. Robert Caro evokes Sam Johnson's world in vivid detail, quoting W. D. McFarlane, a colleague of Sam Johnson's in the legislature. McFarlane recalls a man possessed with helping "the farming people and the working people. . . . They had no one else to look after their interests. And Sam Johnson did speak up on their behalf. I remember Sam Johnson as a man who truly wanted to help the people who he felt needed help."

As a young child, Lyndon Johnson couldn't get enough of his father's political world. One night when the governor of Texas came to visit, nine-year-old Lyndon stowed away under the dining room table so he could listen to the talk. A politician could have greatness, young Lyndon understood, the greatness that came from transforming other people's lives.

But for Sam Johnson, there were other indicators of greatness. There were fine clothes and fancy shoes and other expensive things, all of which he wanted. And he wanted one fine thing above all: a bigger ranch. He was proud of his lineage in the Hill Country, proud of the name Johnson City, proud of the time when the Johnsons had ruled the Pedernales River Valley as prosperous landowners. As his reputation as a man of consequence grew, he thought more and more of the days when his forebears had ruled the Hill Country. He wanted to bring those days back.

And he wanted to do it with land. In the years between 1910 and 1920, he bought up acre after acre adjacent to his ranch on the Pedernales. When hard-up relatives sought to unload their own farms, he'd pay a premium for them so that family land would not pass into the hands of strangers. Soon he was in over his head, mortgaged far beyond his means, but he was confident he would be able to cover his debts with the proceeds of prize cattle raised on his bountiful land. He was confident his ranch would deliver.

And of course it didn't. Like so many ranchers before him, many of them Johnsons, Sam Ealy Johnson, Jr., was devastated by the Hill Country's harsh soil and unpredictable climate. Before long, he had more creditors than he could keep track of. He fell into financial ruin so great that he had to give up not only his land but his political career, too, just so he could pay the bills. A teenage Lyndon Johnson watched in deep shame as his father took any job he could get, even working on a road gang. The man who'd set out to heal the sick, to feed the hungry, to bring money and roads to the poor, had ended up laying down pavement himself.

And those were the Hill Country rules, swirling around in Lyndon Johnson's head as he considered the Kennedy poverty plan. He did not look at the proposal the way Kennedy might have. There was no gray area, no cautious skepticism, no putting off action until the reality became clearer. The story of the Hill Country Johnsons taught that the future could offer only two possibilities: heroic greatness or total disgrace. A great man was the one who could have it all—the ranch, the love of the downtrodden, the dreams. The disgraced man was the one who tried for it all and failed. And when Johnson dreamed for himself and his country, that was what he saw: total greatness. If that vision brought with it a reminder of the other possibility—total disaster and disgrace—well, that was unpleasant but necessary. In Johnson's life, the suppressed fear of looming disaster was always the price of big dreams.

WHEN FEAR DID come to Lyndon Johnson, it usually came with a human face. As he worked with Heller and others that week on the ranch, plotting his great dreams, he did not have to look far for someone to frighten him. He could find him in one of the very men helping to plot the domestic programs on the ranch that Christmas week: Kennedy's counselor Ted Sorensen.

Since the assassination, Johnson had continued to work tirelessly to win over Sorensen, who was, after Bobby and Jackie, the greatest symbol of continuity with the Kennedy legacy. "I think he is going to come around," Katharine Graham told Johnson early in December, "if you just give him a little love." Johnson replied that he had "done as much as I can and have any pride and self-respect left."

Meeting with Johnson in the Oval Office that December, Sorensen mentioned in passing that his three sons were downstairs eating in the White House mess. "Let's go join them!" said the president. Down they went, where Johnson gamely chatted up the young boys before returning to the Oval Office. The children, who had their own magical memories of Kennedy, were unimpressed. "He doesn't look like a president," young Stephen Sorensen observed.

Soon it was clear that Sorensen could not continue in the White House. Johnson agreed to let him go, but he asked Sorensen to first write the State of the Union address and lead the process that would determine Johnson's domestic agenda. On the thirtieth of December, Sorensen and a small group of other advisers joined the president at the ranch in a guesthouse in the middle of a cow pasture to discuss the poverty plan.

Sorensen knew all about Heller's ideas. He had been a chief skeptic of their political viability in the Kennedy White House, and on more than one occasion he had urged Kennedy to deemphasize the issue. When Heller tried to talk about the politics of poverty, Sorensen told him to back off. Up to the last moments of the Kennedy presidency, Sorensen had been focused on the same thing as Kennedy: a second term in the White House.

But since there would be no second Kennedy term, Sorensen now had other priorities. Kennedy's poverty plan was no longer about election year politics, but instead about Kennedy's place in history. It was even more clear by the end of December, after the publication of the "Camelot" story in *Life,* that if history was going to remember Kennedy as a great president, it would not remember him as a centrist pragmatist who'd worried over the men with lunch pails and the shifting American center. The case for Kennedy's greatness would be made by depicting him as a transformational liberal reformer, a man ahead of his time. To make the case for Kennedy's greatness, Sorensen and the other loyalists had to remind the country of the great liberal reforms that, but for Oswald's bullets, President Kennedy had been destined to usher in.

In death, John F. Kennedy would be recast as a man fully determined to end poverty. His disciples were already pushing the revision. In an essay in *The Saturday Evening Post* that December, Arthur Schlesinger wrote that ending poverty had been a signal aim of the

Kennedy administration. He quoted Kennedy in one of their last conversations: "The time has come to organize a national assault on the causes of poverty, a comprehensive program, across the board." In his office, Bobby Kennedy now had framed a scrap of paper on which Kennedy had doodled a single word over and over at his last cabinet meeting: "poverty."

And so, as Heller presented the poverty plan that day, Sorensen offered none of the old political objections. He listened approvingly as Heller described a plan for a war on poverty based on "community action," a program in which the government would provide broad funding for antipoverty centers around the country, run under local control.

It fell to Horace Busby, a Johnson aide of long standing, to voice skepticism about the project's feasibility. After hearing the plans to convert Washington's Union Station into a clearinghouse for employers, the poor and out of work, and experts skilled in matching the two, Busby responded with caustic questions. How would the poor people get to Union Station? Where would they park?

This prompted a flash of anger from the president. Taking Busby outside, Johnson scolded his aide harshly. "Why did you say that?" Johnson asked. "Don't you realize these are *Kennedy's people?*"

To Johnson, watching Sorensen assent to Heller's proposals, the poverty plan began to look like something new: a test. He didn't object to the substance of Busby's questions. In truth, he had his own concerns about the plan. But for the moment, those concerns were beside the point. "Johnson realized," writes the historian Nicholas Lemann, "that the Kennedy people had succeeded in changing the stakes of the poverty program: the question, instead of being whether Johnson could take over what had been a small, stagnating Kennedy idea and make it his first major initiative without one-upping the dead president, became whether Johnson could possibly be as fully committed to fighting poverty as Kennedy had been." He was not going to lose that game. Back in the meeting, Johnson made sure Busby kept his mouth shut.

But Busby was sufficiently concerned about the domestic program to try once more to get Johnson's attention. That night, he stayed up writing a memo to the president cautioning him against making transformative social programs a centerpiece of his presidency in its early days. His words echoed the advice Kennedy's political advisers had given him the previous month, when they had urged him to focus on the men with lunch pails. The poverty program was not fully formed, Busby told Johnson. But more important, it didn't appeal to "the American in the middle. . . . People know instinctively these are your kinds of folks—not the extremes. The politics of the extremes is what the typical American expects you to break away from. If you can do so, you can broaden the Democratic Party base as it has not been broadened in two decades."

If Johnson took the other course, he would face peril. "America's real majority," Busby wrote, "is suffering a minority complex of neglect. They have become the real foes of Negro rights, foreign aid, etc., because, as much as anything, they feel forgotten." If somehow a talented Republican could find a way to speak to those forgotten people, then it would be a very new kind of politics indeed.

It was the kind of warning that might make another president think twice before acting in a bold, dramatic way. The kind of warning that *had* made another president think twice, just a few weeks before. But it was not the kind of warning that would naturally catch the attention of Lyndon Johnson. It was too abstract, too conditional. It relied too much on a murky understanding of what was coming. That wasn't the kind of future Johnson believed in. His visions were always clear ones. Sometimes he saw certain greatness on the horizon, other times certain ruin. But certainty was always there.

He couldn't hold back just for the sake of caution, not when the stakes were so high. That week's issue of *Newsweek* had an article on Jackie Kennedy's new post–White House life on the cover. By then she had purchased a Washington home of her own, on N Street in Georgetown. There, she would be surrounded by the kind of privileged easterners who had looked down on Lyndon Johnson for thirty years. Her new house had a dining room that could seat forty and a nine-hundred-square-foot drawing room. It was the kind of place where a hostess could entertain on a grand scale, the kind of place where a court in exile could plot its return. In the photograph on *Newsweek*'s cover, Jackie was peeking out from a doorway. Half her face was hidden, obscured by the large door. But the other half was filled with contained anticipation. Her eyes, twinkling ever so slightly, were staring straight ahead.

Johnson could not let the Kennedy mythmakers do him in. He had to offer his own story, not about the past but about the future, one that was more glorious than anyone had yet dared to imagine. He sent Walter Heller and the other aides back to Washington with clear instructions: in his State of the Union, he would declare unconditional war on poverty. And the war would be over only when poverty had been eradicated once and for all.

AFTER THE NEW year, the flood of visitors to the LBJ Ranch at last began to subside. Soon it would be time for the Johnsons to return to Washington. But before they left, Lyndon and Lady Bird would play host to one more couple: Sally Reston and her husband, James B. "Scotty" Reston of *The New York Times*.

The senior *Times* man in Washington, Scotty Reston was the most esteemed newspaper reporter in the country. His values were establishment values and his column reflected the Washington establishment position on a given issue more often than not. But he was a perceptive reporter who sometimes challenged conventional wisdom. Already he had taken such a position on the young presidency of Lyndon Johnson. In mid-December, while most other reporters wrote about the active new president and the seamless harmony between the Kennedy and Johnson teams, Reston offered a discordant note. "People here do not like to compare the old and the new, for the time being," he wrote, "but they cannot help it. To talk about President Johnson's genius with Congress somehow seems to imply a criticism of President Kennedy; to dwell on President Kennedy's grace and style similarly seems to suggest a problem of President Johnson."

In the column, Reston wondered if, compared with his now-legendary predecessor, Johnson's emerging presidency might be a practical, placid affair, lacking in the Kennedys' big dreams. He quoted an unnamed correspondent: "Mr. Johnson now seems Gary Cooper as President—High Noon, the poker game, the easy walk and masculine smile. But even Gary Cooper was growing older, and the companions and adversaries around the poker table reflect a less fresh, if no doubt practical and effective mood. All will be well, I feel sure, but it is August and not June."

This was a direct challenge to the story Johnson was trying to tell, in which the time of big dreams and great adventures had just begun. Before Johnson returned from Texas, he intended to make sure Scotty Reston himself saw the proof. On January 3, Reston received a call from Johnson aide Bill Moyers. The president, Moyers said, was hoping to spend some time with Reston to talk about the campaign and the year ahead. Could he and Sally come for a visit at the ranch?

The Restons, who were in Phoenix, Arizona, watching Barry Goldwater officially kick off his campaign for the presidency, made their way to Texas. Their day with the Johnsons was full: a helicopter trip to Austin for a visit with a recuperating John Connally and then the flight home. But first they had to have the tour of the ranch and its environs. Riding along, Lady Bird had one last chance to tell the story of the Johnson heroes, this time with her husband there to help her and the greatest newspaperman in the country as her audience.

In the car, the Johnsons pointed to the old stone fort where Lyndon's settler forebears had taken refuge and fired their rifles at invading Indians. They told of Lyndon's grandmother, Lady Bird later recalled, "hiding with her two infant children in the cellar of the log house, while the Indians stomped outside." They pointed to the old fort's commissary, the place where the Hill Country ranchers had gathered their herds at the beginning of an epic drive.

There, under the Texas sky, Lyndon made it clear to Scotty Reston that his own epic drive was just beginning. Moving briskly across the ranch, he grew animated, talking about his high hopes for his presidency, the reforms he would push through, all the ways he would make America a better place. He was worried about high school dropouts, teenage pregnancy, the rural poor. He believed he could solve each of these problems, and he intended to try. As he spoke, he would pull slips of paper from his pocket, with facts and figures to pepper his arguments. And he was most animated when talking about the war on poverty. This was a monumental problem, he argued, but a solvable one, one that would be solved, by him. He was sure.

The point was not lost on Reston. He could see that there would be more to the Johnson presidency than pragmatism and continuity. President Johnson intended to use his office to solve the biggest problems, to do the biggest things.

Soon it was time for the group to depart the ranch. But moments before he was to get into his helicopter, Johnson held the party up. That morning, during the drive around the area, he had noticed that a nearby patch of land was for sale. It was a parcel that, if absorbed, would increase the acreage of the LBJ Ranch. As soon as he saw it, Johnson knew that he wanted it. He sent a ranch hand to inquire about the price. As the rest of his party waited, Johnson gave instructions for a negotiation. Before long, the land was his.

Satisfied, Johnson stepped onto his helicopter and headed to Austin, then on to Washington and the wider world. Like his proud ancestors, he was ready for greatness. And like his father before him, he wanted a bigger ranch.

PART II

★ ★ ★

Choosing

Reagan at the 1964 Republican Convention.

CHAPTER FIVE

B Movie

February–July 1964

In mid-February 1964, the Young Republicans of California gathered in a San Diego ballroom for a banquet at their annual convention. On the surface, they looked pleasant enough, clean-faced and closely cropped. But the faces in the crowd were mostly male, and some were not far beyond adolescence. Rage was always near at hand.

Standing in front of them as the evening's featured speaker, Ronald Reagan knew what they wanted: a confident voice to affirm the outrage they felt. And he was the one to give it to them.

For months, the press had been filled with saintly remembrances of President Kennedy and laudatory praise for his successor, Lyndon Johnson. All the wise men in Washington agreed that the new president had done a remarkable job of continuing the work of his predecessor, of seamlessly picking up where President Kennedy had left off. That, Reagan's comments suggested, was precisely the problem, a problem worthy of outrage. The work of Kennedy and Johnson was a policy of appeasement and capitulation. A policy of "staving off a direct confrontation with our enemies" in the hope that "Russia eventually will grow to be more democratic, more like us."

The tragedy of this delusion, Reagan said, was "that it doesn't give us the choice between peace and war, only between fight and surrender."

In the hours before Reagan's speech, these young Republicans had been turning their rage on each other. At the convention, they had been waging fratricidal war, tearing themselves to pieces over a pair of hypotheticals—an endorsement they *might* give to someone who *might* win that year's Republican nomination for the presidency. It was still weeks before the nation's first primary voters would go to the polls in New Hampshire, months before the voters of California would have a primary of their own. But a majority of these young Republicans, supporters of the conservative standard-bearer Barry Goldwater, were already vowing to withhold their endorsement should the party's nomination go to Nelson Rockefeller or another moderate Eastern Kennedy-Johnson knockoff, traitor to the cause.

But from the front of the room, these squabbles in the crowd, even the crowd itself, were probably all a blur. Reagan never looked too closely at his audiences. Since childhood, he'd been frightfully nearsighted. His parents paid for thick eyeglasses, which he wore dutifully, but without them, his visible world was mostly blotches of color and drifting shapes. He had adapted without much questioning, the way that children can, forgoing baseball for football, a sport in which you didn't have to see well enough to hit a tiny ball, only well enough to hit another player.

He'd started his show business career on radio, where his audience was invisible. At the audition for his first job at the Davenport, Iowa, station WOC, the Scottish-born program director had explained how things worked. "That's the mike in front of ye," he said. "Ye won't be able to see me but I'll be listenin'. Good luck."

In Hollywood, too, seeing had never been that important. Arriving in Southern California in the late 1930s, he'd looked up Joy Hodges, an acquaintance from back home who was working as an actress in the film colony. "I have visions of becoming an actor," he confessed to her. "What I really want is a screen test." Hodges looked at the man in front of her—dressed like the Midwest, unsophisticated in the ways of the world, but tall, broad-shouldered, and undeniably handsome. "I think I might be able to fix something," she said. "Just don't ever put those glasses on again."

So he'd learned to get by without seeing things too closely. In time, it became the habit of his life. Eventually, he'd gotten contact lenses. Though they could correct his vision, their effect was strangely limited. His children, rushing into a room at day's end to greet their father, would find him looking puzzled, as if they were strangers. *Have we met?* It was as if, after all the years of seeing ill-defined blotches, the part of his brain that processed the particulars of a person's face had corroded irreparably due to lack of use. Or maybe it had never been there at all. Once, at his son Michael's high school graduation, where he was the commencement speaker, he'd greeted a line of graduates. "My name is Ronald Reagan," he said to a grinning boy in cap and gown. "What's yours?" The graduate removed his cap. "Remember me? I'm your son Mike."

When he spoke to large audiences, he didn't focus on the faces before him. Years later, after he'd become a national politician, his aides persuaded him to use a teleprompter. He'd always preferred note cards, filled with his shorthand block writing. But he was not afraid to improve his performance, and he accepted the new technology. Just before going onstage, he would remove the contact lens from his right eye. From the corrected left eye, he read the words from the moving monitor. With his right eye, the one without the lens, he looked at the crowd. He wanted to look at his audience, but he did not want too much detail. Seeing their faces was not important.

What mattered was knowing, *feeling*, just exactly what they wanted most. This was Reagan's great gift. Over the past decade, in his role as GE spokesman, he'd spent countless hours traveling the country. Each day brought a new blur of strangers, more than two hundred thousand of them over the eight years he'd spent in the job.

To get a good reception from these anonymous crowds, he'd learned to intuit quickly who they were and what they longed for—and what they feared.

He didn't have to focus much on the faces of the seething young precinct captains and party chairs who had gathered in the banquet hall that night. He didn't have to dwell on their internecine struggle, their endorsement contretemps. To be sure, he was a conservative and an ardent Goldwater man. He agreed that the party couldn't afford to take a risk on one of those moderates from the East. But there had been plenty of that kind of talk already at the convention, of Republicans fighting Republicans, plenty of proclamations of Goldwaterism as the one true faith.

That wasn't precisely what an audience like this wanted, anyway. They wanted something bigger, something deeper. What conservative crowds like this needed in the spring of 1964 was someone to affirm what they felt most deeply: that things in America had gone terribly, unmistakably wrong. They wanted someone to tell a story they could believe in, a story of a country in mortal danger, and a story of how that country could be saved.

It was a story they could not find in the establishment press. The people in the newspapers, the men on the television screens, they missed no opportunity to tell the country about the splendid job President Johnson was doing, about the broad support he was enjoying in all the polls, about the happy aura that had settled on Washington as both parties put aside their differences. In the press, Johnson quoted Isaiah: "Come now, let us reason together." Goldwater and his angry right-wing maniacs, the press said, had little chance of taking over their party, let alone the White House in November. They were out of touch with the most important fact of American life: that despite the horrors of last November, things in the country were going to be fine.

But the angry young people in the audience didn't feel that way. Things in America were not fine. They weren't fine under President

Johnson, just like they hadn't been fine under President Kennedy, or Presidents Eisenhower, Truman, or Roosevelt, for that matter.

So Reagan gave them what they wanted. That night in San Diego, he delivered a version of the standard political speech he'd been giving in recent years. That speech was a stirring tale of an America in deep trouble, a land desperately in need of salvation before it was too late. It evoked the grandest themes: good struggling against evil, pernicious darkness trying to cover the light. Good was America and its honest, hardworking people. Evil was the totalitarian Communism of the Soviet state. This communism, he told his audiences, sought either to enslave the free world or to destroy it. And it might well succeed unless the creeping socialism of the liberals in Washington was named, condemned, and stopped.

Reagan would name it. He warned his San Diego audience of the dangerous folly of the country's foreign aid program. America was now sending millions of dollars to some hundred and seven countries, including countries that were on the Communists' side. As was his custom, he made his point with vivid proper nouns and precise statistics and facts:

"Our money in Bolivia was simply a means by which the Bolivian government nationalized the economy and went socialist . . .

"We can't justify foreign aid funds which went for the purchase of extra wives for some tribal chiefs in Kenya . . .

"Just as we can't justify the purchase of dress suits for some undertakers in Greece. . . .

"Or just as we cannot justify the purchase of a two-million-dollar yacht for Emperor Haile Selassie of Ethiopia simply by calling it a command vessel."

All of these embarrassments were part of a broader foreign policy that was veering "dangerously close to appeasement." The wise men in Washington, he implied, were making the same mistakes as the men who had appeased Hitler at Munich. They wanted the country to believe that everything was fine, that the days ahead were placid, that peace for all time was at hand. But, Reagan suggested, just as at Munich, the choice between fight and surrender was coming, far sooner than those men could see.

When he finished talking, the room filled with applause. They were all watching him.

LATER IN LIFE, Reagan would give a pithy assessment of his career in Hollywood: "I was the Errol Flynn of the Bs"—the low-budget B movies that ran as the bottom half of a double feature. Performing for the crowd in San Diego that night, he captured his audience's imagination, worked his listeners up, and sent them home happy, just like an A-list heartthrob. But the program itself was unimpressive. In February 1964, a gathering of conservatives in Southern California, or a gathering of conservatives anywhere in America, was a B movie, little loved or seen.

The main attraction was running on the other side of the continent, a sweeping epic of action and triumph starring President Lyndon Johnson. Like many big-budget productions of the era, it was best not to watch it too closely lest you catch the flaws in the script, even the actors wandering in and out of focus. Better just to sit back and take in the feel-good extravaganza for a while:

President Lyndon Johnson Takes Washington
SCENE ONE

INT. THE HOUSE CHAMBER IN THE U.S. CAPITOL: *Midday in early January,* THE PRESIDENT, *Lyndon Baines Johnson, delivers his State of the Union address.*

THE PRESIDENT: Unfortunately, many Americans live on the outskirts of hope—some because of their poverty, and some because of their color, and all too many because of both. Our task is to help replace their despair with opportunity. This administration today, here and now, declares unconditional war on poverty.

JUST OFFSCREEN: After the speech the president calls the columnist DREW PEARSON.

THE PRESIDENT: I got eighty-one applauses, in twenty-nine hundred words. It was a twenty-five-minute speech and it took forty-one because of the applauses.

WAY OFFSCREEN: Senator BARRY GOLDWATER, *campaigning for the New Hampshire primary, pulled off to the side of a snowy highway near the town of Amherst, eats a cheeseburger while listening to Johnson's speech on the radio. With national reporters looking on, he grows outraged over the scale of federal ambitions* THE PRESIDENT *is articulating:*

GOLDWATER: He has out Roosevelted Roosevelt, out Kennedyed Kennedy, and . . . made Truman look like a piker.

SCENE TWO

INT. THE WHITE HOUSE: On the afternoon of February 1, THE PRESIDENT *announces he has tapped Peace Corps head and JFK brother-in-law* SARGENT SHRIVER *to lead the War on Poverty.*

OFFSCREEN: Two hours before the announcement THE PRESIDENT *calls* SHRIVER.

THE PRESIDENT: Sarge, I'm going to announce your appointment at that press conference.
SHRIVER: What press conference?
THE PRESIDENT: This afternoon.
SHRIVER: God! I think it would be advisable, if you don't mind, if I could have this week and sit down with a couple of people and see what we could get in the way of some sort of plan . . .

WAY OFFSCREEN: *Dressed in a tuxedo,* GOLDWATER *appears before the Economic Club of New York.*

GOLDWATER: We are told . . . that many people lack skills and cannot find jobs because they did not have an education. That's like saying that people have big feet because they wear big shoes. The fact is that most people who have no skill have no education for the same reason—low intelligence or low ambition.

SCENE THREE

INT. THE WHITE HOUSE: THE PRESIDENT *conducts a sit-down interview with anchors from the three major networks for a special broadcast.*

ANNOUNCER (V/O): *Mr. Ed* will not be seen tonight.

Close-up on a dark leather chair with an engraved inscription. It reads "The President, November 22, 1963." It is THE PRESIDENT'S *chair in the Cabinet Room which, by custom, bears the date the sitting president came into office. Cut to* THE PRESIDENT, *seated, taking questions from* DAVID BRINKLEY, NBC, ERIC SEVAREID, CBS, *and* WILLIAM LAWRENCE, ABC.

BRINKLEY: Is there any one particular memory that is more vivid than the others for you from those four horrible days?

THE PRESIDENT: (carefully measuring his words) Yes, I have rarely been in the presence of greatness. But as I went through that period I observed Mrs. Kennedy, Jackie Kennedy, I saw her greatness, her gallantry, her graciousness, her courage, and it will always be a vivid memory and I'll always appreciate the strength that came to me from knowing her and associating with her.

OFFSCREEN: JACQUELINE KENNEDY, *widow, taping a confidential interview with the historian* ARTHUR SCHLESINGER, *discussing* PRESIDENT KENNEDY'S *time in office. The interview will not be published for nearly fifty years.*

SCHLESINGER: What sort of a vice president was Lyndon?

MRS. KENNEDY: It was so funny because Jack, thinking of being vice president and how awful it would be, gave Lyndon so many things to do. But he never did them . . . I mean, I think it's so pathetic when all you can find to do with a President who's dying to give you a lot to do, is take a state trip to Luxembourg and Belgium . . .

SCHLESINGER: The story has been printed to the effect that there was some consideration of dropping Johnson in '64.

MRS. KENNEDY: Not in '64. But Bobby told me this later, and I know Jack said it to me sometimes. He said, "Oh, God, can you ever imagine what would happen to the country if Lyndon was President?"

INT. (CONTINUED). *Meanwhile, back in the network anchors' interview with the president, Johnson has grown animated, talking about his domestic program.*

SEVAREID: Mr. President, administrations come to have a handy label: the New Deal or the Fair Deal or the New Frontier. Does any idea come to your mind for the Johnson administration?

THE PRESIDENT: I've had a lot of things to deal with these first one hundred days, I haven't thought of any slogans. But I suppose all of us want a better deal, don't we?

OFFSCREEN: *In the White House pool,* THE PRESIDENT *floats with* BILL MOYERS *and* DICK GOODWIN. *Fog the water to obscure the fact that all three are naked. In speeches he is writing, Goodwin has begun trying out a new phrase—"The Great Society"—to describe the Johnson vision.* THE PRESIDENT *likes the phrase.*

THE PRESIDENT: Now, boys, you let me finish the Kennedy program. You start to put together a Johnson program, and don't worry about whether it's too radical or if Congress is ready for it. That's my job . . .

As the men towel off outside the pool, THE PRESIDENT'S *mind drifts away.*

THE PRESIDENT: They're trying to get me in a war over there. It will destroy me . . .

Goodwin looks confused, not sure where THE PRESIDENT *is talking about when he says "over there."*

SCENE FOUR

EXT. *University of Michigan, May 22.* THE PRESIDENT, *wearing an academic robe, addressing graduates of the university, urges them to join with him in changing the world.*

THE PRESIDENT: The Great Society rests on abundance and liberty for all. It demands an end to poverty and racial injustice, to which we are totally committed in our time. But that is just the beginning. The Great Society is a place where every child can find knowledge to enrich his mind and to enlarge his talents. It is a place where leisure is a welcome chance to build and reflect, not a feared cause of boredom and restlessness. It is a place where the city of man serves not only the needs of the body and the demands of commerce but the desire for beauty and the hunger for community.

OFFSCREEN: GOLDWATER *campaigns like mad in California before the state's Republican primary on June 2. The primary is his chance to knock out his chief moderate rival, Governor* NELSON ROCKEFELLER *of New York, once and for all. Goldwater has a hard time connecting with audiences. They seem to prefer his warm-up act, the well-known face from Hollywood* RONALD REAGAN, *who greets the right-wing crowds with a knowing wink to their reputation in the mainstream press.*

REAGAN: Good morning to all you irresponsible Republicans!

WHO WAS THIS man—Ronald Reagan the actor, or Ronald Reagan the politician? In *The New York Times* that year, he was described as "Ronald Reagan, the youthful-looking former Hollywood actor who has moved to the right wing of the political stage." And he was, in fact, appearing on political stages for Goldwater that spring. But he was not, as we have seen, a *former* actor. He had wrapped production on *Johnny North* only a few weeks before his San Diego speech. Viewers of the program *Kraft Suspense Theater* would see him in several new teleplays that spring.

Later in life, Reagan would claim there was little difference between the jobs of a politician and an actor. Again and again over the course of his political career, he would poke fun at the flimsy line between his two chosen vocations:

Candidate Ronald Reagan, asked what kind of governor he would be: "I don't know, I've never played a governor before."

Newly elected governor Reagan, to California senator George Murphy, like him a former Hollywood star, at Reagan's midnight inauguration: "Well, George, here we are on the late show again."

President Reagan, reflecting on the demands of his job: "How could you do the job if you hadn't been an actor?"

But in the spring of 1964, the difference between politics and acting would have been a meaningful one to Reagan. His future on the screen looked even bleaker than it had a few months before. NBC executives, concerned by the violence and racy content of *Johnny North,* had decided to pass on the film. Wasserman's plan to produce the first full-length feature made specifically for television had fallen apart. With the film already shot, he repackaged the film for distribution in theaters, giving it a new title. That summer, Americans would see squeaky-clean Ronald Reagan appearing as the least likable character in a film called *The Killers.*

Reagan's chances of a third run at Hollywood stardom were slim. But his ambition and his need to play the hero had not died. He'd been working, that winter, on his midlife autobiography. The book's title, borrowed from a line spoken by his character in *King's Row,* was revealing: *Where's the Rest of Me?* Staring out at admiring crowds, like the Young Republicans in San Diego, he must have wondered if the world of politics offered a happier future. Maybe the rest of him would be on these political stages, not just as a speaker but as the star.

He had long since learned that the political arena could offer the same pleasures as movie stardom—the "heady wine" feeling he got when the eyes of the world were on him. He had found that feeling in his days at GE when he'd gotten reacquainted with the pleasures of a live crowd. "Two of the eight years were spent traveling," Reagan would later calculate, "and with speeches sometimes running at fourteen a day, I was on my feet in front of a 'mike' for about 250,000 minutes."

A routine like this can change a man. Making his way from unglamorous hotel to unglamorous hotel in unremarkable city after unremarkable city, a man with a famous face must learn how to connect quickly with strangers. In Reagan, it awoke his old talent for feeling and understanding a room. The actor, said Earl Dunckel, a GE executive who traveled with Reagan, possessed an "almost mystical ability to achieve an empathy with almost any audience." At events, Dunckel would watch as the handsome man from Hollywood was mobbed by the female workers asking for autographs. On the side, Dunckel recalled, the men would stand "together obviously saying something derogatory. 'I bet he's a fag,' that sort of thing." If Reagan knew what they were saying, he ignored it, continuing to chat with the ladies. After a while, though, he would walk over to the men and seamlessly draw them into conversation. "When he left them ten minutes later," Dunckel said, "they were all slappin' him on the back saying, 'That's the way, Ron.'" Reagan, said Dunckel, simply "would not leave a department with the men over there scowling and snarling."

It was on the road for GE, as he learned how to win over anonymous crowds in short periods of time, that Reagan the conservative politician was born. GE had no requirements for the content of his speeches, simply that they generally promote free-market principles. At first, Reagan—alias Mr. Norm—would offer his audiences a defense of the moral values of the movie business. *(Did you know that Hollywood has one of the lowest divorce rates in the country?)* But the more he was on the road, the more he felt his audiences respond when he talked about the Cold War menace. The men and women in Reagan's crowds were eager to hear Reagan's story, for he was offering them a kind of clarity that was otherwise in short supply. The official pronouncements from Washington in the early Cold War were full of frustrating ambiguity. The Soviets were the enemy, of course, but the pragmatists in power counseled that that enemy should be confronted only when strategically necessary. Where the officials dwelled on qualification and complexity, Reagan's message was refreshingly unconditional: America must either vanquish the Soviet threat or perish from the earth.

Soon, international politics was the subject Reagan was talking about the most. In his youth, Reagan, like Lyndon Johnson, had idolized Franklin Roosevelt. He was a devoted listener to the president's Fireside Chats. Roosevelt's genius was for distilling the world's complex problems as vivid moral struggles: the honest Everyman against corrupt big business, the free world against global fascism. Here were stories of the world that Reagan believed in—a world filled with good and decent people, people who needed a leader to stave off insidious conspiracies of evil. And here was a voice speaking directly to the individual listener—"the forgotten man"—making it clear that the president knew that that listener was there, and that he cared. During those broadcasts, Reagan heard the most powerful man in the country doing the thing that Reagan most longed to do: comforting, pleasing, and inspiring people. People he did not know, faces he could not see.

The young Reagan thrilled to Roosevelt's gifts—he crafted an impersonation of FDR, complete with imaginary cigarette holder— and for a time to Roosevelt's politics as well. The world would long note that Reagan started his adult life as a Democrat. When asked to explain his political evolution, he would usually give a variation on the same answer: "I didn't leave the Democratic Party, the Democratic Party left me." It was a good line. It captured not just Reagan's journey but also the journey of millions of Americans who had grown up with pictures of Roosevelt and Kennedy on their walls but would nonetheless vote for Reagan and the Republicans in the later years of the twentieth century.

But that line left a false impression of Reagan as a creature of the center, watching in dismay as his party lurched to the far left. That was never the real Reagan. Throughout his life, Reagan's natural preference for clear drama caused him to view politics as a matter of moral certainty, in which one side was right and the other wrong. Mr. Norm understood the New Deal consensus and was careful to stay within its bounds. But like Johnson, who was capable of operating in a world of compromise and contradiction but fantasized of only total glory or total doom, Reagan saw no beauty in gray areas. For him, the simple was always preferable to the complex. He could find that simplicity only on the edges of consensus politics. And so that was where he felt most comfortable, first on the left edge, then on the right.

In the 1940s in Hollywood, he was a committed New Deal Democrat, a liberal who used his celebrity to point out the corrupt prac-

tices of big business and the mortal threat that moneyed interests
posed to the forgotten man. Campaigning for Democratic candidates, he played up their noble virtues and sought to expose the
greedy interests and secret agendas of their opponents. He had no
great affection for Roosevelt's less media-savvy successor—he called
Harry Truman "as inspiring as mud"—but in the election of 1948,
he headed up the Labor League of Hollywood Voters for Truman all
the same. That same year, he spoke out against Minnesota's incumbent Republican senator Joseph Ball, "the banner carrier for Wall
Street," and urged the election of the liberal lion Hubert Humphrey,
mayor of Minneapolis. "Mayor Humphrey," said Reagan, "is fighting for all the principles advocated by President Truman, for ade-
quate low-cost housing, for civil rights, for prices people can afford
to pay and for a labor movement free of the Taft-Hartley law."

But with the rise of the Cold War, the struggle against Communism captured Reagan's imagination. There was a clear good guy
(the free West), a clear villain (the Soviets), and dramatically high
stakes (the future of American freedom or even the survival of mankind). Talking about the global struggle, Reagan could employ the
kind of urgent drama he preferred: "You have an opportunity to decide now whether you will strike a match," he told an audience in the
early fifties, "and whether you will help push back the darkness over
the stadium of humanity."

In addition, the fight against Communism offered an essential
element for Reagan's worldview: a conspiracy plot. Stories of sinister plans hatched by powerful, hidden interests had long appealed to
him. They became vital to the marriage of his taste for vivid drama
and his notion of the Communist threat. Mr. Norm, who believed
fervently that most people were good, decent, hardworking, and
kind, could not entertain the possibility that evil ideas could win
over the masses. In a good world, evil couldn't ever gain advantage
fair and square; it had to resort to dark magic or dirty tricks. The
foreign treachery of a Moscow cabal played a central part in Reagan's vision of the Communist menace. In America, he wrote in

1951, "the so-called Communist Party is nothing less than a Russian-American Bund owing allegiance to Russia and supporting Russia in its plan to conquer the world. The very Constitution behind which these cynical agents hide becomes a weapon to be used against them. They are traitors practicing treason."

It was strong stuff, driven by motives that were personal as well as political. Reagan had been active in liberal causes in Hollywood in the late 1930s and '40s, a period when it was not easy to keep track of just who was a Communist and who was not. Two groups of which he had been a member—the American Veterans Committee (AVC) and Hollywood Independent Citizens Committee of the Arts, Sciences, and Professions (HICCASP, "pronounced," said Reagan, "like the cough of a dying man")—came under Communist control. Reagan resigned from each group when he learned of its Communist affiliation, and no evidence exists that he ever knowingly supported Communist causes. Still, he could be fairly described as a leftist political activist and labor leader with known Communist associations. In Hollywood, in the McCarthy era, reputations were ruined for far less.

So he had strong personal interest in proclaiming himself a fierce and ardent Cold Warrior, a hard-line anticommunist. And in the process, he began his shift to the political right. Reagan's ideological conversion would not happen overnight. He voted for Dwight D. Eisenhower in 1952 but was no fan of Ike's vice president. "Pray as I am praying," he wrote after the election, "for the health and long life of Eisenhower because the thought of Nixon in the White House is almost as bad as that of 'Uncle Joe.'" ("Uncle Joe" being Stalin—no holding back the drama there.) "Nixon is a hand picked errand boy with a pleasing façade and naught but emptiness behind. He has been subsidized by a small clique of oil and real estate pirates, he is less than honest and he is an ambitious opportunist completely undeserving of the high honor paid him."

But as the decade wore on, Reagan found the left a more and more alien space. The Cold War liberals' case against Communism was aggressive, but it was also nuanced. The totalitarian state that abolished free markets posed a mortal threat to liberty, they argued. But they also believed in the New Deal consensus government: a government that provided a safety net from the market's excesses, a government that could use planning and fiscal policy to preserve and grow the economy, a government that had the power to actively transform the lives of its citizens. "Containment," the government's consensus approach toward international Communism, was, by necessity, complicated and qualified as well. The doctrine held that the expansion of Communism must be met with a willingness to show force around the globe. But it also held that, thanks to the catastrophic potential of nuclear weaponry, force should be avoided at all costs, and conflicts with the Soviets should be carefully and strategically chosen.

Only in the newly radicalized hard right could Reagan find the unqualified moral clarity and dramatic urgency he preferred. By the early 1950s, conservatives had been out of power for nearly a generation. Their worldview was undiluted by the compromise and contradictions that inevitably come with the responsibility of governing. A group of young conservative thinkers—the most prominent of whom was William F. Buckley, Jr., founder of the conservative magazine *National Review*—saw themselves as leading a new, more radical movement. They had little use for classical conservatism's respect for and preservation of existing institutions. Rather, they viewed themselves as an oppressed minority, standing outside the New Deal consensus with no choice but to condemn it in the strongest possible terms. *National Review,* Buckley wrote in 1955, "stands athwart history, yelling stop." The magazine performed "a predominantly monitoring task," observed the writer Garry Wills, who served as a staffer at the magazine in its early days. "It came to accuse."

These movement conservatives accused the governing establishment of creating a leviathan welfare state that threatened liberty. They accused Roosevelt, Truman, and Eisenhower of launching the federal government on a path that would inevitably end in tyranny.

They accused the nation's elite of corrupting that government and of conspiring to obscure its excesses. And they accused the nation's leaders of a dangerous naïveté in foreign policy that would lead inevitably to capitulation and defeat. There could be no compromise, they screamed, in matters of life and death. "The forces of international Communism are . . . the greatest single threat" to liberty, their statement read. "The United States should stress victory over, rather than coexistence with, this menace."

Here was the vivid moral clarity Reagan yearned for. The circumstances of his personal life helped his ideological conversion along as well. From the GE executives who paid his bills, he received a steady diet of pro-business cant. From Nancy's parents and their wealthy friends in conservative Arizona, he heard a mounting cry of indignation at the consensus mush coming out of the Eisenhower administration. Movement conservatism was critical of the East, which Reagan found foreign and unappealing. It lionized the traditional Midwestern values Reagan had long sought to embody, and it romanticized the rugged individualism of the West, where Reagan had proudly made his home. It preached of excessive taxation's threat to liberty, a message that resonated with a high-earning actor who worried about his future earnings. Even the movement's withering critique of those who urged "coexistence" with the Soviet Union—appeasers, the movement had it, who wished for peace and would get war—may have had unique personal appeal. Lew Ayres, the actor with whom Reagan's first wife, Jane Wyman, was rumored to have had an affair, was an avowed pacifist who had been sent to a conscientious objectors' camp during World War II.

But one thing more than any other made the conservative movement a natural home for Reagan: the proud place it gave to a speaker who, like him, could stir dramatic passions. The conservative pantheon of stars was almost exclusively populated by operatic, even hysterical, personalities. First and foremost was Buckley, who lived for experience that revealed vitality—a daring sailing voyage through dark and stormy seas, a motorcycle ride through the streets of

Manhattan—and for moments that hinted at the everlasting—
a Bach concerto played on his Bösendorfer piano, the miracle of the
Eucharist in the Latin mass. In the taut conformity of consensus,
Buckley understood, a political thinker could distinguish himself
merely by being interesting. "For we offer," he wrote in the debut
issue of his magazine, "a position that has not grown old under the
weight of a gigantic, parasitic bureaucracy, a position untempered
by the doctoral dissertations of a generation of Ph.D.s in social architecture, unattenuated by a thousand vulgar promises to a thousand different pressure groups, uncorroded by a cynical contempt
for human freedom. And that, ladies and gentlemen, leaves us just
about the hottest thing in town."

The movement had other hot tickets, too. Conservatives cheered
Wisconsin senator Joseph McCarthy, whose brief and memorable
service as the leading authority on the Communist conspiracy sprang
not from any expertise on the topic but from a search for a campaign
issue that would get him maximum attention. The spirit McCarthy
showed in his infamous Wheeling address—*I have here in my hand
a list of two hundred and five . . . members of the Communist
Party*—was untempered and unattenuated by experience, unbur-
dened by concern for fairness or truth. As such, it made a great show.
Phyllis Schlafly, a grassroots activist from the Midwest, captured the
movement's attention by describing the country's situation as ex-
tremely perilous. The name of her radio show revealed the entire
movement's style: *America, Wake Up!*

Then there was Barry Goldwater, the Arizona senator who, in
the latter half of the fifties, filled the void in the movement's political
leadership left by the death of Senator Robert Taft. Goldwater's
press coverage from the period stressed his rebellious roots. As a
child, writes biographer Rick Perlstein, Goldwater "rubbed shoulders with boys of all classes and races, was a basement tinkerer and
a hellion who fired a miniature cannon at the steeple of the Methodist Church." He became a national figure in the fifties by gleefully
hurling cannonballs at Eisenhower, the sitting president from his

own party. The spending by Ike's government harkened "the siren song of socialism" he declared on the Senate floor. *Conscience of a Conservative,* the slim volume he released in 1960 (actually written by Young Americans for Freedom cofounder L. Brent Bozell), transformed the gray mire of consensus politics into vivid dichotomies:

> I do not undertake to promote welfare for I propose to extend freedom.

> My aim is not to pass laws, but to repeal them. . . .

> Either the Communists . . . will force us, ultimately, to surrender or accept war under the most disadvantageous circumstances. Or we will summon the will and the means for taking the initiative, and wage a war of attrition against them. . . . For Americans who cherish their lives, but their freedom more, the choice cannot be difficult.

"To many young readers," Perlstein observes, "the argument had almost a Gandhian appeal. . . . Freedom was indivisible. It was worth dying for."

By the time 1960, and the choice between Vice President Richard Nixon and Senator John F. Kennedy, came around, it was clear to Reagan: he had become a Republican.

He showed little public hesitation over inverting his allegiances. Now it was Nixon's opponent, not Nixon himself, drawing comparison to famous Communists. "Shouldn't someone tag Mr. Kennedy's 'bold new imaginative program' with its proper age?" Reagan wrote to Nixon, offering his services in the 1960 campaign. "Under the tousled boyish hair cut it is still old Karl Marx—first launched a century ago." Nixon liked this kind of talk. "Use him as a speaker whenever possible," Nixon urged his staff. "He *used* to be a liberal!" (The former liberal, as it happened, was eager to make things official with the Republican Party, but the Nixon camp, believing he could do them more good as a registered Democrat, told him to sit tight.)

Party member or not, Reagan worked tirelessly for Nixon and the Republicans, making speeches whenever his schedule allowed. He liked these political appearances so much he didn't stop them after the election in November, remaining on the Republican speakers' circuit for the early Kennedy years. Now his sinister-sounding proper nouns were attached to the president: Kennedy and aides like *Professor Arthur Schlesinger* were putting programs in place that would inevitably make freedom-loving Americans slaves of the state.

And he learned quickly what an ambitious conservative had to do to advance in the movement. His passion, first and always, was the global threat of Communism, but he backed conservative crusades against statism at home as well. In a 1961 speech, he spoke of the evils of a favorite New Deal consensus cause: a medical-care bill for the elderly. He urged his listeners to block the program, injecting his message with all the drama he could summon: "If you and I don't do this, then you and I may well spend our sunset years telling our children and our children's children what it once was like in America when men were free."

Real conservatives, he discovered, had a long list of people they mistrusted. The kind of conservatives who formed Young Americans for Freedom chapters on college campuses, the kind who were organizing for a Goldwater presidential campaign in 1964—they loathed and mistrusted not just the John F. Kennedys and Adlai Stevensons of the world, but the Dwight Eisenhowers, Nelson Rockefellers, and Richard Nixons, too. These establishment Republicans were hardly better than the Democrats. As proponents of consensus politics, they were naïve appeasers themselves.

Reagan was never quite as enthusiastic about attacking establishment figures as were his movement compatriots. Usually, before he went after a Democrat or wobbly Republican, he took time to note that they were well intentioned but woefully naïve. But he did what he had to do to get along in a movement that valued purity. When Nixon asked for Reagan's endorsement in the 1962 California gubernatorial primary, the actor coolly volunteered that he thought he'd be more help in a general election campaign. Unlike many California conservatives, Reagan did not join the extremist John Birch Society, a hard-line right-wing group whose leadership preached fantastic conspiracy theories, suggesting that Eisenhower was a double agent working on the Kremlin's behalf. But he did campaign for a Bircher candidate, John Rousselot, in the congressional election of 1962.

Before long, he was acquainted with all the movement's leading lights. He struck up a warm relationship with Goldwater, a social acquaintance of Nancy's parents, who had retired to Arizona. Buckley first encountered Reagan as his opening act at a 1960 speech before a group of California doctors. When the loudspeakers wouldn't turn on, Buckley watched as Reagan "cat-walked above the traffic" to the window of the locked control room "and smashed it open with his elbow." Buckley was taken with the handsome actor's heroics: "Turning on the juice," he would note approvingly, "the show must go on."

To the movement's leaders, Reagan's conversion was a boon. Here was a handsome and familiar face who had been in the clutches of the liberal behemoth—only to see the light and live to tell the tale. He told it in a friendly but thrilling fashion, with a seemingly endless supply of facts and figures that made the conservative case sound as indisputable and sensible as they all knew it to be. Who cared if in Hollywood he was a has-been. In the movement, he was a shining star. Right-wing audiences loved him. When he appeared onstage with Goldwater, people wondered: Why didn't Reagan just run for office himself?

Why indeed.

Until the end of his life, Reagan swore that he never imagined a life in politics, not even in the early 1960s. Despite ample evidence to the contrary, this version of events has largely prevailed in histories of Reagan's life. Perhaps this shouldn't be surprising. Both Reagan's admirers and critics share a common interest in a history in which Ronald Reagan's political career just *happens*.

Some facts are indisputable. Sometime before he announced his candidacy for California's governorship in 1966, the idea entered Reagan's head that he could have a career in electoral politics. Some Reagan admirers on the right are inclined to push that date as late as possible. Years spent planning an entry into politics does not fit with his image as a flawless conservative hero—Reagan, after all, was the man who said "Government is not the solution to our problem, government *is* the problem." It is inconvenient for that man to have spent years planning a career in government. They prefer to remember Reagan as a modern-day George Washington, leaving behind his beloved farm and field to heed duty's call, or as the perennial cowboy hero, coming down from the mountains to save California and then the world.

On the left, Reagan's political career is often treated as an accident that he stumbled into. It is difficult for his liberal critics to accept that a B-movie actor, a man who costarred with a chimp, could rise to lead a coalition that would in time roll back a generation's worth of liberal progress. Reagan couldn't have plotted his own ascent. He must have been a pawn for wealthy, well-connected interests, rich men who wrote a script for him and, when the moment was right, told their puppet with his pretty face to look into the camera and smile.

And then, most formidably, there is the narrative put forth by Reagan himself. Again and again, Reagan maintained that a career in politics was something he'd never imagined and never planned. In his postpresidential autobiography, he told of a group of conservative California businessmen coming to his home in early 1965 to speak with him about running for governor of California. "I almost laughed them out of the house," Reagan wrote. He tried to convince them they had the wrong guy. " 'I'm an actor, not a politician,' I said several times, 'I'm in show business.' "

Reagan wrote these words after he had left the White House. He knew his disciples on the right—already out proclaiming him the twentieth century's greatest president—and understood the distaste with which they viewed professional politicians. "I'd never given a thought to running for office," he wrote firmly. "I had no interest in it whatsoever." He recalled the advice of one of his conservative touchstones, Nancy's father, Loyal Davis: "He said I would be crazy to run for office; he said there was no way a man could go into politics without sacrificing his honesty and honor."

Here it is important to recall, however, that Reagan was never inclined to admit he'd plotted much of anything at any point in his life. His was the natural way of the movie star: make it all look effortless. In Hollywood, Edmund Morris notes, the real stars were the ones who don't have to audition. Reagan understood the rules of the game early. Shortly after arriving in Hollywood, he wrote a guest column for a newspaper back in Iowa describing his adventures in the film colony. In it, he excises his ardent efforts to get noticed. Instead, his career is something that happens to him: "I was introduced to Max Arnow, Warner Bros. casting director, invited to make a screen test and suddenly woke up with a movie contract in my fist." And that was how he wanted people to think of his political career, too: that he was invited to run for office and suddenly woke up clutching the keys to the governor's mansion.

Yet Reagan's version of events, wherein he was shocked by the suggestion that he run for office in 1965, doesn't square with the historical record. He had been approached to run for governor of California in the year 1962 (the year, coincidentally or not, that he finally changed his party registration to Republican). The talk of Reagan the candidate was serious enough to reach his adult daughter, Maureen. "Run," Maureen, already a partisan Republican, urged her father, "you can win back California."

"Mermie," her father wrote to her in reply, "I really appreciate your support, but if we're going to talk about what could be, well, I could be President—ha, ha!—but of course, that's not going to happen, is it?"

His other children also remember talk of political campaigns in the Reagan house, at points earlier than in the official narratives. It was obvious to his daughter Patti, who was on the brink of adolescence in the early 1960s, that her father's acting after GE was "a day job, not a passion. Politics was his passion, and it was becoming stronger all the time." His son Michael recalls eavesdropping on a rare argument between Ronnie and Nancy at Christmas 1963 in which Nancy was pressuring her husband to start a gubernatorial campaign: "She said her stepfather was willing to raise $200,000 in campaign money if Dad agreed to run. Personally, I don't think Dad ever had really strong ambitions to be a politician, but Mommy—his name for Nancy—prodded him."

Reagan's version of events—the version in which his political career just happened—is also complicated by the heights to which he aspired. Stuart Spencer, the California political operative, first met Reagan in 1965. Within months, he was convinced that Reagan had his eye on the presidency. And indeed, in two years' time, Reagan would hatch plans for a presidential campaign. The desire to run for president, and the conviction that the presidency can be won, is not born overnight. It is nurtured by mind-altering ego and ambition over years and years. In Reagan's case, it was most likely born in the dark days of the Depression, listening to Roosevelt's wonderful voice on the radio. Here was a man whose office afforded him the grandest stage of all.

That was what Reagan saw in the blurry haze of his political crowds in the first half of 1964: a chance to be the hero once more. It would be impossible for any man to stand on those stages and not think, *What if they were all cheering, and voting, for me?* There is little doubt he would have found that possibility alluring. For Reagan, politics gave him the opportunity that Hollywood couldn't: to spend his middle age as a star.

———————

WANTING A CAREER in politics was one thing. Abandoning his acting career to pursue it was quite another. To do that, Reagan would
have had to look at the opportunities of the modern conservative
movement in a coldly practical light.

Pragmatism is not a virtue people usually ascribe to Reagan. The
Reagan of popular memory is the one the country came to know as
president, the one who preferred to keep things pleasant and let
other people sweat the small stuff. It is certainly true that Reagan
was drawn to fantasies, that he often clung to an oversimplified view
of the world, that he relied on the people around him to understand
the difference between the world as he wanted it to be and the world
that really was. Even so, there was one thing about which Reagan
was usually quite realistic: himself. When it came to his own self-
interest, Reagan the dreamy idealist was a deeply practical man.

It had always been that way. Working as a lifeguard those sweltering summer days in Illinois, the teenage Reagan would resist the
temptation to drop into the water to cool off, knowing that wet
trunks would chafe his skin over the course of his long shift. Upon
graduation from Eureka, he set out for a career in show business, but
he gave himself an ultimatum: if after five years of trying he wasn't
making five thousand dollars a year, he would have to find another
career. (He beat his goal.)

Even in his picture-perfect romances, pragmatism reigned. As
Cannon notes, in the studio propaganda about his marriage to Jane
Wyman, a rare sour note appears when Wyman dishes on their plans
to lavishly furnish a new house they are building in the Hollywood
Hills. "Depends on conditions and prices and war and things," Reagan interjects. "We don't intend to get out on a limb." So, too, in the
early days of his marriage to Nancy, when his Hollywood career was
at a standstill, Reagan was conscious of his financial limitations. "It
was a year and a half," said Nancy, "before we could afford to furnish our living room." His uncommon ambition required him to be
ruthlessly realistic about his own interests. And when his ambition

conflicted with his need for self-preservation, self-preservation usually won out.

Now, too, as politics beckoned, Reagan would have to look squarely at the circumstances of his life. His two children from his second marriage—Patti and Ron Jr.—were attending expensive private schools. His two children from his first marriage—Maureen and Michael—were both having a rough time in their transition to adulthood. He and Nancy were now running in a social circle—wealthy Republican businessmen and their wives—that could make even top tax bracket earners feel destitute. "Money was a big issue in my family," wrote Patti, "a live wire that always seemed to be sizzling." However drawn Reagan was to politics, it was against his nature to let it endanger the security of his family.

By 1964, Reagan had come to understand that self-preservation in politics was no simple task. He had learned that lesson bitterly in his final years at GE. At first, the company's management applauded Reagan's burgeoning interest in politics; they liked his pro-business talk. But as Reagan's tone grew harsher and his politics grew more extreme, he sensed discomfort coming from his corporate overlord. GE did business with the current government, after all, and Reagan's movement talk didn't mesh well with the Kennedy moment.

Reagan felt isolated within GE. He imagined powerful new enemies gunning for him. In a postpresidential memoir he would claim, preposterously, that during the Kennedy years, in any city he spoke in, "there'd be a cabinet member or other high official from the . . . administration who'd be giving a speech on the same day. In the television business, we used to call that 'counter programming,' an effort to knock out the competition with a rival show. I don't have any proof they planned it that way, but I don't think it was coincidental."

Democrats, he believed, were pushing his GE bosses to muzzle him. Like Johnson, he suspected one powerful Democrat in particular of machinations against him. His daughter Patti would later recall her parents' fear that the Kennedy administration was pressuring GE to silence him through threats to the company's contracts:

"Government contracts, my father said one night at dinner. This is exactly what I've been out there speaking about. We're on our way to a controlled society. The government is trying to control everything. And Robert Kennedy is behind this attack on me."

"He is?" I piped up. "Why would he want you fired?"

"Because I'm speaking out against the Kennedy administration and the road they're trying to lead us down."

"*Of course* Bobby Kennedy's behind it," my mother said. "It's obvious."

And so when, in 1962, GE decided not to renew Reagan's television show, he suspected his politics had something to do with it. GE had grown tired of Reagan's political persona. Management also asked that in his appearances as a GE spokesman he refrain from making political statements. This was a deal breaker for Reagan. "There's no way that I could go out now to an audience that is expecting the type of thing I've been doing for the last eight years and suddenly stand up and start selling them electric toasters." He and GE parted ways.

In time, the split with GE would become part of the Reagan legend—how he'd refused to compromise his principles for personal gain. But in early 1964, the split looked like something else altogether. However principled, it was a setback, a failure. And crucially, it was a repeat of the lesson he had learned during the worst days of his movie star career, when audiences had ditched his "Mr. Norm" type for the broody, moody, sensitive male stars. He would long remember the studio bosses who had controlled his career then, how they had failed to see how the preferences of the moviegoing public had changed after World War II. "They thought I was the hottest thing around," he would say, "and didn't realize that the sixteen-year-olds didn't know who I was." In politics, as in Hollywood, it was all the same. Events happened. People's tastes changed. A star could regret the public's mood, but if he wanted to eat, he would respect it.

And so a pragmatic Reagan, considering a life in politics, had to look beyond just the roars of approval he found from his conservative crowds. He had to think about what conservatism meant to the people he'd always cared about the most—the everyday, "normal" people in the American mainstream. Entering politics offered any number of risks. To take the leap, Reagan needed an opening, a moment when his worldview aligned with the public mood.

Could he gain confidence from Barry Goldwater's presidential campaign? Before Kennedy's death, conservatives, having infiltrated the party leadership in key areas of the country, liked their chances of winning the nomination in 1964 and were looking forward to challenging the New Frontier in dramatic style. Kennedy—as aware as anyone of the vast distance between the beliefs of Goldwater's movement diehards and majority opinion in the country—liked the idea of a race against Goldwater, too. At his last political meeting in November 1963, Kennedy had discussed potential Republican opponents in the election. "Give me Barry," said the president; "I won't even have to leave the Oval Office."

At first, it looked as if Goldwater's chances at the nomination had died with Kennedy. The press had stopped holding conservatives directly responsible for Kennedy's death when it was revealed that Lee Harvey Oswald's political views, such as they were, tended toward Marxism. But still, reporters speculated for months about whether extremist politics of the Goldwater variety had contributed to a climate of hate in which minds like Oswald's had flourished. (Johnson gave a nod to this line of reasoning in his January 1964 State of the Union address, saying, "In these last seven sorrowful weeks, we have learned anew that nothing is so enduring as faith, and nothing is so degrading as hate.") In the month after the assassination, Goldwater's standing in national polls dropped by double digits. In a mid-December column assessing the GOP's 1964 prospects, Scotty Reston did not even mention the Arizona senator's name.

Goldwater, who loathed the preening and posing required of

presidential candidates, had been dreading a White House run in the months before Kennedy's death. After the assassination, he wanted to drop out of the race, but his advisers implored him not to give up. They eventually persuaded him the only way you could persuade Barry to do anything—by asserting that it was simply unmanly to drop out of the race at such a late date.

So he stayed in, to the delight of a scornful national press. To political journalists, Goldwater's winter primary efforts were fun to watch, not as a campaign but as a series of comic calamities: Barry stepping on the drama of his January announcement by telling an off-color joke about his own daughter; Barry recovering from a bone spur injury, sliding around the New Hampshire ice on crutches, snarling at any voter who happened into his path; Barry, confused and belligerent in an interview on *Meet the Press,* asserting (incorrectly) that Kennedy had never sent federal troops to the South to enforce the law; Barry reiterating his most controversial established positions, that Social Security should be abolished and the Tennessee Valley Authority privatized, and floating new ones that were even more incendiary, that field commanders should be granted the ability to launch nuclear weapons without presidential approval. "There is no mathematical way of recording the pathetic fate of the Arizona senator's candidacy," wrote the former Eisenhower aide Emmet John Hughes in February, "simply because most of his followers are still unsure of the direction in which they will desert."

That was the urgent question for the Republican establishment: Who was their alternative to Goldwater? Barry's only announced rival was Nelson Rockefeller, the liberal Republican governor of New York. Blessed with his family's resources, Rockefeller bought himself a superb national organization in advance of a 1964 run. But in 1962 he'd doused himself in scandal, leaving his first wife for the married Margaretta "Happy" Murphy. The Kennedy assassination revived his chances, but he had a long way to go to win over traditionalists in his party and overcome a snippy press corps. *Newsweek*'s thinly veiled taunting was typical: "Nelson and Happy

Rockefeller couldn't have been happier. The new year would bring a new heir—in June, the governor and his wife disclosed after the newspapers broke the news—and, on the strength of his weekend reception in New Hampshire, Rocky's political fortunes were showing signs of life too."

Party leaders scrounged for another alternative but had little luck. Thanks to an independent write-in campaign, the New Hampshire primary went to the patrician Massachusetts politician Henry Cabot Lodge, Jr. Lodge indicated his lack of enthusiasm for a presidential run when, shortly after New Hampshire, he announced his intention to stay on as Johnson's ambassador to South Vietnam. Michigan's moderate governor George Romney considered jumping in. The press swooned over a potential run by Pennsylvania governor William Scranton, whose good looks and ample fortune earned him a reputation as the Republican John F. Kennedy.

In the White House, Johnson worried most about the man whom Kennedy had barely beaten in 1960. As 1964 dawned, Richard Nixon was working as a New York lawyer, swearing he was out of politics but acting like an aspiring politician. When the party's financial backers gathered for a meeting that included presentations by Goldwater, Rockefeller, Romney, and Scranton, Nixon appeared by closed circuit television. He was opportunistically ambiguous. "I say with confidence tonight," the noncandidate told the crowd listening to him, "that one of those whom you will hear on this program will be the next president of the United States."

Johnson couldn't quite believe he would be lucky enough to have Goldwater as an opponent. And when Rockefeller upset the Arizonan in the Oregon primary in May, creating momentum that would carry him into the decisive California primary, much of Washington assumed that the Goldwater moment had come to an end.

But they hadn't seen what Reagan saw. They hadn't seen the devotion Goldwater inspired in young conservatives like the ones in that San Diego ballroom. The ones who'd been talking up a Goldwater presidency since before Nixon lost in 1960. The ones who were enthusiastic volunteers in the national Draft Goldwater Committee. Under the leadership of a brilliant organizer, F. Clifton "Clif" White, Draft Goldwater had set out to secure commitments from seven hundred Republican delegates before the party's nominating convention in July 1964 (655 votes would secure the nomination). It was an ambitious target, and it was dependent on strong support from new converts to the Republican Party in the segregationist South. The young Goldwaterites were convinced they could achieve it. They *had to* achieve it. The future of the party, of the country, of civilization itself was at stake.

And more important, the wise people in Washington hadn't seen the California that Reagan knew. They hadn't seen places like Orange County. In those Southern California suburbs, middle-class white refugees from the Midwest had embraced Goldwater's style of conservatism as a modern religion. There, voters needed no convincing that the Communist threat to civilization was real and that conspirators lay within their midst. There, the John Birch Society was no fringe group; it had thousands of county residents on its newsletter subscription list. There, Phyllis Schlafly's manifesto "A Choice, Not an Echo" was passed around like a secret Bible speaking the one true faith in a world of heretics. There, in February 1964, Goldwater supporters set out to collect thirteen thousand signatures to get their candidate on the state's primary ballot. By the end of their first day, they already had close to three times that many. And there, the weekend before the California primary, when Reagan appeared at a rally for Goldwater, the crowd that turned out was twenty-eight thousand strong. You didn't have to look closely at the faces in that crowd to know one thing: Barry Goldwater was going to be the Republican Party's nominee in 1964.

SURE ENOUGH, GOLDWATER won the primary. His victory on June 1 would come almost exclusively from the movement diehards in the southern part of the state: Rockefeller would win fifty-four of the state's fifty-eight counties, but Barry's vote totals in Los Angeles,

San Diego, and Orange counties were large enough to give him the primary victory by a narrow margin. It was the conservatives' day. A poll of California primary voters found that their top issues were, in order, federal spending, Cuba, and Soviet espionage.

The establishment gulped hard. Anything could happen at a convention, but after California, Goldwater would be hard to beat. Barry's true believers rejoiced. At last their moment had come.

Reagan cheered Goldwater's victory, too. For a hardworking Goldwater surrogate like Reagan, it was a happy result. For a conservative true believer like Reagan, the victory was an ideological triumph: finally they had a nominee who would fight for the cause. And for a dramatist like Reagan, it was a delicious story: the man the elites had discounted was getting the last laugh.

But for a pragmatic would-be politician like Reagan, Goldwater's triumph presented a nagging problem: Where did the movement go from there?

After all, you only had to read the newspaper to understand that federal spending and Soviet espionage did not exactly top the list of most Americans' concerns. Goldwater's followers, however many of them there might be, would be working against the public mood, not with it.

That seemed just fine with their candidate. Goldwater had never had much appeal to the faint of heart. His persona was one of adolescent rebellion, the senator bored by the conventions of the staid Senate, the Republican willing to throw rocks at no less a revered figure than Dwight David Eisenhower. "Out here in the West and Midwest, we're not constantly harassed by the fear of what might happen," Goldwater said. "Sure there are risks, but we've always taken risks."

Long before Kennedy's death, Goldwater's supporters in the party were arguing for "a choice, not an echo"—the line Schlafly memorialized in her book. The choice, as they saw it, was clear. On one side were the liberals in both parties who offered appeasement abroad and statist policies at home. On the other side were conservatives who would confront the Communist menace, unchain the spirit of individual freedom in America, and return the nation to its frontier values. Had Kennedy lived, he and his campaign aides would have painted Barry as a dangerous extremist, most likely with great success. But against Kennedy, Goldwater's critique would have garnered a kind of legitimacy from Kennedy's own rhetoric. Again and again, Kennedy argued that the work before the country would be hard, that the country's bright future could not be achieved without sacrifice. The progressive program he envisioned was not possible without risk. The choice in the never-to-be Goldwater/Kennedy election would have been a choice over which side's risks were acceptable, which side's vision was so enticing it was worth taking a chance.

But that choice had died with Kennedy. The public had learned that day in November all about the downside of risk. Now the new president was running a nonstop campaign to convince the public that the time of trauma had passed, that all was fine. With power passing from Kennedy to Johnson, the Democrats' message had changed, and the new message was clearly what average Americans wanted to hear. Yet the Goldwater message didn't change at all. He kept talking of imminent danger, of the nuclear war that was just around the corner, of the liberal policies of appeasement that amounted to a "suicide pact." To believe in Goldwater's vision was to rebel against the great national project of proving that all was right in America again. To believe in Barry Goldwater, you had to believe that things had been going wrong in America for quite some time and that things were about to get much worse. Johnson was the kindly uncle who had come in to take charge of an orphaned nation after the loss of a beloved father figure. Barry was a maniac, rushing in to say the house was burning down.

Reagan understood the rage Goldwater's supporters felt. He shared it. In his speeches before them, he articulated that rage perfectly—so perfectly that his conservative audiences couldn't help but rise to their feet. But he knew, by instinct and by years of training, that there were other audiences that a man in politics would have to appeal to, bigger audiences, with different wants and needs. "There is no point in saving souls in heaven," he wrote in *Where's the Rest of Me?* "If my speaking is to serve any purpose then, I must appear before listeners who don't share my viewpoint." He knew the same thing that the new president in Washington knew: that a preacher who wanted to win converts had to do more than scare people to death.

But no one around Goldwater seemed to know this. They didn't seem to have much interest in converting anyone. At Goldwater's California victory party, Reagan varied his usual speech, trying out a new theme in addition to the familiar encapsulation of outrage. He spoke of unity. "We are going to have to forget an awful lot of bitterness," he told the crowd. "We don't want to win a convention, we want to win an election. Let's start making love to Democrats." He reminded them that he had been a Democrat once, a Democrat who had worked to elect Harry Truman. This was not what the crowd wanted to hear. They booed and hissed in response.

That was the impression in Reagan's mind as he pondered his future that summer: swooning cheers for rage, boos and hisses for "making love."

Reagan was a true believer. He would continue to work for Goldwater, he would keep giving his red-meat speeches, he and Nancy would attend the San Francisco convention as enthusiastic supporters. He believed in the conservative movement, and he fervently hoped that its day would soon come.

But he was not ready to risk his career on it. Not yet. That same year, a new acting job came along. Reagan's advertising executive brother, Neil, was helping to produce a TV Western called *Death Valley Days*, sponsored by one of his clients, the Pacific Coast Borax Company, maker of 20 Mule Team Borax and Boraxo hand cleaner. The show needed a new host, someone who could introduce the short teleplays that ran in each episode. Neil knew his brother needed work, and he tried to persuade him to take the job. As always, Reagan played hard to get, he wasn't sure it was the part for him. But just as had happened with *Johnny North,* after a lunch and some ego stroking, he relented. He signed a contract committing himself to host *Death Valley Days* into 1966, long after the presidential election was over. What else was he supposed to do? It was "good, steady work," his daughter Maureen would later write. Reagan "jumped at the gig."

CHAPTER SIX

★ ★ ★

Everybody's Scared

Summer 1964

As spring 1964 ended and summer approached, more than a thousand young Americans were heading toward Mississippi, hoping to change the world. These were the idealistic college-age volunteers for the Mississippi Summer Project, known as the Freedom Summer in the national press. From late June through August 1964, they would infiltrate the Deep South, educating black voters on their constitutional rights and helping them register to vote. In the process, they knew, they would provoke clashes with white segregationist law enforcement, clashes that would draw national attention and outrage. Most of the volunteers were white middle-class college students from the North. They knew Mississippi only as a ghastly idea. "A desert state," Martin Luther King, Jr., had called it in his 1963 March on Washington speech, "sweltering with the heat of injustice and oppression."

But for one young man working in the Freedom Summer, it had always been a very real place. James Chaney, a native of Meridian, Mississippi, was a black man who knew what the desert state's sun felt like. He was not a college student; he had not even finished high school. His friends and family would later say he signed up in part because he thought it would be a good way to meet girls.

When his mother asked her son if he was frightened by the work

Early in his presidency, Johnson welcomed civil rights leaders
to the Oval Office: (left to right) Martin Luther King, Jr.;
Johnson; Whitney Young; and James Farmer.

© Yoichi Okamoto/LBJ Library

he had taken on, Chaney answered no. "Mama, that's what's the matter now," he told her. "Everybody's scared."

It was a core belief of the civil rights movement—that fear was the problem and that fear was something that could be overcome. But Chaney was also describing the nation in which he lived. In the summer of 1964, America remained as it had been—a nation enjoying unprecedented prosperity, a nation that was firmly committed to proclaiming that everything was okay. But fear remained, unspoken, a kind of background noise. Like the buzz of an old fan in a sweltering room, it would go undetected by placid minds. But in agitated ears, it would stick and smother, until it was impossible to hear anything else. All over the country that summer, people with far fewer reasons to be scared than James Chaney had summoned fear from the background and waited for catastrophe to come.

At some point on June 21, the longest day of the year, fear most likely came to Chaney. We can only speculate as to when. Perhaps it came that morning. At the Meridian office of the civil rights group Congress of Racial Equality (CORE), reports had come in that Mount Zion Methodist, a black church in Longdale, Mississippi, had been burned to the ground by a white mob. CORE had planned a freedom school at the church, and Mickey Schwerner, a young white northerner who headed the group's Meridian office, wanted to find out what happened. With Chaney, and another white volunteer named Andy Goodman, he set out toward Longdale to investigate.

Chaney, the native Mississippian, drove the car. Perhaps fear first came as he and his colleagues crossed into neighboring Neshoba County, known for its heavy Ku Klux Klan activity. Or perhaps fear came in Longdale, where Chaney saw kerosene cans lying near the cold ashes of Mount Zion. "The sixty-five-year-old structure had been totally consumed," write the journalists Seth Cagin and Philip Dray in their definitive account of the events in Neshoba County on the twenty-first of June. "All that remained was the bell, some blackened hymnals and a grotesquely twisted piece of metal that had been the roof." Perhaps fear first came when Mount Zion's parishioners delivered a message to Schwerner, whose activities in the county had raised the ire of its white folk: *The people who did this were looking for you.*

Or perhaps fear came on the long drive back toward Meridian when a police car appeared in Chaney's rearview mirror. Or not long thereafter, when Chaney's right rear tire gave out and the station wagon came to a halt. Or perhaps it came when the police car stopped behind the station wagon and the menacing figure of Neshoba County deputy sheriff Cecil Price emerged. Ordering the three men out of the car, Price told them that they were under arrest. It was unclear exactly what their crime was. They didn't ask. Price was carrying the Southern policeman's nightstick—the leather blackjack.

Behind bars in Philadelphia, Mississippi, the county seat, the men waited out the afternoon. Deputy Price had hauled them into the Neshoba County Jail and then disappeared. When the prisoners asked if they might make a phone call back to Meridian, the local jailers said no. Perhaps there in the quiet of the jail cell, as the bountiful daylight of the summer solstice slowly slipped away, fear came to James Chaney. It was an article of faith among civil rights workers never to let anyone release you from jail after sundown. *You never know who's going to come find you at night.*

At ten o'clock, when full darkness had settled in, a returned Deputy Price informed his prisoners that they were free to go. The three men emerged from the jail into the thick, muddy night, free but not safe. "Now let's see how quick y'all can get out of Neshoba County," Deputy Price had said as they left the jail. As Chaney drove away, he could see the deputy's headlights following behind.

Then, at the edge of town, the lights disappeared. There was only the dark countryside and the desolate road. Somewhere in the distance was the county line and then Meridian—out of sight, but there. The station wagon sped forward. Maybe the men inside thought they would be safe after all. Maybe, for a moment, their fear slipped away.

But then came headlights again, speeding toward the station wagon. Chaney, who knew what happened on dark roads in Mississippi, hit the gas. The safety of Meridian was too many miles away. Most likely out of desperation, he pulled off onto a narrow gravel road, perhaps hoping to lose his pursuer. But the headlights still followed close behind. Then, as the station wagon careened through the darkness, it was suddenly filled with a flashing red light. A police signal. Chaney pulled the station wagon to a stop on the side of the lonely highway, where the three men inside awaited another encounter with their pursuer, Deputy Price.

"I thought you were going back to Meridian if we let you out of jail," the deputy said.

"We were going there," Chaney offered in reply.

"Well, you sure were taking the long way around," said Price. "Get out of the car."

This would have been an unappealing offer, for the deputy was not alone. Shortly after Price pulled the rights workers over, a car pulled up behind him. It was packed with passengers: civilians, not police. There were six of them. And they were all white.

Price ordered his three prisoners to get into the backseat of his own vehicle. The two white men obeyed. For a moment, Chaney held back. Perhaps he was thinking about what happened to black men in Mississippi on dark roads in the dead of night. Perhaps the fear had paralyzed him. Or perhaps he was trying to summon strength.

That's what's the matter now. Everybody's scared.

Then he felt Price's leather blackjack cracking into his skull.

"What do they think happened? Think they got killed?"

Lyndon Johnson was on edge. It was two days later. That morning's *New York Times* bore the headline from Mississippi "3 in rights drive reported missing." All morning, frantic relatives and fellow activists had been badgering the White House for federal assistance in the search for Chaney, Schwerner, and Goodman. Johnson could see trouble coming his way. He asked an aide, Lee White, what exactly the activists' families were suggesting. What did they think had happened to these men?

"So as far as they're concerned," White told him, "they just disappeared from the face of the earth. This means murder, as they see it."

Fear over the young men's fate had spread quickly. In the Meridian CORE office that Sunday, their colleagues began to worry when the men did not return by 4:00 P.M. as planned. They spent that afternoon calling around to local law enforcement authorities, asking if they had the men in custody. A call to the Neshoba County Jail yielded no information. No such persons, said the jailer, were in custody at that time. By nightfall, word was spreading throughout the affiliated groups of the civil rights movement and to contacts in the national press: three of their men were missing in the Mississippi night.

The next day, news came from Neshoba County that the men in fact had been held in custody there. But they had been released after dark the night before. That day, two journalists, Claude Sitton of *The New York Times* and Karl Fleming of *Newsweek,* arrived in Neshoba County to report on the missing men. In Philadelphia, Mississippi, the journalists were greeted by a crowd of hostile white locals. Sitton's dispatch for the next day's paper was coldly factual: "Agents of the Federal Bureau of Investigation began arriving here in force early tonight after the Justice Department offered a full-scale search. The Mississippi Highway Patrol issued a missing-persons bulletin, but a spokesman in Jackson indicated late today that it had no plans at present for further action."

News editors across the country were reading these words and planning their own coverage. That meant that Neshoba County was now Johnson's problem. He knew that the outcry from the friends and relatives of the missing men would only grow. But he remembered well the recent history—and the not-so-recent history—of the

South. He was desperate to avoid a confrontation over federal authority in Mississippi.

The local authority in Mississippi, meanwhile, was disinclined to admit that the men had gone missing at all. Sitton's dispatch quoted Deputy Price's boss, Neshoba County sheriff L. A. Rainey. "If they're missing," said Rainey, "they just hid out somewhere, trying to get a lot of publicity out of it, I figure."

"I don't believe there's three missing," Mississippi senator James Eastland told Johnson on the phone that Tuesday afternoon, "I believe it's a publicity stunt. . . . There's no white organizations in that area of Mississippi. Who could possibly harm 'em? . . . It'll take a crowd to make three men disappear."

"That depends on the kind of men, Jim," an indulgent President Johnson said. "It might take a big crowd to take three like you. I imagine it wouldn't take many to capture me."

Presently, their conversation was interrupted by a call from FBI director Hoover, who had details from his investigators on the scene. Some Choctaw Indians had come upon a burned-out station wagon near a swamp. "Apparently, what's happened," Hoover said, is "these men have been killed. Although, as I say, we can't tell if anybody's in there, in view of the intense heat."

Johnson wondered if he ought to send word to the missing men's families.

"I don't like you having to see these people," Hoover said, "because we're going to have more cases like this down South . . ."

THAT WAS WHAT Johnson feared most. The charred station wagon in the forest changed things. Now there was a picture around which the TV networks could build a story. More reporters rushed to Neshoba County. Soon the newscasts were showing the familiar Southern story: a sinister local sheriff backed by a sullen white citizenry, statements of outrage from civil rights leaders, a swarming federal presence. Hoover would have more than a hundred men in the area by week's end. At Johnson's urging, McNamara would mobilize members of the armed forces in the region to aid in the effort.

But still the missing workers were nowhere to be found. "Officially, at the weekend, they were missing," wrote *Newsweek*; "unofficially, few doubted that they were the first martyrs of a fiery Mississippi summer." The first, the magazine suggested, but hardly the last. "There were those in Washington who feared that the summer so grimly begun might yet end in a Federal occupation amounting to no less than a second Reconstruction."

This was exactly the kind of talk Johnson did not want. The following week, he expected to pass the 1964 civil rights bill, an attempt to bind up the South's wounds once and for all. Johnson's strategy of calling the Republicans' bluff on civil rights—"they're either the party of Lincoln or they ain't"—had paid off. Two months into the Southern filibuster of the bill, the Democrats had offered a new, slightly watered-down bill in hopes of attracting Republican support for breaking the southerners' back. On June 10, the break came in a fiery speech from Republican leader Dirksen on the Senate floor in which he declared, "Stronger than all the armies is an idea whose time has come." It was set to be the signal accomplishment of the Johnson presidency to date.

"We have now come to a time of national testing," Johnson told the country in a televised address before the bill passed the House on July 2. "We must not fail." That day, he signed the bill in a White House ceremony. A Universal newsreel that played in theaters that summer captured perfectly the story that Johnson wanted told:

ANNOUNCER: Congress passes the most sweeping civil rights bill ever to be written into the law . . .

ONSCREEN, WASHINGTON: *A pleasant summer's day. In front of the Capitol dome, a flag flutters in a gentle wind.*

ANNOUNCER: . . . and thus reaffirms the conception of equality for all men that began with Lincoln and the Civil War . . .

Cut to the LINCOLN MEMORIAL: *A wide shot captures the glistening Reflecting Pool and the Washington Monument in the distance. Gone are the urgent masses who filled this setting at the March on Washington in 1963. In their place are summer tourists, ambling happily toward the memorial.*

Cut to a white mother, wearing a white blouse, leading her two daughters toward the seated LINCOLN. *The camera zooms in as they stop and gaze up at the Great Emancipator.*

ANNOUNCER: . . . The Negro won his freedom then. He wins his dignity now.

Cut to interior, a glowing chandelier. Pull back to reveal it is the chandelier in the East Room of the White House, last seen draped in black crape to mark the passing of President Kennedy. Now its gold glitters and the faces in the room are full of smiles.

ANNOUNCER: The Civil Rights Act of 1964 is signed at the White House . . . President Johnson calls for all Americans to back what he calls a turning point in history.

Watch as JOHNSON *sits down at a desk festooned with bouquets of pens and prepares to sign the bill.*

THE PRESIDENT: Its purpose is not to divide, but to end divisions. Divisions which have lasted all too long . . .

Pan back to the audience of assembled dignitaries, rising quickly to applaud JOHNSON. *First to exuberantly pop up is* HUBERT HUM-PHREY, *the jolly-faced Democratic whip.*

ANNOUNCER: There's warm applause from members of both parties as the president sets to work.

In the front row, a glimpse of BOBBY KENNEDY, *staying seated while everyone else stands. The camera cuts quickly away.*

ANNOUNCER: It is work. He uses nearly a hundred pens to affix his signature and date. . . . The president seems to have mastered the art of just touching each pen to the paper.

Watch as JOHNSON *hands pens to* DIRKSEN *and* HUMPHREY *and a crowd of other silver-haired senators.*

ANNOUNCER: Integration leader Martin Luther King receives his pen, a gift he says he will cherish.

Close-up to show KING *approaching over* JOHNSON's *shoulder. His is the first black face we have seen in this newsreel about the rights of the Negro.* KING *receives a warm greeting from the* PRESIDENT, *but when he slips back into the crowd, he looks out of place amid the backslapping bonhomie.*

ANNOUNCER: The Department of Justice will enforce the law, if necessary, and G-man chief J. Edgar Hoover is present.

New camera angle. On the opposite side of the desk from KING *we see the expansive profile of* HOOVER, *grinning obsequiously as he extends his hand downward to the president of the United States.*

ANNOUNCER: Another group of pens is reserved for the Kennedys. And the attorney general is entrusted with a half dozen.

BOBBY, standing slim and straight, his youthful face unexpressive, looks like a petulant little boy amid the gray sea of legisla-

tors. JOHNSON *hands him pens eagerly, as though they were lollipops, meant to coax him out of his ill humor.* BOBBY *takes the pens one by one but is unmoved.*

ANNOUNCER: In this summer of 1964, the Civil Rights Act is the law of the land. In the words of the president—it restricts no one's freedom, so long as he respects the rights of others.

Notably absent from the triumphant newsreel footage was Barry Goldwater. The Arizonan, now the presumed favorite for the Republican nomination, had been one of the six Republican senators to vote against the bill. Reporters assumed he was offering a banner around which the Southern racists could gather in advance of the Republican convention. "If he is nominated for President," Walter Lippmann wrote, "he will stand out as the rallying point of nonobservance and of passive resistance to the law."

But that wasn't Goldwater's intention—it wasn't a crass political calculation. Goldwater didn't do crass political calculations. If he had, he would have concluded that the immediate costs of a no vote on civil rights were too great. He was berated for his vote by no less a figure than President Eisenhower. His own party leader assailed him on the Senate floor: "You can go ahead and talk about conscience," Dirksen said. "It is *man's* conscience that speaks for every generation."

Rather, Goldwater's vote came from contorted constitutional reasoning. His legal advisers had convinced him that he could not vote for the bill—that it constituted an unprecedented usurpation of state powers by the federal government. Before announcing his vote, he was "a shaken man," Perlstein writes, "convinced that the Constitution offered him no other honorable choice."

Characteristically, he expressed his inner turmoil through outward surliness. Asked by a reporter if his position on the bill would hurt him in November, Goldwater exploded: "After Lyndon Johnson—the biggest faker in the United States? He opposed civil rights until this year! . . . He's the phoniest individual who ever came around."

This was the other story Johnson hoped the country would see that summer. The party that had produced two out of every three presidents for the past one hundred years, the party of Lincoln and Teddy Roosevelt, the great Republican Party, was rapidly coming unhinged. After Goldwater's June primary victory in California, the party's moderate establishment wanted desperately to keep him from seizing the nomination at the San Francisco convention. But how? Or, more precisely, with whom?

Scranton, with his fresh, Kennedy-like looks, became the last, best hope of the anti-Goldwater faction when he jumped into the race in June. Rockefeller, conceding defeat after California, pledged the full resources of his campaign organization to the Scranton team. Eager to play the part of a vigorous young statesman in the Kennedy mold, Scranton threw himself energetically into the race. His stroke of luck, he believed, would come in the form of a benediction from Eisenhower, who had watched Goldwater's rise with dismay. But Ike had always preferred to appear above crass politicking. Having seized the cliffs of Normandy and two terms in the White House, he was disinclined in his dotage to give an inch of high ground. Scranton was disappointed to learn Ike's coveted endorsement would never come.

Without it, Scranton had no remaining strategy for stealing the nomination, save what Teddy White would call "the gallantry of hopelessness." Hopeless was the key word. At the party convention, which opened in San Francisco's Cow Palace on July 13, Goldwater's grassroots strategists wrangled his delegates expertly, carefully choreographing the state delegations by radio connection from a trailer adjacent to the convention hall. Goldwater was nominated on the first ballot. In the end, all that the Scranton opposition at the Cow Palace achieved was the thorough discrediting of Goldwater at the hands of much of the party leadership. Scranton, making his desperate case, reminded voters of just how extreme Goldwater was. In a letter published days before Goldwater's nomination, he called Goldwaterism a "crazy-quilt collection of absurd and dangerous positions that would be soundly repudiated by the American people in November."

But it was July, and this kind of talk made the movement diehards hot with rage. It was the kind of anger Reagan had seen in his political audiences throughout the year. Watching the assemblage in San Francisco, millions of Americans got to see the rage for themselves. The television networks, expecting a boring Johnson coronation at the Democratic convention in late August, had pinned their hopes for drama on the possibility of a bloody floor fight in San Francisco. NBC had 173 cameramen navigating the convention floor. CBS laid 180,000 feet of cable inside and outside the Cow Palace, aiming to capture every moment of the convention's experience. "When a delegate goes to the bathroom," producer Bill Leonard said, "CBS wants to know."

Mercifully, this was overstatement, but what the networks did broadcast of the delegates wasn't much more pleasant to behold. Revved up to quash a moderate challenge that didn't need much quashing, the Goldwater army plundered about in search of a suitable foe. They found it in the press galleries. Smarting over the coverage of his primary-season prevaricating, Eisenhower urged the delegates to "particularly scorn . . . sensation-seeking commentators and columnists." Ike was far from a movement favorite, but this message was one the crowd could get behind. *Time* magazine described delegates who "leaped off their chairs, shook their fists at the glass television booths high above," and "jeered newsmen in the aisles on the convention floor." When Rockefeller addressed the convention in support of a platform amendment against extremism, he was shouted down with catcalls. The antiextremism measure failed.

Goldwater, who spent much of the convention holed up in agonizing tedium at the Mark Hopkins Hotel, was in no mood for making nice. Conventions were supposed to feature optimistic tunes like the Democrats' "Happy Days Are Here Again." When Goldwater approached the speaker's stage on the night of July 16, the band blared "The Battle Hymn of the Republic." To his audience, and to the millions of Americans watching at home, the nominee described an America altogether different from the one described in the official narrative of prosperity and good feeling. In his America, the new GOP nominee saw a land marked by "violence in our streets, corruption in our highest offices, aimlessness among our youth, anxiety among our elders."

His words crackled with resistance, the same resistance that had electrified the living rooms of Southern California. "Those who do not care for our cause we do not expect to enter our ranks in any case." Then came the two sentences that would live with Goldwater in history: "I would remind you that extremism in the defense of liberty is no vice!" He paused as the crowd rose in sustained applause. "And let me remind you also: that moderation in the pursuit of justice is no virtue!" More roars as reporters watched in disbelief. Watching from a remote location, Goldwater's chief organizer, Clif White, turned off the television set broadcasting the speech, aware that the Goldwater general election campaign had just died in its infancy.

The nation was shocked by this display of vitriol. The press, feigning horror, was thrilled. *The New York Times* called the Goldwater show "a disaster for the Republican Party and a blow to the prestige and to the domestic and international interests of the United States." The broad consensus among journalists now matched Lippmann's assessment of Goldwater. "He is not a normal American politician who, as election approaches, is drawn toward the center. He is a radical agitator who must stay with the extremists. . . . The prospective nomination of Goldwater is a grave threat to the internal peace of the nation."

From the White House, there was little overt acknowledgment of the Republican horror show. Asked that month about a Goldwater statement that "as of now," Johnson could beat *any* Republican candidate, the president demurred. "I think the Republican Party has enough problems without my adding to them in any way." Like most presidents of his era, particularly those sitting on a comfortable election year lead, Johnson strove to appear above the sordid business of a presidential campaign. "We really won't do any campaigning until after Labor Day," he told House Speaker John McCormack in June. "So we'll let them show all their hole cards and then we'll come in and trump 'em."

It was an act, of course. Out of the camera's view, Johnson thought endlessly about the campaign against Goldwater. Shortly after the Republican convention, Congressman Carl Albert escaped Washington for a vacation in Canada with his wife and son. Hoping to really get away, the congressman did not leave any details of his itinerary with his office or anyone else in Washington. One night, while waiting for Mrs. Albert to get ready in their Quebec hotel room, the congressman turned on the television news. He was surprised by what he saw. "The Canadian Royal Mounted Police are endeavoring to locate Congressman Carl Albert," said the newscaster, "with license plate number PB827 driving a 1964 Thunderbird. . . . Anybody knowing anything about the whereabouts of Carl Albert will please immediately notify the Royal Canadian Mounted Police."

Albert quickly phoned the Mounties, who informed him that they'd been running a national search for him on behalf of the White House. The president, it seemed, was desperate to reach the congressman.

"Boy, you sure are hard to find," said Johnson when the congressman dutifully called in. "What I want you to do is be chairman of the platform committee at Atlantic City, and I need to make the announcement. I hated to bother you . . . but we've got to put this thing together right away."

Still, a winking press corps mostly played along with the notion of above-the-fray Johnson. And so, while the Republicans argued over Goldwater proposals to abolish Social Security and sell the Tennessee Valley Authority, the president nonchalantly informed reporters that government estimates of deficit spending for fiscal 1964 would be $500 million *less* than previously thought.

Subtly, Johnson sought to make Goldwater the face of the un-named, lurking fear so many in the nation felt. "What we really want to do with Goldwater," he told his press secretary George Reedy, shortly after the meltdown at the Cow Palace, "is . . . leave the im-pression we're not gonna do anything to incite or inflame anybody. And let's leave the impression he *is,* without saying so."

AND SO, BY midsummer, it was a truth universally acknowledged that Lyndon Johnson would win in November. Most likely, he would win by a large, even historic, margin. The story he had worked so hard to tell the nation—in which Johnson, with his endless energy and legislative genius, had steered the nation back on a course toward unprecedented prosperity and unimaginable greatness—had taken hold of the nation's imagination. Washington was becoming a Johnson town again. Washingtonians assumed it would stay a John-son town for some time, perhaps into the next decade. In George-town, the rebel outpost languished. Jackie Kennedy put out word in July that after only half a year in Washington, she would leave the capital to make a new home in New York.

And yet the more certain his victory became that summer—the more it seemed that there was nothing and no one who could topple him—the more Lyndon Johnson grew consumed by fear. On the phone with aides, his breathing grew heavier and louder. He com-plained of sleepless nights. His puzzled friends wondered if perhaps the president was in ill health. *Time* reported a rumor "swiftly spread[ing] through the capital and its environs that Johnson, who suffered a massive heart attack in 1955, was ailing again."

His weight, which had dropped considerably during his action-packed first months in office, now soared. An expanding Johnson waistline was always a sure sign of psychological distress. For him, food was not an indulgence but an intoxicant, an object he reached for to fill a gaping void, one that he could never fill up. At lunch meetings in the White House, his secretary Marie Fehmer would often lay a plate of sandwiches on the table in front of him and his guests. Johnson would quickly devour the entire plate and then say to Fehmer, "I'm kind of hungry. Have you got anything to eat?" "But sir," Fehmer would reply, "you had a whole plate of sandwiches." Johnson would show no recollection.

So, too, he devoured any morsel of news that seemed to suggest catastrophe was near at hand, and he'd still want more. The network newscasts on his three television screens and the papers and news-magazines were all reliable sources of worries. There were more stories in the press that summer about senseless crime and brutal killings. There were mounting fears about the inner cities. The same week as the Republican convention, a black student was shot by police in a predominantly white section of Manhattan's Upper East Side. Riots followed, first in Harlem, then in parts of Brooklyn and the Bronx. Days after Goldwater's warnings about a country descending into lawlessness, the television networks showed images that suggested his vision was coming true.

For white people already on edge, the riots hit a sweet spot of anxiety—the unnamed fear that soon the poor black mobs would stop burning and looting their own neighborhoods and come for them. The riots provided the press with a vivid illustration of the fear the nation was feeling. On its cover the following week, *News-week* showed three grim black faces above the headline "HARLEM: HATRED IN THE STREETS." That was the establishment press consensus: it was hatred, deep and irrational—not a racist police force or employment discrimination or substandard housing and schools—that had caused these mobs to riot and loot.

A new word, "backlash," was appearing in the press. The pollster Lewis Harris explained that white ethnics in Northern cities would be particularly susceptible to this phenomenon. By a two-to-one margin, these voters "feel that most Negroes want to take jobs held by whites." Fertile territory for resentment could also be found in the suburbs, where whites "tend to feel that the pace of civil rights is too fast" and "that Negroes are getting 'too uppity for their own good.'"

Johnson lapped up these kinds of dispatches. He was quick to imagine the worst. "If we aren't careful," he told Reedy, "we're just gonna be presiding over a country that's so badly split-up that they'll vote for anybody that isn't us." When Goldwater requested a White House meeting to discuss responses to the riots, Johnson begrudgingly agreed, but he was paranoid about the outcome. "He wants to use this as a forum," Johnson told John Connally. "He wants to encourage a backlash. That's where his future is. It's not in peace and harmony." The president gorged on conspiracy theories. He hoarded rumors that the Texas oilman H. L. Hunt was funding the riots, trying to get the backlash started. Hoover fed him morsels suggesting Communist agitation was to blame. "Hell, these folks have got walkie-talkies," Johnson told John Connally, speaking of the riots. "Somebody's financing them big."

But though it could fuel hours of nervous chatter in White House meetings that summer, the politics of backlash was still too hazy to be a real threat. Fear and resentment in the white American mind were still too removed from its rational decision-making regions to change votes. White Americans in the summer of 1964, looking objectively at their situation, could see that their quality of life was just as Johnson's story had it: quite good, indeed better than it had ever been before. They could stare all they wanted at the horizon, but the black mob was not coming. The looting in the inner cities was happening in black neighborhoods, not white ones. Not yet. "The white backlash itself exists," Harris wrote that summer in *Newsweek,* "lurking more or less menacingly in the background, but it is not yet a major force in the land."

Not major enough to sate Johnson's hunger for fear. And besides, "backlash" was too abstract a concept to embody the anxiety that Johnson felt. He understood the world in human terms. The greatest prize he could imagine was human: winning the votes and the admiring eyes of as many Americans as possible. So, too, his

greatest fear had to take human form. Goldwater, hapless and hopeless, was not terrible enough. Johnson needed a man more worthy of
his growing worry. That man, once again, would be the attorney
general of the United States.

AFTER THE DEBACLE at the Cow Palace, the press had one final
chance at drama in the odd political year of 1964: the mystery of
who would fill out the Democratic ticket as Johnson's running mate.
The logical choices were Minnesota's two senators, Hubert Humphrey and Eugene McCarthy. But as is often the case, the prospect
the press found most exciting was the least likely one. As summer
wore on, Washington grew obsessed with the question of whether
Johnson's running mate would be Bobby Kennedy.

The speculation made Johnson frantic. It was the worst thing he
could imagine. He devoured intelligence reports from aides that suggested Bobby was trying to enlist power brokers like Chicago mayor
Richard Daley to force Bobby's name on the ticket. In late July, Johnson told Connally he had barely slept the night before, his mind had
been so preoccupied by the threat from Bobby. "When this fellow
looks at me," Johnson said, "he looks like he's going to look a hole
through me."

By then, the tension between the president and his attorney general had long been out in the open. Kennedy's friends in the press
had kept his constant muttering about Johnson out of print for the
first months of the new administration. But the split went public in
February when Paul Corbin, a freewheeling Kennedy operative in the
Democratic National Committee, took the independent initiative to
organize a write-in campaign for Bobby on the New Hampshire primary ballot. His goal was to secure the vice presidency for Kennedy,
but Johnson, rightly, viewed the effort as a public challenge to his
legitimacy. In a tense Oval Office meeting, he demanded that Bobby
remove Corbin from New Hampshire and, for that matter, from the
DNC. When Bobby protested that Corbin had been a favorite of
President Kennedy's, Johnson lost his patience. "Do it," he ordered.

"President Kennedy isn't president any more." Bobby was stunned by the challenge. He jabbed back: "I know you're president, and don't you ever talk like that to me again."

A flurry of mutual pettiness followed. Corbin was let go. Kennedy's friends wrote columns suggesting that Johnson was freezing out JFK's staff in favor of his own whoop-hollering Texas posse. Johnson-friendly reporters wrote that the ego and occasionally even insubordination on the part of the Kennedy men was slowing the progress of the Kennedy-Johnson agenda. Kennedy remained Johnson's attorney general, but the two men mostly kept their distance that spring. Johnson's periodic attempts at reconciliation were always rebuffed.

The alienation was inevitable, for Johnson and Bobby were living in different worlds. The death of Bobby's older brother had made him the heir to his family's political hopes. But unlike Jack, Bobby had not been groomed to be a candidate, and he was constitutionally incapable of the empty flattery and false praise with which politicians like Johnson got others to do their daily bidding. Further on in the decade, Bobby's raw emotion and reflexive honesty—what political professionals of a later age would call "authenticity"— would become his greatest asset. But in 1964, it mostly made for uncomfortable scenes. At one point that year, Lady Bird Johnson found herself waiting at Union Station alongside the attorney general, where they were scheduled to greet an arriving dignitary. "We waited quite a while and he leaned over to me and said, 'You're doing a good job,'" Lady Bird would later recall. "Then there was a perceptible pause, and with what seemed like real effort he said, 'And your husband is too.'"

Deeper down, Johnson and Kennedy saw the world through very different eyes. While Johnson was out promoting his wonderful visions of the American future, Bobby was still living in the darkest frontiers of grief. The journalist Murray Kempton, visiting Bobby a few months after the assassination, thought of the epitaph for the three hundred dead at Thermopylae: "Stranger, when you see the

Lacedaemonians, tell them we lie here faithful to their orders." The comparison inverted reality—the *living* Bobby was being faithful to orders, his brother was the one in the tomb. But that was the inverted world Bobby knew. "I'm sure Jack liked it," Bobby wrote to Kempton after his piece appeared. As a belated Christmas gift for aides in the Justice Department, he gave gold cuff links inscribed "Robert Kennedy 1961–1964." It was as though he had died on seeing the first New Year without his brother as president.

Kempton's piece described an "archaic" Bobby Kennedy, and, indeed, in those first months, all of Bobby's allegiances were to the ancient world. In his biography of Kennedy, Evan Thomas reveals how Bobby's attachment to Edith Hamilton's book *The Greek Way* sheds light on Kennedy's thinking in these months. Jackie had given him the book in the weeks after JFK's death, promising it would provide deep wisdom and consolation. For Bobby, "the book, written thirty years before by a Bryn Mawr classicist, was a revelation," Thomas writes. "It is easy to imagine Kennedy, desperate for some meaning in senseless tragedy, transfixed by the morals extracted by Hamilton from the historians Herodotus and Thucydides and the playwrights Aeschylus, Sophocles, Euripides."

In time, the words of Aeschylus—*God, whose law it is that he who learns must suffer*—would help move him beyond the tragedy and give purpose to his life. But in the early months, the way of the Greeks also offered validation for all of Kennedy's worst impulses. Reading Hamilton, Kennedy could console himself that the bitterness and pain he felt were noble. In the Greek way, "there is no dignity like the dignity of a soul in agony," and this dignity belonged only to a privileged few. Pain was human and universal, but tragic suffering was reserved for the rare souls who lived daring lives of passion and gallantry. "Tragedy is enthroned," writes Hamilton, "and to her realm those alone are admitted who belong to the only true aristocracy, that of all passionate souls."

Joseph Kennedy had raised his children to believe that the special vigor within them made them superior to all other aristocratic pretenders, be they the Brahmins of Boston or the elected leaders of the land. So now Bobby would claim the special privileges of his spiritual caste. He referred to "the president" when talking about his brother. He withheld even token deference in the presence of President Johnson. He abstained from all the silly rituals of Johnson's mundane world. All the while he reassured himself that he was not being selfish, but rather dignified and divine. This was the Bobby who, at the Civil Rights Act signing, refused to stoop when Johnson wooed him with his bushel of pens. Hamilton quotes Shakespeare: *"Here I and sorrows sit / Here is my throne; bid kings come bow to it."*

The king would bow to the Kennedys, but only so far. Johnson had always hated the idea of Bobby in the vice presidency. In the spring, he told aides that he would accept Kennedy as his running mate but only if it proved absolutely necessary for him to win. By midsummer, with Goldwater's nomination assured and Johnson's approval rating above 70 percent, it was clear the necessity wasn't there. But the ongoing speculation in the press rattled him. There were reports that Kennedy aides were planning a demonstration in Atlantic City, where they would spontaneously rise up to demand the vice presidency—or maybe something more. He tried to root out accomplices in Bobby's plots. Richard J. Daley, one of the savviest operators in the history of American politics, played dumb when Johnson called to investigate. "The worst city in the United States for rumor and gossip is Washington," the mayor told the president. "And frankly, we out in the prairies don't pay much attention to columnists, the newspapers or anything else."

By indulging his worst fears about the attorney general, Johnson made them real. On its own, the position of vice president was utterly unappealing to Bobby. The job was full of suffering, but not the noble, tragic kind. He knew that Johnson blamed him for the miserable indignity of his own vice presidency and that, as Johnson's vice president, he could count on Johnson to return the favor in kind. At first, Bobby expressed little interest in the job. He could see that in all likelihood Johnson would rule Washington for some time to come. He pondered work in a faraway land—maybe he'd write a book in England. Maybe he could even prove himself a gallant adventurer once more by serving as ambassador to Vietnam.

But then he saw just how desperate Johnson was to keep him off the ticket, and suddenly the vice presidency became the thing that Bobby Kennedy wanted most. He launched a defiantly public effort to force himself on the president. In July, he traveled to Poland, where huge crowds came out to see the brother of America's fallen hero. At the University of Warsaw, he told adoring students that he was "not a candidate for the Vice Presidency" but "if you were in America and could vote for me, I would be." Minds less studied in American politics than Lyndon Johnson's could read these words and remember that there were plenty of other Poles, living in and around the cities of the Northeast and industrial Midwest, who *could* vote for a president and vice president of the United States.

Soon, dark hints of Bobby's intentions were everywhere. Johnson and his staffers were disturbed by a profile in *Newsweek,* written by Ben Bradlee, for which the attorney general had provided extensive access. In it, Bobby talked openly of the impossibility of Johnson's asking him to run on the ticket. "I should think I'd be the last man in the world he would want," Bobby said in the piece, "because my name is Kennedy, because he wants a Johnson Administration with no Kennedys in it . . ." But there were other ways to become his party's vice presidential candidate. "Most major political leaders in the North want me," he said. "All of them, really." The threat was subtle but unmistakable: "I have this feeling that I am going to end up in government," he said. "These things have a way of solving themselves."

All of this was too much for Johnson to take. The fear that, like so many others in the country that summer, he had kept in the back of his mind, now took hold of his thoughts. In mid-July, he told John McCormack he was hearing consistent grumblings that party bosses were going to force Bobby onto the ticket in Atlantic City. "I don't want the presidency if they do," he said. "I don't want to have to sleep with a woman I don't trust."

With a month to go before the convention, the uncertainty became unbearable. On July 29, he invited Bobby for a private meeting in the Oval Office. As the appointed hour drew near, Johnson's nerves took hold of him. Clark Clifford, who, save for Johnson's longtime friend Abe Fortas, was Johnson's closest outside adviser, had offered constant counsel on the Bobby Kennedy threat. Waiting for Bobby, Johnson called Clifford to unload his anxiety. "He's got [Jackie] thinking about going to the convention," Johnson said. "He thinks that most of the delegations are for him, and this is the thing he wants more than anything in his life."

Clifford advised Johnson to take a hard line. "Now I think it appropriate and courteous for you to give some reasons for your decision," he counseled the president. "But you are not asking him at any time for his reaction."

Bobby had a good idea what he was walking into when he entered the Oval Office that day. Still, he grew uncomfortable. He glanced at what appeared to be a recording device on Johnson's desk and wondered if the president was recording the exchange. (In fact, no known recording of the meeting exists, but as John F. Kennedy's brother, Bobby should not have been surprised by the idea of a president's recording a meeting with a political foe.) He had the impression that someone—Johnson's right-hand man Walter Jenkins?—was listening in and taking notes. Later, he would say that an agitated Johnson, gripping prepared remarks, subjected him to a strange exegesis on the vice presidency before making it plain that Bobby would not be his choice. Bobby was pleasant in response, but once again he showed no interest in the politician's obligatory fakery. "You didn't ask me," he said, walking out the door. "But I think I could have done a hell of a job for us."

After the meeting, a triumphant Johnson rushed to call Clifford.

"I was very firm and very positive and very final," he said. He re-counted Bobby's final words and his own reply: "Well, I think you *will* do a hell of a job for us . . . and for yourself too."

It was clear who was boss.

Clifford had been a force in Washington since the Truman ad-ministration. To sustain a career that long in the capital requires a keen sense for where power resides. "Oh, I'm just so gratified," the lawyer cooed. "Let me say, right away, that this was not an easy task for you. It took courage and forthrightness and it just makes me very proud." It was indisputably clear who had won the battle between Lyndon Johnson and Bobby Kennedy. With Johnson, Clifford spared no flattery: "This is the kind of president I want."

But, like the plate of sandwiches, even the praise from Harry Truman's man did not leave Johnson satisfied. He scavenged for more, which only caused him more trouble. The whole point of tell-ing Bobby he wouldn't get the job, after all, had been to end public speculation. Now he needed to make the news public, but in a way that didn't seem personally vindictive toward the Kennedys. So John-son devised a broader rationale to explain his decision. Later that afternoon, he announced that, for the sake of continuity in govern-ment, he would not consider any sitting member of his cabinet as his running mate in 1964.

"He had communicated that decision personally," said the next day's *New York Times,* "to Mr. Kennedy and to Secretary of State Dean Rusk, Secretary of Defense Robert S. McNamara and Secre-tary of Agriculture Orville L. Freeman." This was true, but only barely. "While I'm thinking about naming him," Johnson joked an hour before the announcement, "I'm gonna try to get ahold of Rusk."

He couldn't leave it there. The next day he called in a select group of reporters to brag, off the record, about how he'd crushed Bobby. With heavy embellishment, he walked them through the Oval Office meeting, beat by beat. "When I . . . told him it would be 'inadvisable for him to be on the ticket,'" Johnson told the stunned newsmen, "his face changed and he started to swallow. He looked sick. His Adam's apple bounded up and down like a yo-yo."

Quickly, inevitably, word of this performance spread to Bobby. In the version the attorney general heard, Johnson portrayed Bobby as "a kind of stunned semi-idiot," journalist Stewart Alsop was later to recall. Bobby was furious. "This," said Alsop, "was the final break." Soon Bobby's friends in the press were lobbing their own bombs back at Johnson. Bobby, they claimed, had never thought about challenging for the vice presidency. "Mr. Johnson may have been seeing goblins where none ever existed," Evans and Novak wrote. "The vice presidential choice was the president's own from the beginning without any need for all the political gymnastics."

Johnson knew that Bobby was angry. He feared further escalation in their conflict. He obsessed over reports that Kennedy lieutenants were meeting to plan some kind of effort at the Democratic convention. "I think we ought to just watch that just like hawks," he told an aide. He looked at the horizon—August, Atlantic City—and saw disaster coming for him.

ON THE OTHER side of the world, in the last days of July, the American destroyer *Maddox* approached the Gulf of Tonkin, the broad inlet enclosed by the Chinese island of Hainan and the mainland coastlines of China and North Vietnam. From the edge of hostile territory, the *Maddox* would lead an American intelligence operation, gleaning information on the coastal defenses of the Vietcong. The mission would require the *Maddox*'s chief officer, Captain John Herrick, to dance around the precarious border between international waters and North Vietnam's sovereign territory. It was a dangerous task. The North Vietnamese had massed protective forces throughout their gulf coastline. The *Maddox* was huge and easy to spot on radar. In the early morning hours of August 2, ten miles from North Vietnam's Red River Delta, a feeling of imminent danger came to Herrick. And when his radar interceptors informed him that enemy forces had been ordered to attack the *Maddox*, he knew that the danger was real.

The Americans fired first as he dashed back to sea. Under pursuit from the North Vietnamese, Herrick requested reinforcements from U.S. bombers in the vicinity. The Communists fired torpedoes at the destroyer in response to the American attack but were unable to reach their target. Soon, the American bombers had downed a Communist ship, the *Maddox* was safe within international waters, and the frightening incident was over.

But Herrick and the other Americans remained on nervous watch. Under the order of the Pentagon, they were now joined by another destroyer, the *Turner Joy,* to undertake a new mission in the Gulf. As the historian Stanley Karnow demonstrates, this new charge was designed to provoke North Vietnamese aggression: "The two destroyers would stage direct daylight runs to within eight miles of North Vietnam's coast and four miles off its islands, as if defying the Communists to 'play chicken.'" The American vessels "were effectively being used to bait the Communists."

It is hard, when you are the bait, not to obsess over encircling sharks. On the evening of August 3, waiting for the enemy in a darkening, thunder-filled gulf, the crew of the *Maddox* sensed that it was under attack. Along with the *Turner Joy,* the *Maddox* launched a furious counterattack, firing its torpedoes into the dark abyss. The two destroyers engaged with a phantom enemy for hours on end until Herrick concluded that the danger had passed. In truth, he wasn't sure *what* had just happened. The *Maddox* had not sustained any hit. None of his crew was certain they had seen the enemy at all. "The entire action," Herrick advised his superiors, "leaves many doubts."

But back in Washington, there was little doubt. President Johnson had been presented with an apparently brazen attack on American forces. On the morning of August 4, he prepared a resounding response. American allies and congressional leaders were informed of a coming bombing campaign against North Vietnam.

All summer long, Johnson had obsessed over murky facts, ambiguous signals, and unspoken threats at home. By contrast, the path forward from Tonkin seemed quite clear. He had been trying to draw as little attention as possible to the continued American presence in South Vietnam, to the perennial instability of the nation's South Vietnamese allies, and to the growing threat that American forces would be enmeshed in a wider war. But he also heard the ominous talk from Goldwater, and Goldwater allies like Reagan, about the dangers of Communist appeasement. "Make no bones of this," Goldwater had said in his convention speech. "Don't try to sweep this under the rug. We are at war in Vietnam. And yet the President, who is Commander-in-Chief of our forces, refuses to say . . . whether or not the object over there is victory."

Johnson had been in Washington for the entirety of the Cold War. He had seen the persecution of Dean Acheson over the Truman administration's China policy. He had lived through the McCarthy period in the Senate. He understood one simple rule about the politics of Cold War foreign policy: Democrats lost when they looked weak. The facts from the Gulf of Tonkin were far from clear. But there was no real debate over what to do: Johnson's government would treat the incident as an act of calculated belligerent aggression, and Johnson would respond with clear and commanding force.

"My fellow Americans," Johnson told the nation in a televised address on the evening of August 4, 1964. "As President and Commander in Chief, it is my duty to the American people to report that renewed hostile actions against United States ships on the high seas in the Gulf of Tonkin have today required me to order the military forces of the United States to take action in reply. . . . That reply is being given as I speak to you tonight."

Indeed it was. As Johnson spoke, American bombers from the aircraft carriers *Ticonderoga* and *Constellation* were in the air over North Vietnam. They would fly sixty-four sorties that night, destroying North Vietnamese PT boat bases and an oil depot at a place called Vinh. There, David Halberstam wrote, "the smoke was observed rising to 14,000 feet."

Soon, a resolution that the Johnson administration had prepared in anticipation of an act of North Vietnamese provocation was sailing through the Congress. It would give the president broad war-making powers in Southeast Asia without actually having to declare war.

Soon, no less than Barry Goldwater himself was calling to commend the president on his strong response to the incident. "You've taken the right steps," said Goldwater, "and I'm sure you'll find that everybody will be behind you."

Soon, a triumphant Johnson was bragging to reporters about the American triumph. "I didn't just screw Ho Chi Minh, I cut his pecker off."

It was only years later, after exhaustive examination, that experts determined that there had in fact been no attack on the *Maddox* or the *Turner Joy* by the North Vietnamese.

In the meantime, there was only glory for Lyndon Johnson. The news from Tonkin dominated evening newscasts, the next day's papers, the newsmagazines the following week. For a moment, at least, the troubles in Vietnam were at the forefront of the American mind. They even obscured an important bulletin that reached Johnson in the White House during the first hours of the American response on August 4. On a tip from an informant, federal agents in Neshoba County had searched in a dense forest not far from Philadelphia, Mississippi. There they'd found the bodies of Andy Goodman, Mickey Schwerner, and James Chaney.

After striking Chaney in the head on the dark country road that night in June, Deputy Price had shoved him into the back of his car with the other two men. Then, followed by the vigilantes, members of the Neshoba County Ku Klux Klan, he had driven his prisoners down a lonely dirt road that cut deep into a dark pine forest. There, the posse pulled each man from the car—first Schwerner, then Goodman, then Chaney—and murdered them, one by one. Moments before he was shot, Mickey Schwerner looked into the eyes of his killer. "Are you that nigger-lover?" the killer asked. Schwerner's studies in nonviolence taught him to be compassionate in the face of aggression. "Sir," he said to his murderer, "I know just how you feel."

THE NEWS FROM Mississippi was disturbing, but it did not alter most Americans' determination to be cheerful, to ignore any lingering anxiety. Tuesday, the twenty-fifth of August, 1964, was bright and hot on the East Coast. In the seaside resort of Atlantic City, New Jersey, delegates to the Democratic Party's thirty-fourth nominating convention were putting on a gala affair. There was much for them to celebrate. Their nation was the richest and the freest on the planet. Urged on by their president, they imagined a future that was brighter, bigger, and better than any ever before imagined by humankind. And their party, the party of Jackson and FDR, the party that controlled the White House and both houses of Congress, was the clear favorite of the American people to usher in the glorious days to come.

Had it really been only nine months since that awful day in Dallas when shots were fired and the president was killed? Who hadn't wondered on that appalling November afternoon if things would ever get back to normal? Who hadn't wondered if there would ever be celebrating again?

Well, they were celebrating now, and for that they had one man to thank: Lyndon Johnson, who had stepped into the presidency and offered steady leadership, who had seized Kennedy's unfinished program and challenged the nation, *Let us continue!* Continue he had, passing a tax cut and a civil rights bill that had seemed hopelessly marooned in Congress under President Kennedy. He'd urged the nation to dust itself off and get moving, to get back to the business of being America.

And so this convention—the largest one in the nation's history, all the newspapers said—was all about the wonders of LBJ. Reporters described it as "a coronation, not a convention"—there would be none of the usual horse-trading, none of the usual first, second, third ballot suspense. There were no other candidates—Johnson's picture was the only one on display. And it was everywhere: on hand-held signs, on hats and masks, on posters that hung three stories tall beside the giant organ at the center of the convention hall. He had earned the loyalty and respect of his party, and according to every poll, soon enough he would have so much more: his own presidential term. Millions of Americans would be pulling levers, not for Kennedy, but for him. It was the one thing he wanted most in the world. And it was coming soon.

But the president did not share in the joy. As the delegates swarmed the boardwalk that Tuesday afternoon, Johnson, still in Washington, climbed the stairs to his White House bedroom, where he drew the shades and lay down on the bed. His mind drifted to the crowds gathered in Atlantic City. He was weary. What if he didn't go to accept the nomination? What if it all just went away?

He'd stayed up much of the previous night, scrawling a short and stunning statement on a yellow lined pad:

> Forty-four months ago, I was selected to be the Democratic Vice President of the United States . . .
>
> On that fateful November day last year, I accepted the responsibility of the Presidency, asking God's guidance and the help of all of our people. For nine months, I've carried on as effectively as I could. Our country faces grave dangers. These dangers must be faced and met by a united people under a leader they do not doubt . . .
>
> I am not that voice or that leader.

He thought about doing something with the statement. He could go downstairs to the press room, gather the newsmen with their cameras, and announce: he would not be going to Atlantic City, he would not be a candidate in 1964, he would simply serve out the rest of President Kennedy's term and then retire.

And then it would be done. The eyes of the party, the love of the nation, all of it would move on to someone else. Most likely, it would be Bobby, Johnson knew. But maybe even that didn't matter. What mattered was that the presidency would soon belong to another man. In the darkness, Johnson imagined what that would feel like.

On the other side of the White House, Johnson's aides were starting to get nervous. The president had been in a funk for several days. He was obsessed with a festering dispute on the convention floor. Members of Mississippi's renegade Democratic Freedom Party, an integrated alternative to the state's all-white Democratic Party, were protesting the seating of an all-white Mississippi delegation. The dispute had turned into a televised spectacle, highlighting the competing pressures weighing on the Democratic Party around the difficult issue of race.

It was an ordeal, but in the long run, it would be a blip, a footnote in the wearying but worthy struggle over civil rights. And yet, bizarrely, Johnson was talking as if his presidency itself was at stake. In fact, he was talking as if his presidency had already been ruined. That morning, he'd been making cryptic calls to West Wing staffers. "I'm just writing out a little statement that I'm gonna make," he'd said, his voice straining to sound casual, even bored, "either at press conference here or go up to Atlantic City this afternoon to make." He wasn't asking for their advice on this statement. He was acting as though it were a fait accompli. His questions were about process, as though this was just another matter for the schedulers: have a chopper ready, at some point this afternoon I need to go up to Atlantic City and blow up the Democratic Party.

Experience had taught Johnson's aides not to be overly concerned. The president had a terror of public failure. It was just like him to convince people he didn't want something—even the presidency—until he was sure he was going to get it. He would try to convince even himself. When you worked for Lyndon Johnson, you learned to live with empty threats.

But if the aides had listened closely to Johnson, they would have heard something else, something more unsettling: fear of the presidency itself. He returned to the list of threats he'd kept track of all summer—the cities exploding with racial tension, right-wing agitators urging it along, Vietnam spinning into a nuclear conflict with China or the Soviets, Bobby scheming and plotting. He was worried about that word in the newspapers, "backlash." It was all too much for him, he told one of his lieutenants. "I do not believe I can physically and mentally carry the responsibilities of the bomb and the world and the Negroes and the South."

He reached back into history for affirmation of a curse on his head. He thought about that other Johnson, Andrew, who'd been thrown into the presidency after the death of the heroic Lincoln. Andrew Johnson, who'd left the White House a failure and disgrace. "I deeply feared," he would later recall, "that I would not be able to keep the country consolidated and bound together." His mind moved toward frightening fantasies. In the darkness, he envisioned catastrophe coming to his country, to his presidency, to himself.

Someone had to pull the president back into reality. Not for the first time, nor for the last, the duty fell to Lady Bird. In the darkness of his bedroom, Lyndon talked to his wife of his troubles. She implored him to get out of his funk, but he persisted, saying he wanted it all just to be done. It was painful to listen to, Lady Bird later told her diary. "I do not remember hours I ever found harder."

After a time she left him, but she did not let the matter go. She wrote him a letter, telling him it was beneath his dignity to drop out now. As always, she was loving and admiring, but this time she was forceful, too. "To step out now would be wrong for your country," she wrote, "and I can see nothing but a lonely wasteland in your future. Your friends would be frozen in embarrassed silence and your enemies jeering." She could not force him to be president. She could only force him to see the world as it was. "I can't carry any of the burdens you talked of," she said; "it's only your choice."

Eventually, he made the right one. Johnson sent word to his aides that he would go to Atlantic City after all. He did go, and he saw the crowds and the giant portraits and the thousands of faces cheering for him. At the climax of the week, the convention hall echoed with applause for Johnson and his newly announced running mate, Hubert Humphrey. Years later, Johnson would remember how he felt as he accepted his party's nomination, staring out into the crowd. "As I stood there warmed by the waves of applause that rolled in on us, touched to the heart by the display of affection, I could only hope that this harmonious spirit would endure times of trouble and discouragement as well." But for Lyndon Johnson, waves of hope always signaled a larger storm of fear, out of sight but arriving soon.

CHAPTER SEVEN

Sacrifice

October–December 1964

On the evening of October 7, 1964, Walter Jenkins, special assistant to President Johnson, left his White House office and turned onto Pennsylvania Avenue. He was leaving work at an unusually early hour, headed toward what was, for him, an unusual destination: a party to celebrate the opening of a new Washington bureau for *Newsweek*.

Jenkins was not a habitué of parties thrown by the press. Really, he was not in the habit of doing much of anything besides working for Lyndon Johnson, an obligation that consumed nearly every hour of his day. He was often the first Johnson aide to arrive at the White House in the morning, and he was known to stay at his desk until midnight or beyond. Even when he did leave the office, he knew he was never free of it. He'd long since grown accustomed to getting calls from Johnson at any hour, asking him to track down so-and-so and make sure he knew such-and-such. For a while he'd enjoyed a brief nightly reprieve from presidential interruption on his short drive from work to home. But then Johnson had him put a phone in his car, and the peaceful interlude came to an end.

On this particular autumn night, however, Jenkins was able to make an unmolested escape. The president, fully engrossed in the fall campaign, was busy barnstorming the Midwest. Mrs. Johnson, too, was away, off on a campaign railway tour of the South. Leaving

Johnson watches election returns at Austin's
Driskill Hotel, November 3, 1964.

© Cecil Stoughton/LBJ Library

word with his secretary that he would be back later that evening, Jenkins headed out into the cool fall air.

It was a good thing, that October, for Johnson men to get out, to be seen at Washington parties. With just weeks to go before the election, the president was soaring far above Goldwater in the polls. Hungry for the appearance of inevitability, his aides were projecting total confidence. What better way to demonstrate their favored position than to have Johnson lieutenants chatting away at Washington parties as if they had nothing more pressing to do?

You could see that same Johnson assurance on television, in campaign advertisements for the president scattered across the airwaves. Johnson's face was everywhere—serious, responsible, *presidential.* Long gone was the cautious delicacy the Johnson aides had exercised in the first hours of his presidency. Gone, even, was the old story of those hours, replaced with a new one more to Johnson's liking. One campaign advertisement, fittingly titled "Johnson Accomplishments," reordered the awful events of the previous fall. It began with the familiar image of Air Force One landing at Andrews Air Force Base on that terrible night. But what came next was new. There was no shot of the coffin of John F. Kennedy being carried off the plane; no widow centering the camera as she followed behind; no Bobby Kennedy looking on. All of that had been excised. Instead, viewers saw only the Johnsons coming down from Air Force One. In this story, the president coming off the plane was alive, not dead. He climbed aboard the presidential helicopter, leaving Andrews behind. In the air, he journeyed five days forward in time, skipping neatly over the murder of Lee Oswald and Jackie Kennedy's passion play. The story skipped straight to Johnson in the Capitol, delivering his "Let us continue!" message of resolve.

An announcer narrated: "The promises made that November day were strong promises. One by one they have been kept . . ."

The ad ended with a close-up on the back of the president's Cabinet Room chair. It bore the insignia THE PRESIDENT, NOVEMBER 22, 1963. And when the camera pulled back to reveal the chair's occupant, Lyndon Johnson, even those words seemed to have a new meaning. In this story, November 22, 1963, was not the day the Kennedy presidency ended but the day the Johnson presidency began.

"Vote for President Johnson on November 3," said the announcer. "The stakes are too high for you to stay home."

The ad did not explicitly state what those stakes were. It didn't have to, for they were thoroughly explicated elsewhere in the fall campaign. In early September, Americans watching NBC's *Monday Night at the Movies* saw another ad, an ad that would air only once but that would define Johnson's campaign for the voters in 1964. This commercial, known as "Daisy," was so memorable that five decades later, it remains the best-known political advertisement in the history of American television. A little girl pulls petals from a daisy, counting each one as she goes. When she gets to "nine" her words are overtaken by a stern male voice coming over an amplifier, counting down "nine, eight, seven . . ." As the countdown approaches one, the camera zooms into the pupil of the little girl's eye until the screen is filled with darkness. From this darkness erupts the fiery mushroom cloud of a massive nuclear explosion. Then comes Johnson's voice: "These are the stakes: to make a world in which all of God's children can live or to go into the dark. We must either love each other, or we must die." The advertisement ended with the familiar refrain: "Vote for President Johnson on November 3. The stakes are too high for you to stay home."

An enormous audience—perhaps as many as 50 million people— saw "Daisy" on TV that night. Most were shocked by what they saw. Even the parents of the little girl picking the daisy petals were surprised. They had taken their daughter to shoot a scene for a commercial for an undisclosed client. No one had told them what their daughter would be selling: the possibility of her own annihilation, along with that of the rest of the human race. Many viewers thought the ad far outside the bounds of good taste. Angry callers jammed the White House switchboard. Noting the public reaction, the campaign did not air the ad again.

It didn't have to. All that "Daisy" had done, in its particularly memorable fashion, was the same thing Johnson had done when kicking off his fall campaign in a rally at Detroit's Cadillac Square. "I am not the first president to speak here," the president told the crowd, "and I do not intend to be the last." It was the same thing just about every communication from the Johnson campaign sought to do: to take an already anxious electorate and ensure that when it thought of Goldwater, it got so scared so quickly that it didn't want to think about him ever again. "FACT," wrote Jack Valenti in a blunt memo to the president on September 7. "Our main strength lies not so much in the FOR Johnson but in the AGAINST Goldwater. . . . We must make him ridiculous and a little scary: trigger-happy, a bomb thrower, a radical . . . not the Nation's leader, will sell TVA, cancel Social Security, abolish the government, stir trouble in NATO, be the herald of World War III." In a memo to the DNC, Bill Moyers laid out the Democrats' central message: "He *could* do these things— but only if we let him. Vote for President Johnson on November 3. The stakes are too high to stay home."

Through September and the early weeks of October, the Johnson campaign jammed the airwaves with that message. Another ad, "Confessions of a Republican," showed a neatly dressed man smoking a cigarette, looking unsettled, as though even by talking about Goldwater he was inviting some sort of danger. "But when we come to Senator Goldwater," he said, "this man scares me . . . President Johnson—now, Johnson, at least, is talking about facts." Thus the stripped-down message of the president's campaign: "Goldwater scares me! . . . Johnson, at least . . . But Goldwater!" It was not inspiring stuff, but it was remarkably effective. By the end of September, polls showed Johnson beating Goldwater by as much as thirty points.

Goldwater continued to be the Johnson campaign's best surrogate. When he attempted to soften his image, he ended up sounding even less appealing. Sucking up to peanut farmers on the campaign trail, he declared himself "probably the most violent advocate of peanut butter in history. On a dare from my son, I even shaved with it once, and it was all right, except that it smelled."

The press, growing bored with the hapless Republican candidate, tried out new terms—"frontlash" for Republicans abandoning Goldwater for the Democrats—and strained for ever more macho metaphors to describe the president's triumphs. In *Newsweek,* Johnson was "this big, booming, leonine Texan, this Paul Bunyan of politicians . . . gobbl[ing] up cities, crowds, distances, and issues with the uninhibited relish of a cormorant at a smorgasbord. He oozed restraint, responsibility, and reason at every pore—and he exuded confidence like a rooster in a henhouse."

Outwardly, Johnson seemed to glory in his triumph. Through the fall, he continually frustrated the Secret Service as he plowed into crowds. Some presidents seeking reelection recoil from hand-to-hand politics, finding it drains them of life. But Johnson's validation, and thus his strength, came only from other people. A crowd was an endless feast. "He needed contact with people," said his secretary, Marie Fehmer. For Johnson, tactile campaigning "was like a B-12 shot."

But in Johnson, blissful ecstasy and crushing anxiety were never far apart. He could feed his hunger for affirmation all day long. After a certain point, he would start craving things to fear.

And fear was surprisingly easy to find in that fall's campaign. When a political candidate is sitting on a comfortable lead in the polls, the final weeks in the election are like a sleepless night in an old, empty house. Time stands still while stray sounds and unaccountable movements gnaw at the nervous mind. Rational adults grow deeply superstitious; responsible professionals become haunted by the memories of races that seemed like sure things—and then weren't. Everyone obsesses over any small signal that the public mood could be heading for a dramatic shift.

And so, like many campaigns enjoying fabulous success from a negative advertising push, the Johnson camp began to worry that they were being too negative, that they had not said enough about what Johnson was *for*. People respected Johnson's performance, his aide Horace Busby told him that fall. But there was danger in the fact that "people don't fully know this man whose performance they respect."

This was a notion that had been floating around the Johnson campaign for some time. The polling after Johnson's convention acceptance speech had been unimpressive. "There was nothing in particular that people *disliked* about the speech," reported the campaign adviser Robert T. Bower, but "there was no central focus for the favorable response. The reaction, in sum, was one of moderate undifferentiated approval."

As the campaign entered its final weeks, Johnson and his aides projected total confidence to the outside world, shaking hands and attending parties and acting as though they intended to remain fixtures in the Washington swirl for some time to come. But internally, they launched an intense debate over how they might be more specific about what electing Johnson would mean, what kind of mandate an elected Johnson would have. How could they make the country *really* love him at last?

Johnson's aides debated the particulars: How specific should he get? What explicit promises should he make? But the real question was for Johnson alone: What kind of president did he want to be?

It was a new sort of problem for Lyndon Johnson. All his life, he had found his way out of difficult situations by determining what people wanted and then convincing them that he was the best one to provide it. Then he'd go ahead and provide it, even if the providing meant walking the narrowest of paths. But the abundance of his electoral opportunity created an altogether new kind of challenge. There was no narrow path in front of him. There was no path at all. He had to create it. He had to decide what he wanted, and to try, like Kennedy and FDR before him, to persuade the nation to come along.

For Lyndon Johnson, this would have seemed the most frightening proposition of all. He had the opportunity, with his comfortable lead, to tell his people how things really were in America, and how things might get better from there. But to do so, he would have to turn the same realism on himself: to be not the president people wanted, but the president he really was. And that would mean risk: the risk that once they saw him, they would not want him at all.

FEW PEOPLE WERE as intimately familiar with the debate within the Johnson campaign—or any debate concerning the interests of Lyndon Johnson—as was Walter Jenkins. His title—special assistant to the president—was one of those opaque Washington designations. But Jenkins was indeed special. For nearly twenty-five years, he had been Johnson's keeper of the guard. He could listen to just about any Johnson phone call, give an order to just about any Johnson aide, and read just about any piece of paper headed to or from Johnson's desk. No one was closer to the president. Johnson once called Jenkins "my vice president in charge of everything."

That evening in early October, four weeks before the election, the vice president in charge of everything attended the *Newsweek* party in the company of his wife, Marjorie. Jenkins was a proud family man; he and Marjorie had six children. But Mrs. Jenkins had learned early on that their family would have to sacrifice much in the service of Lyndon Johnson. She and Walter were married in 1945. Three days into their honeymoon, a call came from a certain congressman in Washington. "I need you badly," said Johnson. "Can't you cut it short?" By the time her husband hung up the telephone, Marjorie's honeymoon was over.

In time, Marjorie would grow friendly with Lady Bird, and her children would grow up alongside the Johnson girls. When the period of mourning for President Kennedy made it impossible to celebrate Lady Bird's first birthday as First Lady in the White House, the Jenkinses offered up their own home as an alternative locale. They named a young son Lyndon. They were Johnson people through and through.

Now these two Johnson people made their way through the *Newsweek* party. Walter did not possess flawless social graces. But in the brutal thrust of a Washington cocktail party, a man had to use whatever assets he could muster.

Alcohol helped. The room was filled with the well groomed, the wellborn, and the well-positioned. Jenkins clutched a martini glass in his hand.

It helped, too, to have a familiar face. Jenkins certainly had that. Practically all of official Washington knew him. He had stumbled into town in the late 1930s, twenty-one years old, just out of the University of Texas at Austin. At the university, he'd fallen into the orbit of John Connally, the tall, handsome student body president. After graduation, Connally was headed to Washington, where he had a job in the office of a young, ambitious Texas congressman. Jenkins, without a better plan, followed along. In that congressman's office, Walter Jenkins would find a calling. And in that congressman— Lyndon Johnson—he would find a cause to define his life.

In Jenkins, meanwhile, Johnson found a man with any number of invaluable qualities: a strong work ethic and cool efficiency, a fierce loyalty and perfect discretion. And, perhaps most important, Walter Jenkins had an uncommonly high tolerance for pain. By the time Johnson reached the Senate, Jenkins was his closest aide. Officially, he was in charge of the "Texas office"—Johnson's Senate Office building lair—but unofficially he was a second set of eyes for every aspect of Johnson's life. He dealt with the Johnson family's taxes, their Texas business holdings, the LBJ Ranch. In time, Jenkins earned a reputation around town as the man to see on all things Johnson, a man who knew Johnson's mind well enough to answer questions and fulfill requests on his behalf. For the other guests at the *Newsweek* party, Jenkins's face was indeed familiar. It was the face you saw when you needed something from Lyndon Johnson but weren't quite up to facing Lyndon Johnson himself.

There is one asset, however, that provides greater confidence at a Washington cocktail party than any other: power. And despite all the things he had seen, despite his extraordinary ability to get things done, power was not the first thing anyone would think of when they looked at Walter Jenkins. Too many people in Washington had watched Lyndon Johnson berate Jenkins in their presence. Too many had seen Johnson treat him, as one Jenkins friend put it, "like a nigger slave." Too many people had seen the way Jenkins jumped when Johnson gave an order. Too many had heard the old knock on Johnson—he was such an awful boss, he could only keep mediocre men, *like Walter Jenkins,* on his staff. Washington is a ruthlessly transactional city. As Jenkins made his way through the *Newsweek* reception, people smiled. But they were smiling at the proximity to power, not at power itself.

To the people who worked for Johnson, however, Jenkins did have power—the power of mercy, and salvation. Over the years, more than one hapless staffer was saved when Jenkins decided to pocket an order Johnson had given in the heat of anger. They knew that Jenkins could be counted on to pick up the slack if something came up, or, if they were in the doghouse, to put in a kind word with the boss on their behalf. And they knew that when Johnson's rage came raining down, Jenkins would stand in the full force of it, absorbing as much as he could.

That was what Walter Jenkins did better than anyone else: suffer, and carry on. The sacrifice was physical. His body grew hunched, his face became covered in blotches. In time, the agony of Walter Jenkins became an insiders' joke. Tax time was always a stressful period for Jenkins. He had to ensure that the Johnsons' complicated business interests did not leave an impolitic paper trail. One year, as April 15 approached, an exhausted Jenkins stole a quick nap on an office couch. Entering the room, Bill Moyers discovered the slumbering Jenkins and crept back outside. Then, Harry McPherson would later say, he threw open the door and, in an impersonation of Johnson, bellowed: "Goddamn it, Walter, what are you doing out here? Aren't you working on my taxes?" Jenkins, said McPherson, "came off the sofa, levitating . . . just came right straight up off of it in total terror of Lyndon Johnson."

It was perhaps this capacity for suffering that made Walter Jenkins so uniquely valuable to Lyndon Johnson. In three decades in Washington, Johnson had worked harder than anyone else, ruffled more feathers than anyone else, encountered pressure that would have toppled anyone else. It had come with a cost—harsh attacks, wounding criticism—that he had counted on Jenkins to bear. In Bill Moyers, Scotty Reston once wrote, Johnson saw his "ideal of what the President himself would have liked to be at 29": quick-witted, composed, and urbane, a polished Texan who was going places. Jenkins was the other side of the coin. When Johnson looked at *him*—lumpy and provincial, weak and worn down—he saw the man that he secretly feared he was. He would do anything not to be that man in the eyes of the world. He hated that man. And he let Jenkins know how much.

The *Newsweek* party wore on. There was Katharine Graham, the evening's hostess, the owner of the magazine and of *The Washington Post*. There were seven members of the cabinet, and leading lights of the press. Jenkins had another martini and then another after that.

Marjorie had dinner plans in another part of town. At eight o'clock, Walter took her downstairs and put her in a taxi. He then returned to the gathering. But when a man filled with alcohol steps out of a party and then reenters, he can find the room subtly but irrevocably altered. Friends have vanished; something darker reigns. After just a few minutes, Jenkins was back outside again on Pennsylvania Avenue, alone.

It was not yet nine o'clock. He did not go to join Marjorie at dinner. He did not head home to his children. He did not return to his office, to the pile of papers and to the ringing telephone and to the voice at the other end of the line that very well might be the president of the United States. He was steps away from the White House, the pulsing center from which Lyndon Johnson ruled over the city, over the country, and over him. And for once, he turned away.

For there was another city near at hand, a city that only certain men could see. It was a city where strangers sat quietly on the benches of Lafayette Park after nightfall, waiting. A city where anonymous faces, peering through the glass of telephone booths, made brief eye contact and then quickly darted their glance away. A city filled with strangers hurrying into alleys, stairwells, and restrooms. A dark city where Walter Jenkins had no famous boss and no important title saying just how special he was. It was a city where he did not even have a name.

It was toward that other city that Jenkins now turned. As he stepped onto G Street, he could see it in the sign over the entrance to the YMCA. He knew this place; it had been the scene of a great catastrophe in his past. And he had some idea what he would find inside. He passed through the doorway, walking toward danger, self-destruction, and desire. For certain men, on certain nights, they are all the same thing.

ONE WEEK LATER, Lyndon Johnson was resting in his hotel room at Manhattan's Waldorf Tower when he received a phone call from Abe Fortas, his old friend and counselor. Explaining that Clark Clifford was in the room with him, Fortas told the president they had a "very serious problem" to discuss.

Johnson listened, weary and weak. It had been an exhausting fall of flying back and forth across the country, trying to run up his margin against Goldwater. At stop after stop he'd refused to leave until he'd shaken nearly every hand. Inevitably, he'd come down with a bad cold.

He was trying to get some rest before leaving for an evening at Jackie Kennedy's new apartment with his predecessor's widow and brother. It didn't promise to be an easy event. Leaving the Justice Department a few weeks earlier to launch a campaign for a Senate seat from New York, Bobby had written an almost hostile letter of resignation. The best that Johnson could hope from the evening ahead was civility.

The truth was, he needed the Kennedys less now than ever before. Three weeks earlier, on September 27, the Warren Commission had published its final report on the events in Dallas. The next day, twelve thousand people crowded the Government Printing Office to buy copies of the 888-page report. Most were there to buy a piece of history. Hardcover copies—at a cost of $3.25—outsold $2.50 paperbacks by a two-to-one margin.

"WARREN COMMISSION FINDS OSWALD GUILTY AND SAYS ASSASSIN AND RUBY ACTED ALONE" read the banner headline in that day's *New York Times*. Press coverage of the report was almost exclusively adulatory. In the write-up of the report that led the *Times*, Anthony Lewis claimed "the commission analyzed every issued [*sic*] in exhaustive, almost archeological detail." "From Mexico City to Moscow and Minsk," wrote David Kraslow in the *Los Angeles Times*, "the Warren Commission probed for any shred of evidence to support the theory that Lee Harvey Oswald did the bidding of others. The commission found none." In a twenty-four-page cover story on the report, *Newsweek* declared that "most Americans . . . will probably agree with Lyndon Johnson's words discharging the commission last week: 'You have earned the gratitude of your countrymen.'" The cover image for the story was a new bronze bust of JFK by the artist Robert Berks. The late president looked like a figure of antiquity. The Kennedys were the past.

Bobby Kennedy was learning that reality the hard way. He had jumped into the New York Senate race in late August, making fun of his own carpetbagger status: "Now where is the Hudson River again?" But by mid-September, it was clear that the campaign would be no lark, nor an easy restoration of Camelot. Polls showed him trailing the Republican incumbent, Kenneth Keating. Relations between Bobby and Johnson had never been worse, but with less than a month to go before the election, it was clear that the popular president could help the struggling candidate. Bobby Kennedy relying on Lyndon Johnson for help: more than any poll, this made the president feel on top.

But then Fortas's voice came over the phone line in the Waldorf and the bottom dropped out. "Walter came over to see me this morning," the attorney told the president, "and he got involved in a quite serious situation. We hope that we have it under control."

The details of the situation were so serious, and so clearly uncomfortable for Fortas to discuss, that it was several minutes before Johnson could gather what on earth Fortas was talking about. Eventually he got the salient details of a complicated story: a week earlier, Jenkins had attended a party for *Newsweek*'s new Washington offices. Apparently he'd been drinking heavily. Afterward, he'd gone to, of all places, a nearby YMCA known to be a favorite haunt of homosexuals seeking clandestine assignations. And that was where plainclothes policemen had discovered Walter Jenkins, the quiet family man, the most understated man on the Johnson staff, the closest aide to the president, in sexual congress with another man.

Both men were arrested promptly and hauled into police custody. Jenkins paid a fine and was released. He returned to his desk at the White House that night. For a week he'd gone about his business as usual, telling no one what had happened. But that morning, after the White House had received word that *The Washington Star* planned to print an article on the event, Jenkins had come to Fortas, desperate. Fortas and Clifford soon learned that the story had been circulating in the capital for several days. Not only did the *Star* have it, *The Washington Post* and the *Washington Daily News* did as well. Worse, the *Star* had the record of a prior Jenkins arrest, in 1959, in the same location on a similar charge.

The two lawyers believed they had persuaded the papers to kill the story. With the help of Jenkins's family doctor, they'd persuaded him to check in to George Washington University Hospital, where he was undergoing treatment for nervous exhaustion. There, he would be away from the prying eyes of reporters.

The president, taking this all in, spoke softly. Despite his famous temper, it was usually dumb quiet that first came over him in moments when catastrophe seemed at hand. He groped for more information. "Does his wife know about this?"

"We're not going to ever tell her anything," said Fortas, "except that he was exhausted and in the hospital."

Johnson's mind was turning over. "I just can't *believe* this!"

The implications for Johnson of Jenkins's troubles were significant—anyone could see that. In recent weeks, Goldwater, desperate to make something stick on Johnson, had been talking up other scandals surrounding the president. A year earlier, Bobby Baker, a colorful Capitol Hill fixture who'd served as secretary to the majority leader, had come under investigation on corruption charges and had to resign. Baker had been a Johnson retainer during his years in the Senate, and there were rumors that he'd also done dirty dealing at Johnson's direction and with his assent. The Republicans had been looking for anything they could find to suggest Johnson lacked morality. Now, in Jenkins, was the proof.

In a way, the whole business had a sort of ironic justice. For months on end, Johnson had been unable to accept the pleasant forecast for the November election. He'd waited with vigilance and apprehension for something that could destroy his chances, for a nameless, faceless phantom to appear. Now at last it had come. It had a form and a face. A face he had been staring at every day.

Johnson's voice took on a tone of fatalism. "You don't foresee that you can keep this lid on for three weeks, do you?" he asked. It was more a statement than a question.

"No sir," Fortas replied. "I think that, however, if we can keep it out of the news stories that it won't assume a great deal of dignity. And I think that Walter ought to stay in the hospital a while, and then be sent off somewhere . . . to recuperate."

It was fantasy to believe that a story like this could stay out of the news pages. Johnson had been around Washington long enough to know that. Sure enough, shortly after eight o'clock, the wire service UPI published a bulletin obliquely describing Jenkins's arrest.

Later that night, from the Waldorf, Johnson spoke to John Connally, the one person in Johnson's political world who went further back with Walter than he did.

"Now, I don't think I have any choice, once I know the facts, but to have him resign, do you?"

Connally answered with quick certainty: "None whatever."

"And I ought to do it tonight, don't you think—"

"Yes, sir!"

The two time frames Johnson mentioned—*once I know the facts* and *I ought to do it tonight*—could not long coexist. Talking with Clifford and Fortas, Johnson had expressed little interest in Walter's well-being and no interest in making a call to his room at the George Washington University Hospital. "Tonight" was all that mattered. As Johnson and Connally spoke, editors in various newsrooms throughout Washington and New York were working to get the breaking Jenkins news into their morning editions. Everyone thought this story would be big. In the coming days, journalists would stretch the art of euphemism to simultaneously preserve the standards of a family newspaper, titillate their readers, and make naughty in-jokes. Jenkins, said *Time,* had been caught in the YMCA's "basement men's room . . . a 9-ft. by 11-ft. spot reeking of disinfectant and stale cigars . . . a notorious hangout for deviates." *The Wall Street Journal* would write that Jenkins's crime could range "from the seemingly trivial—'reaching over and touching a person's leg'—to the unprintable."

In his hospital room, Jenkins was saying he did not want to go on living. He said he couldn't remember much from that night. That was convenient, but also understandable. It had been a harrowing ordeal. He had no prior acquaintance with the other man, a sixty-year-old Hungarian immigrant who lived in Washington's Old Soldiers Home. They had rendezvoused in a pay toilet stall, unaware that they were being watched by three policemen—two through a peephole, with the third hovering on a stool outside the stall. These observers had come in search of easy prey in a locale known to be favored by men of a certain kind. Finding their quarry, the cops had barged in and arrested the two men and taken them to the police station. There, they had asked Jenkins what he did for a living. He replied that he was a clerk at the White House. He accepted the charge, paid his fine, and went on his way, praying that somehow the whole thing would stay out of the papers.

Now, as the night wore on in New York, President Johnson was working to ensure that when the name Walter Jenkins did appear in the papers it would be as a *former* White House aide. On the phone from Washington, Clifford read him a prepared statement:

> Walter W. Jenkins submitted his resignation this evening as Special Assistant to the President. The resignation was accepted and the President has appointed Bill D. Moyers to succeed him.

After requesting some minor changes, Johnson approved the statement. They all agreed it was best for it to go out that night.

In passing, the president wondered if there was something they could whisper to reporters, off the record, to urge charity, reminding them that "nearly every family has had some problem."

"No," said Clifford, flatly. "Every family has problems, but they don't happen to have *this* kind."

George Reedy, the press secretary, read the statement to reporters later that night, tears in his eyes. Walter Jenkins's twenty-five-year term of service as Lyndon Johnson's closest aide had come to an abrupt end. The political world would convulse in the coming days, trying to absorb the implications. But in Jenkins's hospital room, the change was already unmistakable. For once, there was not a single call from Lyndon Johnson all night.

EARLY THE NEXT morning, Liz Carpenter found the First Lady in her bedroom, looking as though she'd barely slept. She had just spoken with a confused and angry Marjorie Jenkins on the telephone. Marjorie felt her life was ruined. And she felt the Johnsons were to blame.

The call had left Lady Bird distraught. It had been a long month, and a long year. In that year, the country had seen Lyndon as the picture of confidence and calm, collected certainty. She alone knew how frequent and how deep had been his moments of despair: in those agonizing first days in office, in the endless days of conflict with Bobby, in the awful last days of August when he'd almost thrown off the presidency altogether. She had sat with her husband through all of it, abiding witness in his time of trial.

Meanwhile, she had borne trials of her own. Her whistle-stop tour of the South that month had been hard. She had known at the outset that her journey would be a daring one, so daring that Southern politicians were reluctant to guarantee her safety. There was too much hostility toward the president in the South, they said, too many people who thought Lyndon was a traitorous native son. But the First Lady knew her husband. She knew that no matter how large his margin of victory in the election, a Goldwater sweep of the South—the Johnsons' home territory—would leave Lyndon's pride bruised. So she had brushed off the warnings and set out to make her case as a fellow southerner. On a train dubbed the *Lady Bird Special,* she headed deep into the old Confederacy, carrying six thousand straw hats stitched with the initials *LBJ*.

The South did not welcome her with open arms. At Charleston, South Carolina, she encountered protesters, indignant over Lyndon's policies on civil rights. A sign in the crowd called the First Lady BLACK BIRD. In the state's capital, Columbia, she'd struggled to be heard over a booing mob. Pleading for silence, she held her white-gloved hand in the air. "This is a country of many viewpoints," she said. "I respect your right to express your own. Now it is my turn to express mine. Thank you." And, miraculously, the startled mob had hushed.

Now, back in Washington, came the hardest trial of all. Her heart ached for Marjorie and Walter. Never mind what little she knew of what went on in YMCA basements. In a way, there was no one better suited to sympathize with Walter Jenkins than Lady Bird. After all, there was no one but Walter Jenkins whose role in Lyndon's life more closely resembled her own. Both of them worked

tirelessly to handle the countless details and arrangements to which
Lyndon never deigned to give a second thought. Both of them praised
Lyndon and soothed him. Both of them, on so many occasions, had
absorbed the full force of his rage. And both of them had stood by
him even in the darkest hours when he could not stand by himself.

Now she would stand by Walter. With Carpenter's help, she set
to work on a statement of support. And to make sure he and Marjorie were provided for, she would offer him a job at the Johnsons'
television station in Austin, KTBC. She had spoken to Fortas and
Clifford. She knew that her speaking out would not go over well
with them. She had to go over their heads. She had to reach out to
Lyndon. She did not like to quarrel with her husband; she sought,
whenever possible, to do his will. But sometimes she had to displease
him. Sometimes she was the only one brave enough to tell her husband what was real—and what was right.

She reached him that morning. "I would like to do two things
about Walter," she said. The connection was bad and she had to fill
her words with force. "I would like to offer him the number two job
at KTBC." She paused. "Do you hear me?"

The president was wary. His wife was forcing him to admit what
he'd been doing: giving preference to his own interests above those
of a man who had served them for so many years. "I wouldn't do
anything along that line now," Lyndon said. "I'd just let them
know . . . that they have no problem in that connection. Go ahead,
next?"

"I don't think that's *right,*" said Lady Bird. Her voice swelled
with emotion but she went on stating her case. "Second, when questioned, *and I will be questioned,* I'm going to say that this is *incredible* for a man that I've known all these years. A devout Catholic.
The father of six children. A happily married husband. It can only
be a . . . period of a nervous breakdown, balanced against—"

"I wouldn't say *anything,*" interrupted the president. "It's not
something for you to get involved in now." He advised her to leave it
to the lawyers.

Lady Bird was silent. She knew what the lawyers were working on—and it didn't concern the best interests of Walter Jenkins.

Seeing that he wasn't getting through to his wife, Lyndon tried another, softer approach. "I don't want you to hurt him more than he's hurt. And when we move into it, we do, we do that." His words came haltingly, as though he were trying to convince himself.

"All right," said Lady Bird, refusing to match the gentleness in her husband's voice. "I think that if we don't express some support to him, I think that we will lose the entire love and devotion of all the people who have been with us. Or so drain them—"

Johnson cut her off. "Well you get ahold of Clark and them and . . . see what advice I'm getting. And I'm late now and I'm going to make three speeches and you can imagine what shape I'm in to do it. So don't create any more problems than I've got . . ."

No one was more willing to listen to the woes of Lyndon Johnson than Lady Bird. But this time she would not give in. "All right," she said quickly, playing a new card. "Abe approves of the job offer. Abe approves of the statement."

Johnson, hearing something he didn't like, suddenly was having trouble with the phone line. "What?" he asked.

Lady Bird said it again, slowly and loudly. *"Aaa-be . . . approves . . . of the job offer . . . Aaa-be . . . approves . . . of such a statement . . . when questioned."*

They volleyed back and forth for some time. But Lady Bird would not be deterred. "I think a gesture of support," she insisted, "on some of our part is necessary to hold our own forces together."

At last Lyndon's voice sank into resignation. "Well, talk to Abe and Clark about it. And, uh—"

He sounded tired. And he sounded as if he might give in. For Lady Bird this was enough. Lyndon was not going to be brave, but he was not going to prevent bravery on her part. "My poor darling," she told her husband. "My heart breaks for you, too."

Later that day, Liz Carpenter delivered a statement from the First Lady. "My heart is aching today," it read, "for someone who has reached the end point of exhaustion in dedicated service to his country. Walter Jenkins has been carrying incredible hours and burdens since President Kennedy's assassination. He is now receiving the medical attention he needs."

LADY BIRD'S POLITICAL instincts were superior to those of her husband, and to those of the rest of Washington as well. The print publications, assuming their readers would be equal parts titillated and horrified by the Jenkins news, played up the moral outrage. "If any responsible person," *The Christian Science Monitor* editorialized, "most of all the President, knew of Mr. Jenkins' trouble, he was inexcusably reckless in permitting him to remain in office."

To the political establishment, the broader implications were obvious. In America in that era, homosexuality was synonymous with conspiracy. The city swirled with speculation about who else had shared in Jenkins's secret. George Reedy chased down rumors of other alleged White House connections to the gay underworld. Most of this talk never made its way into the press beyond snide nudging and winking. *Time* noted that in the hospital, Jenkins received "a bouquet of mixed fall flowers. With it came a card signed 'J. Edgar Hoover and Associates.' There was some doubt about just who those 'associates' might be."

But the country wasn't interested. As the scandal broke, word came from Moscow that Soviet leader Nikita Khrushchev had been ousted. Shortly thereafter came the news that China had successfully tested an atomic weapon, joining the nuclear club. The two events reinforced the central message of the Johnson campaign, that an era of fragile global peace was no time to have a dalliance with extremism. A week after the Jenkins incident first came to light, Johnson's poll numbers were the same.

It helped that Barry Goldwater had refused to use the Jenkins episode as ammunition against Johnson. High officials in his campaign tried to push it. "Walter Jenkins came to the White House," his running mate, Bill Miller, told a crowd in Dayton, Ohio, "and ever since has attended meetings of the National Security Council, the Cabinet of the United States, and has had access to information vital to the security of all mankind and to the survival of the world . . . Can we stand for four more years of that?" But Goldwater himself hated this kind of talk. "What a way to win an election," he said with disgust, "Communists and cocksuckers." Showing a private decency that belied his harsh public persona, he forbade his aides to take advantage of Jenkins's plight.

For once, Goldwater saw things the same way the voters did. "The really remarkable thing was the mail that came to the White House in the aftermath," Liz Carpenter said later. "So many people saying, 'I have that problem in my family.' . . . People are more civilized if you give them the chance to be."

The last-minute reversal in campaign fortunes wouldn't happen. The Johnson landslide was now inevitable. Inside the Goldwater campaign the mood was bleak. "If they don't want us," the candidate concluded, "they don't have to take us." On the stump, he appeared more and more unhinged. "Just think about it for a moment," he implored. "Do you want my opponent to 'let us continue'? We *simply* can't continue!—unless we want to commit *national suicide!*"

Yet if there was one clear consequence of the Jenkins affair, it may have been the marked shift in Johnson's tone in the final days of his campaign. After the news broke, candidate Johnson seemed to grow more manically intense. And, significantly, his promises grew more extravagant, his optimistic prophecies more and more certain. The closer he got to the election, whose outcome was no longer in doubt, the more he dispensed with all responsible caution when describing the great things that were soon to come.

You could hear it in his words the night after the Jenkins scandal broke. "The Great Society is not something brand new," he told a huge crowd at Madison Square Garden. "It is a dream as old as our civilization. The difference is, *for the first time in man's history* we really have the resources to make it possible, to make the Great Society a reality."

The debate over what kind of vision Johnson should run on, it seemed, had been settled. He would not look within himself to see what he truly believed in. He would not ask the country to take on a great risk. He would not echo Kennedy, the old president who'd asked for sacrifice and risk in exchange for a chance at uncertain but unmatched reward. Instead, he would promise a bold and fantastic future that was certain to come.

It was as if the Jenkins ordeal had given him an out. When it seemed that he couldn't lose, he had been forced to contemplate talking to the country about reality, to contemplate what was real and true. But the scandal, and its attendant danger, had taken care of all that. He was free to revert to what came naturally to him, saying whatever he had to in order to earn the people's love. He could give them a fantasy and call it the future.

His extravagant visions grew and grew until, in the final week of the campaign, they reached the highest heights. On October 27, he began a cross-country campaign swing in Boston, appearing at a rally on behalf of Teddy Kennedy, who was up for reelection as senator from the Bay State. "I am not a prophet," Johnson told a crowd of 350,000, "but in due time he will lead a lot more people than those of Massachusetts." But by the time the president reached Pittsburgh, later that day, prophecies were indeed flying out of his mouth. There, *The New York Times* reported, Johnson described a "utopian society" that was about to arrive. "Here is the Great Society," he told his audience. "It's the time—*and it's going to be soon*—when nobody in this country is poor. . . . It's the time—*and there's no point in waiting*— when every boy and every girl in this country . . . has the right to all the education that he can absorb. . . . It's the time when every slum is gone from every city in America, and America is beautiful."

There, a week before Election Day, the president promised the people that they could banish uncertainty, that they could triumph even over fate. "It's the time when man gains full dominion under God over his own destiny," he said. "It's the time of peace on Earth and good will among men. *The place is here and the time is now.*"

A FEW HOURS after the president had finished speaking that night in Pittsburgh, Americans watching NBC at home heard an altogether different vision of the nation's future. "Now, one side in this campaign has been telling us that the issues of this election are the maintenance of peace and prosperity," a speaker told them. "The line has been used, 'We've never had it so good.' But I have an uncomfortable feeling that this prosperity isn't something on which we can base our hopes for the future."

The broadcast, viewers were told, was paid for by "TV for Goldwater-Miller." It carried the Goldwater message: the perils of overtaxation, the ballooning national debt, the rapacious spending of the federal government. It emphasized the existential threat to freedom posed by the Communist bloc. But in this broadcast, Goldwater's best chance to make his final pitch to a national audience, the Goldwater case was not coming from Goldwater. It was coming from Ronald Reagan.

It was, in fact, not altogether different from the speech Reagan had delivered to the audience of Young Republicans eight months earlier. In basic outline, it was The Speech, the statement of Reagan's political vision he'd developed while traveling the country for GE. Reagan, who was working again as actor, had been squeezing in appearances for Goldwater when he could that summer and fall. Late in the summer, he'd delivered The Speech to the kind of audience he usually gave it to, a group of wealthy Goldwater backers who had gathered at the Coconut Grove nightclub in Los Angeles. Afterward, a group of the supporters approached the Hollywood star. Barry needed serious help, they believed, help that Reagan could provide. They asked if Reagan would be willing to deliver The Speech again for a television broadcast. "Sure," said Reagan, "if you think it would do any good."

He sounded innocent, but Reagan had very specific notions of how to do the telecast. He knew how he benefited from the feel of a crowded room. This speech would work best, he said, in front of a live audience. So his backers purchased airtime on NBC and filled a studio at the network with friendly Republicans who cheered excitedly at the beginning of the actor's address.

For a time, it looked as though the studio audience would be the only ones to see Reagan speak. In the final stretch of the campaign, months after they'd lost the battle to define their candidate, Goldwater's advisers suddenly began to worry about making their candidate look like an extremist. They feared that Reagan's broadcast hit too shrill a note, that it dwelled too long on the topic of Social Security. Better, the Goldwater high command told the California donors, to use the airtime for a reairing of a different broadcast. In that special, Goldwater appeared with Eisenhower at the ex-president's Pennsylvania farm. Ike, the voice of reasonable moderation, embraced his party's nominee and discussed with him the Republicans' issues in the campaign. It was intended as a rebuttal to the extremist charge, to get voters to think: *if I like Ike and Ike likes Goldwater, then maybe I can like Goldwater, too.* But neither of its two leading men, aged Ike or irascible Barry, was very good at faking emotion. They spoke nicely of one another, but their faces contorted in pain. The whole thing looked like an excruciating postmodern prison drama in which the audience, scrutinizing two adversaries, is meant to determine who is the prisoner and who is the guard. "I'd seen the film showing Barry's meeting with Eisenhower at Gettysburg," Reagan would later write, "and I didn't think it was all that impressive."

Neither did the donors writing the checks for the airtime on NBC. They told the Goldwater campaign to stick with the Reagan plan. But the Goldwater hacks wouldn't give in; they had their candidate phone Reagan to request he pull out. "Barry," Reagan said gently when Goldwater called, "I've been making the speech all over the state for quite a while and I have to tell you, it's been very well received." Goldwater admitted that he hadn't actually seen the broadcast in question and agreed to review it himself. After listening to the audio, he was confused: "What the hell's wrong with that?"

And so, on the night of October 27, millions of Americans

watched Reagan give his alternative vision of America's future. It was indeed unsettling. He used his standard trick of clumping together statistics in rapid succession to make them appear more distressing than they would if presented on their own:

> Today, thirty-seven cents out of every dollar earned in this country is the tax collector's share, and yet our government continues to spend seventeen million dollars a day more than the government takes in. We haven't balanced our budget twenty-eight out of the last thirty-four years.

He barely paused for breath between a string of sinister quotes from his opponents.

> They have voices that say, "The cold war will end through our acceptance of a not undemocratic socialism." Another voice says, "The profit motive has become outmoded. It must be replaced by the incentives of the welfare state." Or, "Our traditional system of individual freedom is incapable of solving the complex problems of the twentieth century."

But The Speech did more than just confuse, obfuscate, and scare. It also inspired. Reagan framed the conservative cause in a kind of moral urgency the nation had not heard much of in the past year:

> You and I know and do not believe that life is so dear and peace so sweet as to be purchased at the price of chains and slavery. If nothing in life is worth dying for, when did this begin—just in the face of this enemy?

It was, to be sure, the hard-line anticommunist message. But it also revived the sentiment of moral clarity that Kennedy had evoked so well—that the purpose of a meaningful life was not to avoid suffering, but to find something that was worth suffering for.

And as delivered by the handsome actor with his warm, textured voice, the conservative message sounded altogether different from what had been coming from Goldwater. In response to Johnson's enticing promises, Goldwater had offered only depressing attacks: *Don't you see it's national suicide? Don't you see it's not true?* "In Your Heart, You Know He's Right," went the Goldwater slogan. But Goldwater failed to see that the electorate of 1964 didn't *want* to listen to sinking feelings in its heart. It wanted to believe in something good. Reagan's speech showed him to be keenly aware of this fact. It offered voters something good to believe in, something different from Johnson but something just as fantastical and fantastic. At the conclusion, Reagan, the man who had imitated the speaker as he listened in awe to the Fireside Chats, imitated Roosevelt once more: "You and I have a rendezvous with destiny. We'll preserve for our children this, the last best hope of man on earth, or we'll sentence them to take the last step into a thousand years of darkness."

The response to the speech, called "A Time for Choosing," was overwhelming. Goldwater's campaign headquarters was jammed with calls asking when it would be rebroadcast. Donations came flooding in through the mail. Barry's campaign reversed itself entirely on Reagan. Dean Burch, running the Republican National Committee, sent Reagan a telegram at home:

I JUST WANTED YOU TO KNOW THAT YOUR SHOW HAS BEEN WONDERFULLY RECEIVED AND WE APPRECIATE SO MUCH THE FINE WORK THAT YOU HAVE DONE ON OUR BEHALF. WE ARE MAKING EVERY EFFORT TO SEE THAT YOUR SHOW GETS NATIONWIDE COVERAGE BEFORE TUESDAY.

In the end, it wouldn't matter what kind of coverage they got before Election Day. For most of the nation, the time for choosing Goldwater had long since passed, if it had ever occurred at all. Reagan's address seemed to acknowledge as much. In the forty-six-hundred-word speech, the name "Goldwater" appeared only seven times, and the name "Johnson" did not appear at all. On the other hand, Reagan used the word "I" fully thirty-two times. Indeed, at the opening of his remarks, Reagan seemed at pains to make clear he was not just an actor anymore: "The sponsor has been identified, but unlike most television programs, the performer hasn't been provided with a script. As a matter of fact, I have been permitted to choose my own words and discuss my own ideas regarding the choice that we face in the next few weeks."

Something was changing in Ronald Reagan. Perhaps there could be a future in politics after all. For the pragmatic Reagan, so deeply intuitive of the shifts in public mood, could sense that something had changed in America. By propelling politics into the realm of fantasy, Johnson was creating an opportunity for the conservative worldview that hadn't been there even a few months before.

Perhaps, in fact, the "time for choosing" was just beginning. In the course of a few hours that night, the country had heard two new and radically different visions of what America was becoming. From Johnson in the East, they'd heard prophecies of a coming era that looked like God's kingdom on earth, arriving shortly. From Reagan in the West, they'd heard of the potential for calamity and the extinguishing of freedom, coming soon. Both visions could not stand. Here was the beginning of a great drama. The time for choosing would be a time for watching, and waiting, to see which vision would prevail, and to see who would play the hero in the end.

A JOHNSON VICTORY on November 3 was inevitable. Still, it was spectacular when it came. He beat Goldwater with 61 percent of the vote, the largest popular vote landslide in American history. Goldwater had carried his home state of Arizona, but only by a single percentage point. Other than that, his victories were confined to the Deep South: South Carolina, Georgia, Alabama, Mississippi, and Louisiana. In Johnson's home state of Texas, which, since the Kennedy assassination, the country had come to think of as a hotbed of reactionary radicalism, the president outperformed his national margin, securing 63 percent of the vote.

But Johnson's appeal had no regional accent. He did well in California, earning 59 percent of the vote, and in the Mountain and Middle West, and in New England—with more than 65 percent of the vote in Vermont and Maine, the two states that had prevented Franklin Roosevelt from securing a national sweep in his reelection year, 1936. (Johnson would be the first Democratic candidate to win the state of Vermont since the founding of the Republican Party, in 1854.) In 1960, Kennedy had won a respectable 60 percent of the vote against Nixon in his home state of Massachusetts. Four years later, Johnson had beaten Kennedy's margin in the Bay State by a whopping sixteen points. "The returns," said *Newsweek,* "read like tall tales from Texas. They spelled the victory of a Southerner who won 97 percent of the country's Negro vote; of a Protestant who won more Roman Catholic votes than the Catholic President he succeeded."

Of perhaps even greater significance, Johnson's Democratic Party had also won the largest majorities in both houses of Congress of any time since FDR, picking up thirty-six seats in the House. In the Senate, the party retained a two-thirds majority, large enough that if (and it was a big "if") Johnson could maintain an alliance between Southern conservatives and Northern liberals, there would be a filibuster-proof path for any legislation the president put forward. The incoming class of Democratic senators would include Bobby Kennedy, whose 53.5 percent of the vote in New York paled behind Johnson's 68.5 percent. ("Listen, I pulled you through up here," Bobby self-consciously joked to Johnson in an election night call.) Of twenty-five governor's races that year, the Republicans managed to win only eight.

It seemed clear that the public had rejected the conservative worldview, completely and perhaps forever. In the press, columnists and scholars competed for who could be more over-the-top in their predictions of the long liberal era to come. "Barry Goldwater not only lost the presidential election," Scotty Reston wrote the next day, "but the conservative cause as well." In *Newsweek,* the columnist Kenneth Crawford quoted a "Dixie politician" saying that Goldwater's Deep South route would prove "a one-shot affair" driven by bad blood over the civil rights betrayal. "They were spitting in Johnson's beer. Now they've got that out of their system." "By every test we have," said the historian James MacGregor Burns, "this is as surely a liberal epoch as the 19th century was a conservative one."

Goldwater's running mate, Bill Miller, saw a more prosaic reality at work: "The American people were not prepared to assassinate two Presidents within a year."

Johnson read press accounts of his triumph with relish. Jack Valenti prepared a packet of postmortems, with selected passages underlined that he thought the president would particularly appreciate:

His margin of victory was greater in each of twenty-two states than Kennedy's was in the entire nation . . .

Had it not been for Johnson, such Democratic Senators as Young, Yarborough, Cannon, Proxmire, and Robert Kennedy, who ran far behind the national ticket, would probably not be there at all . . .

Despite the physical resemblance, Mr. Kennedy is a less attractive figure than his brother.

"J," Johnson scrawled on the memo, "thanks much—excellent idea L."

In his postelection messages, Johnson urged unity in the country. But he had a very definite idea of what the country was unifying behind. In his moment of personal triumph, he clung tight to the vision of glory he had promised to his nation. Indeed, he suggested that his promise would soon be fulfilled. In the days after the election, he set his aides to work, drafting bills to pass in his first days in office in order to bring his Great Society vision to life. On December 18, he appeared triumphant on the Ellipse outside the White House for the lighting of the Christmas tree. The temperature was below freezing, but in the fashion of the Kennedys, he wore no hat or coat. That year's tree, a two-ton Adirondack, the largest in the history of the White House, sparkled with 7,500 lights. Just before he and Lady Bird pushed the button to illuminate them, the president expressed unbounded optimism for the coming year, 1965.

"These are the most hopeful times," he cried, "since Christ was born in Bethlehem."

"I don't see any way of winning": By mid-1965, Johnson (shown
in the Cabinet Room with Secretary of Defense Robert McNamara)
had grown deeply pessimistic about the war in Vietnam.

© Yoichi Okamoto/LBJ Library

CHAPTER EIGHT

Valley of the Black Pig

January 23–April 9, 1965

At nearly half past two in the morning on Saturday, January 23, 1965, a Navy ambulance pulled away from the South Portico of the White House. Escorted by a Secret Service motorcade, it headed north toward Bethesda Naval Hospital, speeding along streets lined with dirty slush, through a slumbering city that was unaware of the ambulance or its patient. Seated inside, in a robe and pajamas, was an ailing president of the United States.

Three nights earlier, the night of his inauguration, a triumphant Lyndon Johnson had stayed up late celebrating. At a ball at the Mayflower Hotel, he had danced exuberantly, exchanging partner after partner, nine of them in thirteen minutes. At one point he'd coaxed Harry Truman's daughter, Margaret Truman Daniel, over the rail of her observer's box down onto the dance floor. He took her on his arm and they flitted across the floor gaily. The band played "I've Got the World on a String."

The temperature had been just above freezing when Johnson delivered his inaugural address. The grounds of the Capitol were flooded in a persistent chill wind. At his brother's grave at Arlington, where he fled after Johnson's speech, Bobby Kennedy knelt to grab a fistful of snow. But Johnson had insisted on passing the long day outside without a coat or hat. On Friday, two days later, he could feel a distinct pain in his throat.

By evening he was stricken with illness and he went to bed without dinner. The private quarters of the mansion were uncommonly quiet. Lady Bird had been feeling unwell herself that morning. She had left for Camp David lest she infect the president. From the residence, Johnson summoned the White House physician, complaining to him of a cough and chest pains. The doctor inspected his patient and told him not to worry. It was merely a cold, one that could be treated with aspirin and cough syrup.

The doctor left Johnson to get some rest. But the president could not sleep. There was nothing he hated so much as a night spent alone. Normally, when Lady Bird traveled, he would ask friends to stay in her bedroom, making them promise to leave their door open and listen for cries in the night. But Lynda, also sick, had accompanied her mother to Camp David, and Luci was out on a date. Even Jack Valenti had left on a late flight to New York for an evening out with his wife. Johnson was totally, horribly alone. As the agonizing, lonely minutes slumped onward, he felt a fever taking hold.

Eventually, he summoned the doctor back. When the physician arrived, a worried Johnson explained that his condition was deteriorating. The doctor didn't want to take any chances; he suggested hospitalization. By three o'clock that morning, Johnson was in Bethesda's seventeenth-floor VIP suite.

Hours later, the city woke to the news of the president's illness and panic blossomed everywhere. Press secretary George Reedy was ready with quick reassurances—Johnson was in no danger, he had only gone to the hospital out of an abundance of caution, he had *walked* out of the White House into the ambulance and through the front door of Bethesda. But the press pack remained skeptical. Kennedy's assassination was still fresh in their minds. Johnson's room at Bethesda was in the same suite where Jackie Kennedy had received friends and family while she waited out the long hours of her husband's autopsy. And many reporters could remember the myriad health crises President Eisenhower had suffered when early, optimistic assurances from aides and doctors always masked a far more grim reality.

Now, too, the reporters had reason to be suspicious. Briefing the press on the president's health earlier that month, Johnson's physician had asserted that the president enjoyed an occasional bourbon and branch water, was able to relax easily, and only "infrequently" was forced to postpone his regular bedtime on account of work. This rosy account struck the press corps as vaguely ridiculous. (For one thing, *Newsweek* noted, Johnson's drink was "not bourbon but Scotch.") They shrugged off Reedy's happy talk and covered the initial hours of Johnson's illness as a crisis. They turned the Naval Hospital's movie theater into a makeshift newsroom. The networks broke in for special bulletins throughout Saturday morning's broadcasts.

As soon as Lyndon had arrived at the hospital, he'd called Lady Bird at Camp David. By the following afternoon, the First Lady had come back and checked herself in to the hospital, too. Ostensibly she was there to seek treatment for her own head cold. Really she was there to make sure her husband was all right.

She always went to Lyndon when he was ailing, to tend his illness and contain his mood. In the late spring of 1948, just as he was launching his campaign for the Senate against former Texas governor Coke Stevenson, Lyndon had felt the staggering pain of a kidney stone. At first he chose to ignore it and kept campaigning full tilt. It was a poor decision, one that resulted in a ghastly, fevered ride on an overnight train, an infection, and eventually an emergency hospitalization in Dallas, where he learned that he would probably have to undergo surgery followed by a long period of recovery. Worse, news of his condition had reached the press. He grew despondent as he considered the implications for his race. He told Warren Woodward, a campaign aide, to take down a statement announcing he was dropping out. Stunned, Woodward ventured that perhaps the president ought to wait for Mrs. Johnson. She would want to be present for her husband's withdrawal.

In a panic, the aide bolted for the airport to fetch Lady Bird, who, on news of Lyndon's hospitalization, had jumped on a flight from Austin. Driving her to the hospital, Woodward gave a frantic account of Lyndon's mood and his dramatic declaration. Woodward would tell Jan Jarboe Russell years later that Lady Bird had listened coolly. "Settled in her seat," she "told me to relax, that she would take care of it." Sure enough, not long after arriving at the hospital, Lady Bird emerged from Lyndon's room with the news that all was well. There would be no withdrawal.

It was much the same seven years later in 1955, when Lyndon suffered a massive heart attack on a friend's plantation in Middleburg, Virginia. At Bethesda Naval Hospital, Lady Bird found her husband, who, for the sake of time, had been rushed in from Middleburg in an undertaker's hearse. Lyndon, who had always feared an early death from a heart attack, was talking as though the end had surely come. He told Lady Bird that he'd seen a tailor that morning to be fitted for two suits, one blue and one brown. "Tell him to go ahead with the blue," Lyndon said. "We can use that no matter what happens." As her husband headed to surgery, Lady Bird insisted on calm. "Honey," she said, "everything will be all right."

So although she herself was still ill and exhausted, when she arrived at Bethesda, she checked on Lyndon straightaway. She found that this time everything was in fact all right. Indeed, Lyndon was trying to do some soothing himself. He had invited four reporters to visit him shortly after noon on the seventeenth floor. There they found the president of the United States leaning over on his elbow so he could get his face close to a vaporizer. "I think we'll be all right in a day or two," he told the reporters. "It may just be a bug that all of you get." The reporters could see pain in the president's face when he coughed, but he assured them the situation wasn't serious. "I wouldn't hesitate at all to put on my britches now and go back to the office if something had to be done. But it is Saturday and a good day to rest."

In time, it became clear that the president really was just suffering from a bronchial infection. "By evening," *The New York Times* reported, "concern about the president's health had subsided."

Reedy, briefing reporters that evening, not so subtly underscored that there was no hidden heart attack. He had seen the president only moments before, he told them, enjoying a steak sandwich.

Johnson's doctor told the press he'd advised the president to stay in the hospital for five days of recuperation. Johnson lasted three. Discharged on the afternoon of January 26, he insisted on walking out of Bethesda on his own two feet. He did agree, though, to put on a coat and hat. When reporters asked how he was feeling, he winked at them but did not speak. A UPI photographer snapped a photo of the Johnsons leaving Bethesda that ran across several columns in the next day's *New York Times*. It was not an entirely comforting image. The president's face looked drained, gray, and thin. The circles under his eyes drooped deeper, making his whole face seem longer and hollowed out. But the First Lady was a truly arresting sight. Dressed in black, Lady Bird had her eyes fixed on her husband. She seemed pained, clearly holding back anguish—or fear.

The truth was, for all of the optimism she was quick to dole out for Lyndon, Lady Bird was apprehensive by nature. When friends and acquaintances would call to congratulate her or Lyndon on some piece of good news, she would sometimes express her thanks and then remind them that of course less happy days were sure to eventually come. As First Lady, she popularized an old expression— "The Lord willing and the creek don't rise." Many southerners used this expression as affectionate hyperbole. Lady Bird, who along with her daughter had once been trapped inside her home for a full day by a Hill Country flood, knew it to be literally true. More than once in her diary she referred to a good day of Lyndon's presidency as a peak or pinnacle—an unspoken reminder that a fall back to earth was sure to come.

Long experience had taught her to be wary. As a child who'd lost her mother in an accident, she knew that life could be altered irreparably in an instant. As the wife of a man with heart disease, she knew that that instant could be coming soon. As the wife of a president, she was painfully aware of the perils her husband faced. She could think of the presidents brought low in her lifetime: Woodrow Wilson, who'd left the White House an invalid; Dwight Eisenhower, who'd left it a victim of stroke and heart attack, his bowels and intestines wrecked; Warren Harding and Franklin Roosevelt and John Kennedy—who'd left the White House dead.

And as the wife of Lyndon Johnson, she was always ready for the turmoil of an ever-changing mood. She knew that triumph could morph into dejection in a moment, cruel indifference into desperate need. She had spent her life with a man of extremes, who looked to the future and saw total victory or total disgrace. In time, that became her world, too.

Now she had to worry about what this illness might mean. After his first night back in the White House, she expressed concern to her diary. "Last night was not a good night. An old enemy returned. Lyndon sweated down two or three pair of pajamas. This has been a symptom of his illnesses for all the years I have known him, so I should have expected it." These words suggest a deeper awareness: that the various ailments of Lyndon Johnson sprang from a common place.

What could this place have been? It was impossible to spend thirty years with Lyndon Johnson and not develop a healthy appreciation for the effect of nervous anxiety on physical well-being. The 1948 kidney stone had come at the outset of a seemingly impossible quest—the Senate race against Stevenson he'd ended up winning by 87 votes found in a box in Jim Wells County. The heart attack had come when floor leader Johnson was entertaining another grand ambition—a run for the president in 1956 against the hero of Normandy, Eisenhower. It was as though when Lyndon Johnson saw a great opportunity in front of him, the forces inside him divided. His mind moved with determination to do the impossible; his body revolted, to ensure that he could not.

These same forces were at war inside Johnson that January, and he was paying the price. "With LBJ's history of physical and emotional maladies when he is under political pressure," Michael Beschloss writes in his authoritative study of the Johnson White House tapes, "one must wonder whether the illness, coming so soon after the inauguration, has been aggravated by his painful awareness of the challenges he is about to face."

Lady Bird took the aggravation for granted. "This week's mood is not good," she worried in her diary a week after Lyndon entered the hospital. "It's sort of a slough of despond . . . The 'Valley of the Black Pig.' The obstacles indeed are no shadows. They are real substance: Vietnam, the biggest. Walter. The need of getting really superior people . . . and bringing them into the government. The carping of the press. . . . And someday we may really know a storm."

Johnson resumed his normal manic schedule, but it took him longer than usual to bounce back fully from the illness. As February began, he admitted to reporters that he still felt only "80 percent normal." Lady Bird bought a new black dress that she did not wear for months and months. Later, she recounted "the grim, unacknowledged thought" that had compelled its purchase: "I might need a black dress for a funeral."

To MOST OUTSIDE observers that winter, Lady Bird's fatalism would have been astounding. What was the impossible challenge facing Lyndon Johnson this time? He was president of a supremely prosperous country in an apparently peaceful world. He had won the largest landslide in American history, on his own terms. He had not retreated from his extravagant expressions of confidence in the nation's future. "Is our world gone?" he asked in his January 1965 inaugural address. "We say 'Farewell.' Is a new world coming? We welcome it—and we will bend it to the hopes of man." These were the words of a man at the stunning summit of his presidency, not of a man stuck in "the valley of the black pig."

In those first months of 1965, it looked as if he really *could* bend history to the hopes of man. As the new year began, Johnson and his aides alerted the press to the major areas of focus in their Great Society domestic program. On January 7, Johnson sent a special message to Congress on "Advancing the Nation's Health," a plan to create Medicare and grant health insurance coverage to all American senior citizens. Five days later, the Congress received another special message, this one calling for $1.5 billion in federal spending on education. In addition, the administration was pushing a massive $1.1 billion bill aimed at alleviating poverty in Appalachia. And while Johnson's aides had decided not to press for a voting rights bill—the last remaining legislative opportunity on civil rights—in the first months of the term, most in Washington expected an effort before the end of 1966.

Getting this extraordinary program through Congress would be no small task. Harry Truman and John Kennedy had tried and failed to pass Medicare, stymied by the powerful efforts of the American Medical Association, a doctors' trade group that was preparing for an encore performance. In the modern era, no president had produced a major bill for education funding, thanks to the great political might of the Catholic Church, which objected to a large taxpayer expenditure that benefited only students in public schools while neglecting the millions of American families who sent their children to parochial schools. As a Democratic politician who'd grown up outside the party's Catholic-heavy urban machines, Johnson knew that the Church would be wary of any such push from his administration.

Still, the odds of his passing a strong progressive package seemed good. His November landslide had extended to the Congress, where Democrats now held a staggering majority of 295 to 140 in the House and 68 to 32 in the Senate. An influx of new blood meant liberals now had the numbers to break the Southern-conservative alliance that had, for all practical purposes, controlled the Congress since Roosevelt's second term. Among the 91 new House members, 71 were Democrats.

The strong majorities meant that Appropriations and Ways and Means—the key House committees where generations of progressive bills had gone to die—would now be stacked with Great Society liberals. The Ways and Means chairman, the Arkansan Wilbur Mills, was cautious and conservative. He had successfully blocked a Medicare bill in the Kennedy administration. But Mills could sense that public opinion favored action. Early in the year he signaled he would be willing to make a deal.

Everywhere in Washington that winter, people were comparing the first days of Johnson's new term to the famed one hundred days of concerted action with which Franklin Roosevelt had commenced his presidency in 1933. It was an imperfect analogy: Roosevelt had urged swift action in his first hundred days in response to the consuming crisis of the Great Depression, while Johnson was urging swift, strong action in a time of unprecedented prosperity. Also, there was the small fact that at the time of his 1965 inauguration, Johnson had already *been* president for well over four hundred days. Still, the comparison was one that Johnson's aides, mindful of the boss's Rooseveltian ambitions, encouraged. In the White House, two consecutives dates loomed largest on the calendar: April 12, the twentieth anniversary of Roosevelt's death, and April 13, the hundredth day of the new term. The goal was rarely stated but known to all: have a record by that date that could stand up against FDR's. Or surpass it.

To the press, it seemed that the president faced little danger in pursuing such grand ambitions. Certainly the Republicans could pose no immediate threat. Their new House leader, genial Gerald Ford from Michigan, had let it be known that obstructing the Democrats' agenda would not do; the Republicans must instead offer a "constructive" alternative. But given the paltry size of the Republican caucus, the press took few of these alternatives seriously. To some in the Eastern media, the party's problems seemed epitomized by ever-growing chatter out in California that the actor Ronald Reagan would mount a serious campaign to be the party's nominee for governor in 1966. "Republican rank-and-file enthusiasm for [Reagan] continues to swell," *Newsweek* reported in early February, "but the party pros feel differently. They find three things wrong with

Reagan: 1) his close ties with the right wing; 2) possible anti-Hollywood feeling in view of the fact that song-and-dance man George Murphy is already in the Senate; and 3) Reagan's refusal to fly—a tough campaign hurdle in a state almost 800 miles long." Writing in *Life* magazine, the journalist Shana Alexander found the idea laughable. Reagan, she said, "shouldn't even be *cast* as governor."

In a series of private sessions with reporters just before his inauguration, Johnson was careful to stress the lessons he'd gleaned from history about taking little for granted in ensuring passage of the legislation. "The history that interests Mr. Johnson," wrote the columnist Drew Pearson, a sometime Johnson favorite, "is how Roosevelt, re-elected by a landslide vote in 1936, slipped so badly that he lost 88 congressional seats to the Republicans." LBJ was determined "not to make Roosevelt's error and squander the great potential of his landslide over Goldwater," wrote Evans and Novak in their 1966 book *Lyndon B. Johnson: The Exercise of Power*. "The power derived from his election victory, Johnson felt, must be employed judiciously. To a visitor at the LBJ Ranch shortly after the 1964 election, Johnson compared that power to a bottle of bourbon. 'If you take it a glass at a time,' he said, 'it's fine. But if you drop the whole bottle you have troubles. I plan to take it a sip at a time and enjoy myself.'"

But the reality in the Johnson White House that winter and spring of 1965 was not conscientious caution but panicked urgency. Meeting with his congressional liaisons in the Fish Room of the White House in early January, Johnson impressed on them how easily the tide could turn. "I was just elected by the biggest popular margin in the history of the country—sixteen million votes," he said. "Just by the way people naturally think and because Goldwater had simply scared hell out of them, I've already lost about three of those sixteen. After a fight with Congress or something else, I'll lose another couple of million. I could be down to eight million in a couple of months." The sense of accomplishment Johnson had felt after the election had seemingly vanished. "I knew from the start that the

'64 election had given me a loophole rather than a mandate," he told Doris Kearns Goodwin, "and that I had to move quickly before my support disappeared."

Larry O'Brien, a rare Kennedy aide who had decided to stay on for the new Johnson term in his role as congressional liaison, would later compare the attitudes of Kennedy and Johnson with regard to the Congress. In selling the New Frontier to recalcitrant congressmen, O'Brien would have to make special requests for more of Kennedy's time. "With Lyndon Johnson it was the reverse," O'Brien would later say. "He felt that I ought to be using him more, that I ought to have him more deeply involved." Johnson could grow irritated if O'Brien "wasn't informing him on an hourly basis." Johnson was the rare president who began each day perusing the *Congressional Record* and who wanted summaries of staffers' daily contact with legislators each night. This, he believed, was the only way for a president to operate. "If it's really going to work, the relationship between the President and the Congress has got to be almost incestuous," Johnson would later tell Doris Kearns Goodwin. "He's got to know them even better than they know themselves."

Staffers learned to keep the president in the loop on all things pertaining to the Congress. O'Brien recalled one occasion when a bill he was shepherding for Johnson went down to defeat well after midnight. Heading home, O'Brien found a sandwich shop that was open at that late hour and stopped in for a bite. "I didn't need anything to eat," he recalled, "it was just a matter of trying to unwind. Then I waited until 6:30 or 7:00 A.M. to call the president . . . I wanted to wait until he would have awakened." Finally, he called Johnson, who wanted to know when the vote had come in. When O'Brien told him, Johnson was surprised. "God, you should have called me right then and there," he admonished. "When you're bleeding up on that Hill . . . I want to bleed with you."

This president—bleeding for his program, working the Congress day and night, convinced that his tenuous majority could easily slip away—was not the president seen by the press, much less the public.

Mostly what people saw of Johnson that winter and spring was a man with ever more glowing words about the coming conquest of man's ills. Heralding a raft of encouraging economic data that spring, Johnson suggested that, thanks to the wonders of Keynesian economics, economic downturns might be a thing of the past. The unprecedented prosperity the nation was enjoying could go on and on. "Economic policy can more than ever become the servant of our quest to make American society not only prosperous but progressive," he said. "Not only affluent but humane, offering not only higher incomes but wider opportunities, its people enjoying not only full employment but fuller lives."

IF THERE WAS one visible sign that all was not quite right with the president, however, it was the moments he chose for these prophecies of greatness. Early in the afternoon of March 1, Johnson came to the Cabinet Room to address a group of high school students who had won that year's Westinghouse National Science Prize. This group, leading lights of the coming generation, represented the best hopes of the oh-so-hopeful age, and Johnson was expansive in his description of the Great Society they would surely know. "Peace on earth, good will toward men," he told them. "That must be our objective and that must be the pledge of my generation, and yours." Declaring that their lifetimes would surpass the age of Columbus as an age of discovery, he imagined what the four hundredth anniversary of the explorer's voyage to America would look like:

> By 1992, distances on earth will have lost all meaning. Man will be moving purposefully among the planets; man will be farming the beds of the sea. He will be inhabiting the reaches of the Arctic and the Antarctic. He will be tilling the deserts and he will be taming the jungles. . . .
>
> I think that as a result of your experiences and your dedication and diligence and what is going to come out of the efforts that you make, that that just may be possible; that when you sit

in your rocking chair talking about what used to be in 1992, that you can say: "Well, I was at the White House and I talked to the President. He remembered a good many combats, a few offensives that he engaged in, and he remembered two wars. But I have lived my life and I haven't known any."

"Peace on earth, good will toward men . . ." This was a nice thing for a president to say, and a bold one. Later in his speech, he even dared to echo the words of Neville Chamberlain after Munich, expressing hope that in their "twilight years," the students could say they'd known "only peace in [their] time."

"He remembered two wars. But I have lived my life and I haven't known any . . ." And this was a deeply dishonest thing for this president to say. Only hours after Johnson finished speaking to these students, the military he commanded would commence a sustained bombing campaign against North Vietnam.

The military's code name for the operation was "Rolling Thunder." Johnson's hope was that the Vietcong, witnessing the Americans' power, would suspend their guerrilla efforts in the south. But it would not be that easy. The prediction Johnson gave the students—that next year the money for tanks and bombs could go to education instead—would prove empty. The bombing campaign, scheduled to last eight weeks, would in fact go on for three years. And the students, just shy of fighting age, would not know "only peace" in their time. For the next eight years they would know war, a war in which hundreds of thousands of their peers would be drafted to fight, a war in which, as the journalist and historian Stanley Karnow notes, the U.S. military would deliver to "an area the size of Texas, triple the bomb tonnage dropped on Europe, Asia and Africa during World War II."

The Johnson presidency had been heading straight toward that war for months. After his show of strength in the Tonkin Gulf incident the prior August, he had tried to keep Vietnam out of the headlines before the November election. The Vietcong did manage to grab attention to the conflict on November 1 when they launched a surprise attack on an American air base twelve miles north of Saigon, killing four Americans and two South Vietnamese. It was clear to anyone who bothered to read the news stories from Southeast Asia that the situation there was slipping out of control. Throughout 1964, a massive and well-organized Vietcong army grew in strength, swelling with indigenous South Vietnamese recruits, bolstered by supplies ferried in from the north along the Ho Chi Minh Trail.

The North Vietnamese watched as a calamitous succession of weak governments rose and fell in the American-backed south. They believed that Communist domination across Vietnam was within reach. America, with its guarantees to the governments in Saigon, was the great remaining obstacle. As 1964 drew to a close, the Vietcong grew ever more bold, hoping to puncture the notion that America had built an impenetrable fortress in the south. On Christmas Eve, they took provocative action, exploding a bomb in Saigon's Brinks Hotel, home to American military personnel. The bomb, which killed two Americans and injured fifty-eight others, was intentionally detonated at a quarter to six in the evening—precisely the moment when American officers were known to gather for happy hour in the hotel bar.

By then it was clear to American officials in Washington and Saigon that the Johnson administration's Vietnam policy needed fixing, fast. "We are presently on a losing track," cabled Ambassador Maxwell Taylor in early January. "To take no positive action now is to accept defeat in the fairly near future." By month's end, McNamara and Bundy had come to the same conclusion. "Both of us are now pretty well convinced," Bundy wrote to Johnson, "that our present policy can lead only to disastrous defeat."

And so at precisely the moment when Johnson was preparing his August push for the Great Society, he had to decide whether to escalate or withdraw in Vietnam—to choose, as he saw it, full-on war or disgraceful defeat. The timing would seem a tragic coincidence, the beginning of an awful split in the story of the Johnson presidency. On one side of the screen are the triumphs of his domestic program, on the other the morass of Vietnam. The Vietnam side slowly creeps over the dividing line until, before long, it is all the eye can see.

Students of history are no doubt familiar with this split. It is standard practice in assessing the Johnson presidency to put Vietnam and the Great Society on opposite sides of the historical ledger. His great domestic achievements are weighed against his failings in Southeast Asia. His lies about Vietnam are weighed against his transformational impact on civil rights. The two President Johnsons—liberal reformer and Vietnam warmaker—are seen as combatants, forever locked in a push-pull struggle in which one's loss is always the other's gain.

Yet here, too, is a moment when history was shaped by a convenient overlap in the interests of opposing parties. Progressives, when accounting for the backlash against Johnson's domestic policies in the latter part of the 1960s, can blame public dissatisfaction with Vietnam. *If only he hadn't gotten bogged down in the war, he could have exerted his full energy and attention on the administration of the Great Society.* Vietnam hawks, meanwhile, can explain the war's failure as a product of Johnson's reluctance to put the country on a war footing for fear that those steps would endanger his Great Society aims. *If only he had leveled with the American people about the need to fight, then the war could have been won.*

Many of Johnson's biographers have leaned toward this divided view as well. The first wave of Johnson scholars to work with a generation's distance was in the 1990s, a moment uniquely suited for a split understanding of his presidency. In comparison to the politics of the nineties, marked by partisan stalemate and small ambitions for government, the great hopes and legislative successes of the Johnson years seemed to shimmer. At the same time, after the rapid, dramatic collapse of the Soviet Union, it began to look in retrospect as though America's triumph in the Cold War had been assured all along. In that light, Johnson's preoccupation with the "domino theory" and the high stakes in South Vietnam looked silly and his prosecution of the war in Vietnam unforgivable.

The 1990s also saw the release of the Johnson tapes, which revealed a stunningly paradoxical president—a man who could be charming, cunning, and coolly rational one moment and alarmingly crass, cruel, and paranoid the next. Johnson's apologists suddenly had to account for auditory evidence that the president and his advisers had held grave doubts about their chances for success in the war even as they had committed American forces to die. Baby boomers who had grown up thinking of Lyndon Johnson as a lying warmonger were stunned to find themselves in the thrall of this captivating man giving the Johnson Treatment over the phone. There were too many sides to this new Lyndon Johnson, too many angles that didn't add up. It was best—and easiest—to understand him as a man hopelessly divided between the best and worst of impulses. *The Triumph and Tragedy of Lyndon Johnson,* the title of a memoir published by Johnson aide Joseph Califano in 1991, summed up the established view.

In a way, this was how Johnson himself wanted to be remembered. In the last years of his life, as he watched American forces struggle on in Vietnam during his retirement at the LBJ Ranch, he knew that the war would be a black mark on his legacy. He hoped, though, that history would cover the Great Society and his civil rights bills in gold. The Vietnam sections of his memoirs drip with fatalistic sorrow: it was a war that cruel fortune forced him to fight. He encouraged the notion that his domestic and foreign presidencies had been in perpetual conflict—for his time and for his soul. Vietnam, he told Doris Kearns Goodwin, was "that bitch of a war on the other side of the world" that kept him away from "the woman I really loved—the Great Society."

There is no denying that Johnson's triumphs in the Civil Rights and Voting Rights Acts stand in stark contrast to his failures of credibility and creativity as commander in chief. Still, to accept that the good and the bad of the Johnson presidency are irreconcilable and separate is to erect a wall across the Johnson presidency that wasn't really there. In fact, there was only one Lyndon Johnson who served as president, both at home and abroad, in the years 1963 to 1968. And the best and worst moments of the Johnson presidency came from the same man and sprang from the same place.

In the spring of 1965, the key moment of decision making, Johnson's Vietnam and Great Society policies were not in conflict. Rather, they worked hand in glove. Since 1945, Cold War liberals had accepted as an article of faith that a progressive domestic program could only be passed if it was matched with a muscular anticommunism abroad. That conviction had animated the writings of liberal intellectuals like Schlesinger and Galbraith and had guided Democratic officeholders from Truman to Kennedy. It was no coincidence that Truman had fought the Korean War even as he tried to pass the Fair Deal through Congress, just as it was no coincidence that Kennedy's first push for the New Frontier coincided with his great anticommunist misadventure, the Bay of Pigs. Johnson understood the rule better than most. He was not willing to risk a new approach. "I knew that Harry Truman and Dean Acheson had lost their effectiveness from the day that the Communists took over China," Johnson told Doris Kearns Goodwin. "I believed that the loss of China had played a large role in the rise of Joe McCarthy. And I knew that all these problems, taken together, were chicken shit compared with what might happen if we lost Vietnam."

And so, as he considered how to address the deteriorating situation in Vietnam, Johnson's determination to produce a historic domestic program in early 1965 propelled him *toward* escalation, not away from it. His advisers understood as much and made their recommendations accordingly. After the November election, Assistant Secretary of State for the Far East William Bundy (Mac Bundy's older brother) convened a study group on the situation in Vietnam. The group presented the senior figures of Johnson's national security team with three policy options going forward. Option one was for the United States to maintain the course it was currently on in

Vietnam. Option two was to escalate dramatically and commence a broad offensive against the Vietcong all at once. Or, option three, the United States could commence a flexible, incremental offensive increase, starting with select targets in Laos and North Vietnam. "Bundy," Karnow writes, "had resorted to a classic bureaucratic device known as the 'Goldilocks Principle.' By including one choice 'too soft' and one 'too hard' he could plausibly expect the upper-echelon 'principals' to go for the 'just right' option—in this case, the third, which he himself favored." The principals, and Johnson, favored it, too. By February 1965, they had determined on a course of deliberate, calibrated escalation. All they needed was an event that could provide the pretext for a strike.

It came early in the morning of February 7, in a place called Pleiku. There the Vietcong used purloined maps to launch a prolonged mortar attack on an American garrison. "We're going to die," an American voice shouted as enemy forces stormed the compound, "we're all going to die." Eight Americans were killed, and the dramatic attack at last captured the attention of the American media. The assault had been meticulously planned: the invaders had a detailed knowledge of the garrison's layout. The timing also seemed suspicious, and provocative. At the time of the attack, McGeorge Bundy had been visiting Saigon to assess the situation firsthand. Twenty-four hours earlier, Soviet premier Alexei Kosygin had arrived in North Vietnam to consult with the Communist leadership.

Suddenly the stakes in Southeast Asia seemed very high. Many Americans had managed to get to that point in time with only a dim awareness of what was happening in Vietnam. No longer. "Not only Americans," declared *Newsweek* in the following week's edition, "but people everywhere on earth felt the sudden chill that makes living in the second half of the twentieth century a new departure in man's experience: a chill born of the awareness that any small localized war, may, through misjudgment or mischance, flare up into a holocaust that could blot out civilization."

In Washington, Johnson sought immediate action. He ordered retaliatory bombing and asked for plans for the prolonged campaign that would become Rolling Thunder. The National Security Council considered a request from General William Westmoreland, the American military commander in Southeast Asia, for two Marine battalions that could fortify the air base at Danang.

Here was a Rubicon to cross—once Johnson deployed ground forces, he would be in an Asian land war. But the president hurried across to the other side. Invited to join a National Security Council meeting, Senate Majority Leader Mike Mansfield played the role of skeptic—worrying over the dangers of the war widening to include the Chinese and the Russians, wondering if a negotiated settlement could be reached. "Even as he finished, the others at the meeting could tell that Johnson had welcomed his dissent," David Halberstam wrote in *The Best and the Brightest,* his classic account of Vietnam decision making. "It was a desired part of the scenario because it permitted Johnson to do his performance, which he now did. No, there was no alternative. We had tried to be peaceful, we had tried to disregard provocation in the past, but now it had gone too far. Lyndon Johnson, he said, was not going to be the President of the United States who let Munich happen."

And that was the same president of the United States who spoke of the bright future on the first day of March. When Johnson addressed the science prizewinners and spoke of peace in their time, he echoed Neville Chamberlain because he could. Soon the bombs would be dropped. Who would dare call him an appeaser then? He was encouraging the contrast: Chamberlain had refused force and gotten war; he would use force and get his glorious peace. There was no coincidence: Vietnam would be the handmaiden of the Great Society to come.

Yet Johnson's foreign war and his domestic ambitions were also interlinked in another, different place that spring: inside Lyndon Johnson's fearful mind. Whenever the public Johnson attacked some great challenge, the private Johnson fixed his mind on some awful force that might make the challenge impossible. In the summer of 1964, as he'd neared the party convention at Atlantic City, it had been Bobby Kennedy and the fractured South. In the fall, as he'd looked toward his landslide victory, it had been the threat of disgrace in the Jenkins affair. Now, as he rushed through his hundred days, within reach of the greatness to which he'd always aspired, he needed some evil force with the power to destroy it all. And in his private agony, that force had a name: Vietnam.

The truth was that for all his confident talk, for all his swaggering refusal to cower in the face of an enemy's aggression, even by the winter of 1965 Johnson had grave doubts that the war in Vietnam could be won. He was trying to prop up the Saigon regime, but he had few illusions that Saigon would ever be able to control the country. He was ordering up bombers, but he no longer believed that bombs would persuade the North Vietnamese to come to the peace table. "Now we're off to bombing these people," he told McNamara four days before the bombs began to drop. "We're over that hurdle. I don't think anything is going to be as bad as losing, and I don't see any way of winning." No chance of winning, no hope after losing. In his dark private moments, the certainty of disaster was the only certainty he could see.

That was the real split emerging in the Johnson presidency—not between Vietnam and the Great Society, but between the outward Johnson who proclaimed unmatched greatness ahead and the inward Johnson who saw despair. It was the split between the man who raced through his hundred days and the body that revolted in fevered sweats. Between the president who insisted on marching out of the hospital with a smile on his face and the First Lady who looked on in horror. Johnson was divided between two fantasies— one of utopia, the other of ruin.

In his public meetings he would wave off the dissenters—Mike Mansfield or Undersecretary of State George Ball. But in private, he had a hunger for some of the most uncomfortable aspects of the war. As the Rolling Thunder bombing mission launched in the early morning hours of March 2, he called the White House Situation Room. "How long before you should hear something?" he asked the duty officer. The officer told Johnson it would be 5:00 or 5:30 in the morning before they had an account of any lives lost. "Call me," Johnson ordered.

And, in private, Johnson was willing to explore the hopelessness of the Vietnam situation in depth. A few days after the Rolling Thunder mission began, he spoke on the phone with his old mentor, Senator Russell. "We're going to send the Marines in to protect the Hawk battalion, the Hawk outfit at Danang," he told Russell. "I guess we've got no choice, but it scares the death out of me. I think everybody's going to think, 'We're landing the Marines. We're off to battle.'"

"We've got so damn far, Mr. President," Russell said. "It looks to me like we just got in this thing and there's no way out."

It was telling that Johnson chose Russell as the rare confidant for his Vietnam doubts. True, he had always looked to the Georgian for counsel in times of need. And he knew that Russell, long a skeptic of U.S. involvement in South Vietnam, could be counted on to give him hard truth. But there were deeper forces guiding their gloomy conferences. By 1965, Russell was old, tired, and defeated. His great cause, defending the white South in the Senate, was lost. His other strong passions—a restrained foreign policy abroad, the promotion of agrarian interests at home—were fading into the past. Everyone else in the capital and the country could talk about the great future that was coming. To Russell, the American future was a sad, bleak thing to behold.

And he saw that bleakness when he looked at Lyndon Johnson. Russell had once embraced Johnson as his heir, a great Southern hope in the Senate. He understood why Johnson had embraced civil rights in his presidency, but it still came as a hard blow. To colleagues, he would describe Johnson as "a turncoat if ever there was one." He was perhaps the only person close to Lyndon Johnson that spring who looked at the Johnson presidency and saw a great tragedy. When he spoke to Lyndon now, he was helpful and kind. But there was a touch of sadness, too, the pain of a father whose son has traded away his inheritance.

Johnson could hear all of that in Russell's voice. And perhaps that, too, was why he confided in him. The president had grave doubts about Vietnam. Had he engaged with William Fulbright or George Ball or Lippmann or any of the other prominent skeptics, he could have heard what he could do about those doubts, how he could get out of the war and still be all right. But perhaps that wasn't what he needed when the darkest thoughts came. Most likely, all he wanted to hear was that it was hopeless. In his moment of greatness, while the world said he was capable of everything, he needed to hear that he was doomed.

Russell would not disappoint him. "I don't know, Dick," the president went on. "The great trouble I'm under . . . A man can fight if he can see daylight down the road somewhere. But there ain't no daylight in Vietnam. There's not a bit."

"There's no end to the road," agreed the old man. "There's just nothing."

The true breach that spring was within Johnson himself. In public, the president worked through his hundred days, delivering his vision of greatness to the nation, talking of peace on earth. Doubts belonged to the part of himself he believed least worthy, the part he suppressed so the world would not see.

Lady Bird was one of the few people who crossed back and forth between the two sides of her husband. At dinner the night after his conversation with Russell, Johnson was still speaking in dismal tones. "I can't get out and I can't finish it with what I've got," he said. "I don't know what the hell to do." Her husband's dark imagery crept into her diary that night: "Lyndon lives in a cloud of troubles, with few rays of light."

It was agony, living in the valley of the black pig. At times, a far-off future was her consolation. "I am counting the months until March 1968 when, like Truman, it will be possible to say, 'I don't want this office, this responsibility, any longer, even if you want me. Find the strongest and most able man and God bless you. Good-bye.' "

THEN, FROM THE fog of Johnson's dueling fantasies, reality broke through. And it summoned a kind of greatness the world had not seen from Lyndon Johnson before.

It came in an Alabama city called Selma. There, in early January 1965, two civil rights groups—the Southern Christian Leadership Conference (SCLC) and the Student Nonviolent Coordinating Committee (SNCC)—had formed an uneasy alliance to launch a voting rights campaign. As with Mississippi in the summer of 1964, they had chosen their target strategically. Segregation in Selma was vivid and monstrous. It was typified by James Gardner Clark, sheriff of Dallas County, the face of white law enforcement. Clark was a made-for-TV racist, with a bulging waistline and a fondness for the night-stick, which he often waved at television cameras. He did not have the ability to control his impulses, nor did his city. On January 8, Martin Luther King, Jr., arrived at Selma's segregated King Albert Hotel at the beginning of the campaign, hoping to check in. "Get him! Get him!" a woman in the lobby screamed, and a young man obliged, punching King repeatedly and kicking him in the groin.

Selma's voter registration practices were grotesquely unjust. *Time* magazine observed the activists' efforts in the city in January of 1965:

> Negroes stood in line for up to five hours a day waiting to enter Room 122 in the courthouse. During the two weeks only 93 got in, since only one applicant was admitted at a time. Each had to answer a series of biographical questions, then provide written answers in a 20-page test on the Constitution, federal, state and local governments. (Sample questions: Where do presidential electors cast ballots for President? Name two rights a person has after he has been indicted by a grand jury.) To prove literacy,

each applicant had to write down passages from the Constitution read to him by the registrar. The registrar was the sole judge of whether the applicant's writing was passable, and whether his test answers were correct.

Selma was, in other words, the kind of place that could make the country care about the fact that millions of its black citizens had been denied the right to participate in their democracy, the kind of place that could take a country that had turned a blind eye toward the violation of its Constitution for a century and finally force that country to see. As January turned to February, the press became transfixed by the barbarism of Clark's forces: their eagerness to assault black citizens who were simply waiting in line, their tendency not to calm white mobs but to whip them up. The Johnson administration had made noises about a push for a voting rights law as part of its hundred days agenda. But conventional wisdom was that Johnson would not risk further full-scale combat with the Southern bloc in the Senate so soon after his 1964 civil rights success. The movement activists wanted to make it impossible for Washington to wait. From the pulpit in Selma's Brown Chapel, King used a familiar phrase to make the case for moral urgency: "We've gone too far now to turn back. And in a real sense, we are moving. And we cannot afford to stop because Alabama, and because our nation, has a date with destiny."

Destiny came on March 7 on Selma's Edmund Pettus Bridge. The movement activists had set out on a march to Montgomery, the Alabama capital, where they would demand that the state's governor provide protection against white mobs, protection that Clark's forces certainly would not provide. In response, Clark effectively declared a race war, announcing that all of Dallas County's white male citizenry would be deputized under his command. The two sides met at the bridge. At the front line, the marchers were quiet as they stood erect. At first, when the police force charged them, the nonviolent protesters simply toppled over and let their persecutors tread upon them. Then everything was swallowed up by a high, unified shriek—the sound of a mass of demonstrators suddenly engulfed in chaos. It was the sound of ordinary men and women on a public thoroughfare coming under attack.

For history, that day in Selma would be Bloody Sunday. The mangled faces on the television broadcasts that night showed why. Subsequent generations of American schoolchildren would be shown the footage from the Edmund Pettus Bridge in order to learn what courage looks like, and what evil looks like, too. Johnson watched from Washington. "America didn't like what it saw," Johnson aide Richard Goodwin later wrote. "And neither did Lyndon Johnson, who witnessed not a revelation (he had grown up in the South), but an affront to the sensibilities and moral justice of the country he now led."

He knew he had to act. In an immediate sense, his path forward was treacherous and complex. The situation in Alabama could not be allowed to spin further out of control. The protesters were determined to march to Selma. Alabama governor George Wallace, the great segregationist demagogue of the era, would not rebuke Clark and would not offer protection to the marchers. But he fancied himself the grand ambassador of states' rights, and he did not want to appear incapable of preventing his state from descending into lawlessness while the world looked on.

That was exactly how it was starting to look. On March 9, Unitarian minister James Reeb, one of many white clergymen who had joined the Selma protest, was savagely beaten by white segregationists chanting "Nigger lover." Two days later he would succumb to his injuries. Privately, Wallace hoped that Johnson would send federal troops to restore order. Johnson, always wary of reviving the ghosts of Reconstruction in the South, could do no such thing. He would send troops, but only if Wallace asked for them.

The matter was resolved in a legendary showdown between Wallace and the president at the White House on March 13. Wallace had requested the meeting, but on arrival he was sly and noncommittal.

He was startled by a full Johnson assault. "What do you want left after you when you die?" the president asked the governor. They were both seated, but Johnson had positioned himself in a high rocking chair and he looked down at the Alabaman as he spoke. "Do you want a *great, big, marble* monument that reads, 'George Wallace—He built'? . . . Or do you want a little piece of scrawny pine board lying across that harsh, caliche soil, that reads, 'George Wallace—He hated'?"

"Hell," said Wallace after the meeting concluded, "if I'd stayed in there much longer, he'd have had me coming out for civil rights." Within days, the governor of Alabama would submit a public request to the president for federal assistance in providing for the court-ordered security of the marchers in Selma.

In a larger sense, Johnson's path forward from Selma was simple. The men and women on the Pettus Bridge had said everything that needed to be said about the urgency of voting rights. Like the brave men of Lincoln's Gettysburg, their suffering was above even a president's power to add or detract. All that was really left for Johnson to do was the hardest thing, the most important thing, that any president can do. He had to look at his country as it really was and not shrink from what he saw. King and the marchers in Selma, the protesters just outside the White House gate—they were all saying they could not wait for justice in the South a moment longer. And suddenly, neither could Lyndon Johnson. He knew he had to act.

That weekend, word came from the White House that the president would address a joint session of Congress on the evening of Monday, March 15. Before a televised audience, he would ask the Congress to take immediate action on a sweeping voting rights bill. Lady Bird marveled at the swiftness with which her husband would need to pull together a speech. Still, she said in her diary, "I am glad that he is launched, that he is being intensely active. It is the milieu for him. It is his life. He is loosed from the bonds of depression."

It fell to Richard Goodwin, the talented speechwriter and former

Kennedy aide, to craft Johnson's text. Arriving at his office that Monday, the very day Johnson would give the speech, Goodwin felt the terrible pressure of his task and the terror of his approaching deadline. But then he started to think of Selma, and the busy world hushed. Years later, in his memoir *Remembering America*, Goodwin would remember the rare speechwriter's gift he had been given that day: "There was, uniquely, no need to temper conviction with the reconciling realities of politics, admit to the complexities of debate and the merits of 'the other side.' There was no other side. Only justice—upheld or denied."

"I speak tonight," Johnson said that evening from the House floor, "for the dignity of man and the destiny of democracy. . . . At times history and fate meet at a single time in a single place to shape a turning point in man's unending search for freedom. So it was last week in Selma, Alabama."

The room was deathly quiet. "Pulses quickened," *Time* would later note, "as it became obvious that Johnson had discarded the syrupy quality that has marked many of his earlier speeches. With painful poignancy, he pricked his country's conscience, uttering the unutterable":

> Rarely in any time does an issue lay bare the secret heart of America itself. Equal rights for American Negroes is such an issue. And should we defeat every enemy, and should we double our wealth and conquer the stars, and still be unequal to this issue, then we will have failed as a people and as a nation. For with a country as with a person, "what is a man profited if he shall gain the whole world and lose his own soul?"

From a gallery high above, Lady Bird scanned the chamber as her husband spoke. So many of the Southern senators she and Lyndon knew well had stayed away from this speech. Richard Russell was gone. Harry Byrd was nowhere to be seen.

This time on this issue there must be no delay, or no hesitation, or no compromise with our purpose. We cannot, we must not, refuse to protect the right of every American to vote in every election that he may desire to participate in . . .

The break from the Southern Democrats was not easy for Lady Bird. She was descended on her mother's side from a proud Alabama family. When she'd come to the strange new world of Washington, she had found her way by making friends with the wives of other Southern congressmen, women whose warmth and easy intimacy she had easily understood.

But now this was Lyndon's cause, and her cause as well. Earlier that winter, Lady Bird had convened a meeting in the Queen's Sitting Room of the White House to discuss the new program she had launched to improve the beauty of the American landscape. Outside it was cold and snowy. Waiting for the First Lady to arrive, Sharon Francis, an Interior Department employee, heard the sound of civil rights protesters singing outside the gate. When Lady Bird entered, she heard the sound as well. "What are they doing?" the First Lady asked. Francis turned to a window, pulled back the curtain, and looked out. "They're singing 'We Shall Overcome,'" she said, "and they're kneeling in the snow." Francis turned back toward the First Lady. A tear was running down Lady Bird's face.

Their cause must be our cause too. Because it's not just Negroes, but, really, it's all of us, who must overcome the crippling legacy of bigotry and injustice.

And we shall overcome.

For a moment, all was silent. Then Johnson was engulfed by that greatest of treasures, applause from the hundreds of listeners he could see and the millions he could not. Watching from a living room in distant Birmingham, Martin Luther King, Jr., began to weep. By adopting the words of the civil rights anthem, the president had changed the movement forever. Its leaders were now American heroes. Its dead were now martyrs for the American idea. The story of civil rights was now part of the American story.

And part of Lyndon Johnson's story, too. As he concluded his speech, Johnson recalled the young Mexicans he had taught in Cotulla, Texas, in the school year 1928–29. Those students were poor and hungry and "they knew even in their youth the pain of prejudice." As their teacher, Johnson said, it had never occurred to him that he would one day "have the chance to help the sons and daughters of those students, and to help people like them all over this country. But now I do have that chance. And I'll let you in on a secret—*I mean to use it.*"

When he'd finished speaking, Johnson knew he had given one of the great speeches of his life. "It was terrific, magnificent, and impressive," Mayor Daley told him afterward. "The greatest speech you ever made," said California's governor, Pat Brown. "Your speech was beyond belief!" Jackie Kennedy cooed.

Even Dick Russell called to congratulate his old protégé. Goodwin would recall the smile on Johnson's face when he got off the phone with the Georgian. "That was Dick Russell," Johnson announced. "Said that though he can't be with me on the bill, it was the best speech he ever heard any president give." Johnson was plainly thrilled: "Let's have a little whiskey, boys, looks like we've got something to celebrate."

Indeed they did. By summer, the legislation would pass both houses. The dramatic moment occasioned by the speech reinvigorated Johnson's entire legislative program, just as he reached the final stretch of his one hundred days. On April 8, the Medicare bill made it out of the House. The next day, four days before the hundred days ended, Johnson reviewed his record with Larry O'Brien. "Roosevelt's got eleven," said the president, referring to the number of bills passed. "They were not major bills at all. But you have one major one really with education. Now, Appalachia's a super-major one, and then the others are about like Roosevelt. But on the twelfth, you'll have the best Hundred Days. Better than *he* did!"

That night, Lady Bird recorded in her diary: "Lyndon talked of the last week. He said, 'Never has there been such a Hundred Days.'" So vast was his triumph that for the moment, Lyndon could see only greatness ahead. For the moment, his persistent visions of ruin were put to bed. It fell to Lady Bird, always careful to be prepared for anything, to remember the other side. "This was a week to put a gold circle around. So let us remember it, because there will be many ringed in black."

PART III

The Cost

The world aflame: California National Guard troops took the
streets of Los Angeles during the Watts riots of August 1965.

© Hulton Archive/Getty Images

CHAPTER NINE

Lonely Acres

Summer 1965

The months that followed were hard on both Johnsons. The bombing of Vietnam continued apace. At night, Lyndon haunted the halls of the White House, often heading for the Situation Room, where a military aide could provide up-to-the-minute reports from the war. From her bed, Lady Bird could hear the ring of the telephone in the earliest hours of the morning, bringing news of a plane shot down on the other side of the world. Lyndon was always eager to answer. Vietnam was now his constant companion, the third party in their marriage. "He can't separate himself from it," the First Lady told her diary. "Actually, I don't want him to, no matter how painful."

Lyndon's anxiety was hard for Lady Bird to bear. She was happy to retreat to the peace of the ranch in Texas. There she spent much of the summer, leaving Lyndon to worry away in Washington, though she knew her absence wore on him. In early July, their daughter Lynda spoke to her father on the phone. He sounded lonesome, Lynda told Lady Bird afterward. "Mother," she said, "he's never the same without you." Lady Bird knew it was true. "I feel selfish," she told her diary, "as though I was insulating myself from pain and troubles down here. But I know that I need it." Just as she had foreseen in April, there had been many dark days.

To be sure, that spring and summer had seen plenty of glorious moments, days that, in another presidency, would have indeed been ringed in gold. There was April 11, when the $1.3 billion elementary and secondary education bill became the first federal law to fund education on a large scale nationwide. Seated on a wooden bench beside the old Junction schoolhouse in Stonewall, Texas, Johnson signed the bill into law, amid an elaborate display of his lifelong commitment to education. In the audience were some of the Mexicans the president had taught in Cotulla, Texas, and at his side was the seventy-two-year-old Mrs. Kate Loney. Mrs. Loney was the former "Miss Kate" Deadrich, the teacher who'd coaxed young Lyndon to read by holding him on her lap in front of her class. For the ceremony, Johnson broke with his usual custom and signed the bill with only one pen, which he then handed gratefully to his teacher. "She seemed not to realize it was meant as a souvenir," observed *The New York Times,* "and left it on the table as she walked away."

There was July 30, when Johnson signed the bill establishing a system of Medicare for seniors. "No longer will older Americans be denied the healing miracle of modern medicine," Johnson proclaimed in the auditorium at the Harry Truman Library in Independence, Missouri. "No longer will illness crush and destroy the savings that they have so carefully put away over a lifetime so that they might enjoy dignity in their later years."

Johnson had chosen the Truman Library out of respect for his only living Democratic predecessor. As president, Truman had felt the fury of the medical lobby when he'd tried to pass Medicare himself. As Johnson signed the bill, he was joined by the eighty-one-year-old Truman, a man whose own later years had not been entirely happy. Johnson felt a special affection for the only other living Democratic president. So much of Truman's story was his own: an old-school politician thrust into the White House by a charismatic president's death; a president who came from humble origins and fought for the common man; a man weighed down by an awful Asian war. Johnson's praise for the ex-president was sincere and generous, and revealing. "The people of the United States love and voted for Harry Truman," he said, "not because he gave them hell but because he gave them hope." Truman was so moved he could barely speak. "I thank you all most highly for coming here," he told the crowd. "It's an honor that I haven't had done to me—well, quite a while, I'll say that to you."

And there was August 6, when, under a glittering chandelier in the President's Room off the Senate chamber, Johnson signed the voting rights bill into law. On the same day a hundred and four years earlier, the White House staff informed the press, Abraham Lincoln had signed a bill emancipating black slaves who had been conscripted to fight in the Confederate Army. Moments earlier, Johnson had addressed the nation from the Rotunda. "Today is a triumph for history as huge as any victory won on any battlefield," he said. "Today we strike away the last major shackle of those fierce and ancient bonds. Today the Negro story and the American story fuse and blend." He spoke in front of John Trumbull's oil painting *Surrender of Lord Cornwallis,* depicting George Washington astride his horse as the British army capitulated at Yorktown. On Johnson's left as he spoke was a likeness of the head of Lincoln sculpted by Gutzon Borglum for Mount Rushmore. On his right was a standing marble statue of Lincoln by the nineteenth-century sculptor Vinnie Ream.

Washington standing over him, Lincoln on either side—subtlety was not the order of the day. But for once Johnson's extravagant stagecraft didn't feel like overkill. With the stroke of a pen—or, rather, the strokes of several pens—Johnson had ended poll taxes and literacy tests and all of the violent indignities that for nearly two centuries had denied millions of American citizens the greatest promise of their nation. For a moment, Lyndon Johnson had earned the right to be mentioned in the same breath as the father of the nation and the man who had ensured it did not perish from the earth.

Yet he could not remain with them. And in the long story of America, the summer of 1965 would not be ringed in gold. In that story, as we now know it, the summer of 1965 would be the moment when troubles overtook the country, troubles that would remain for years to come. We have come to think of that summer—the middle of the year in the middle of the decade—as the moment when Americans began to choose sides. Hope or fear, young or old, black or white, violent or nonviolent, radical or reactionary, student dissident or silent majority.

To Americans living through the summer of 1965, however, things were not so clear. In many respects, their lives looked the same as they had the summer before. Most of them were not fighting or dying in Vietnam. Most of them still enjoyed the benefits of a prosperous country with a stable government—their trash was collected, the water ran clear in their pipes, order was kept, and domestic peace was preserved. Most Americans still expected the policemen and the politicians to be trustworthy, decent, and good.

But, as in the previous summer, there remained a nagging fear that things were changing too fast, that some catastrophe loomed. The pitch of the anxiety had grown higher in the intervening year. Now everyone was talking about it, the causes of mistrust and worry, all the possible reasons for fear. Despite all the assurances of the prior twenty months, despite all the talk of the powerful president with his glad tidings of great joy, there was no use pretending anymore. Something was wrong in America. They could see it with their own eyes.

They could see it on their television screens, in the unsettling images coming out of Vietnam. The Rolling Thunder campaign had earned the conflict a regular spot at the top of evening newscasts and on the front pages of the papers. Fighting on the ground had been sporadic all spring, but Americans were warned of a coming summer offensive in which guerrilla fighters would emerge from the jungle to attack American holdings in South Vietnam with terrible force. Sure enough, in mid-June, Vietcong battalions had appeared as if from nowhere. They proceeded to destroy much of the South Vietnamese army, barely reconstituted from the offensive of the previous year. From the sky, Saigon's American allies continued to pound targets in the north, but the bombardment seemed to have little effect on the Vietcong's morale. If anything, the bombing had brought more recruits into the Vietcong ranks. It was clear that without further American intervention, the Saigon government would fall. In July, the press reported that the number of troops in Vietnam would soon top 75,000. For the moment, Johnson announced no further commitments, but he looked truly grim on television. "Incidents are going up," he told the nation. "The casualties are going up. . . . We expect that it will get worse before it gets better."

It was clear that the South Vietnamese would not be able to charge through to victory on their own. So tenuous was Saigon's hold on the country that it was barely safe for Johnson administration officials to visit. In July, McNamara arrived for a fact-finding mission. While he was there, Vietnamese security officials learned of a plot, mere moments from being launched, to assassinate Ambassador Maxwell Taylor. The more the public learned about Vietnam, the more it seemed rigged with trip wires that extended far out from the jungle. There were Soviet-piloted jets on the ground just north of Hanoi; there were Chinese air defenses massing on the island of Hainan. That summer, the frightful reality sank in—the fighting in this faraway land could somehow trigger a nuclear war.

Criticism of the war was starting to come from more and more respectable quarters. The press complained about the lack of candor from the Johnson administration. "Vietnam is a different kind of a war from Korea," editorialized *The New York Times,* "but it is a war—one the nation must recognize as such; and it is time to say so." In June, Senator William Fulbright, chairman of the Foreign Relations Committee, declared that "military victory in Vietnam, though theoretically attainable, can in fact be attained only at a cost far exceeding the requirements of our interest and our honor." He thought further escalation would only lead to "a bloody and protracted jungle war in which the strategic advantages would be with the other side."

The sharpest establishment critic was Walter Lippmann. The progressive lion had been cheered by Johnson's landslide the previous November and thrilled by his hundred days' domestic push in the spring of 1965. But he was quicker to sound a note of caution on the Johnson presidency than younger liberal intellectuals, who were still confidently predicting in the summer of 1965 that a progressive golden age had arrived. At the age of seventy-five, Lippmann had lived through two previous hours of liberal triumph, during the presidencies of Woodrow Wilson and FDR. The twentieth century had taught him that progressive golden ages are always shorter than predicted. By summer, he was writing columns that got at the heart of the Johnson administration's problems: its unwillingness to accept its own fallibility. In Vietnam, he wrote, "we have set ourselves a task, which, like squaring the circle or perpetual motion or living 200 years, is impossible to do. . . . To say that something ought to be done does not make it possible to do it."

Lippmann knew that his words did not please the president. He was in frequent contact with enough administration officials, including an old protégé, Mac Bundy. It was painful for the century's greatest progressive writer to take a hard line against the most effective progressive politician in a generation. Still, he wrote with moral clarity, and foreboding, "it is essential that the President should not talk himself into a position where he has foreclosed a rational and workable solution of the war. He will be doing just that if he continues to say that our honor is at stake."

Johnson acted as if the criticism didn't bother him. He assured the country that he was doing everything he could to sue for peace. He looked, as always, for the deal. He tried to entice Ho Chi Minh to the peace table with promises of American investment in a giant Mekong Delta Project, modeled on the TVA. In May, he announced a pause in the bombing in hopes of jump-starting negotiations. Through his ambassador in Moscow he sent word to the North Vietnamese that he hoped they would reciprocate with an "equally constructive" act of good faith. The message came back to the ambassador unopened. Before long, the American bombers were back in the air.

In private, Johnson raged at his domestic critics. The Communists were holding out, he believed, precisely because they believed Americans lacked the will to stay and fight. Any critical word, any suggestion that military victory was hopeless offered strength to the Vietcong. A story circulated of a testy exchange between the president and Frank Church, a senator from Idaho and an emerging Democratic critic of the war. At a White House reception, the president had buttonholed Church to complain about a recent antiwar speech. "Mr. President," Church protested, "if you read the speech all the way through, it isn't the same as the headlines."

Johnson was unimpressed: "The headlines are all I read and all anybody reads." He could remember when Church had been a green freshman and had to learn the ways of the Senate from the master of the Democratic caucus, Lyndon Johnson. "When you were in trouble out in your state, Frank, I used to come out and give you a hand, didn't I?"

Church tried again to defend himself: "Mr. President, what I've been saying isn't much different from what Walter Lippmann has been writing."

"Walter Lippmann is a fine man," Johnson replied. "Next time you're in trouble out in Idaho, Frank, you ask Walter to come help."

Polls showed a consistent majority of Americans supported the president's course in the war. This was true in part because for most Americans, the war was not yet a question of life or death. Some 1,928 Americans would die in Southeast Asia by the end of 1965, an alarmingly high figure, nine times as many as had died there the year before. But most on the home front could hardly imagine that the death toll in the conflict would eventually exceed 58,000.

The war was hell for those fighting it; as yet, it was only confusing and unsettling for those back home. The newspapers were filled with strange Asian names with misplaced vowels and extraneous consonants. The fortunes of the United States depended on a ro-

tating cast of shady figures who made up the Saigon government.
Buddhist monks were incinerating themselves in protest of sup-
pression by the Catholic government. Catholics suspected the premier of having Buddhist sympathies. American men fighting to
keep South Vietnam free faced an enemy whose ranks were swelling with South Vietnamese recruits. All of it was an indecipherable
jumble that left the nation confused, and uneasy about what was
coming next.

War correspondents, meanwhile, were growing pessimistic about
the whole enterprise. The gap between the conflict they saw and the
one described in official communiqués had grown appallingly large.
From their reports, American readers began to sense that this war
was different from others—deteriorating, disorganized, and altogether foul. "The sky over Saigon is alive with noisy aerial boxcars,
stuttering helicopters and flashing Skyhawk fighter-bombers," wrote
Scotty Reston during a late summer visit to Southeast Asia. "The
airports, the bars and the restaurants are now all a little high—not
to mention the G.I.'s on leave—and even the fancy hotels are beginning to smell like a men's locker room."

Bleak as the situation in Vietnam was, the most vividly frightening tales in the papers that summer came from much closer to home.
In early July, the national press grew fascinated with the troubles of
the O'Neal family of Los Angeles. Nineteen-year-old Shirley O'Neal
had been brutally raped by a gang of young men on June 29 in the
suburb of Northridge. She had been going door to door selling
cookbooks when a young man lured her into his home on the premise that his "uncle" would want to buy one. Inside, five men dragged
her into a bedroom, where they threw her onto the floor and proceeded to torture and rape her. She escaped with her life but was
psychologically shattered. A few days later, her father, a lieutenant
with the Los Angeles Police Department, entered the department's
West Valley station where her assailants were being held. Mistaking
a young man with a "Hellbound" tattoo for one of his daughter's
attackers, Lieutenant O'Neal pulled his service revolver and began

to shoot. As he fired, fellow officers would later say, he looked "like a man in a dream."

Something was happening to the nation. Neighbors could no longer be trusted, good people were at their breaking point, sick minds roamed the land. A report showed that in the course of the year 1964, serious crime had risen 13 percent over the prior year. In August, *Newsweek* ran a cover story on "Crime in the Streets." The story began with the tale of one Chester E. Pierce, Jr., of Worcester, Massachusetts, who'd "strolled coolly" into a police station and announced that "that very morning" he had stolen from the sidewalk a five-year-old boy whom he had sexually abused and strangled to death and stuffed into a closet.

"And so it went," the *Newsweek* story continued, "with astonishing variety and numbing repetition—across the U.S. in midsummer." Moving on from the poor little boy in Worcester, the magazine provided a ghastly roll of crime victims across the country. Suellen Evans, on her way home from summer school in Chapel Hill, North Carolina, who'd "encountered a swarthy man who attempted rape and stabbed her fatally in the neck and heart." Mary Ellen Bay, twenty-seven, stabbed to death with a screwdriver by a nineteen-year-old rice mill worker. Two "pretty . . . University of Texas coeds" found dead, their bodies "blackened" and only "partly clad." These attacks and others like them, said *Newsweek,* left "an impression of U.S. society slipping into a condition of epidemic criminality."

Never mind that, as the magazine noted briskly, "many observers believe [the impression] is distorted." What mattered wasn't the reality of violent crime—"a malignant enemy in America's midst," said President Johnson—but its effect on the nation's imagination. "As the malignancy spread," *Newsweek* observed, "it was inevitably outdistanced by anxiety and apprehension." Most Americans were at no greater risk of falling victim to gruesome violence than they had been the year before or the year before that. But they *believed* they were. They grew afraid of something unknown but awful, lurking just out of sight.

Feeding the fear was now a chief pastime in the culture. That summer, *The New Yorker* had plans for a four-part excerpt of a new work of nonfiction by Truman Capote. The book, *In Cold Blood,* described the terrible fate of the Clutter family of Holcombe, Kansas. Herbert and Bonnie Clutter and their two teenage children had been murdered, one by one, by two paroled convicts who'd come to their isolated farmhouse for a hoard of cash they'd heard was in the Clutters' safe. Capote's tale, published in book form the following January, would become a classic for its deep reportage from inside the minds of the Clutters' killers. But it grabbed readers in the 1960s with its terrible premise: a normal family, living in their unremarkable home, unaware of the evil agents on the highway getting closer by the second. "I've been staggered by the letters I've received," Capote would say after the book's publication. "About 70 percent . . . think of the book as a reflection on American life, this collision between the desperate, ruthless, wandering, savage part of American life, and the other, which is insular and safe, more or less." The tale of the poor Clutters spoke to people because "there is something so awfully inevitable about what is going to happen: the people in the book are completely beyond their own control."

So much of life, it seemed, was like that—slipping beyond control. No one knew what to make of what was happening to the nation's youth, who seemed to be turning toward coarse and dangerous pursuits. In July, *Time* reported that "resort towns" all over the nation had been besieged by mobs of young people who had celebrated the Independence Day holiday in rollicking, disorderly fashion. The crowds were "college students from middle-class families with middle-level incomes" who had nonetheless dissolved into angry riots, shouting things like "We want booze!" and "We want beer!" prompting a rebuke from police and, in more than one case, the National Guard. "The state with the most trouble was Ohio," *Time* said,

> where 590 National Guardsmen were mobilized to restore peace
> to two different towns—Russells Point and Geneva-on-the-Lake.

Before they did, 1,500 youths at Russells Point had broken the glass of every store front in town, set fire to homes and businesses, driven firemen away with rocks. At Geneva-on-the-Lake, some 8,000 students rioted for three hours, mauling three police cruisers, smashing shop windows, and keeping residents awake with blasts from three-foot-long plastic horns.

Of course, most of the nation's youth had more serious concerns than the absence of beer. Most American colleges in 1965 were not yet the hotbeds of civil disobedience they would become by decade's end. But a few campuses were on the leading edge. At the University of California, Berkeley, in the fall of 1964, students in the "Free Speech Movement" had launched a series of protests against university policies that banned political activity on campus. That December, when some four thousand students staged a sit-in at the university's Sproul Hall, hundreds were arrested in the early morning hours under the authority of California's governor, Pat Brown. In the spring, the protesters were reorganized, with an agenda that extended beyond California—protesting, in particular, American policy in Vietnam.

Everyone was worried that summer would mean more unrest in the nation's cities. In New York, home to the worst rioting in the previous summer, Congressman Adam Clayton Powell, Jr., warned that the city was facing another "summer of discontent." The first weeks went by without incident, but apprehension rose with the temperature. "The fuel of unrest and injustice is still here," said an unnamed Harlem political leader in *The New York Times*. "There's been improvement but the fuse can be lit by any random spark."

Detroit authorities, concerned that rioters would barricade bridges, made plans to deploy amphibious landing craft for crossing the Detroit River when an emergency struck. In Chicago, civil rights activists protesting the city's housing laws came into bitter conflict with Mayor Daley, who arrested 252 protesters in June. The arrests left the black community inflamed. "We're going to see to it that it will be a long, hot summer for Daley," said one protester. "Every Negro who cannot march will be asked to turn on all his faucets and drain the water." City officials across the country urged calm, arguing that fear of unrest could be self-fulfilling. In Rochester, New York, where hundreds had been injured in riots the prior summer, the departing city manager, Porter W. Homer, decried the periodic rumors sweeping the city that "this or that date is to be the time for another outbreak of violence." Rochester, he observed, was "tragically close to talking itself into another riot."

"Positive hope," the *Times* declared in June, "seems to be the key to the coming summer. Where it exists, there is less talk of the possibility of riots. Where it does not exist, predictions about long, hot summers are heard with increasing frequency." By that standard, vast expanses of the American north could expect fire in the sky by summer's end. Following the cues of civil rights leaders, the national press was now opening its eyes to the fact that the "negro problem" extended beyond the segregated South to Northern cities where abysmal housing, mass unemployment, and lax law enforcement made a mockery of the term "equality."

This new awakening posed a serious threat to the Johnson story. The Johnson vision for liberal reform, like much of postwar liberalism itself, had taken for granted that America could afford to solve the problems of its worst off because things in the country were better than they had been before. The nation's problems were solvable, and would be solved soon. In June 1965, Johnson had set out even grander aims for solving those problems in an ambitious speech at Howard University. Noting that true equality of the races would be fulfilled only when African American families could achieve "not just legal equity but human ability—not just equality as a right and a theory but equality as a fact and equality as a result," he'd pledged to bring together leading experts to devise a series of programs that would transform black family life in the country.

A year before, when willing away anxiety had been a national project, this would have seemed a laudable goal and a reasonable one. But as the troubles mounted in the summer of 1965, Johnson's confidence began to look strange. Did he really think it would be as simple as bringing together the best minds to solve the problem? Besides, the best minds had already spent a good deal of time thinking about the problems of the poor and the black in America. When would their attention turn to the problems of everyone else?

The Johnson story was further undermined by leaks in the press that summer of a provocative forthcoming report from the Department of Labor entitled "The Negro Family: The Case for National Action." Its author, Daniel Patrick Moynihan, was a leading liberal intellectual from the Kennedy circle, but the report nonetheless challenged the basic assumptions of contemporary progressive thought. While noting the great advancement in the rights of black people in the 1960s, Moynihan predicted that blacks would be inhibited from making further gains by limitations in their own education and skills. "We have been in the business of breaking down job barriers to Negroes for four years now," Moynihan wrote in a confidential memo to Johnson in March 1965. "We can no longer deny that our hardest task is not to create openings, but to fill them."

Moynihan believed the lack of black advancement could be explained by deep-seated problems in American black culture. "We feel," he wrote to Johnson, "that *the master problem is that the Negro family structure is crumbling.*" Noting that "the richest inheritance any child can have is a stable, loving, disciplined family life," he compared the 43 percent illegitimacy rate in Harlem with the 3 percent of whites nationwide born out of wedlock. He believed the disparity was a consequence of a crisis in black manhood. Too many adult males were out of work and unable to provide for a family. That itself was a consequence of slavery and segregation, but it now exercised its own insidious, independent effect on the black community.

And, pointedly, Moynihan told Johnson that government aid programs, like the ones in the Great Society, weren't helping; in fact, they might be part of the problem. "Most of the welfare assistance,"

he wrote, "the special education efforts, the community action programs which we are now doubling and redoubling are essentially the
provision of surrogate family services. Society is trying to do for
these young persons what in normal circumstances parents do for
their children. . . . We can go on providing this kind of welfare assistance forever. The evidence is it does not change anything."

The implications of this assessment for the Great Society were
immediate and profound. In a letter to Johnson enclosing Moynihan's memo, Labor Secretary Willard Wirtz was succinct: "The attached Memorandum is nine pages of dynamite about the Negro
situation." Initially, Johnson was intrigued by Moynihan's findings—
they helped to form his Howard University speech. But, clinging to
his optimistic vision, Johnson excised from his speech Moynihan's
gloom about the efficacy of government programs to solve the problems of the black family. Rather, it took for granted that, under his
leadership, the centuries-old problems of inequity could be dealt
with once and for all.

To Americans, that seemed an increasingly dubious and improbable prospect. But most were willing to give Johnson a bit more time
to bring his grand promises to pass. They waited to judge, but they
waited anxiously. As the summer reached its midway point, none of
the many trouble spots on the American scene had fulfilled their
terrible promise. The Saigon government hung on, the fire in the
cities did not light, the evil intruders did not burst through the door.
So the country went on waiting for what was awful and inevitable,
the thing they could not yet see.

IF YOU WERE looking for a real, visible sign that something had
changed in America that summer, there was one place you could find
it: the White House. The signs of trouble were now unmistakable in
the president's face. In early July, *Time* described a "brooding" President Johnson who "sat glumly in the Cabinet Room, his chin on his
fist." The president was "mercurial" and "given to periods of great
ebullience and monumental gloom." Johnson was now "more som-

ber, subdued and preoccupied than at almost any time" since Kennedy's death. He'd taken to calling the White House "Lonely Acres."

The president's portrait in the press had changed, as if overnight. Johnson's "stock on the gossip market in chronically tattletale Washington," *Newsweek* observed in early July, "was near an all-time low." The nastiness, said the magazine, "skittered from lawn party to luncheon, and finally into the press. LBJ . . . had turned moody and depressed under the pressure of his high office. He was given to frightening temper tantrums. . . . He took credit for other people's triumphs, blamed others for his own mistakes." The magazine related a favorite new joke about a police officer who'd pulled over a Lincoln Continental for speeding. When the officer realized his offending driver was the president of the United States, he exclaimed, "Oh my God!" The driver's curt reply: "Yes, and don't you forget it again!"

This new Lyndon Johnson—arrogant, abrasive, sensitive to the smallest slight, prone to the darkest depression—was of course not new at all. It was the same Lyndon Johnson who had been in the White House since November 22, 1963, and the same Lyndon Johnson who'd been in Washington for thirty years. But the Lyndon Johnson who'd been a character in the press for months on end was the Man-in-Motion Johnson, the legislative wunderkind, the cool-headed "let us reason together" dealmaker, the strong and prudent commander in chief. For the first year and a half of his presidency, he'd been a winner in the eyes of the public. And the wise press corps, always careful not to get too far in front of public opinion, had written about him as a man who didn't—indeed, couldn't—lose.

But Johnson wasn't untouchable anymore. Now Americans seemed to be tiring of his gooey, hopeful speeches. Now the country seemed to be facing a tangle of emerging, intractable problems—Vietnam, ongoing racial conflict in the South, the tinderbox cities of the North—that could bring Johnson down. And so the press quickly reversed its assessment of him. Tom Wicker, writing in *The New York Times,* was straightforward in describing the abrupt shift:

> While he had so much going for him for so long, Mr. Johnson also built up without difficulty an "image"—a word heard often in the White House—of a sort of super-Lyndon, wise, experienced, responsible, a wizard in politics and with Congress, a veritable maestro of the Presidency. Now that the triumphs have slacked off and the toughest problems persist, super-Lyndon has disappeared like stage scenery and there stands plain old Lyndon—the hard-driving, explosive difficult man he always was.

Most other reporters, following the custom of their trade, offered no explanation of how they'd gotten it wrong in the months before. Many, in fact, told their readers that really, they'd seen the problems with this Johnson fellow all along. Twenty months' worth of unused anecdotes and unflattering adjectives suddenly found their way into print. "It is said," the *Newsweek* columnist Kenneth Crawford wrote of Johnson, "that he is a hard, even harsh taskmaster to his subordinates: that he is secretive to the point of obsession; that he is hypersensitive to criticism; that he is petty in his attitude toward rivals, or fancied rivals, for power."

Joe Alsop was one of the earliest and harshest Johnson critics. In February, he had complained about the president's obsession with message control. Johnson was a man with an "irrepressible longing to have every story in every newspaper in the United States written exactly as he would write it. The amount of the President's time that is thus devoted to what is now called the President's 'image' is almost alarming to contemplate." By summer, the Johnson in Alsop's columns had started to sound like a dangerous, mad king. "To those beyond the limits of the ingrowing American political community, it will surely come as a shock that there are serious reasons to worry about Lyndon Johnson's frame of mind."

To loyalists in the Johnson White House, it was fitting that Alsop—a Kennedy courtier—would be leading the charge against them. As the press turned, Johnson staffers closely tracked Kennedy contacts with prominent members of the press corps and reported them to the president, who lapped up the intelligence.

That summer, *Life* and *Look* magazines published dueling excerpts from two forthcoming books on President Kennedy, one by Arthur Schlesinger and the other by Theodore Sorensen. Both men had secured large advances for their accounts, and their imminent publication titillated the incestuous circles of politics, publishing, and the press. ("The major industry in New York this summer," said columnist Jimmy Breslin, "is handling words about John F. Kennedy.") Sorensen's was a Kennedy-family-approved venture. He had written the book in a small cottage in Hyannis Port and Jackie Kennedy was a close editor of his manuscript, providing handwritten comments on yellow lined paper. In her notes, she displayed the same vigilance over her family's image that she had exerted toward Teddy White's "Camelot" draft a week after her husband's death:

> "*He thought* The New York Times *was the greatest newspaper in the world*"—Are you sure? He had a great deal of disillusionment about them . . . just don't give them that much of a plug—perhaps 'one of the greatest newspapers' (he liked *Le Monde*).
>
> "*John-John, as his father called him.*" His father never called him John-John—only John. That nickname now plagues the little boy—who may be stuck with it all his life.
>
> Not vodka and tomato juice in the afternoon . . . On vacations he had a drink before lunch—otherwise never—just one before dinner . . .
>
> You are wrong—he read poetry a lot—at least with me.

Sorensen would say four decades later that Jackie had also asked him "to tone down my references to JFK's praise of LBJ." As Sorensen himself was hardly inclined to write anything admiring of Lyndon Johnson, Jackie's standard of "praise" must have been very low indeed. In the end, little Kennedy affection for Johnson graced

Sorensen's pages. Self-consciously, Sorensen sought to rebut the notion that Kennedy's presidency had lacked substance, that compared with Johnson's emerging record as a progressive reformer Kennedy lacked liberal greatness. "Most insidious," Sorensen at one point told a reporter, "is the myth that Kennedy's cool, analytical manner meant that he had no heart, that he didn't commit his heart, that he didn't feel passionately about issues. This just wasn't true."

Schlesinger produced the better book. He understood that the case for Kennedy's greatness would be found in his more human moments, not the ones where he'd resembled a marble god (though *Newsweek* clucked over the "mawkish, tasteless" ending to the Bay of Pigs section in which Kennedy, "distraught over the defeat in Cuba, went into the bedroom with Jacqueline, 'put his head into his hands, almost sobbed and then took her in his arms'"). But the ultimate project was the same as Sorensen and Jackie's. The book recalled the Kennedy presidency as a golden age of mythic promise, cut tragically short after just 1,036 days in office, an age followed by days less vital, graceful, and true. The image was cemented by the book's mystical title, featured on the cover of *Life* that July above a portrait of the smiling, living Kennedy: *A Thousand Days.*

Johnson, witnessing the impressive progress of the Kennedy mythmaking machine, was more convinced than ever that if only he had a similar apparatus, his public image problems would be solved. Johnson envied Kennedy's press coverage and was convinced that his predecessor had earned it through brilliant, strategic stage management. His staff encouraged the perception. "Images do not spring full-blown," Jack Valenti wrote in a memo to the president after the 1964 election. "President Kennedy was conscious of this—and courted newspapers and magazines that had been screened by his people. In the doing, he began the creation of the Kennedy legend."

Any problems with Johnson's public image, Valenti told his boss, came from his lack of a similar strategy. How could it be otherwise, for a president whose "style" was "Jacksonian and Rooseveltian in the mainstream of American tradition and scope rather than Ivy

League gloss and splendor"? Valenti suggested that "if the President will allow the construction and execution of carefully prepared programs of public imagery we can begin now to establish the real and enduring Lyndon Johnson instead of the callous and the spiteful sketching that will spill out from cynics in the White House lobby." Valenti knew his audience. "Excellent Approved" Johnson scrawled across the memo.

But manipulating the press is rather like training a goat—possible, but not worth the bother if you don't enjoy spending time with farm animals. Kennedy did enjoy it. He liked joking with reporters and canvassing them for gossip. He wooed them for strategic reasons, but he wasn't faking it when he acted interested in what they had to say. His congenital confidence helped him to see that the best way to control his press was to give up control. He acted as though he didn't expect anything from reporters, except a chance to say his piece and, of course, to enjoy the pleasure of their company. They liked him, because everyone liked him. And, because he hadn't asked them to, they protected him in their prose.

Harnessing power by surrendering control—that would never work for Lyndon Johnson. For him, life was transactional. He was capable of dogged loyalty and sincere friendship, but only to those he knew would be 110 percent loyal to him. He was a funny, engrossing storyteller, but his stories did not exist to amuse or entertain, they drove home a Johnson point. As Senate majority leader, transactional relations with the press had served him well. They needed a way to bring the byzantine legislative process to life. He gave them conflict and drama, access and color, and wicked off-the-record asides. In return, they wrote stories in which he was the brilliant master legislator hero. And woe to the offending reporter who dared to write a negative Johnson story when the majority leader came to settle the account.

Johnson never fully grasped that a president cannot count on the same tidy commerce with his press corps. The presidency is inherently interesting, whether the president cooperates with the press or not. And even presidents who tend to the care and feeding of their press corps must resign themselves to their share of nasty, unfair stories. Johnson was stung early in his presidency, when he'd taken a group of female reporters for a ride in his convertible on the LBJ Ranch, popping open a beer can as he drove. His guests had seemed to enjoy themselves. But the result was a disastrous story in *Time* with the sneering title "Mr. President, You're Fun!"

Valenti's "image" campaign was doomed before it began. On a moment's notice, reporters would learn they had been granted some special audience with the president, watching him as he went about his life or performed the solemn duties of his job. Usually, they'd find they'd been invited to observe a president who was annoyed by their presence, or a president who was obviously false or intolerably controlling. Helen Thomas, a correspondent covering the president, recalled marches around the White House lawn behind the president. "He first called his dogs, and then he called us. He'd talk in a whisper, which was deliberately sadistic, and then he'd put everything either on background or off the record, which left everybody totally confused. . . . The whole thing was, I thought, an exercise in showing us who was boss."

Television proved especially frustrating. Everyone in the White House understood the tremendous power of the emerging medium. And everyone in the White House understood that it was a miserable format for the president. He looked smaller on the screen. His eyes narrowed, his voice extended like a high school orator's. His aides and family members tried everything to fix his performance: new venues for press conferences, instructions on pacing, thicker or thinner eyeglasses. None of it worked. They often gave him so many contradictory directions before television appearances it's a wonder he was able to summon his words.

Inevitably, a staff member became a casualty of the president's nasty publicity. That summer, Johnson's long-suffering press secretary, George Reedy, announced that he was leaving to address long-festering health issues. He was replaced by no less a figure than Bill Moyers—the best face Johnson could present to the press.

Moyers could see that all the manipulating and dissembling were the problem. In his new post, he absorbed Johnson's conspiracy theories about Kennedy-friendly staffers speaking out of turn to Kennedy-friendly press. Mac Bundy was saying things he shouldn't. *Time*'s White House correspondent was "an awfully strong Kennedy man."

Moyers clearly did not want to spend his time chasing down Kennedy plots. "I think there's a lot can be done with just more candidness," he ventured. "I think that's our basic problem. . . . Our images do result primarily through their interpretation of our being overly secretive." The best way to help the president's image was not loyalty probes or publicity campaigns. Johnson could best help himself with "more candid, sincere discussion."

And thus the challenge facing President Johnson was a familiar one: in a time of great peril, he could save himself by leveling with the American people. It was clear to Americans, watching the awful scenes from Vietnam and witnessing the appalling conditions of their cities, that their president was no longer the Lyndon Johnson of Texas Tall Tales, the Man-in-Motion who could do no wrong. But he still had his hulking majority in a Congress that he knew better how to maneuver than perhaps any of his predecessors. The momentum for the Great Society had slowed, but not stopped. His massive store of political capital from the election was depleted, but not gone. The decline in his image was, in fact, an opportunity. He could put aside the mythmaking and the gauzy promises and say what he really wanted to do. He could say who he really was.

JUST BEFORE DAWN one morning that summer, Lady Bird was awakened by the sound of Lyndon's voice. "I don't want to get in a war and I don't see any way out of it," he said. "I've got to call up six hundred thousand boys and make them leave their homes and their families." Lady Bird listened to her husband with wonder. "It was as though," she later told her diary, "he were talking out loud, not especially to me."

At other low moments of Lyndon's presidency—the panicked hours before the Democratic convention, the morning after he'd let Walter Jenkins go—Lady Bird had summoned the strength to cut through her husband's warring fears and fantasies and force him to see the world as it was. Now again he was grappling. Should he summon the strength to rise to another challenge? Or should he give in to his fear that he was doomed?

But this time, as he pondered the request for additional forces in Vietnam, she would not be the strong voice urging him to see the hard truth. Lyndon already had so many people he consulted on Vietnam—McNamara, Mac Bundy, Rusk. There were generals with statistics and cool certainty. Lady Bird was not an expert on guerrilla warfare or the domino theory. She did not question her husband's handling of the war. Sometimes that summer, when the phone rang and Lyndon tossed and turned with Vietnam worries, she would leave to go sleep in another room.

Officially, Westmoreland's request was for fifty thousand more troops. Really, he was asking for assurances from Johnson that he would deploy a hundred thousand additional forces and then perhaps an additional hundred thousand a year after that. (Thus Johnson's fears of calling up six hundred thousand boys.) The order was a loaded gun. All Johnson had to do was pull the trigger. As the end of July neared, the decision-making scenario was set to play out much as it had before. McNamara and Rusk and Bundy were advocating that he accede to the request from the field—more bombing, more troops. George Ball was the voice of dissent. Johnson was expected to hear both sides, to weigh the options. The Goldilocks Principle had been reduced from three options to two—too small, and just right.

This time, at least, Ball would have an ally: Johnson's confidant, Clark Clifford. In a series of National Security Council meetings, culminating with a dramatic debate against McNamara at Camp David, Clifford passionately argued the case against escalation:

> I hate this war. I do not believe we can win. If we send in a hundred thousand more men, the North Vietnamese will match us. If the North Vietnamese run out of men, the Chinese will send in "volunteers." Russia and China don't intend for us to win this war. If we "won," we would face a long occupation with constant trouble. And if we don't win after a big buildup, it will be a huge catastrophe. We could lose more than fifty thousand men in Vietnam. It will ruin us. Five years, fifty thousand men killed, hundreds of billions of dollars—it is just not for us.

But Johnson's mind was made up. He felt he had no other choice. Earlier that summer, Lady Bird recalled to her diary a conversation with Lyndon. "He said, 'Things are not going well here . . . Vietnam is getting worse every day. I have the choice to go in with great casualty lists or to get out with disgrace. It's like being in an airplane and I have to choose between crashing the plane or jumping out. I do not have a parachute.'"

On July 28, Johnson told the nation that he would grant the request to send additional forces to Vietnam. He spoke in a midafternoon press conference rather than a televised address in prime time. This time, he did not want the nation's eyes on him.

In his speech, he used the same florid prose that had bogged down his past speeches. It compounded the unpleasantness of the message he had to deliver. "I do not find it easy to send the flower of our youth, our finest young men, into battle," he said. "I have seen them in a thousand streets, of a hundred towns, in every State in this Union—working and laughing and building, and filled with hope and life."

Once more, as he spoke of Vietnam, his grand ambitions and bold promises for the home front were on his mind. In the speech, he recalled his great goals: "healing to the sick and dignity to the old," education for the young and equal rights for blacks. "That is what I have lived for, that is what I have wanted all my life since I was a little boy, and I do not want to see all those hopes and all those dreams of so many people for so many years now drowned in the wasteful ravages of cruel wars. I am going to do all I can do to see that that never happens."

TWO WEEKS LATER, the awful, inevitable calamity the country had been waiting for that summer finally came to pass in the Watts section of Los Angeles. In that predominantly black neighborhood, a white highway patrolman arrested a young black man on suspicion of drunk driving. When the young man's mother arrived at the scene, she got into an altercation with the officers and was arrested herself. By then, hundreds of residents of the neighborhood had flooded its streets to witness the commotion. Their agitation quickly boiled over. By the next night, five thousand people were rioting in Los Angeles. The city was in flames. Over the next five days the rioting mushroomed—a combined force of fifteen thousand National Guard and police troops could not bring the city under control.

California's governor, Pat Brown, was on vacation in Greece at the time the rioting broke out. After being alerted to the initial incident, he thought things were under control and continued to enjoy himself, unaware that a full-fledged crisis was breaking out. When he did realize the gravity of the situation, he scrambled to get back home. But the long journey took two days, during which time he was largely unreachable.

In his absence, the public face of authority in Los Angeles was Chief William Parker of the LAPD, who fanned the flames of racial conflict on television as well as any sheriff of the Deep South. The black rioters, he said, were acting like "monkeys in a zoo." Rioting of this sort was inevitable, Parker suggested, "when you keep telling people they are unfairly treated and teach them disrespect for the law."

Clearly, the president had to do something about the crisis. Johnson was spending the weekend at the LBJ Ranch, so his aide Joseph Califano monitored the situation in Los Angeles. Through Bill Moyers, Johnson released a statement that the events in Watts were "tragic and shocking." On Saturday, the rioting reached its worst. The pictures on television were gripping—the skies themselves seemed to be on fire. Califano frantically called down to Texas, trying to reach the president. But he was told the president was unavailable. He waited for Johnson to call him back with direction, but the call never came. It was not a busy day filled with other meetings and decisions—Johnson spent that day walking with Lady Bird and driving alone in his car. Califano dialed the ranch again and again. But Johnson never came to the line.

In a matter of a few short days, the Watts riots would deal a grievous blow to Johnson's presidency and the story he had been trying to tell the nation. Los Angeles, whose population had boomed in recent decades with middle-class Americans seeking a better life, was the embodiment of postwar American affluence. With its modern architecture and its carefully planned communities, the glittering suburban metropolis looked like the magnificent future to come. Its descent into chaos and carnage was not what was supposed to happen in an America that, according to the president, was on the brink of the greatest glories in the history of civilization. Even worse, the riots attacked the most basic project Johnson had pursued since the first hours of his presidency: to assure the country that he was in control, that security and stability reigned. For the scenes from Watts left viewers all over the country with one unmistakable impression: there was no one in charge.

The next day, Califano finally reached Johnson on the telephone. The president was "deeply distressed" and "sorrowful" but strangely detached from what was happening to his country. The sense of foreboding he had described to Lady Bird earlier that summer was at last coming to fruition. His plane was crashing. All summer, he had been hurtling toward the ground. Here at last was the impact—and the fire.

On the trail in 1966: Reagan's training as an actor made
for an easy adjustment to the candidate's life.

© *Bill Ray/Getty Images*

CHAPTER TEN

Like a Winner

September 1965–June 1966

In late September 1965, Ronald Reagan was back onstage. It was twenty months since he'd appeared before the California Young Republicans in San Diego. The crowd in front of him was still a blur, but everything else had changed.

He had a different kind of audience now. He'd come to the Statler Hilton in Boston to appear before the New England convention of the Federation of Republican Women. Now he was wooing comfortable middle-aged ladies, not anxious young men. His message was different, too. He was deep in the belly of moderate and liberal Republicanism, sharing the dais with the Massachusetts party's establishment—Governor John Volpe and Lieutenant Governor Elliot Richardson. And Reagan himself was different, too. Twenty months earlier, feeling the rush of standing in front of a crowd this size, he'd had to wonder how much longer it would last. But ever since "A Time for Choosing"—known everywhere now as "The Speech"—the requests for appearances before big Republican crowds had been constant. Now he could look to the future and see bigger and grander crowds to come. For the third time in his life, he had become a star.

Thanks to some wealthy benefactors and the political consulting firm Spencer-Roberts, he had also become a politician. Back home in California, where he was running an unannounced but nonetheless intense campaign for governor, he liked to stress that he was a citizen called to service, not a professional politician. But it was clear, listening to him that night in Boston, that he had learned all of the politician's tricks. His speech showed a perfect mastery of all the obligatory little rituals in which a politician seeking office must engage.

First, he heaps praise on the high official sharing the dais with him.

> Governor Volpe—

And then heaps a little patronizing chauvinism on the high official's wife:

> —and she who governs the governor, Mrs. Volpe.

He loosens the crowd up with some self-deprecating humor. He's a film actor? Fine, he'll mention some of his old films:

> There [were] some that the studio didn't want good—it wanted them Thursday. And in the old days we could always count on the passing years taking all of the [less than good] pictures out of your mind. Now you just stay up late enough at night in front of the TV set and they all come back to haunt us. . . . I've got a friend in the business who stays up late at night just to watch his hairline recede.

He plays to his strengths, always. He's a handsome movie star. It's a room filled mostly with women:

> I tell you there was one disappointment, though. When I was invited to come to a six-state convention of women Republicans, I didn't know so many men were going to stick their noses

in too. It sounded to me like the kind of a dream that a man could have all his life, and then you had to show up.

But he doesn't take it too far. He brings it back to the realm of respectability with a little more of that patronizing gender talk:

I'll tell you this, though, seriously, I am very happy to be here and to be talking to you. And the men aren't going to like me for this, but they know what I say is true. That there is a certain amount of housekeeping connected with the political activity— a party of the nation. And every man knows way down deep in his heart that if it wasn't for you gals, we'd still be walking around carrying clubs.

And then he pivots into the meat of his speech:

And so you are the ones who will do what has to be done, I am sure.

He had mastered all these tricks so that the words seemed to come effortlessly off his lips. This was the easy part. These little rituals came as naturally to him now as they did to any seasoned pol. And the rest was fairly straightforward, too. It was what he'd been doing since he'd launched his unofficial campaign for the governorship earlier that year, the same thing he'd done all those months ago in San Diego, the same thing he'd been doing, really, since he'd addressed the students and faculty of Eureka College all those years ago. Standing in front of the nice ladies of New England, he felt the energy coming off his audience. And he gave them what they wanted most.

It wasn't hard for him to figure out what that was. The audience needed a new hero. All through that fall of 1965, the Errol Flynn of the B movies watched as the feature attraction team in Washington continued to sputter out duds. The plotlines were depressing, the characters' motivations convoluted, the scripts increasingly irrelevant and absurd. They still had the grand set pieces. They still had the highly produced shots. But growing clamor from offscreen intruded and spoiled the effect:

SCENE ONE

EXT. THE ROSE GARDEN. *The second week in September,* THE PRESIDENT *gives brief remarks as he signs legislation creating a new Department of Housing and Urban Development. His administration is promoting the department as a headquarters for key Great Society programs and a sophisticated solution to the complex problems facing the nation's deteriorating cities.*

THE PRESIDENT: With this legislation, we are—as we must always—going out to meet tomorrow and master its opportunities before its obstacles master us.

FLASHBACK: *The last weekend of summer.* THE PRESIDENT *celebrates his fifty-seventh birthday at the LBJ Ranch. He admires gifts from his family including a white-leather-bound book of poems written by his younger daughter, Luci.*

LUCI JOHNSON (V/O):

Admiration flows abundantly
From this pen of mine
For the man who's giving all he's got
To try to save mankind.

OFFSCREEN INT. THE OVAL OFFICE. THE PRESIDENT *reads a memo prepared by his staff on recent changes in public opinion.*

People just aren't going to get excited or go crusading for an antipol-
lution program, for beautifying America, even for bettering its
educational standards.

SCENE TWO

INT. THE PENTAGON. *It is November 2, 1965, a year since* THE
PRESIDENT's *historic landslide victory over* BARRY GOLDWATER. *In
his large office on the third floor of the Pentagon's E-Ring, Secretary of Defense* ROBERT S. MCNAMARA *works at his desk. Early
reports show a sharp uptick in casualties from Vietnam. By
week's end, seventy Americans will be dead, the highest combat
losses of any week in the war to date.* MCNAMARA *speaks on the
phone to* THE PRESIDENT.

THE PRESIDENT: How's your battle going out in Vietnam?
MCNAMARA: Well, uh, pretty well, Mr. President . . . The problem is
that it's not producing the conditions that will almost surely win
for us. It may but it probably won't. And therefore we're going to
have to propose the problem to you and suggest some alternative
solutions to it . . .

Cut to EXT. THE PENTAGON.

Flames erupt within forty feet of MCNAMARA's *office window.*
NORMAN MORRISON, *a Quaker, sets himself on fire, in protest
over the killing of innocents in Vietnam.*

It was not a movie in which Reagan would have wanted to star.
There was another movie coming, with a more enticing script.
Reagan was a conservative politician from Southern California,
where, a month earlier, the horror of the Watts riots had so vividly
punctured the promises of utopia that Johnson and the liberals had

made. In the immediate aftermath of the riots, some of Reagan's
fellow conservatives had tried to encourage backlash and tastelessly
overdid it. (The managing editor of the conservative magazine
American Opinion, visiting Los Angeles, joked about making millions by selling spears in Watts.) Reagan, meanwhile, took the opportunity to reach out immediately to black businessmen in Watts,
saying that these upright, respectable citizens, not bureaucrats from
the government, were the neighborhood's best hope of recovery and
revival. On his trip to Boston, he posed for pictures with Ed Brooke,
the Republican who would soon launch a campaign to be the first
African American elected to the U.S. Senate since Reconstruction. In
the process, he'd instantly established himself as a respectable and
authoritative voice—an alternative to the reactionary crazies and an
alternative to the tired leadership coming out of Washington. He
was beginning to sound like the kind of person these respectable
New England Republicans could not just approve of, but follow.

He knew his partisan Republican audience was rooting for him.
A year earlier, after the Goldwater debacle, they had resigned themselves to a fate of losing national elections for some time to come.
But now, for the first time in a while, they were beginning to believe
they could regain power in Washington. He knew what they wanted
from their hero: a stirring attack on the sitting president of the
United States. So he gave it to them with his usual assortment of
tools.

He attacked Lyndon Johnson with biting humor:

Our president is fond of quoting from Isaiah, "Come let us reason together." Doesn't that sound cozy? But our President does
not drop down a line further to quote "If ye refuse ye shall be
devoured by the sword."

He attacked Johnson's record with his familiar cascade of numbers, leaving the impression of irrefutable precision:

We are told we enjoy unprecedented prosperity, but at the same time the Federal Government reveals that there are 42 Government agencies spending $70 billion a year on public welfare.

He used the righteous indignation of Mr. Norm, enraged that the architects of the Great Society had called someone like *him* an extremist in the last presidential campaign:

We, on the other hand, were presented, for the most part, as radicals who were going to bring about great changes and cataclysmic upheaval. Well, now the wraps are off the Great Society and a multitude of messages have made it plain that we are to have a welfare state with an unprecedented federalization of American life.

He employed his old habits, using vague language to mask factually dubious claims:

A serious discussion by supposedly learned men was given to the idea that income should no longer be dependent on the need to work and that we should evolve some system whereby a man is entitled to an annual income just by reason of being born.

And he attacked with the sweeping, dramatic imagery he most favored, and which he believed the moment required:

You and I have come to a moment of truth. Does man exist by permission of and for the sake of the group marching toward eternity in a super-ant heap, or does he control his destiny. . . . This question must be answered by us all, regardless of party.

He attacked Lyndon Johnson and the entire mythic vision of the American future Johnson had worked so hard to spread. When he'd finished, his audience gave him a standing ovation. In the next day's *Boston Herald* he was "the one-time motion picture star who often played the guy who didn't get the girl" but who "overwhelmed more than 1,400 of them" in his speech. "From sub-debs to septuagenarians," the *Herald* wrote, "the female hearts fluttered as he told them what they wanted to hear: that theirs was the historic role of saving the Republic from a government 'that tends to grow until freedom is lost.'"

IT WAS ALWAYS nice to get a standing ovation, but there were plenty of cheering crowds in California. His trip to Boston was part of a larger East Coast swing, during which he could attract national media attention and talk to wealthy conservative easterners who'd write checks for his gubernatorial campaign. But more important, he had come to places like Boston to prove a point. He wasn't a conservative fringe candidate who could only play rooms in San Diego or Santa Rosa. He could stand before a group of New Englanders, moderate and conservative alike, and bring them all to their feet. This was his most important message that fall: he didn't plan on being in B movies forever. Ronald Reagan didn't want another campaign like Barry Goldwater's. Ronald Reagan was going to win.

Reagan could win—it had been the guiding principle of his candidacy since its inception. The first person in need of convincing had been Reagan himself. Two months after Johnson's 1964 landslide, a group of millionaires convened at the house of Holmes Tuttle, the Los Angeles car dealership mogul, to commiserate over the Goldwater embarrassment. Among Republican donors, this was a rarefied group. And its members had a unique perspective. Across the country, in those first weeks after the Johnson landslide, mainstream Republicans like Nelson Rockefeller and Michigan governor George Romney were taking a hard line against conservatism. To survive, they argued, the party had to rein in its extremist right wing. Tuttle's group of hard-line conservatives did not share in this view. But they also did not agree with movement activists who thought that the way forward was to demand that the party become more pure. Among Goldwater's mistakes, Tuttle believed, had been his tendency to double down on extremism in the general election. Instead of the horror show at the Cow Palace, Goldwater should have changed the subject from the divisive primary by adding a moderate like William Scranton to the ticket. For conservatism to triumph, Tuttle and his friends maintained, it had to seek out alliances with the party's mainstream. They set their sights on the upcoming California governor's race in 1966 as their best shot to prove their theory.

They had been at the Coconut Grove fund-raiser that spawned the "Time for Choosing" telecast. They understood that Reagan had superior gifts of communication. "Reagan," said Cy Rubel, another supporter, "is the man who can enunciate our principles to the people." Some of "the people" already agreed. Grassroots activists in the party were talking up Reagan as a candidate before Johnson's hundred days of progressive legislative action had even begun. Maureen Reagan, a plugged-in Republican, urged her father to jump into the governor's race. "Oh, my God," Reagan said to Nancy, "they're closing in all over."

He'd been hesitant in those early months. Later he would claim he was shocked when Tuttle and his friends approached him with their plans. "I almost laughed them out of the house," he wrote in his memoirs. "I'd never given a thought to running for office and I had no interest in it whatsoever." This, as we have seen, rings false—he would have jumped at a chance to run for office if he'd thought he could do it and still manage to support his family. But his practical concerns were real. A campaign for governor would be a lengthy commitment. The television show he was hosting, *Death Valley Days,* had proved a reliable source of income. Once he announced his candidacy for governor, he would have to give up the show lest his opponents demand equal time on the public airwaves. Reagan, realistic as always about his own interests, was not going to make the leap unless he believed he had a decent shot at winning.

In those early months of 1965, it was not at all clear that he did.

California's Republican Party was badly divided after the Goldwater campaign. Conservatives had grabbed hold of much of the party apparatus in the state, but moderate voters remained a major force in the GOP. Thomas Kuchel, the state's moderate Republican senator, had been making noises about coming home to run for governor. Reagan, who some still saw as a John Birch Society–supporting extremist, would potentially face a long, bloody primary fight that might end in an embarrassing loss.

Even more daunting was his probable general election opponent, the sitting governor, Pat Brown. In the winter of 1965, there were few liberal politicians in the nation as formidable as Brown—perhaps none besides Johnson and Hubert Humphrey. Brown had already established himself as a national figure when, in 1962, he had run for reelection against no less a figure than Richard Nixon, who'd planned an easy victory in the governor's race as a launching pad for a second try at the White House. Brown won the election by nearly 300,000 votes. It was this stunning defeat that prompted Nixon's retreat from politics in the infamous "You don't have Nixon to kick around any more" rant. At that time, Brown's future had seemed bright. "Double parking in Sacramento on the way back to Washington," an aide had quipped. In 1965, even as Brown considered running for an unprecedented third term as governor in 1966, he was at the top of the list of potential successors to Johnson in the White House in the long Democratic era to come.

For Reagan, then, life as a political candidate still meant risk—the risk of failure or ruin. He was hesitant to jump in. So, with the help of Tuttle's group, he found a way to run without really running. The wealthy benefactors would form a group, Friends of Ronald Reagan, to supply Reagan with enough funds to acquire the best political assets available. Reagan would spend much of 1965 traveling California, meeting with party officials, and trying to determine whether there was sufficient support within the party for him to run as a serious challenger to the Democrats, not just as a factional favorite of the conservatives. He would effectively *be* a candidate for governor without ever outright declaring it, a distinction that would allow him to keep receiving checks for *Death Valley Days* into 1966.

This solution suited Reagan. It would be a campaign designed for a proud actor: he could *suggest* himself to the people without having to audition for their support. As he began his travels, he explained that he hoped to meet a cross section of California Republicans to determine who could best run as the party's unity candidate. The press quickly realized that Reagan himself was a candidate in all but name. What if, one reporter asked him, after meeting that cross section of Californians, he determined that the best candidate was someone other than himself? "Oh gosh, Jack!" Reagan replied. "You've asked me one I've never even thought about. Maybe I'm naïve, but I just sort of figured that if, when I found out who the cross-section wanted, it wasn't me, they at the same time, would indicate who it was and I guess that's the way I go."

Clearly, he wanted the choice of the cross section to be no one other than himself. To help things along, Friends of Ronald Reagan enlisted the help of Spencer-Roberts, a highly regarded political consulting firm headed by two young stars, Stuart Spencer and Bill Roberts. The firm had run Nelson Rockefeller's campaign against Goldwater in the photo-finish 1964 California primary and resided well outside the sphere of alternative reality from which had sprung the calamitous Goldwater candidacy. The firm's sterling reputation was well known in Southern California—and beyond. While visiting Nancy's parents in Arizona, Stu Spencer would later say, Reagan had paid a call on Goldwater. "I'm thinking of running. What would you do? Tell me." Goldwater's reply, according to Spencer, was simple. "I'd hire those sons of bitches Spencer-Roberts."

Spencer-Roberts had also been approached to run a primary campaign for George Christopher, the moderate mayor of San Francisco. Christopher was not a thrilling candidate, but he was a far safer bet than Reagan. Still, the fact that Reagan wanted to work with a bunch of Rockefeller Republicans surprised them: he was more practical than they'd thought. After a two-hour meeting at the

Cave du Roy in Beverly Hills, they found that Reagan had charmed them. "We had heard," one of the partners said, "that Reagan was a martinet, a conceited ass, that he would be hard to work with. We found this was totally false. There's not a phony bone in his body." It didn't hurt that Reagan's backers would cut substantial checks to a firm whose young partners were looking to grow their business. Asked later in the campaign to explain the ideological gap between the Spencer-Roberts partners and their conservative candidate, Bill Roberts shrugged: "We are mercenaries."

But the governor's race was more than a paycheck: Spencer-Roberts wanted to win. And after a few more meetings, they came to believe they *could* win with Reagan. The more they talked to him about the issues, the more they came to see that he was no rigid ideologue. "He was obsessed with one thing," Stu Spencer would later explain, "the Communist threat. He has conservative tendencies on other issues but he can be practical."

Reagan's new team knew that their first order of business would be removing the taint of extremism from their candidate. Grassroots activists loved him. Voters in the middle remembered him fondly from television and found him likable. The immediate problem was with the elite. To the establishment, Reagan's embrace of the hard right during the heyday of the Kennedy-Johnson era still seemed bizarre. National elites thought of him as a failed actor who could give a good speech but who had gone off the Goldwater deep end. Reagan was the "darling of the Goldwaterites and the choice of the John Birch Society," Evans and Novak wrote in 1965, a man whose primary victory would signal "rightist control of the Republican party in the nation's most populous state." Reagan's advisers knew that if that was how donors and primary voters thought of him, he would be dead in the water.

So they focused their initial energy on removing the odor of extremism. Traveling the state that spring and summer of 1965, Reagan began preaching against "hyphenated Republicans"—those who regarded themselves as conservative-Republican or liberal-

Republican or moderate-Republican voters. They should all just be Republicans, he said. The line had a sort of genius to it. It was a message of unity, meant to appeal to moderates. But it had unconscious echoes of Teddy Roosevelt's early-twentieth-century worries about unassimilated "hyphenated Americans." To California conservatives, who'd gone to war rather than accept "unity" with moderates in the past, Reagan's preaching sounded like just the thing: he wanted a party that was more pure!

What they didn't notice, for the most part, was the moderation creeping into his words. "I'm sure that we all recognize that as the state grows," he told one group, "we must have growth in government also and in government services. But there should be some proportionality." Asked what caused the Watts riots, Reagan was careful with his words. "I think you have to preface anything you say about Watts with the recognition that ninety-nine percent of the people there are fine, responsible citizens and had no part in the trouble," he said. "We're talking about a one percent minority."

He was even wary of being called a conservative. When a reporter asked if the term applied to him, Reagan dodged: "You'd have me going counter to the talks I've been giving to Republican groups. I have been saying to all Republicans who'll listen that the descriptive adjectives and the hyphens have no place in our party. I actually believe they were first foisted off on us by . . . opponents, and that we should give them back and from now on just be Republicans."

It was easy for Reagan to say this sort of thing, because he actually believed it. After thirty years as a Democrat he had converted and was proud to wear the label of the Republican Party. He was Mr. Norm, convinced, always, that he shared the values of the good and decent majority. He knew he was a Republican; therefore, by definition, the majority of Republicans must see the world the way he saw it. What was the point of squabbling when there were evil conspiracies to stop? Better for him to play the role of unifier, healer of the party's wounds. *That* was a hero's role, one he knew he could play.

And as he played that role, he would accept no carping from the right. "I have no intention of compromising my beliefs," he wrote testily to a rare conservative critic, "but I do know this. If we are to have the constitutional government we all desire, then we of the so-called conservative philosophy must recognize we have to convert those people of a more liberal view. We don't win elections by destroying them or making them disappear."

Mainstream Republicans were pleasantly surprised by this kind of talk. Never mind that the policies Reagan advocated differed little from Goldwater's. To candidate Reagan, Social Security was necessary but horribly construed. Medicare was an atrocity that should be dismantled. The Civil Rights Act was well intentioned but unconstitutional. The problem with Johnson's policy in Vietnam was a lack of resolve to *win,* come what might. And the federal government was an encroaching behemoth, steadily enslaving the people it was supposed to protect.

Never mind all of that. Reagan didn't sound like Goldwater when he talked, and he didn't look like him, either. He sounded, and looked, like a winner.

And that was what he desperately wanted to be. If all he wanted to do was make speeches, raise his profile, and cement his status as a darling of the hard right, he could have looked to New York City. There, in the summer of 1965, William F. Buckley, Jr., had announced his intention to run for mayor in the November elections on a conservative party line. It was, self-evidently, a fruitless task. But winning was not the point for Buckley. "Do you really want to be mayor?" a reporter asked the *National Review* editor as he announced his campaign. "I've never considered it," Buckley replied. Elsewhere, he admitted that for a conservative candidate to win in New York City would take "a miracle." But, the devout Catholic added, "I happen to believe in miracles." Buckley's platform, *The New York Times* noted, included "a ban on mid-day truck deliveries; the sale of narcotics to adult addicts who submit to a doctor's care; the abolition of rent controls; a constitutional amendment, if necessary, to permit school prayers; separate schools for laggard students and city clean-up work for those on relief." He would entertain, he would provoke, he would draw attention to movement principles. He would hopefully win some converts. And then he would go home. It was, in a sense, a mannerist, erudite updating of the Goldwater effort: winning was not the point of his campaign. His campaign was the point of his campaign.

Once, Reagan, too, had sought nothing more than to win converts to the true faith. No longer. His break with the hard-line conservatives had its awkward moments. When a reporter asked him if he was a candidate in the Goldwater mode, he grew uncomfortable. "I don't think it's very pertinent," he said. "This is the present and the future now, and the problems of California." It was awkward with his friend Goldwater, too. "I have received some kick-back," he wrote to Barry during the campaign, "and in checking it out, discovered some of my remarks were quoted by the press as indicating you might be unwelcome in California. This, of course, I'm sure you know is untrue, but just for the record, I tried to keep my answer to the question regarding your possible participating in line with your own remarks on this subject, namely that the forthcoming primary was a California affair between California Republicans and their candidates, and that you had expressed yourself as believing it would be improper for anyone from another state to intervene." This was a weak excuse for keeping the Republican Party's most recent presidential nominee out of the state, and Reagan knew it. "Nancy sends her best. Please give Peggy a kiss from both of us, and I hope we'll be seeing you soon."

Movement conservatives could see what Reagan was doing. They knew that by distancing himself from the movement's touchstones, he was conceding the moderates' point about conservatism being toxic. But for the most part, they didn't complain about his abandonment of movement principles. They had heard him speak and they knew he was one of them. And they wanted a winner, too. Writing in the movement journal *Human Events,* the conservative pamphleteer Lee Edwards mentioned the long list of moderates that

Reagan's consultants had represented. "Spencer Roberts does not handle any Democrats, but quite obviously does service a wide variety of Republicans. However, *all* Republicans are agreed that the firm is first in political management in California."

Reagan's early adjustment to the candidate's life was not flawless. He struggled with the gripping and grinning that fill any politician's days. From a speaker's rostrum, he could form an instant connection with his audiences, but when he walked into a roomful of strangers, he was sometimes shy and tended to keep to himself. He prided himself on appearing always decent and respectful. He was repulsed by the politician's "Hey there! I'd appreciate your vote!" Plus, he was Ronald Reagan, the star—he wanted people to come to him.

Eventually he learned to introduce himself, reverting to his standard routine of friendly comments and silly jokes. His preference was always to keep things as light as possible. Supporters who tried to engage him on substance were disappointed. "I think he should have been briefed on the people he was talking to," one potential donor wrote to Bill Roberts. "Admittedly, we were a rather unimportant group, but the magnitude of his impression would have been much greater had he had even the slightest idea who we were and why we were there."

It was clear, too, that he had little passion for the parochial issues that are the bread and butter of any governor's race. "If he can zero in on California as he has done [on] the national and international problems," one supporter tactfully observed to Stuart Spencer, "we should have a winner." His benefactors were less circumspect. At a meeting at his house in late November, the donor Henry Salvatori expressed concern that Reagan's candidacy lacked sufficient substance. W. S. McBirnie, a right-wing radio host, was present at the meeting. "I think Henry tried to say that he had no criticism of *you*," he told Reagan afterward, "but he was waiting for a definite *program* which would stamp you as electable."

Reagan tried to do the work required. Spencer and Roberts hired

BASICO, a team of behavioral scientists, to help Reagan flesh out his positions on local issues. BASICO developed a file system for candidate Reagan with index cards containing digestible bits of information on a variety of issues. With his photographic memory, he crammed facts and figures to develop positions on water policy and early childhood education. But his heart wasn't in it. "Damn," he exclaimed to BASICO co-founder Stanley Plog, "wouldn't this be fun if we were running for the presidency."

So, to solve the problem, they started to act as if they were. They nationalized the governor's race. After the November 1965 meeting at Reagan's home, McBirnie proposed "a positive direction" for Reagan's campaign. "Almost every successful candidate of any historic importance in modern times has offered a positive program, packaged in some kind of slogan or neat description: New Deal, Fair Deal, New Frontier, Great Society, New Order, etc. Why not try: 'The Creative Society.' "

Stu Spencer saw the opportunity right away. "The Great Society," he later explained, "which was Lyndon Johnson's, was going on at the time. Everybody liked it conceptually, but it didn't work out. We were taking advantage of the society aspect, not the great."

They would offer an alternative to the Johnsonian vision, on Johnson's own terms. The goals were the same: a better country, a fuller, more meaningful life. So was the basic assumption: that a magnificent future was possible, that soon Americans could master their own fate. The difference was in the means of doing it. "You could base it upon the firm belief that there exists within this state the resources," McBirnie advised, "to solve any problem—without the growth of bureaucracy. But to release this tremendous latent, creative power, more citizens must be *led* by the 'Creative Society' type of government to organize in volunteer associations to deal directly with these problems."

And so Reagan was unleashed to do what he loved—to tell a story about the threat facing the country under its current president, and the way that *he* would stop it. As 1965 came to a close, the voters who, a year earlier, had thrilled to Johnson's message in the aftermath of his landslide election—"These are the most hopeful times in all the years since Christ was born in Bethlehem"—were rapidly giving up faith in the president's promises. Offering his alternative vision, Reagan told the voters of California they didn't need to give up their hope, they just had to look for it to be delivered in another form. "We must show the voters," he told an audience, "that major issues cross party lines. Almost half of them have grown up under a planned society leaning toward a socialist system. We must match dreams of utopia with the hard facts of actuality, and show them that a free economy is far more attractive than the deadly dullness of a planned society."

ONE MAJOR PROBLEM remained for Reagan as he sought to prove that he could be a serious candidate. It was the most basic: What was a B-movie actor doing trying to run the country's largest state? In many press accounts from 1965 and early 1966, the idea that Reagan could fancy himself a candidate for high office played as a bad joke. "The idea of an actor named Ronald Reagan becoming the next governor of America's largest state evokes a political vision approximately as radiant as a nomination of Rock Hudson to be the next Secretary of State," Emmet John Hughes wrote in *Newsweek*. *The Saturday Evening Post* quoted an anonymous Reagan rival: "Sure he's drawing the crowds . . . so would Jayne Mansfield."

In Sacramento, Pat Brown acted as though he barely knew who Ronald Reagan was. He'd seen the actor only once onscreen, he said. "It was on the late show," Brown recalled. "He played a sheriff. . . . He was a very attractive sheriff. He was shot in the end, though." (Watching Brown's remarks, Reagan pointed at the screen: "In the back. I was shot in the back.")

Reagan's "actor problem" came with two dangerous prongs. First, it invited the notion of Reagan as an intellectual lightweight. A bad day on the campaign trail inevitably ended with this conclusion. "Ronald Reagan," wrote one critic in January 1965, "who recently announced he was seeking the Republican nomination for governor of California, proved he might be able to portray a politician, as an actor, but also that every actor needs a good script—which he did not have when he faced several newsmen Sunday on . . . 'Meet the Press.'"

The second, more dangerous concern was that Reagan was acting out the part of politician too well. "He is assiduously playing the role of a political figure up and down the State of California," *The Fresno Bee* worried in the summer of 1965. The paper compared Reagan's performance as a politician to Raymond Massey playing a doctor on television. "What happens when an actor simulates a role so well he is called upon to perform it off stage in real life? Then you have Raymond Massey actually attempting an appendectomy or Ronald Reagan actually making crucial decisions of government. Frightening thoughts."

Attacking the "actor problem" became a central focus of the campaign. Humor was a first line of defense. The candidate had any number of canned jokes at the ready. He would tell crowds that his son Ron Jr. thought his father, the *Death Valley Days* star, should "just go up to Sacramento, stand in the street and call out to the governor, 'Pat, one of us has to be out of town by sundown.'" Or he'd try to beat those who questioned his qualifications to the punch: "I've never played a governor." Or he'd joke that the concerns about his background signaled progress: "Only a generation ago, people in my profession couldn't be buried in a churchyard."

After a life spent trying to get onto Hollywood's A list, he suddenly found himself scrambling to get off. In campaign materials, he was listed not as an actor but as "an actor-rancher." A campaign résumé made the most of his non-Hollywood professional life. It was thin gruel. Entries included "Operates horse breeding and cattle ranch" and "Member Board of Directors International Holding Company & Coast Life Insurance Company." His Midwestern radio career merited two separate entries. These billowed with extraneous nouns in a manner familiar to job applicants in their early twenties:

"Radio sports announcer and editor—Central Broadcasting Company" and "Broadcast Chicago Cubs & White Sox home games, Big Ten and Notre Dame Football." At *GE Theater,* he had been not just host or actor but "Production Supervisor." Meanwhile, a single entry in the middle—"Motion Pictures, Warner Bros., Universal and free-lance. Appeared in 50 featured pictures"—encapsulated his entire movie career.

As a last defense, the campaign actually made the case for actors. For help in the cause, they enlisted no less a figure than John Wayne, who put on his cowboy costume to cut a Reagan ad. "So what's this empty nonsense about Ronald Reagan being just an actor?" asked Wayne, standing in front of a desert backdrop. "I've watched Ronald work his entire adult life preparing for public service." Reagan was no lightweight, the ad suggested. Anyone arguing otherwise would have to talk to the Duke.

Still, the actor attacks stung Reagan. It had been more than twenty years since the brief moment he'd been a hot-ticket movie star. In several of those years, he'd struggled to make a living as an actor at all. But to listen to his critics, he'd been a matinee idol all along. "I'll probably be the only fellow who will get an Oscar posthumously," he joked, only half concealing his bitterness. He would grow testy at the suggestion he was just looking for another stage. "There are no jobs in politics," he wrote to one critical newspaper editor, "that offer comparable rewards to those obtainable in show business."

But that was the biggest problem Reagan faced when fighting the actor charge. The rewards of the job—the job itself—*were* similar to being a Hollywood star. Certainly there was plenty of Hollywood staging. In January 1966, when he finally made his campaign official, he announced it in a highly produced television special taped in the same studio as *Death Valley Days.* Hours before the telecast, the campaign held a premiere for two hundred reporters in the Pacific Ballroom of the Statler Hilton in Los Angeles. "Roll it," Bill Roberts ordered, and the broadcast began to play on a movie screen. In the program, Reagan appeared on a set made to look like a comfortable upper-middle-class living room, complete with books, framed pictures, and a roaring fire. He moved effortlessly around the set as he spoke.

> California also leads in some things that unfortunately give us no sense of pride. The only thing that's gone up more than spending is crime. Our city streets are jungle paths after dark.

As he spoke, he tilted his head down, strolling slowly but purposefully toward the other end of the room, as though this carefully coded racial imagery had just now popped into his head.

And the greatest reward of a campaign was the same as the greatest reward of the movie business: he got to be the star. Often, a powerful man who starts a second career in politics chafes when the professionals try to handle him. He is accustomed to being the boss in all areas of his life. Indeed, he has been the boss for such a long time that he has come to think of it as his natural state. But a candidate has so many places to go, so many performances to give, he must hand over large areas of his life to other people. He struggles with one of politics' most basic truths: to win, you must surrender control—first to the handlers, then to events, and eventually to the voters.

For Reagan, this was nothing new. He didn't expect to be the one deciding which donors to woo or which cities to speak in any more than he'd expected to write a script or set up a shot or handle negotiations for his next contract. A movie actor learns early on that he cannot take care of everything. Too much worry, too many sleepless nights, too many stressful details—it will all show up on his face, the face he needs to be perfect for the camera, and the world. He didn't want or need control. He just needed to be the star. And in a campaign—where his name appeared on every piece of paper, where his photo could be seen on thousands of brochures and flyers—he was the biggest star around.

Reagan's advisers quickly understood the parallel. Spencer found it easiest to explain the structure of a campaign to Reagan in show business analogies. "I would say, 'This is like a stage play in New York and then we'll take it out of town. We're going to go out of town to Visalia and to all these little burgs up in Northern California and try out your act. If you screw up, only a small number of people will see it, and if it's good, we can keep it.'"

At times, indeed, Reagan's campaign organization looked like a giant fan club for the movie star candidate and his beautiful wife, Nancy, who was his costar in every respect. In meetings with advisers she would mostly stay quiet on policy. "She'd say something every now and then," Spencer was to recall, "and he'd look at her and say, 'Hey, Mommy, that's my role.'" But Reagan's advisers came to see that Nancy was no shrinking violet. Her instincts on matters of personnel and strategy, it turned out, were superior to her husband's. "She thinks very well politically," Spencer observed. "She thinks much more politically than he thinks."

The campaign built a kind of cult around the Reagans. Campaign materials showed Ronnie and Nancy feeding their horses and posing for pictures with their children, Patti and Ron Jr. Nancy, a campaign brochure noted, was "the daughter of one of the world's great neurosurgeons" who "shared the stimulating association of the scientific world. As a pretty and popular debutante, she enjoyed the fun of campus life, attending exclusive Girls Latin School and graduating from Smith as a theater arts major."

Young female supporters were encouraged to be "Reagan Girls," lithe young hostesses at campaign events. "Reagan Girls represent the young, wholesome, vivacious, natural, all-American girl," a flyer for the position advised. Their uniforms—"selected by Mrs. Ronald Reagan" and available only in waist sizes under twenty-five inches— were to be kept immaculate at all times. "A clean and neat appearance is a must," the Reagan Girls were warned. "Giving out of phone numbers and addresses, and making dates are not permitted during appearances."

Just as he had in his movie career, Reagan allowed his campaign publicists to take liberties with the details of their star's biography. The résumé that Reagan's campaign distributed noted that he had been named Father of the Year for the motion picture industry by the National Fathers Day Committee in 1957. Meanwhile, a line in the "Personal History" section noted that he was "Married to Nancy Davis Mar. 4, 1952. Daughter, Patricia, and son, Ronald." The two children from the Father of the Year's first marriage were left unmentioned.

Most likely, this was not a clerical error. California Republicans had fresh memories of the Rockefeller-Goldwater drama, with its complicated marital subplots. Reagan's advisers were loath to draw excessive attention to their candidate's two marriages. And a complicated personal life only exacerbated the frivolous Hollywood idol problem. So Reagan's campaign, with the implicit approval of Ronald and Nancy, mostly expunged his first marriage and his first family from the record. It was a brutal excision, even by the standards of 1966. It was particularly hard on Reagan's elder daughter, Maureen, who was an enthusiastic Republican and who longed to be close to her father's campaign, and close to her father. Unwilling to blame him for her banishment, she fixed her fury on Spencer-Roberts. After a pitched battle, she was offered a chance to introduce her father to a conservative group of which she was a member. Her feeling of triumph ended when she was handed the introduction the campaign had prepared for her to deliver: "Ronald Reagan and his wife Nancy have two children, Patti and Ronnie."

In the end, it was impossible to fight the actor problem. All of Reagan's advantages as a candidate were completely tied up in the fact that he had been an actor. In time, Reagan's campaign found that here, too, they could make a virtue of his defect. As 1966 dawned, it was clear that politicians were failing, in California and the country. Lyndon Johnson was thought to be among the greatest politicians of his generation, and look what *that* had gotten America. Maybe it was a *good* thing that Reagan had no experience in the political realm. The problem with California politics, Reagan started to argue, was that it had been hijacked by career politicians like Pat Brown. As he traveled, he began to emphasize the distinction, describing himself as a "citizen-politician." He was, he said, "an ordinary citizen with a deep-seated belief that much of what troubles us has been brought about by politicians, and it's high time more ordinary citizens brought the fresh air of common sense thinking to bear on these problems."

In making the "citizen-politician" case, they were helped by an unlikely source: Reagan's ongoing Hollywood career. In the first year of his campaign, 1965, when he had still not officially entered the race, he continued to appear as both host of and a player on *Death Valley Days*. After officially announcing his candidacy in early 1966, he could no longer appear as host in California, but he continued to appear as an actor in pretaped episodes of the program.

The show turned out to be a political plus. Sure, there were awkward moments, like the ads he was contractually obliged to cut for Boraxo, the show's sponsor. "Here's Boraxo waterless hand cleaner," chirped a tan Reagan, wearing a grandfatherly peach cardigan in one of the commercials. "New Boraxo waterless hand cleaner removes the toughest dirt or stains!" But the actual programming on *Death Valley Days* usually fit the Reagan campaign message perfectly. The program featured weekly teleplays, stories of daring and heroism from the real-life history of the Old West. Often, the heroes were a classic Western type—the decent, soft-spoken man who reluctantly answers the call of duty to stand up for justice in the rough frontier. As a consequence, the characters Reagan played on television seemed to speak roughly the same words as the character he was playing in the campaign.

In one episode he played the nineteenth-century senator George Vest. "I'm a citizen first," Vest explains early in the episode. "And a candidate after that."

Here, cut to an ad from Reagan's campaign, showing the candidate in a crowded banquet hall, addressing the crowd:

I don't believe that just holding public office is the only way by which you can get experience for public office. If we are to place political experience as the only criteria [*sic*] for making our decision, we have in Sacramento men with eight years political experience and I think that's what's wrong with California.

In another episode, he played the naval hero David Farragut. As the teleplay begins, Reagan's Farragut, commanding a U.S. Navy ship in San Francisco Bay, has grown disillusioned with the captain's life. "I've made a decision," Farragut informs his wife. "I'm going to buy as much land in California as we can afford. And when Commodore Mervine gets back from Panama, I'm going to hand in my resignation, effective immediately."

"David," replies his worried wife, "the Navy is your heart and soul. To start all over again way out here in the West!"

Farragut is not deterred. "Everyone in the West is starting new."

Another flash, from Reagan's telecast announcing his candidacy for governor:

People have been coming to this place and to this way of life for a hundred years. . . . Even when we've been here thirty years, as I have, we still refer to ourselves as being "from" some place. We're "from" Illinois or Iowa. Kansas, Ohio, New Jersey. But we're here to stay. And our children are native born Californians. And California's problems are our problems.

Even as he dreams of retirement, Farragut receives word that San Francisco has been overrun by an unruly vigilante mob that is threatening to destroy civil government in California. He reluctantly puts aside his plans to retire to the land. Coming ashore, he discovers that the city fathers have grown corrupt and weak and are unable and unwilling to maintain order while the mob takes free rein.

Another flash: Candidate Reagan at the San Francisco Cow Palace in 1966, preaching about a favorite campaign issue, the student unrest at the University of California, Berkeley, and the incompetent administration of the university:

> You have read about the report of the Senate Subcommittee on Un-American Activities—its charges that the campus has become a rallying point for Communists and a center of sexual misconduct. . . . How could this happen on the campus of a great University? It happened because those responsible abdicated their responsibilities.

With no one else willing to do what is necessary, it falls to Farragut to subdue the bad guys. And he does it, confidently, by threatening force. The unruly crowd disperses. "That's the way you lose a mob," he explains to their ringleader. "One man comes to his senses. Then two. Then a dozen. Then a hundred."

Reagan couldn't have put it better himself. And that, in the end, was why Reagan's "actor problem" was really no problem at all. Show business had taught him how to relate to the voters as a politician. And it had taught the voters how to see him as a politician, too.

At first the press missed it. In March 1966, it seemed that Reagan might have torpedoed his campaign when he appeared with his primary opponent, George Christopher, before the National Negro Republican Assembly. Highlighting Reagan's opposition to the 1964 Civil Rights Act, Christopher tried to paint Reagan as a Goldwater clone. Goldwater's position on the bill, Christopher said, "did more harm than anything to the Republican Party . . . Unless we cast out this image, we're going to suffer defeat."

At that Reagan shot up. "I resent the implication that there is any bigotry in my nature," he insisted. "Don't anyone ever imply I lack integrity!"

He was yelling. He continued:

"I will not stand silent and let anyone imply that—in this or any other group!"

He was walking out the door.

There it was. The unity candidate, the mainstream Republican who had promised to build bridges and work with anyone and everyone in his party, had dutifully gone to meet with a bunch of black Republicans—and had stormed out of the room. He knew right away that he'd made a disastrous, amateurish mistake. Political reporters wondered if he'd killed his chances. In the *Los Angeles Times,* a cartoon recalled the title of Reagan's memoir when it depicted Reagan with his head cut off with the caption: "I'm looking for the rest of me." Pat Brown, watching, was convinced that Christopher would be the tougher opponent in the general election, and most likely the opponent he'd face.

He was wrong. In June 1966, Reagan defeated Christopher in the primary by a far larger than expected margin of 700,000 votes. In the end, the voters just didn't buy the idea that Ronald Reagan was a hothead extremist. They *knew* Ronald Reagan, and that wasn't the Reagan they knew. "We did some studies through the ad agency, Hixson and Jorgenson," Spencer later said. "He had an approval rating with women in 1965 of 93 percent. . . . That was purely based on the roles he played in the movies, the nice guy versus the bad guy. He never played the bad guy."

The conventions of show business were all working in Reagan's favor. His surprising margin of victory had given him juice. This would be a surprise twist. Adding to the effect, Brown had been through a nasty, divisive Democratic primary against Sam Yorty, the conservative Democratic mayor of Los Angeles. Brown had squeaked by with only 52 percent of the vote.

Suddenly, there was a great national story coming out of California. A Universal Newsreel summed it up:

ANNOUNCER: In California, actor Ronald Reagan and Mrs. Reagan arrive to cast their votes in the state's primary election. He's the Republican nominee for governor, it's his first political contest.

Watch as a pair of sun-dappled Reagans walk hand in hand to their polling place and enter side-by-side curtained voting booths. Moments later, they each pull back their curtain at the same moment and look at each other lovingly, breezily evoking the fun, twin-bed sexuality of the Production Code.

ANNOUNCER: Reagan's Democratic opponent in November will be Governor Edmund Brown, who's trying to become California's first three-term Democratic governor. Experts now rate him as the underdog.

In a parallel scene, the Browns walk into their polling place. Mrs. Brown is holding her handbag, not her husband. Goaded by photographers, the Browns stand outside their voting booth, not knowing what to do. Finally, the governor awkwardly shakes Mrs. Brown's hand.

ANNOUNCER: November's showdown election between Reagan and Brown may well forecast an exciting '68 presidential fight.

PAT BROWN WAS on the phone from California.

"Are you feeling all right?" President Johnson asked.

"I never felt better in my life and had less," Brown said. "Between you and me."

This was not what the president wanted to hear. Brown was underconfident, far removed from the governor who had showered praises on Johnson after his landslide election two years before. It was June 1966, a week since the California primary. "President Eisenhower and [Republican Party chair] Ray Bliss have already begun to call liberal Republicans . . . to put the heat on them," Joe Califano had informed the president in a memo. "Brown is very nervous about the election, is running scared and thinks he will lose many of the votes that Yorty got in the campaign." The day before, Johnson had watched on television as Yorty continued to criticize the governor, making it quite clear there would be no happy Democratic unity any time soon. Brown was saying that a race against Reagan would be his toughest as governor.

Now Johnson urged him to buck up.

"You're selling everybody on the fact that you can't win!" he said. "And I'm against that kind of stuff coming out of California. I think we gotta get the tail up, get bushy tailed, and high behind, and chin up and let's go . . . I think that we've just got to quit thinking about the possibility that they could beat us, because they can't. You've got a good administration, you've got the best state in the Union, you're way out in front and the people know it."

It sounded as though he was trying to convince himself—and as though he was talking about more than just the troubles of Pat Brown. "California is the most populous state in the Union," the *San Diego Union* would observe the next day, "and a Republican victory in November would most certainly signal the beginning of the end of the political extravagances of the Great Society."

Johnson wasn't about to let Reagan do that to him. "We've just got to go after him," he scolded. "And . . . put him right where he belongs: with Goldwater around his neck."

Brown agreed. "I spent all day Sunday reviewing Mr. Reagan's record. And this fellow is a part of the kook crowd in the United States! He's to the right of Goldwater!"

"No question about that," said the president. "He's got a better television personality and he's more effective. But he's more dangerous."

They were making themselves feel better. But the president and the governor were already several steps behind Reagan and the press. As Johnson and Brown spoke, Reagan was headed back to the East Coast. There he would continue his I'm-Not-Goldwater campaign, jumping toward the middle in the most ostentatious fashion possible. Later that week, he'd head to Gettysburg to receive formally the establishment blessing from Eisenhower. Unlike Goldwater's wretched and desperate performance with the general late in the

1964 campaign, this visit would produce great pictures. "Here in a brick house on a shaded lawn," a *Washington Post* correspondent wrote from Gettysburg, "he humbly paid his respects to Gen. Eisenhower, respectfully listened and eagerly posed for photographs with him."

Reagan continued the theme the next day in Washington, where he addressed a crowd at the National Press Club that included many leading lights of the Eastern media, coming to scout the new talent. He was eager to show that he was no radical. "I've never advocated selling the Post Office or abolishing Social Security," he said. "Nor do I believe in some conspiracy theory that all who favor increased government planning and control are engaged in a devious plot."

It worked like a charm. "Right-winger," the columnist William S. White observed, was "far too strong" a term for Reagan after Gettysburg. "In consequence," White wrote, "he enters what has become known as 'the mainstream of Republicanism' and cannot be symbolically dislodged from it."

Indeed, the talk in Washington that week was not whether candidate Ronald Reagan was too extreme to win the governor's race in 1966, but whether *Governor* Ronald Reagan would be his party's *presidential* nominee in 1968. At Gettysburg, Ike had said he saw nothing to prevent such a possibility if the circumstances were right. "Even a Reagan in the clothing of a right-winger," White wrote, "would have been a strong force at the 1968 Republican National Convention. In such clothing, however, his power would have been largely that of veto. In his present posture of mainstreamism that power could become something else again."

Richard Nixon, already eyeing 1968 with dogged focus, was nervous about what that something else might be. Once, Reagan had written flowery notes to Nixon offering campaign advice. Now it was Nixon gushing in a lengthy letter to Reagan after the primary. "I was unable to reach you by telephone Tuesday night and Western Union is on strike. Consequently, I must resort to the uncertain delivery schedules of the U.S. mails," Nixon wrote. Nixon knew that as governor of California, Reagan could control the state's delegation and, if he wished, scuttle Nixon's chances at the nomination. In characteristic fashion, he tried to suck up to Reagan by speaking what he thought was Reagan's language. "As I am sure you know the assault on you will reach massive proportions in the press and on TV as Brown and his cohorts realize that they are going to be thrown off the gravy train after eight pretty lush years. There is an old Mid-Western expression (my roots also are in the Mid-West) which I would urge you to bear in mind as the going gets tougher. 'Just sit tight in the buggy!'"

Reagan's response to the former vice president might as well have been a form letter: "I won't try to write much of a letter since we'll be seeing each other on the 23rd, but I want you to know how much I appreciated hearing from you and how grateful I am for your very good suggestions."

Reagan knew it was bad politics to indulge the presidential chatter. With the press, the citizen-politician made sure, as always, to keep his ambitions hidden. "It has taken me all of my life to get up the nerve to do what I am now doing," he answered when asked about the '68 talk. "I just feel there are problems I'd like to clean up in California. That's as far as my dreams go."

But it was plain from listening to him in Washington that June of 1966 that his dreams went much further. At the Press Club, he offered his most explicit attacks on Johnson yet. "The Great Society grows greater every day," he said. "Greater in cost, greater in inefficiency and greater in waste."

Summer had arrived. The images from Vietnam were awful. The cities were more on edge than they had been in either of the summers before. Reagan looked toward November and then beyond. Timing and shifting public tastes—the forces he revered most—at last were on his side. He was fifty-five years old. For the first time in a long time, he looked like a winner.

Another land-
slide: The
Reagans cele-
brate victory in
the California
governor's race,
November 8,
1966.
*Courtesy Ronald
Reagan Library*

Johnson in the Oval
Office in early 1966.
The 1966 election
brought an end to
the grand ambitions
of the Johnson
presidency.
*© Yoichi Okamoto/
LBJ Library*

CHAPTER ELEVEN

A Thousand Days

August–December 1966

Wednesday, August 17, 1966, was Lyndon Johnson's thousandth day as president of the United States. The administration did not acknowledge the occasion publicly, but inside the White House the date loomed large. To mark the event, Johnson aide Robert Kintner asked each member of the cabinet to write a lengthy summary of what his department had accomplished in the course of the thousand days. He arranged these summaries into a formally divided book and presented it to Johnson on the evening of the seventeenth. He knew to tread carefully. "While this period constitutes a thousand days," Kintner wrote in a memo to the president, "I would doubt if this title should ever be used in any public way because of the connotation re President Kennedy."

A thousand days later, it was still the same story: Johnson people horrified at the thought of public comparison to the Kennedys. Johnson people privately obsessing over how they measured up against the Kennedys all the same.

On paper, it was not even close. By any standard of material accomplishment, Johnson's tenure in office through August 17, 1966, far outshone his predecessor's gilded thousand days. Kennedy had won the presidency by the tiniest of margins, with heavy debts to the unsightly practices of urban Democratic machines. Johnson had won with the largest popular margin of any president in history,

with support that cut across age and ethnic groups, geographic regions, and even political parties. Kennedy had struggled to get even
trivial legislation out of the Congress. Johnson had amassed a string
of legislative successes that rivaled the glorious domestic record of
FDR's first term. Kennedy had dithered and dragged his heels on
civil rights; he had at times scorned the movement's activists as a
distracting nuisance and had died without any major legislative accomplishment in the fight against state-sanctioned segregation.
Johnson had committed his presidency to the cause of racial equality, had embraced the movement for racial justice in dramatic fashion on a national stage, and had won more rights for black Americans
than any other president since Lincoln. Kennedy had spoken in inspiring tones about teaching the young, healing the sick, feeding the
poor. Johnson had passed programs to see that it was done.

Yet Kennedy belonged to the angels, while Johnson was sinking
on earth. No one seemed inclined to make the case for his greatness.
He wanted the Eighty-Ninth Congress—the Congress he had ushered in with his 1964 landslide, the Congress he had dominated like
no president had before or since—to be known as "the Great Congress." Historians would in time come to view the Eighty-Ninth
Congress as perhaps the most productive legislative session in American history, and for later generations of progressives, the Congress
that produced the Voting Rights Act, Medicare, and so many other
programs would come to seem the greatest Congress of all time. But
in the fall of 1966, as chaos engulfed the nation's cities and the war
in Vietnam raged, the Eighty-Ninth Congress was deeply unpopular.
Even the liberal commentators who shared its goals were qualified in
their assessments. The "B plus Congress," *The New Republic* called
it, "not excellent, better than fair, very good." The journal *The Progressive* concurred: "We prefer to call it the foot in the door Congress, because so many of the laws it passed represent a significant if
modest effort to cross a threshold of social welfare legislation."

Johnson faced the reverse fortune of his predecessor. At the end
of his thousand days, Kennedy became instantly greater than his ac-

complishments. Johnson, at the end of his thousand days, was somehow less.

To the Johnson loyalists, this revealed the same old double standard. He was being measured against a man that the Kennedy family and the Eastern media had conspired to make a saint. It was unfair, they protested, and some in the press were inclined to agree. In *The New York Times Magazine,* the presidential scholar Thomas A. Bailey wrote a long essay on Johnson's thousand days, arguing that Johnson's substantive accomplishments in the period were remarkable. Still, he said, "Historians in future decades will probably rate Kennedy somewhat above and Johnson somewhat below their deserts. History is written by intellectuals, and Kennedy's style, crowned by mysterious martyrdom, has an irresistible appeal."

If Johnson was being overshadowed by the enduring power of the Kennedy myth, though, he had himself to blame. He had, after all, accepted the terms of that myth in the earliest hours of his presidency. That was the deal he had struck: he would encourage the myth of Kennedy the martyr so that he could be the martyr's redeemer. *That way Kennedy would live on forever, and so would I.* He had seen his country searching for a story to believe in, and, seizing a moment of opportunity in the chaotic aftermath of the assassination, he had promised it the grandest story of all.

A myth's allure and authority depend on its power to explain the mysteries of the world. In some cases, this power is self-sustaining: the story of Helios driving his sun chariot across the heavens can endure through the centuries as it literally illuminates the visible world every single day. But most myths lack this certainty. Indeed, myths are often born when certainty is most absent. In a parched land, a man who offers a story to explain the drought makes good use of people's anxiety. They feel powerless and ignorant. Why have the gods forsaken them, when will they be delivered? In comes the would-be mythmaker to offer the people assurance. Some unseen mystical force, he explains, is the cause of their suffering. He offers the steps they can take to make it end. And as the days go by and the ground grows harder, the mythmaker's power at first increases, for there are more people desperate for relief.

But if enough time goes by and the skies still do not open, the power of uncertainty starts to work against the mythmaker. The people begin to contemplate the worst possibilities—they see their lives given over to famine, their lands aflame, their livestock slaughtered, their children dying of thirst. They are more anxious than ever, and now they are angry, too, angry at the man who offered them false prophecies and grand promises. Both fear and hope depend on an uncertain future. The man who seeks to profit from uncertainty with seductive, hopeful promises is ultimately vulnerable to the ungovernable force of human terror.

So it was in America in 1966—the year that *Time* asked on its cover, "Is God Dead?" Fear about the future was not a new thing for Americans. It had been present for some time, at least as long as Lyndon Johnson had been president. Johnson had assumed the presidency as a fearful nation faced the greatest uncertainty in the awful hours after the death of President Kennedy. How would they make their way forward in a rapidly changing world without their vital young leader in the White House? Johnson, desperate to start a new story, had taken advantage of that anxiety, and that unknown future, to craft his original mythic vision: the nation would have nothing to fear from the future, as long as it followed him.

And the nation did follow him as he set about passing his program of liberal dreams. Americans embraced their active, ambitious president and convinced themselves that the transformative future would be something great. Only rarely did people acknowledge the lingering anxiety that had been pushed to the edge of consciousness but not eradicated. "That's what's the matter now," said James Chaney, "everybody's scared." Johnson had been far more scared than he'd ever let on. But he had not acknowledged the fear, neither the nation's nor his own, and he had offered no wisdom on how to live with it as his Democratic predecessors, Roosevelt and Kennedy, had done. Instead, he had tried to root fear out, promising an end to all worry straightaway. "It's the time of peace on Earth and good will among men," he said the week before his landslide. "The place is here and the time is now!"

The people had wanted to believe he was right, even though, deep down, they suspected he was not. So the uncertainty persisted and spread, and with it, of course, the fear. And in the months and years that followed Johnson's grand proclamations, tension over what the future might bring continued to accrue. By the latter half of 1966, that tension was impossible to ignore. Fear itself became a subject of national concern. "Disunity, frustration, suspicion and fear permeate the nation," *The Saturday Evening Post* editorialized that fall. "It seems as if an air of unreality is settling over us all. For, very clearly, things are not what they had seemed two years ago."

Suddenly, Lyndon Johnson was the man who had promised the rain that did not come. The country could not believe his story any longer. There was simply too much reality for which he could not account. He was on the unfavorable end of the comparison that every sitting politician must face: between what he had once promised and what had actually come to pass. And, thanks to his mythic ambitions, Johnson was held responsible for an even broader deficit, one he had little ability to address: the gap between the way things had once seemed and the way they now were.

Once, standing in front of that enormous White House Christmas tree, Johnson had declared his moment in history was "the most hopeful . . . since Christ was born in Bethlehem." Now he was living in a country where everything was filtered through the possibility of coming catastrophe. *The New Republic* captured the mood well that fall: "You have a home, but what about interest rates? You live in a fairly orderly community, but how about the riots nearby, or a thousand miles away?"

Once, Johnson had declared war on poverty and had promised "we shall not rest until that war is won." Now riots in the worst neighborhoods of the nation's cities had revealed people living in conditions irreconcilable with America's early-sixties self-image as a land of unprecedented affluence and opportunity. The conditions in the cities were not in fact much worse than they had been three years earlier, when Kennedy was president, but three years earlier, the collapsing urban centers hadn't been on television every night. Now they were, and as a result, a thousand days after Johnson had launched his poverty efforts, it seemed that poverty in America had actually gotten worse.

Once, the press had published sensational stories, wondering about a psychotic madness festering in the nation, ready to strike at random, God knows when. Now, it seemed, the madmen had arrived. Late that summer of 1966 at the University of Texas at Austin, Charles Joseph Whitman, a twenty-five-year-old architectural engineering student, climbed to the observation deck of a three-hundred-foot limestone tower overlooking the university. From his perch, he shot indiscriminately at the busy crowds below. During the tower assault, he struck forty-four people, killing fourteen. Earlier that day, Whitman had purchased ammunition at a local hardware store. What did he need the bullets for? the clerk asked. "To shoot some pigs," the killer replied.

Once, white "backlash" against policies that benefited minorities had been something the press and the pollsters warned about, but it was a phenomenon that had failed to show up on Election Day. Now, with astonishing speed, that backlash had become the country's dominant political force. In a survey in 1966, two out of three Americans would say that the cause of racial equality was being pushed "too fast" in America.

That summer, the Congress considered another Johnson administration–backed civil rights bill, this one attacking the issue of housing discrimination. As was his custom on these matters, the eighty-three-year-old Virginia segregationist Howard Smith had spoken against the bill in the House. "Now we come here with mobs in the streets," the Virginian warned, "with further mob violence threatened, and no word is spoken of courage to defend the American way of Government." When he'd finished speaking, his colleagues in the House gave him a standing ovation. On the Senate side, the Republican leader Everett Dirksen, who had broken the dam for Johnson's first civil rights bill, now took the opposite view of the administration on the new civil rights effort.

Once, Democrats had hoped that the newly enfranchised blacks in the South could come together with moderate, reasonable-minded whites to begin a postracial era in Southern politics. Now white backlash was empowering the very worst kind of racists of all. In Georgia, once home to moderate white politicians like former governor Ellis Arnall, the new face of the Democratic Party was a man named Lester Maddox. Maddox, an ardent segregationist, was well known to the Northern press thanks to his operatic racism—he had chased blacks away from his Atlanta restaurant with an ax handle. Maddox, *Newsweek* observed, "had never won anything much grander than the Fourth Annual East Point, Ga. bicycle race and the chairmanships of a succession of right-wing citizens' committees he organized himself." But after defeating Arnall by seventy thousand votes in a runoff for that year's Democratic primary, Maddox was the sure favorite to be the state's next governor.

The national face of the resurgent segregationists was Alabama governor George Wallace. Prevented from seeking reelection by term limits, Wallace was backing his wife, Lurleen, in that year's Democratic primary for governor. Once, at the height of the Selma crisis, Johnson had forced Wallace to back down, prompting hopes that the governor's power in Southern politics would begin to wane. Now Wallace was looking toward a run for the presidency in 1968, offering himself up as the choice of white backlash voters, not just in the South but nationwide.

Once, Johnson had seemed to erase the distance between the nation's political leaders and the civil rights movement simply by uttering three words in the House chamber: "We shall overcome." Now Martin Luther King, Jr., was in a state of open warfare with the Democratic Party's most formidable power broker, Mayor Daley of Chicago, a city where white mobs were using physical violence to

prevent African Americans from integrating all-white neighborhoods. "They're just out here for no other purpose than to have a
race riot," Daley complained to Johnson that August about King's
protesters. He warned the president that his white constituents
would be willing to exact a price. "They put all of this on the Democratic Party. [People say] 'Oh, what the hell. If we get rid of Johnson . . . and we get rid of Daley and the whole outfit because . . .
they're not doing anything for us, and they're doing everything for
the Negro.' "

Once, presiding over the greatest boom the country had ever
known, Johnson had wondered aloud if the marvels of modern economics had made recessions a thing of the past. Now prices were
rising and people were worried about paying their bills. Economists
warned that heavy government spending on Vietnam was overheat-
ing the economy, causing inflation that would lead to a recession.
Walter Heller, architect of the Kennedy-Johnson tax cut, now returned to academic life, was arguing for the necessity of a tax hike
to cool the economy down. President Harry S Truman, to whom
Johnson had extended so many kindnesses, was setting off loud
alarm bells. "There is a matter," he said, "about which I am so deeply
concerned that I feel it has become necessary for me to speak out."
In imagining the dire effects of a tight monetary policy, he used the
one word any president dreaded most: "The result could be a serious
depression."

And, in the end, everything came back to Vietnam. Once, worries about America's involvement in that faraway land had only hov-
ered somewhere in the ether. Now Vietnam had become the ether
itself, the awful atmosphere, touching everything. "From Vietnam,"
Bailey wrote in his essay on Johnson's thousand days, "flows a river
of woe: inflation, the price-wage pinch, mounting strikes, restric-
tions on credit, the need for increased taxes, the further drain of
gold, pressure for calling up the Reserves, dissatisfaction with the
draft, and a drumfire of world criticism, much of it from allies."

The bombing continued over North Vietnam, tonnage falling

from the sky on a scale Johnson could not have imagined when he'd commenced Operation Rolling Thunder a year and a half before. On the ground, the Army and Marines continued to sustain heavy losses. More than six thousand American men would die in Southeast Asia in 1966. Once, Johnson had suggested to a group of high school students that they could live to old age and say "I knew only peace in my time." Now young men who were contemporaries of those students were being sent off to distant jungles where they would fight, and where many of them would die.

Once, Johnson had been able to manipulate Vietnam politics effortlessly, using the conflict and the Tonkin Gulf incident to demonstrate his toughness in the 1964 campaign. Now the politics of Vietnam had become a shifting mirage. The antiwar movement was getting all the attention in the press. Angry students demonstrated against the administration at colleges and universities, and protesters were now stationed at the White House gates. But that wasn't what made Johnson worry. "Don't pay any attention to what those little shits on the campuses do," he'd said to George Ball. "The great beast is the reactionary elements in this country. Those are the people we have to fear."

He was largely right. In mid-1966, large majorities of American voters still broadly supported the war. In fact, Johnson's polling showed that a majority of those who disapproved of his handling of the war felt that he "should go all out, short of nuclear attack" in order to win it. Republican candidates shrewdly handled public opinion on Vietnam. They voiced a general frustration with Johnson's war even as they suggested that the way to end that frustration would be to fight harder. "Bomb the devil out of Haiphong Harbor!" urged Minority Leader Dirksen. President Eisenhower, who himself had been a master of talking tough and doing very little in Southeast Asia, now told reporters that the United States ought to consider any means necessary to secure victory, including the use of nuclear weapons. Richard Nixon, in the midst of a remarkable comeback as a national political figure, appointed himself a spokesman for the hard-liners. He visited South Vietnam that summer. "For the first time now," he said, "I am leaving Vietnam with confidence that it is not possible for us to lose this war from a military standpoint."

Johnson would never say it publicly, but he did not share Nixon's confidence. He wasn't sure it would ever be possible to win the war. He had not been sure for some time. And lately, it wasn't clear who was. McNamara, for so long his brilliant hawk, had started to go wobbly. What Johnson did know was that he was under tremendous pressure from the Joint Chiefs to call up the reserves. He knew that at some point he would probably give in. And he knew that if the current estimates were correct, by the next year there would be more than half a million Americans on the ground in Vietnam. And even then, Nixon and the hawks would keep telling him *Fight harder!*

At times, Johnson still indulged dreams of being the peacemaker in Vietnam. As always, his dread about the conflict there was interwoven with his hopes for the Great Society—and now with his fears and his regrets for the Great Society, too. He knew that the disturbances and exertions of the war were draining him, distracting him from focusing on the domestic program he loved so much. There were complaints coming in from all over about the Great Society—of funds that were held up, of programs that were poorly organized, of antipoverty volunteers being corralled together with nothing to do and nowhere to go. Johnson believed these were all solvable problems. And he knew that he could solve them, as long as he had the necessary time.

Once, the country might have believed in that. Now the bristly tangle of Johnson's foreign and domestic policies had made that kind of faith impossible. For three years, he had told the nation of its favored position in history. This was a country that could solve most any problem it faced. The public had listened to him; some of them had even believed him. And now they were following his prophecies to their logical end. Most Americans understood, vaguely, what their country was doing in Vietnam. What they could not understand was why such a mighty nation, in such a hopeful time, could still be stuck fighting this war. Voters, Bill Moyers told the president, "do not understand how a country of our size and power can seemingly make so little progress in Vietnam."

Everywhere Johnson looked was an unhappy reality, compounded by all the happy promises he'd made that hadn't come true. And yet, in the face of it all, he still clung to his old grand ambitions. He had even made an effort of late to rival the Kennedys in regal pageantry and pomp. In August 1966, Lyndon and Lady Bird's younger daughter, Luci Baines, had married Illinois's Patrick Nugent in an elaborate ceremony at the National Shrine of the Immaculate Conception. It was followed by a White House reception where more than seven hundred guests gawked at a three-hundred-pound, eight-foot-tall wedding cake. The press, briefed in copious detail on every aspect of the occasion, was no longer inclined to indulge the president's pretensions. The wedding was a "semimonarchical event," *Time* said disapprovingly, noting that Luci's bridegroom had "a modest background and an unchartered future" that set him apart from the "mature, professionally established, wealthy, patrician" mates typically favored by White House brides.

For the occasion, reporters were presented with glowing quotations from the beaming father and mother of the bride. The president volunteered that he was "as proud as a man can be when his youngest daughter is doing the most wonderful thing in the world: beginning a life with the man she loves." The First Lady, who'd worked tirelessly on the preparations for the wedding, was pleased as well. "The wedding day will be something beautiful to remember," she said, "and I want Luci to have it."

As always, Lady Bird's happiness carried with it a tiny suggestion of fatalism—a happy memory might come in handy some day. But this time, the fatalism was understandable and needed no explaining.

For, once, the president's approval ratings had reached as high as 80 percent. Now he had dipped below 50 in many pollsters' surveys.

Once, Lyndon Johnson had looked like a man who couldn't lose. Now, as the fall arrived and he looked toward the midterm elections, it was clear that he could.

THERE ARE FEW things less pleasant for a sitting president to contemplate than the national midterm elections that occur halfway through his term. Even when the inhabitant of the White House is well loved, his party's results in the midterm congressional races are usually disappointing. Without the president's name on the ballot, his steadfast supporters stay home. The voters most likely to turn out are the disaffected ones, looking to lodge a vote of protest. A party that has won the presidency two years earlier in a landslide will almost always lose seats at the midterm, giving back the districts the party had no business winning but had collected in the presidential year's unusual surge.

Nevertheless, the press inevitably interprets the midterm results—not just the results in Senate and House races but also in faraway gubernatorial contests and even battles for control of state legislatures—as the country offering a verdict on the person in the White House. An especially bad set of results can make a president look humbled, weakened, and vulnerable. And in presidential politics, as in all power games, the appearance of vulnerability and the fact of it are usually the same thing.

All of this creates a dilemma for a president. The midterms can have a significant impact on his ability to pass legislation, to win reelection, and to secure a favorable place in history. And yet if he actively inserts himself in the campaign—campaigning for party candidates, using the bully pulpit to remind the country of why the elections matter—he raises the stakes even more. The hacks' political columns write themselves: "The results were a particularly stunning rebuke to a president who had invested significant time and the prestige of the presidency in the results." Many presidents conclude it isn't worth the risk. Publicly, they act dimly aware that there is some sort of election coming in November. Privately, they obsess over it and demand all the intelligence they can get on what particular issues are helping or hurting particular party candidates in particular districts around the country.

Thus, for much of 1966, the public President Johnson appeared far too concerned with Vietnam and the burdens of governing at home to think about partisan politics. Meanwhile, the private Lyndon Johnson was brooding over the same thing Lyndon Johnson always thought about: whether the voters would still love him come next Election Day. "What do you think about the elections?" he had asked Dick Russell in June. "How many seats you think I'm going to lose in the House?"

"In the House?" replied Russell. "About twenty-eight."

Johnson was surprised. "Our boys say that we're going to pick up eight or ten, going to lose ten or twelve." That would mean a net loss of at most four seats.

"Well," said Russell, "I think you'll lose twenty-seven, twenty-eight seats in the House. And I don't think you're going to lose anything in the Senate."

It was significant, the difference between losing four seats and losing twenty-eight. Four seats was entirely manageable, not a bad showing for a president's party at the midterm. It might mean some diminished expectations for the next Congress, that they might get fewer bills passed in the next two years than they had in the two before. But it was survivable. Twenty-eight seats, on the other hand, would be a disaster. It would mean, effectively, losing control of the House to a revived alliance between conservative Southern Democrats and Republicans. If true, Russell's offhand prediction of a loss of twenty-eight seats would prove the end of the Great Society.

Back then, in June 1966, it just sounded like Dick Russell being Dick Russell—the tragic conscientious objector to Johnson's triumphs. Now, as summer ended, it looked as if Russell was going to be right, at least about the House. During July and August, as the cities burned and the fears rose and the war dragged on and on, Johnson had lost all control of his story. Now there was more of the kind of talk that had cropped up after Ronald Reagan's surprising primary victory in California. Reporters were talking about the November elections as a national referendum on Johnson's presidency. "This is the off-year," *Life* observed that fall, "and thus the issues . . . ought to be local, regional and variously personal. Instead, by a strange sort of political transmutation, the biggest issues looming over most of them have become singularly personalized in the tall Texas shadow of Lyndon Baines Johnson."

Johnson's aides scrambled to come up with a national strategy for the fall campaign. "John Gardner has talked to Bill Moyers and me about a problem of great concern to him," Douglass Cater wrote to the president, referring to Johnson's secretary of health, education, and welfare. "He is worried that the Administration is suffering from a feeling in the nation that the domestic program has lost its momentum. He fears that when momentum slows down, people become pre-occupied with selfish problems. He has submitted a memorandum on this, suggesting ways that you may create the spirit of a new burst of momentum that will carry the nation into the 1970s. He thinks the time is now to create a 'Spirit of 1976.'"

It was the same old Johnson message: the future is coming, and it will be beyond your wildest dreams. Yet it was hard to find anyone who truly believed in that message, even on Johnson's staff. Bill Moyers would soon leave the White House, nursing grave private doubts about the justness of the cause in Vietnam. But the president would accept no strategy that deviated from his orthodox policy. He was left to get political advice from the likes of Walt Rostow, his ultra-hard-line national security adviser. "My proposed theme is: We are on the way to solving great national and international problems; we are making great progress: let's stick together and see it through."

Meanwhile, after years of silence, Republicans were tripping over each other to make the case against Johnson's vision. The most prominent was Nixon, who had spent most of 1966 appearing on behalf of Republican candidates around the country. By Labor Day, he had visited thirty out of fifty states. The press, so certain that Nixon's political career was over after the disastrous 1962 gubernatorial loss to Pat Brown, was at first stunned and then ultimately charmed by Nixon's refusal to accept the verdict. "This stubborn, yearning man," marveled Tom Wicker, "plunging on in the loneliness of the long-distance runner, somehow is out there in front of the pack again." Older reporters could see that Nixon was following a strategy similar to the one he'd used to secure the Republican nomination in 1960—travel the country, swearing off any talk of higher office, all the while accruing debts from delegates and party organizers nationwide. On the stump in 1966, he declared himself "a dropout from the electoral college" and asked audiences to "forget about 1968 for now and concentrate on 1966."

Yet, while the broad outlines of Nixon's strategy might have been similar to his earlier effort, he understood that his party and the country had changed since 1960. His strategy would have to change, too. He could not count on the support of the Republican establishment to win the nomination; the party's moderate and liberal wings would most likely offer their support to George Romney. To overcome Romney, Nixon would need to appeal to a new, more conservative Republican majority with its roots in the South and West. He had to offer warm refuge to the white southerners fleeing Johnson's Democratic Party. That summer, Nixon traveled to the Municipal Auditorium in Birmingham to appear at a dinner for the Republican Party of Alabama. John Grenier, the party's candidate for Senate that year, saw great things in Nixon's future. Should the party select Nixon "to lead this great country from the swampland of socialism to the bright sunshine of liberty," Grenier told the crowd, "the electoral vote of Alabama would be cast for Dick Nixon." Wealthy white folks in Birmingham speaking of threats to *their* liberty: a year earlier, with the awful images of Selma's Bloody Sunday still fresh in everyone's mind, a statement like that would have been farcically ironic. Now it was the reality of American politics. And the odd sight of Richard Nixon listening earnestly while those wealthy white southerners spoke of those threats? That was a glimpse of the America to come.

Meanwhile, to Johnson's left, Bobby Kennedy was making his own audacious claims. By the fall of 1966, it seemed that the moment for Bobby's national ambitions had at last arrived. He was a ubiquitous presence on the midterm campaign trail, stumping for Democratic candidates. Traveling with a large contingent of the national press corps, he prompted ecstatic reactions from crowds. They mobbed his car and pulled at his clothing. In Columbus, Ohio, a group of young people waiting to greet him at the airport grew so enthusiastic it overturned a snow fence. Bobby, whose politics was moving further and further to the left, was becoming a symbol of progressives' distaste for Johnson. RFK MINUS LBJ IN 1972 read one sign in a Kennedy crowd. Another was more pointed: KENNEDY FOR PRESIDENT ANYTIME. Pat Brown, fighting hard for his political life against Reagan, grew increasingly irritated that summer when the aid that Johnson had promised after Reagan's primary victory failed to materialize. Brown knew how to sting Johnson. When asked by reporters if he'd appreciate a visit from the president of the United States, the governor replied, "We need help wherever we can get it, but the guy I'd really like to see come to California is Bobby Kennedy."

Bobby still had a lot to learn about being a presidential candidate. In West Virginia, the state whose primary had proven crucial for President Kennedy's campaign, Bobby announced that "there is no Kennedy who does not feel that West Virginia is his second home." A good line, until you thought about it. Bobby kept his primary home in one state (Virginia), hailed from another state (Massachusetts) where his family had its famed compound, spent sun-drenched winter holidays at another sprawling estate in a third state (Florida), and served as the junior senator from a fourth state (New York). For another patrician candidate—like Bill Scranton or Nelson Rockefeller—this kind of error would merit a fistful of mockery from the national press. But with Bobby, reporters were endlessly forgiving. *Newsweek* tsk-tsked the "unrealistically far-out school that feels Kennedy might even be contemplating a coup so grand as to displace Mr. Johnson from the ticket . . . two years hence."

From inside the Johnson White House, that possibility looked not so far out. By mid-1966, the Harris and Gallup polls both showed Bobby leading the president as a favorite for the Democratic nomination in 1968. There would be no more talk of softening tensions between the president and his former attorney general. Johnson was convinced that Bobby would be his mortal enemy for life. He even abandoned the theme of continuity in the "Kennedy-Johnson program" around which he had once shaped his presidency. When speaking of his own White House record, Johnson now talked up improvements over the performance of the "previous administration"—the administration that came to an end on November 22, 1963.

A revivified Richard Nixon, an advancing Bobby, a formal schism between the Houses Johnson and Kennedy: all of the imaginary goblins Johnson had once conjured were now real, human threats. This change had its benefits. For most of his presidency, Johnson had pretended outwardly that all was peaceful, while within he'd felt besieged. Now, at least, he didn't have to pretend anymore. The time had come to stand and fight.

For a moment, it looked as if he would. In late summer, he moved buoyantly though campaign stops in New England. The trip seemed to revive him. Soaking up the crowds, he seemed poised to start a "Give 'Em Hell, Harry" campaign against the elitists and naysayers. "This," he told one crowd, "is what every officeholder should do, to remind himself where the *power* is in this country." He hoped to campaign in all fifty states "before the leaves turn brown."

But then the post–Labor Day polls showed further slipping in his approval, and the potential for an even greater midterm disaster than previously imagined. The president resumed acting as if he was unfamiliar with the electoral calendar. In early October, as the leaves were turning, *Time* recalled Johnson's late summer promise. "Instead of fifty states," the magazine noted, "he has so far campaigned in only one."

Instead of fighting, he fled. The White House sent word that just weeks before the election, the president would depart on a seventeen-day, seven-country tour of Asia. Ostensibly, he was on a mission to sow goodwill with America's Pacific allies. At a conference in Manila with Asian heads of state, he would seek solutions to the conflict in Vietnam. But none of the leaders with any influence in the matter—those from China, the Soviet Union, and of course North Vietnam—would be present in Manila. To some observers, it seemed clear what Johnson was really doing: putting eight thousand miles between himself and the coming electoral calamity.

He kept up appearances, posing for a goodbye shot as his helicopter left the South Lawn, observing a twenty-one-gun salute and "Hail to the Chief" before departing on Air Force One from Dulles Airport. He flew west, high above his troubled country, while down below hundreds of candidates from his party struggled on through the final days of their campaigns. He did not stop until he had long since cleared the continent and reached Hawaii, the magical outer reach of his realm. And from there he voyaged farther, out of his grim world of troubles, into a fantasy.

In the Pacific, he was not an embattled politician, but the mighty leader of a mighty superpower. He commanded enormous crowds. In Honolulu, four hundred thousand people came to see the president. A two-hour layover in the tiny American Samoan island of Tutuila brought out a quarter of the island's population. In Seoul, the South Korean city protected from its northern neighbors by a formidable American army, a crowd of two million came to cheer Johnson. Their signs were worshipful: ALL HAIL TO JOHNSON, read one. WELCOME, KING OF DEMOCRACY, another. A band serenaded him with a familiar tune, "He's Got the Whole World in His Hands." At the Malacanang Palace in Manila, his hosts placed sampaguita flowers around his head. This crown, a writer for *The Progressive* noted, captured the spirit of the trip: Johnson as Caesar, "conferring with his proconsuls . . . and accepting the homage of the subject peoples."

He accepted it with relish, of course. Johnson treated the trip as an extended campaign stop, handing out his signature LBJ pens, rubbing shoulders and shaking hands until blisters formed on his hands. In the Australian capital of Canberra, he stopped his motorcade nine times for impromptu visits with onlookers. "I'm glad you're not standing for Prime Minister," exclaimed the actual inhabitant of that office, Harold Holt.

His speeches in the Pacific nations were essentially a stump speech, quite possibly the speech he would have given in the midterm campaign had the mood of the country allowed. "I have said so often," he told an audience in Sydney, "that if you want to know what our foreign policy is, look at our domestic policy." He went on to list the many gifts he had bestowed on the American people. He had brought "food for hungry people . . . jobs and good wages . . . seventy-seven million of our people are working, more than ever in history." He had guaranteed "medical care for all of our senior citizens, modern hospitalization, increased nursing training, and nursing homes for all of our elderly people." He had offered "eighteen educational measures . . . picking [up] the youngster at four years of age and carrying him through a Ph.D. in college, giving him all the education he can take." Here, for a moment, was a rare glimpse of the old Johnson, showing off his accomplishments, speaking of the better world on the horizon, the miracles soon to come.

This, perhaps, was what he really sought on his journey. Perhaps he thought that the passage of miles and the expanse of the oceans could take him not just out of his country but out of the present, back in time. Back to that moment, glorious and vanished, when he had promised everything, and people had believed.

As always, Johnson expected the looming danger to come in human form. As the troubled year 1966 wore on, a new face joined the familiar crowd of potential threats. In a confidential memo to Johnson that summer, Robert Kintner related an account from the publisher Walter Ridder of a recent meeting with Ronald Reagan. "He went in," the memo read "prepared to dislike Reagan but found him interesting, well-informed, articulate, with a political philosophy a bit left of Goldwater, but basically a strong conservative. . . . He also believes that if Reagan were elected, he would be a good and a strong candidate for the Republican nomination in 1968."

As the fall campaign took off, Johnson, reading the press along with everyone else, watched Reagan emerge as the most exciting story in American politics, the icon of resurgent Republicanism. In October, his face was featured on the cover of *Time* in a long profile titled "California: Ronald for Real." It was a glowing portrait of the leading man at work. Here was Reagan "engulfed" by adoring crowds. Women exclaimed "You're wonderful!" and men "Good luck!" Next he was performing "a stagy caricature of an ancient-sounding Pat Brown that is true to the last creaky quaver." Then he was "hunched over 3-in. by 5-in. index cards, laboriously printing capital letters with a nylon-tip pen—'my speech for the next town.'" And here he was running with a pithy summary of the "citizen-politician" theme: "Don't forget," he says, "there weren't any professional politicians when this country started."

The strategy Johnson and Brown had plotted in the early summer, to tag Reagan as the second coming of Barry Goldwater, wasn't working out so well. *Time* readers got through eighteen hundred words of the story before the name "Goldwater" even showed up. When it did, it was a chance for Reagan to express that "removed from the passions of 1964," he'd learned an important lesson: "Perhaps we needed the bloodbath. Perhaps we needed the bitterness on both sides. I think it made us all realize that we have too much in common to be separated by intolerant differences." Hang him around his neck, indeed.

None of Brown's tactics against Reagan worked, mostly because they weren't any good. He mocked the notion of a citizen-politician—

should Californians have citizen-doctors, too? What about citizen-pilots? It was sort of funny, for a minute. But it missed Reagan's true meaning, which voters instantly understood. Reagan wasn't using "citizen-politician" to emphasize the special virtues of the citizenry. He was drawing attention to the fact that there were *professional* politicians, people whose only career had been subsidized on the taxpayer dime. Brown, he said, was the worst of that bunch. And with his analogies to doctors and pilots, people with lifelong, specialized professions, Brown was conceding the point.

Even more disastrous was Brown's attempt to make use of the actor problem. He started off okay, drawing attention to the slick, overproduced qualities of Reagan's campaign. "The governor's office . . . is not a movie set with painted doors and an artificial fire in the fireplace," a Brown ad noted, bringing to mind the stage set from which Reagan had announced his gubernatorial campaign. "It's a real room. And into this room, every day, come real people—Californians—to discuss real problems with a real governor."

But then Brown's campaign took it too far. Trying to make up for its candidate's communications deficit in comparison with his opponent, the campaign ordered up a thirty-minute documentary that it broadcast on TV. The film, titled *Man v. Actor,* showed Brown addressing a group of black and white children. "I'm running against an actor," the governor told the children, "and you know who shot Lincoln, don't ya?"

These were costly, amateur mistakes, the kind a candidate makes when his opponent has gotten deep inside his head. Brown's problem was a fatal one in politics: he didn't respect the man he was losing to, and it showed. When Brown looked at Reagan he saw the ultimate phony and fraud, a man who would clearly be a disaster for the state. He felt the same way fringe conservatives had felt in the Kennedy era—that the voters had somehow allowed themselves to be duped. The conclusion served him just as poorly as it had served conservatives before. To voters, Brown looked contemptuous, suggesting that he was somehow more serious, that he knew better than they.

From Washington, the Johnson administration could see Brown flailing. Aware of how bad it would look if the Democrats lost the nation's most populous state to a candidate from the reactionary right, they sent Hubert Humphrey to California to try to help. Appearing beside Brown, Humphrey recalled some of the old, extremist Reagan's greatest hits: "Who was it," Humphrey asked, "who said, 'It is a strange paradox, with our complete tradition of individual freedom, parents being forced to educate children'? Who was it who called California's elderly citizens and children and the maimed and the handicapped receiving welfare payments 'a faceless mass waiting for handouts'?"

But it was too late. After more than a year of campaigning, Reagan had convinced Californians that he was no radical, not in personality and not in politics. To the last, establishment Democrats underestimated his ability in both realms. They thought Reagan was hoodwinking good California Democrats into supporting an anti-government orthodoxy to which they couldn't possibly subscribe. "Reagan is anti-labor, anti-Negro, anti-intellectual, anti-planning, anti-20th Century," wrote *The New Republic*. "We rather suspect Brown will take him. We can't really believe the old bogey of federal government still scares Californians."

It wasn't an old bogey, though. It was a new one. What the establishment left could not understand was that Reagan's campaign against the state was different from the paranoid Goldwater attack on the New Deal consensus. Reagan wasn't urging Californians to reject the evils of Social Security or internationalist foreign policy, to turn away from federal spending on highways and dams and power plants. He could, when necessary, talk to a conservative audience about how any of those things were an affront to liberty, and he would mean it. But he was realistic enough to understand that those government functions were there to stay. Instead, Reagan told Californians all the ways the contemporary federal government, the government Johnson had built, had turned away from them. It had rejected them in favor of *new* programs, programs that were meant to help minorities but actually left them no better off.

The more that Brown and the visiting Johnson administration officials painted Reagan as a threat, the more they fed the backlash. *Reagan wants to destroy government programs,* they said, thinking that good New Deal voters would understand that an attack on government programs was an attack on them. But these weren't New Deal voters anymore. The people who gave Reagan his majority in the polls were white workers in the suburbs whose top issues were crime, drugs, juvenile delinquency, racial concerns, state taxes, and welfare programs. Reagan was winning with the men with lunch pails Kennedy had worried about all those years ago.

THE CAMPAIGN HAD been a thrilling ride for Reagan, the kind of adventure in which he had always longed to be the star. It was probably too much to expect that Election Day would bring more drama. The Reagans had planned to have dinner that night with friends before heading to a party with supporters. As they drove from dinner to the party at the Century Plaza Hotel, they heard the news come over the radio: Ronald Reagan had defeated Pat Brown and would be the next governor of California. "I had always thought you waited up all night listening to the returns," Nancy would write, "and although this may sound silly, I felt let down. After so much hard work, Ronnie's early and overwhelming victory seemed almost an anticlimax."

Reagan had not only won, he'd won big. The B-movie actor, the extremist, the citizen-politician, had won the largest state in the nation by nearly a million votes—a landslide. Orange County, the funny anomaly Brown had idly mentioned to Johnson after Election Day in 1964, no longer seemed so strange. Reagan had secured an astounding 72 percent of the vote in Orange County—despite the fact that half of the county's voters were still registered Democrats.

It had been a great night for Republicans across the country. The

GOP had defended all but two of their existing governorships and added eight new ones nationwide. ("I AM LOOKING FORWARD TO WORKING WITH YOU IN THE REPUBLICAN GOVERNORS' ASSOCIATION," another new winner, Spiro T. Agnew of Maryland, cabled Reagan on November 9.) Republican governors were winning in all sorts of strange new places. In Arkansas, Winthrop Rockefeller became the first Republican elected statewide since Reconstruction. In Massachusetts, John Volpe was reelected with a commanding margin, winning even the city of Boston, homeland of Kennedy Democrats. In governor's races across the country, the GOP received 54 percent of the statewide vote, a showing not seen since 1952, the year of Eisenhower's first sweeping presidential victory.

Meanwhile, the results in the congressional elections were as bad as could be for Johnson and the Democrats. In the House, the Democrats had sustained losses far worse than even the twenty-seven or twenty-eight seats Dick Russell had imagined, losing an astounding forty-seven seats altogether. Only fourteen of the seats they'd wrested from the Republicans in the landslide year of 1964 remained in Democratic control. Johnson's Democrats still controlled the Congress in name, but for the next two years, at the very least, the conservative bloc would be running the show.

The Republicans had also added three Senate seats, along with 557 state legislative seats nationwide. Altogether, the party had received four million more votes than the Democrats in races across the country. Two years after respected commentators had openly wondered if the GOP was finished as a national party, the Republicans seemed poised to form a new majority in American politics.

Most remarkable of all was the face of that resurgent Republican Party: Ronald Reagan. More exciting than any vote margin was the story of how a former actor and a committed Goldwaterite had won the favor of the Golden State. Predictably, the talk of a Reagan for President campaign in 1968 that had surrounded Reagan since his victory in the primary now grew louder. "In these circumstances," wrote *The New York Times,* "Ronald Reagan may hold something like the balance of power. A hero to the Goldwater conservatives, he could assist Mr. Nixon mightily by supporting him early and strongly; or he could cut into the Nixon base and open the way for Governor Romney by becoming a candidate or letting himself be 'drafted'; or he could even make a party unity move by trying to align himself with Mr. Romney."

The party's big names stumbled over each other to get in Reagan's good graces. Romney called him on election night. "CONGRATULATIONS ON THAT GREAT VICTORY," cabled Nelson Rockefeller. "THE RESULTS OF THE ELECTION IN CALIFORNIA AND THROUGHOUT THE COUNTRY SIGNAL THE RESURGENCE OF OUR PARTY TO ITS HISTORIC POSITION OF STRENGTH AND INFLUENCE."

Nixon stayed in close touch. "I thought you would be interested to know that since returning to my office after a post-election vacation," he wrote to Reagan in November, "I have heard a number of very favorable comments from some of the political 'pros' in the New York area with regard to your appearance on *Issues and Answers*. I only wish I had the opportunity of seeing it because from all accounts you hit the curves as well as the fast balls over the fence." Just as before, he was cloyingly obsequious, but this time there was an added edge: *Don't forget who worked hard in this election, too.*

As always, Reagan was careful not to look as if he wanted the big part. He brushed off the presidential talk and told friends and supporters how daunting he found his pending responsibilities in Sacramento. But he was careful to nurture his party relationships outside California. In response to a congratulatory telegram from Governor James A. Rhodes of Ohio, a state of the utmost importance to Republicans seeking the presidency, Reagan was fawning. "I think more than any other governor of a major state you have proved that sound, fiscally-responsible government is indeed appreciated by the people," he wrote. "I hope to see you at the Republican Governors Meeting . . . and I would like at some time to sit down and discuss with you your approach to state government."

Behind closed doors, he was already running. Less than two

weeks after the 1966 election, Reagan met at his home with a group of political advisers to discuss a run for the presidency in 1968. Spearheading the effort was Tom Reed, described by Theodore White in *The Making of the President, 1968* as "a distinguished physicist turned successful industrialist, now urged into politics by his conviction that Lyndon Johnson was an incarnation of evil." Reed's first move was to recruit a key strategist for the cause: Clif White, the architect of Goldwater's 1964 convention strategy, the one man in the country who knew how to take a conservative candidate national. White had been devastated when Goldwater failed to make an appeal to the voters in the middle, presaging his disastrous '64 loss to Johnson. Reagan, White knew, would not make the same mistake.

While these underlings worried about the details of a campaign, Reagan kept his eyes squarely on Lyndon Johnson. He urged fellow Republicans to make the case that the election results were more than a vague expression of dissatisfaction. They were the public rising up against the administration in Washington. "I've been a little disappointed at how slow we are to respond to all the Liberal pundits who are trying to explain what happened," he wrote to Senator Carl Curtis of Nebraska. "I think we should start making a case that what happened was a turning away from the Great Society by the people." Writing to another member of Congress, he was even more direct: "I think we can claim a mandate from the people; that if any backlash was present, it was a backlash against the Great Society."

ON THE PHONE from Chicago, Mayor Daley was giving the president forceful advice. "Some way," the mayor said, "somehow, you should drop this Great Society. And pick up something else."

It was December 17, 1966, just over a month after the midterm elections. Through those long weeks, Johnson had heard repeatedly what a disaster the results had been for the party. And how he, Lyndon Johnson, the greatest Democratic president since Roosevelt, was to blame.

To the end, he had dithered over whether or not he should insert himself into the campaign. After returning from his trip to the Pacific, he'd decided to make a last-minute push. From the ranch, where he'd retired in advance of an upcoming hernia operation, he staged a hurried revival of the old Man-in-Motion Johnson Show. In the three days before the election, he flew in an array of cabinet members to try to create the impression of major substantive progress as voters went to the polls. "The mimeograph machines," wrote the *Times,* "churned out bullish statements on nearly everything the voters could conceivably have been worried about—white backlash, Vietnam, the draft, high food prices."

Then the devastating results came in and it was even easier for reporters to pin the blame on him. "There was no question," observed the *Times,* "that the Republicans . . . capitalized on the 'anti votes'—those who turned against the Johnson Administration and the President himself." His old enemies spared no extravagance detailing Johnson's failure. Ted Sorensen, addressing New York Democrats, was near apocalyptic in describing the effects on the party. "It was . . . far worse than the usual midterm slide," he said, "far worse than the issues required; and it spread disaster and disarray into our party in every section of the country and in every normally Democratic state."

Newsweek summed it up best: "In the space of a single Autumn day . . . the 1,000 day reign of Lyndon I came to an end: The Emperor of American politics became just a president again."

Johnson was a man whose myths had left him behind. For progressives, the election was liberation—no longer did they have to qualify their critique of the Vietnam War; no longer did they have to claim Lyndon Johnson as one of their own. In fact, by turning on Johnson, they could cling to their old utopian ideas and simply say it was Johnson and his war that had prevented that utopia from coming to pass. The problem wasn't the program, they could say; it was Johnson and his war. And so they began. "The election results," wrote Walter Lippmann, "are a tremendous demonstration of how in the atmosphere of war it is impossible to pursue the tasks of peace." Johnson, the liberals felt, was incapable of pursuing those tasks. "The feeling is widespread," observed *The Progressive,* "that he is much too devious and domineering, too crafty and calculating to capture the admiration and affection he so passionately desires."

Some were more realistic. Michael Harrington, the journalist whose reporting on poverty in the late fifties and early sixties had punctured his fellow liberals' breezy confidence, once again was more pessimistic than his peers. He feared that a permanent shift had occurred. The old Goldwater movement had been "a fantastic mood rather than a program," Harrington wrote in an essay after the election. But the conservatism that voters had embraced in 1966, particularly the "Creative Federalism" Reagan had promoted, was something real: a program that would move resources away from federal projects helping the underprivileged in the cities and toward state programs that benefited more affluent voters in the suburbs. "If the Dixiecrat-Republican coalition adopts a version of 'Creative Federalism' they will have come up with a workable and reactionary alternative to social progress."

Conservatives were eager to describe a version of that "workable alternative"—that the future now belonged to men like Reagan, that a definitive move to the right had begun. William F. Buckley concluded a column in the *National Review* with an anecdote about a "young conservative" who had run for State Assembly in the '66 election in a district that included Harlem. "A Negro woman advanced on him and growled that he was a Nazi," wrote Buckley. " 'Look, madam,' the young and engaging Yale graduate said, 'it's not right to call me a Nazi, any more than it would be right for me to call you a Communist.' 'But I AM a Communist,' she answered exultantly." After long decades in the wilderness, the taint of extremism had shifted to the other side.

The old New Deal consensus had cracked. Johnson's majority had vanished. There were challenges to his authority everywhere. The day before Johnson spoke with Daley, a caucus of Democratic governors, meeting at the Greenbrier resort in West Virginia, had released an ostentatious statement explicitly saying that Johnson was responsible for the party's poor showing the month before. Iowa's Democratic governor, Harold Hughes, serving as a public spokesman for the group, would not even say whether Johnson could win reelection. "I don't know," Hughes said. "If he had a respectable opponent who was acceptable to the American people, he would have a very tough race."

Now here was Mayor Daley: "The Great Society is tarnished," he said. "It's been hurt. . . . I don't think we can keep pushing this Great Society idea because it hasn't worked. It's stumbled and fumbled and in many places, it's fallen down."

Johnson breathed deeply while he listened. This was the new reality: he was expected to sit back and take this kind of talk. Two years ago, Daley wouldn't have dared tell the president what he should call his prized domestic program. He probably would have told him how wonderful he thought the name "Great Society" was.

But no one was thinking about 1964 anymore. As Johnson knew better than anyone, no one in Washington was ever thinking about the last election. They were thinking about the next one, 1968, about the increasing likelihood that Johnson would face a primary challenge, quite possibly from Bobby Kennedy. That would be the ultimate indignity: a sitting president losing his party's nomination and Bobby triumphing over Johnson in the end.

Johnson had reasons now to placate people like Mayor Daley.

Anyway, Daley wasn't the only one saying this sort of thing to Johnson. To survive, his advisers told him, he had to find a new message, one that spoke to the Americans in the middle. He had to forget about the editorial writers and heed the message of the voters, to scale back his domestic agenda, to focus his energy, to bring some sort of resolution to the war in Vietnam. And yes, he had to lay off the Great Society, at least for a while, and give people a new story in which they could believe.

Johnson said that he agreed, he would change his story going forward. But his preoccupation was with the past. In the final weeks of 1966, his mind drifted back in time. Back before the miserable midterms. Before people talked about Ronald Reagan as anything other than an actor. Before Vietnam had tainted everything. Before the triumphs: Medicare and the Civil Rights Act and the Voting Rights Act. Before the crises, before Pleiku and Rolling Thunder and the Gulf of Tonkin; before the marchers on the bridge in Selma, before those kids had gone missing in the Mississippi darkness. Before he'd lost Walter Jenkins. Before that gold-ringed morning in November 1964 when he'd woken up a reelected president, the owner of a record landslide. All the way back to the place where his thousand days had begun.

Back to Dallas.

As 1966 came to an end, the talk of Washington was a new book by the journalist William Manchester, *The Death of a President*. It was an authoritative recreation of the events before, during, and after the killing of President Kennedy, informed by interviews with one thousand people, including nearly everyone who'd been near the fallen president and his family in those dark days. It was the cooperation of one person in particular that made the book unique. Personally selected by the Kennedy family to write the authoritative account, Manchester had spent long hours in the company of Jacqueline Kennedy in her Georgetown home in the months following the assassination, reliving each moment of November 1963.

The book was not due out until the spring of 1967, but it was already a sensation. *Look* magazine planned to publish an excerpt in a January issue (it had bought the first serial rights for $665,000 and had already earned back half the purchase price in overseas sales). Jackie's participation fueled public interest—she had not talked at length about the assassination in public since her Camelot interview with Teddy White. In Washington, fascination with the book swirled around rumors that it revealed tensions between Johnson and the Kennedy family in the first hours of the Johnson presidency.

Indeed it did. Manchester's 654-page book, which remains the definitive account of the Kennedy assassination and its immediate aftermath, included the Kennedy loyalists' version of events in Dallas in which Lyndon Johnson commandeered Air Force One, installed himself in Jackie's bedroom on the plane, and generally acted like a greedy usurper throughout the long weekend of mourning and transition. There was a lengthy description of Jackie, in a hotel room the night before her husband's death, listening to her husband berate Vice President Johnson in a nearby room. A strong contempt for all things Texan pervaded Manchester's emotional prose, suggesting that the culture of the Lone Star State had played a part in Kennedy's murder. This implied culpability extended to the nation's most famous Texan, the president of the United States. An early version of the book began with a vignette, provided by Jackie, of JFK visiting the LBJ Ranch in 1960 and growing appalled by the way Johnson hunted deer. The meaning was subtle but clear: the new president practiced the same kind of brutality that had taken the old president's life.

Never once in Manchester's story did Jackie Kennedy put a foot wrong. And yet she and the Kennedy family quickly realized that the human messiness of Manchester's account was a threat to their most valuable asset: the Camelot myth. Relying on reports of the book's contents from Kennedy family loyalists, Jackie filed suit to prohibit its publication, an ultimately unsuccessful effort that only increased the public's appetite for the tale. The advance orders reached four hundred thousand.

In public, Johnson acted as though he'd paid little mind to the entire affair. He wrote to Jackie, telling her not to think that he'd taken any offense:

My dear Mrs. Kennedy,
Mrs. Johnson and I have been distressed to read the press accounts of your unhappiness about the Manchester book. Some of these accounts attribute your concern to passages in the book which are critical or defamatory of us. If this is

so, I want you to know that while we deeply appreciate your
characteristic kindness and sensitivity, we hope you will not
subject yourself to any discomfort or distress on our
account. One never becomes completely inured to slander,
but we have learned to live with it.

This was a familiar Washington transaction—political families
papering over an embarrassing incident by blaming the wretched
jackals of the press. There were hints that Johnson still longed for
intimacy with the former First Lady: the typed "Mrs. Kennedy" was
crossed out and replaced with a handwritten "Jackie"; "Mrs. Johnson" was replaced with "Lady Bird." But the cool, businesslike tone,
compared with Johnson's extravagant courtship in days of old,
showed he was not quite so untroubled as he protested. His line "one
never becomes completely inured to slander" contained a perhaps
unconscious slip that may have revealed how Johnson really felt
about all the things Jackie had told Manchester. A person who writes
untruth is guilty of libel. "Slander" comes from the person who
speaks it.

In private, of course, Johnson was obsessed with the Manchester
book. He pressed for any intelligence his associates could gather on
the contents. "What are the damaging things to us in there?" he
asked Abe Fortas. "Is it the plane incident in Dallas?" Fortas struggled to narrow down a long list of damaging material. "The basic
damage of the thing is the portrayal of you." Johnson devoured gossip about Manchester, whom he denounced as "a fraud." Naturally,
Johnson assumed Bobby was responsible for the entire project. The
book was "vicious, mean, dirty, low-down stuff," Johnson said,
planted by Bobby to delegitimize Johnson's claim for reelection in
1968.

But what was truly damaging about the Manchester book was
not its implication for the future—it was what it said about the past.
Whatever the public thought of Johnson's program—and in late
1966, they did not seem to think much of it—most Americans had

always appreciated the way Johnson had handled himself in the first, difficult hours of his presidency. In his nation's time of sorrow, Johnson had been silent but strong, and then at just the right moment he had urged the country to continue. Now, through Manchester, the Kennedys were denying him even that achievement. They were taking the heroic beginning of Johnson's story away.

Perhaps for the first time, Johnson fully realized what had been clear in the last line of Teddy White and Jackie's story in *Life* magazine: *for one brief shining moment that was known as Camelot.* He couldn't be a hero in that story. There was no place for him in the Kennedy myth. His bitterness toward the family was total. "They're going to write history as they want it written, as they can buy it written," he said. "And I think the best way we can write it is to try to refrain from getting into an argument or a fight or a knockdown, and go on and do our job every day."

But for how long? That was what the political world wondered as 1966 came to an end. Two years before, when he'd won his landslide, it was unthinkable that Lyndon Johnson could be scared out of running for reelection. In that moment of triumph, it was a near certainty that Johnson would choose to run for reelection in 1968, win another landslide, and stay in the White House for a remarkable nine-year run. But after the Republican triumph in the midterms, it seemed possible that the president would not seek reelection after all.

Lady Bird found that prospect appealing. Earlier that fall, she had met with the landscape architect Lawrence Halprin about a project he was to design as part of her efforts to beautify Washington, D.C. At one point, she asked Halprin how long it had taken him to design a similar project, San Francisco's Ghirardelli Square. Listening in, Sharon Francis, a staff assistant on the beautification project, knew why the First Lady was interested in timing. Lady Bird was always a careful planner. She wanted to know whether this project could be completed before she left the capital in two years' time.

Lyndon's thoughts about the future were harder to read. He nodded along when his aides talked about a shift in strategy, the course of prudence that would win public opinion back. He agreed vacantly. But then he would talk about some big new bill he wanted to get through Congress, some new program he needed to start. It was as if he believed that if he could only get one more great accomplishment under his belt, one more remarkable program, then people would forget about the war and the riots and the heavy fear they felt. Then they would see that all the great things he had promised were coming to pass. If only he could do something bigger and better, then they would love him again. His instinct at the end of the thousand days was just the same as it had been at the beginning: all would be well if he could just capture the nation's attention, if he could just start his story over.

There was, however, one small hint that his perspective on the future had changed. It came when people asked him to explain himself. Why was he trying to accomplish the big things now, why not slow things down and wait for a while? *What was his hurry?* The answer should have been obvious. The Man-in-Motion had always been in a hurry, ever since that day in November when he'd spied morning light on the White House as president for the first time. It was his natural state of being. He was Lyndon Baines Johnson, he had been in a hurry all his life, hurrying toward greater and greater things. Now, though, something was different. He hurried, he said, because "I have so little time."

Epilogue

R onald Reagan was sworn in as governor of California shortly after midnight on January 2, 1967, in the rotunda of the state's capitol building. Already, however, his mind was drawn to an even higher office. With Reagan's blessing, Clif White and Tom Reed had developed a detailed campaign timeline for the coming year, leading up to the Republican convention in the summer of 1968. There, Reagan hoped to win his party's nomination and challenge Johnson for the presidency.

Throughout his first year as governor, Reagan declared himself focused on his substantial duties in Sacramento, too busy to consider a run for the presidency. But reporters noted that he never offered an outright refusal to run in 1968. Press interest in a Reagan candidacy grew steadily, thanks in part to not-so-subtle encouragement from Reagan himself. At a meeting of the nation's governors aboard the SS *Independence* in October 1967, a tanned and smiling Reagan appeared before the national press. "Governor Rockefeller of New York said yesterday that he does not want to be president," said one reporter. "Do *you* want to be president?" Reagan laughed and paused. "Well," he said, "there's one carry-over I have from my previous occupation: I never take the other fellow's lines."

Final days: Johnson at
the LBJ Ranch in 1972.
© Frank Wolfe/LBJ Library

The long run:
Reagan with
supporters in
1968.
© AP Photo

Off camera, he was more overt. Despite the demands of his office, he found time for periodic trips around the country, gathering support for a potential run. His aim, in part, was to recreate Goldwater's strategy for capturing the nomination: secure the overwhelming support of the conservative grass roots, and of the white voters flocking to the party in the South. "Most South Carolinians are, as I am, relatively new converts to Republicanism," he told an audience in the Palmetto State in 1967. "Somehow the Democratic Party went away and left us. It left us when it switched to philosophies and policies that we could not accept . . . the philosophy that whoever the Democratic president may be, he knows best."

Lyndon Johnson was always on his mind. As an unannounced candidate, Reagan could not overtly criticize his more moderate rivals for the Republican nomination—Richard Nixon, George Romney, and Nelson Rockefeller. Instead, he stirred conservative passions with an unrelenting critique of the Johnson administration. His office maintained a thick file of index cards to aid in the effort. Each card contained a thematic title printed in capital letters followed by a statistic, quotation, or set of facts that illustrated some aspect of the Johnson administration's record of failure. Strung together, the titles formed a scripted account of the Johnson presidency for Reagan to perform. Reagan was a B actor no longer; now the script on his cards told the main story of American politics and the declining fortunes of the Johnson presidency:

POVERTY NEEDS TOO EXPENSIVE

ADMINISTRATION SHORTCOMINGS ENHANCE RIOTING

LBJ HAS NOT FULFILLED GREAT SOCIETY CLAIMS

Meanwhile, on their TV screens, viewers see that rioting becomes the norm in cities across America in 1967. . . . A presidential task force reports to Johnson that if current trends continue, by 1983, the nation's major cities will be 40 percent poor.

HARMS OF INFLATION ON FULL EMPLOYMENT ECONOMY

YOUTH UNEMPLOYMENT GOING UP

LBJ INCREASES FEDERAL SPENDING

Facing a projected 1968 budget deficit of $28 billion, Johnson announces he will request that Congress pass a tax surcharge.... LBJ, fearing a political backlash against government spending, tells aides he is prepared to "slash the hell out of domestic programs if necessary."

"ADMINISTRATION HAS MISLED THE PUBLIC ABOUT

     VIETNAM"—W. CRONKITE

LBJ HAS ACUTE SENSE OF SECRECY

LBJ'S BIGGEST PROBLEM IS LACK OF CREDIBILITY

After a tour of Vietnam in early 1968, Walter Cronkite reports to his audience that "it is increasingly clear to this reporter that the only rational way out then will be to negotiate, not as victors, but as an honorable people who lived up to their pledge to defend democracy." ... Under duress, Robert S. McNamara resigns as secretary of defense, to be replaced by Clark Clifford at the Pentagon.

In travels across the country, Reagan assailed Johnson's out-of-control spending, the "matchless boondoggle" that was his War on Poverty, and a "leadership gap" in the White House that was "on a scale we have never known and should no longer tolerate." He spared no drama in playing up the urgency of the moment, of the crossroads America had reached: "There is a question abroad in the land—what is happening to us?"

WHAT WAS HAPPENING to America? That *was* the question asked everywhere in 1968. And before long, Johnson's failure to provide an answer would prove his undoing.

Following the disastrous 1966 midterm results, Washington had entertained the possibility that Johnson would not seek reelection in 1968. He often appeared listless and beaten down. His mood grew darker, his temper shorter, his waistline larger yet again. He watched helplessly as his presidency was swallowed whole by Vietnam—the war he hadn't wished for, the war he struggled to control, the war he could not win. In late January 1968, the Vietcong and North Vietnamese launched a surprise, coordinated attack on more than a hundred locations in South Vietnam. The attacks marked a new, bloodier phase in the already gruesome conflict. In a single week in February, 543 Americans were killed. The Vietcong and North Vietnamese initiative, which came to be known as the Tet Offensive, deeply damaged morale on the American home front, underscoring the hollowness of the administration's claims of improving fortunes in the conflict. In a poll taken early in 1968, just 35 percent of Americans approved of Johnson's handling of the war.

Throughout 1967 and early 1968, Johnson refused to announce himself as a candidate for reelection. He was keeping to the old customs, the ones that had served him well in 1964, by which a president refrained from unseemly politicking until his party commanded him to seek the office again. This time, though, it was unclear if a resounding command from the party would actually come. Johnson quizzed friends on whether he ought to run. Recalling that few Johnson men lived past the age of sixty-five, he wondered if he had four more White House years in him. In January 1973, the end of the next term, he would be sixty-four. Lady Bird made no secret of her desire to leave at the end of the term; John Connally advised Johnson that if he did run, he probably would not win.

It was far from clear that he could even count on the nomination of his party. Eugene McCarthy, the liberal Minnesota senator, launched a campaign for the Democratic nomination centered on his opposition to the Vietnam War. In the March 1968 New Hampshire primary, McCarthy stunned the nation by winning 42 percent of the vote to Johnson's 49. Shortly thereafter, the dire blow Johnson had always imagined at last was delivered: Bobby Kennedy announced himself as a candidate for the presidency in 1968.

On the last day of March, a weary Lady Bird Johnson found her husband in his bedroom. Their daughter Lynda had just described the harrowing ordeal with the press she'd endured while saying goodbye to her husband, Marine Corps Captain Charles S. Robb, who was leaving to serve a tour of duty in Vietnam. Lyndon's "face was sagging," Lady Bird told her diary, "and there was such pain in his eyes as I had not seen since his mother died." That night, Johnson planned to announce a partial halt in the bombing of North Vietnam in a renewed effort to start peace talks with the Hanoi government. But the pain in Johnson's face, Lady Bird knew, had a deeper root.

That day, March 31, 1968, would be a river cutting across their lives. Lady Bird passed the day in a nervous bustle. Just before nine that evening, she went to the Oval Office with her children and a gaggle of Johnson aides. Under the glare of the television lights, her husband was waiting to give his speech. "Remember," Lady Bird told him softly, "pacing and drama."

Johnson delivered the substance of his Vietnam proposal like a news report: he would introduce limits on bombing as a genuine signal of his desire to reach accommodation with the North Vietnamese. Then the drama came.

"With American sons in the field far away," the president told his people, "I do not believe that I should devote an hour or a day of my time to any personal partisan causes or to any duties other than the awesome duties of this office, the presidency of your country. Accordingly, I shall not seek, and I will not accept, the nomination of my party for another term as your president."

The nation was stunned: President Johnson was not going to run again after all. Johnson intimates staggered at the turn. He was giving up on what had once been his grandest ambition—to serve nine great years in the White House, to be as great a president as FDR, to transform his country and the world.

Lady Bird left the Oval Office in a daze, floating on a tide of sadness, shock, and relief. To her, this was a moment of true courage and greatness in her husband's life. Watching the speech, she thought and later recorded in her diary, "those who love him must have loved him more. And those who hate him must at least have thought: 'Here is a man.'"

LYNDON JOHNSON WAS a man whose ambition could overcome almost any obstacle, save the course of history. History was simply moving too fast. Americans were still absorbing the news that the president had decided not to run when, four days later, even more shocking news came from Memphis: Martin Luther King, Jr., the leader who had survived years of terror and intimidation in the South, had been shot dead while standing on the balcony of a motel.

It was early April, warm enough for rioting, and the nation's cities braced themselves for a grievous blow. Appearing that night at a campaign stop in a rough neighborhood in Indianapolis, Bobby Kennedy had to inform his audience of the news. "For those of you who are black," he said, his hands and voice shaking from the deep emotion he felt, "and are tempted to be filled with hatred and distrust at the injustice of such an act, against all white people, I would only say that I can feel in my own heart the same kind of feeling. I had a member of my family killed, but he was killed by a white man. But we have to make an effort in the United States, we have to make an effort to understand, to go beyond these rather difficult times."

Soon enough, though, the times would claim Bobby too. Two months later, just after declaring victory over McCarthy in the California primary on June 4, 1968, Bobby Kennedy was shot in the head while exiting his victory party at Los Angeles's Ambassador Hotel. Like his brother before him, Bobby had been killed by a deranged assassin acting out a fantasy. The fierce and fearsome spirit that had inspired a nation and tormented its president was gone.

"Too horrible for words," Johnson said when he first learned Bobby had been shot. Though it was quickly apparent his wounds

were mortal, Bobby's body lingered for more than a day before finally succumbing. In those hours of waiting, Johnson was less dignified. "Is he dead?" he asked his aides. "Is he dead yet?" Once again,
as the nation mourned a Kennedy struck down in the prime of life,
Johnson had to stand by silently as a complex muddle of emotions
swirled in his head. Once again, a Kennedy was destined to live on as
a martyr, with a posthumous reputation that barely resembled the
man Johnson had actually known. Once again, Johnson's nation
was in trouble, and he was helpless to do little more than watch.

The Johnsons attended Bobby's funeral service in New York.
They entered without ceremony and Lyndon did not speak. After
the service concluded, Lady Bird found herself face-to-face with
Jackie Kennedy. "I called her name and put out my hand," Lady Bird
noted in her diary later. "She looked at me as if from a great distance, as though I were an apparition. I murmured some word of
sorrow and walked on."

The troubles persisted through the last months of Johnson's
presidency. Bobby's death left McCarthy as the leader of the antiwar
movement within the party. Hubert Humphrey became the stand-in
for Johnson, the candidate of the status quo. When the two sides
met at the Democratic convention in Chicago that summer, bitter
rancor broke out on the convention floor. Outside there was blood.
Young dissidents protested the war on the city's streets; urged on by
Mayor Daley, the Chicago police and Illinois National Guard met
them with shockingly brutal force. "The whole world is watching,"
the protesters screamed, and the whole world was. Americans were
watching in horror, wondering if their democracy, their country itself, was coming apart.

Johnson grew more and more weary in the final months of his
presidency, thwarted in all his ambitions, beaten down by events. In
the end, he at last allowed a bit of reality to temper his grand dreams.
"I hope," he told Congress in a farewell address, "it may be said, a
hundred years from now, that by working together we helped to
make our country . . . more just for all of its people, as well as to

ensure and guarantee the blessings of liberty for all of our posterity. *That is what I hope.* But I believe that at least it will be said that we tried."

The Johnsons left the White House on January 20, 1969. They arrived at the LBJ Ranch in Texas as night was falling. A group of five hundred Hill Country neighbors had come to welcome them. Happy as always to have a crowd, Lyndon lingered with them in the ranch's airplane hangar. He was glad, he told the visitors, to be home. That evening, after five years of often sleepless nights, Lady Bird retired early to the comfort of her own bed. As she drifted off she recalled a line of poetry: *"I seek to celebrate my glad release, the tents of silence and the camp of peace."*

AMERICANS HELD THE Democrats to blame for much of what was happening in the late 1960s. But Reagan would not be the one to profit from the other party's collapse, not in 1968. His strategy was all wrong for the moment. It was not a year to run quietly for the presidency, not a year to do much of anything quiet at all. While Reagan dropped hints and winked at the press, Richard Nixon went straight to Reagan's strongest supporters—Southern conservatives— and sewed up commitments for support. No doubt the sons of Dixie loved Ronald Reagan far more than they would ever love Dick Nixon, but there was more than personal feeling to consider. "The Southerners," wrote Theodore White, "had had enough of gallant lost causes; they wanted winners." Nixon, for all of his defects, was a former vice president who had come within a hair's breadth of the presidency eight years before. Reagan was two years out from *Death Valley Days.* By early August 1968, when the party gathered in Miami Beach for its convention, it was clear that Nixon would be their choice.

Some of Reagan's aides urged him to make the best of the situation in his signature dramatic form, turning away from his supporters on the convention floor and asking the convention to nominate Nixon straightaway. It was good advice that would have earned Rea-

gan a morsel of goodwill with Nixon, possessor of one of the longest memories in American politics. But for once, Reagan's knack
for timing was absent. Uncharacteristically, he failed to intuit when
it was time to subvert his ambition in the name of self-preservation.
As the delegates gathered in Miami, he clung to his dream and suddenly announced his intention to be considered as a candidate.

Reality intervened fast. Nixon won the nomination on the first
ballot, swamping Reagan, who came in an embarrassing third behind Rockefeller. He scrambled to clean things up, quickly proclaiming his support for the nominee. For the rest of his career, he would
downplay his efforts to seek the presidency in 1968, suggesting he
had simply allowed his name to be put forward as a "favorite son"
candidate of the California delegation.

But the damage was done. Nixon defeated Humphrey in the November election. He was backed by disaffected members of the white
middle class, the men with lunch pails Kennedy and his aides had
worried about, the concerned suburbanites Reagan had so artfully
courted. It was the beginning of a generational realignment. In five
of the six presidential elections in the period 1968–88, these voters
would deliver the White House to the Republicans, just as they had
delivered it again and again to the New Deal Democrats in the generation before. The sixties closed out in appalling style. The decay
persisted in the cities, the new president expanded the war in Vietnam, violence and killing continued at home. But Nixon so effectively channeled the resentments of the forgotten middle—the "silent
majority," as his base came to be known—that he entered the 1970s
a popular president, well on his way to reelection.

In California, Reagan remained popular as well; he was elected
to a second term as governor in 1970, albeit with a smaller margin
than he'd enjoyed in his 1966 landslide. But his ultimate dream, the
White House, seemed to have slipped from his grasp. Nixon was
governing not as a new, Reagan-style conservative, but as a sort of
Southern fried modern Republican. His White House was friendly
to business and to whites in the Old Confederacy, hostile to what

was left of the civil rights movement. But it was expansive in its vision for the federal government, taking on broad projects in education, public works, and environmental regulation. Overseas, Nixon shocked the hard-line anticommunists by visiting Red China and reaching an accord with the Soviets on reduction of antiballistic-missile systems.

None of this was the glorious future Reagan had imagined. After winning reelection in 1972, Nixon even envisioned the rise of a new majority party in the United States that eschewed the influence of both the radical left and the reactionary right, Reagan's hard-line base. Nixon had no intention of letting a conservative like Ronald Reagan follow him in the White House. In fact, his preferred successor was Lyndon Johnson's old protégé John Connally. Connally, like so many other southerners of his generation, became a member of the Republican Party in the 1970s. After Nixon's resounding reelection victory in 1972, Reagan's dream of the presidency seemed increasingly far-fetched.

But once a man starts running for president, he never really stops. He keeps running until he wins or he dies. And in the 1970s, the country would learn the same simple fact it had learned in the sixties: the future never turns out the way people think it's going to. The Watergate scandal and Nixon's subsequent resignation in August 1974 left the Republican Party decimated. For Reagan, the GOP's decline was yet another moment of opportunity. Just as he had after the Goldwater disaster of 1964, Reagan positioned himself as a fresh face, someone who could bring the party back from the brink. He challenged Nixon's successor, Gerald Ford, for the GOP nomination in 1976, running a serious and spirited primary campaign. At the party's convention in Kansas City, he lost the nomination to Ford by only 117 votes. When Ford went on to lose the November election to Democrat Jimmy Carter, many in the party wondered if they hadn't made a mistake in passing Reagan by.

Reagan was eager to show them they had a chance to rectify their mistake. He turned sixty-nine in 1980, the year of the next election, but he ran again anyway and finally captured the party's nomination. The mood in the country that year was similar in many ways to the mood in 1966, when Reagan had won his first California landslide. The American economy was in trouble, roiled by inflation and unemployment. The country's position in the world was in doubt, as was painfully illustrated by the humiliating failed attempt to rescue Americans being held hostage inside the U.S. embassy in Tehran. America seemed to have lost its way.

Reagan, by then an old pro at presidential politics, ran an artful campaign against the unpopular Carter. He tossed aside the academic question of whether the country's economic woes were best described as a recession or a depression with a clever pivot: "A recession is when your neighbor loses his job. A depression is when you lose yours. A recovery is when Jimmy Carter loses his."

And yet, in a sense, the campaign he ran had very little to do with his opponent Carter. Really, it was the same campaign he had been running since the mid-sixties. The succession of recent failed presidencies—Johnson, Nixon, Ford, Carter—allowed Reagan to run not just against the record of the last four years, but against an entire era of broken government promises. The root of the country's problems, Reagan suggested, was in the arrogant ambitions that the Democratic Party had staked out in the mid-1960s.

Reagan's 1980 campaign was a campaign against those ambitions, against the myths of Lyndon Johnson's thousand days. He ran against the Big Government that stifled innovation and threatened freedom. He ran against appeasement of a resurgent Soviet threat. He ran against the liberal promises that had not come to pass. He ran against the government elites who had overtaxed hardworking Americans in the name of helping the poor but had only created a class of dependents living off the government dole. He ran as hard as he could against all of Lyndon Johnson's dreams.

"We have a group of elitists in Washington," he said in 1980, in words that he could just as easily have uttered in 1966, "who . . .

think they must control our destiny, make all the rules, tell us how to run our lives and our businesses. And it is time to have a president who will take the government off the people's backs and turn the great genius of the American people loose once again."

Sometimes, his campaign against the Johnson-era vision was so literal it was crass. Running against Carter, an evangelical Christian from Georgia, Reagan's campaign knew that they had to make a hard play for the white vote in the South. Thus for his first stop after the Republican convention in August of 1980, Reagan went to Mississippi. And not just anywhere in Mississippi: Reagan chose to begin his general election campaign at the Neshoba County Fairgrounds, just a few miles from the lonely country road where James Chaney, Andrew Goodman, and Mickey Schwerner had breathed their last breaths. There, Reagan greeted an almost exclusively white audience and spoke the code words that had signaled resistance to federal civil rights efforts since the sixties: "I believe in states' rights."

Mostly, though, his campaign against the old Johnson vision took place on a higher plane. Like Johnson, he sought to inspire the nation with a mythic promise. "For those who have abandoned hope," he said, accepting the Republican nomination, "we'll restore hope and we'll welcome them into a great national crusade to make America great again. . . . Can we doubt that only a Divine Providence placed this land, this island of freedom, here as a refuge for all those people in the world who yearn to breathe freely: Jews and Christians . . ."

Just as they had for Johnson in 1964, the American people listened to Reagan's promises of hope, destiny, and the divine and gave him a landslide in return. Carter and Reagan had been close in the polls going into the fall campaign, but after a solid debate performance in which he came across as reasonable and mainstream, voters flocked to Reagan. He swamped Carter on Election Day, securing 489 electoral votes to the incumbent's 49. Unlike Goldwater, who had made Johnson wait until the next day for his concession in 1964,

Carter didn't even wait until the polls closed. When he called Reagan to concede, the president-elect was dripping, having just emerged from the shower.

It was clear from the dramatic words in Reagan's 1981 inaugural address that his presidency would be devoted to undoing the legacy of the past two decades. *In this present crisis, government is not the solution to our problem, government* is *the problem.* That spring, Reagan was shot by a would-be assassin after a speech in Washington. The president suffered a serious wound but made a full recovery. To some Americans, this seemed a mystical endorsement of the Reagan project. The time of trouble had begun when a president was shot and killed; it would end with a president who was shot and lived.

Reagan's advisers knew that after the Kennedy assassination, Johnson had used the swell of public support for his administration to force through his ambitious agenda. They moved to do the same after Reagan's assassination attempt, pushing forward a program that brought Reagan's vision to life: a defense buildup to more aggressively confront the Soviets abroad, and a shrinking of government at home. The centerpiece of this effort was the largest tax reduction in American history, which Reagan signed into law in the summer of 1981.

Like Johnson before him, Reagan applied his mythic vision at the expense of reality. Johnson's War on Poverty took an untested idea, community action, and applied it on a large scale without waiting to see if it would work. So, too, the Reagan administration brushed off concerns that the massive tax cut would shrink federal revenues to unsustainable levels. Government expenditures could be dramatically reduced, Reagan believed, by eliminating the wasteful programs for the poor that had metastasized since the Great Society. Reagan embraced a faddish conservative theory, supply-side economics, which held that a large reduction in marginal income-tax rates would create such significant economic growth that the federal government would in the end receive *greater* revenues. There was scant factual support for the theory—running against Reagan in the 1980 primary campaign, George H. W. Bush had dubbed it "voodoo economics." But as with the Great Society programs, the Reagan administration implemented its theory as though it were fact, willing a fantasy to come true.

The results were catastrophic. The tax cut reduced government revenues to approximately 18.5 percent of gross domestic product. The accompanying cut in federal expenditures never came: while Reagan did cut discretionary spending on Great Society domestic programs for the disadvantaged, he made no serious effort to alter federal spending on middle-class entitlements, and his defense buildup more than offset any cuts he'd made. At the end of his term, federal spending would amount to 22.5 percent of GDP. Reagan's policies had created unprecedented federal deficits. When Reagan assumed office, government debt was a manageable one third of GDP. During his time as president, Reagan would add more debt to the nation's ledgers than had all of his predecessors, going back to George Washington, combined. In a moment of crisis, Reagan had promised to restore fiscal responsibility to an out-of-control federal behemoth. But, as with Johnson, the real world never matched the mythic vision he espoused.

Unlike Johnson, however, Reagan did not pay a political price. By the 1980s, the fracture in the nation's governing consensus—the fracture that began in Johnson's thousand days—had grown so large that reality was no longer something for which politicians had to account. The public had gotten used to the politics that Reagan and Johnson had pioneered in the mid-sixties, wherein two sides told competing fantastic stories of great days to come and the party with the more enticing and believable story would win. The same qualities that had fueled Reagan's rise in the sixties—his intuition for the national mood, his ability to tell a clear and dramatic tale—served him well as his policies went into effect. In 1983, when the economy at last began to recover from the 1970s doldrums, Reagan was quick to interpret it as a vindication of his vision. The story of mythic resurgence he prophesied was coming to pass.

As always, he made sure the villain in his story, the same villain that had always been at the center of his story, was exposed: Johnson-era Big Government. Looking toward his campaign for reelection in 1984, Reagan reshaped the story of recent history to fit the contours of his vision. "The simple truth is that low inflation and economic expansion in the years prior to the Great Society meant enormous social and economic progress for the poor of America," he told an audience in 1983. "But after the gigantic increases in government spending and taxation, that economic progress slowed dramatically. . . . Today, because of our attempts to restrict and cut back on government expansion and to retarget aid toward those most in need, and away from those who can manage without Federal help, the working people of America are directly benefiting."

In the new political fashion, he expressed certainty that the country had chosen wisely, that the best days were yet to come. The slogans in his 1984 reelection campaign echoed the assured optimism Johnson had used two decades before: "It's Morning in America," "America Is Back," "You Ain't Seen Nothin' Yet." Once more, the country wanted to believe in the grand vision, to believe that the time of endless prosperity had arrived. Reagan won reelection that year with a landslide that in some ways outdid Johnson's, capturing all but one of the fifty states.

LYNDON JOHNSON DID not live to see that landslide. He did not live to see the dawn of the Reagan presidency and Reagan's attack, as president, on the Great Society and the prized programs Johnson had passed. After leaving the White House in January 1969, Johnson intended to retire from public life, the heroic rancher returning to his ranch. His life there was quiet, or at least as quiet as anything concerning Lyndon Johnson could be. He became a sort of commander in chief of Stonewall, Texas, taking an interest in everything within his line of sight: the management of the ranch, the construction of his presidential library, the particulars of Lady Bird's wardrobe.

Unsure what to do with his golden years, he seemed determined to make them brief. After leaving the White House, his health declined, and his habits of healthy living, always tenuous, disappeared. He'd given up smoking after his 1955 heart attack when doctors warned him that cigarettes could kill him, but he resumed the habit in his final years. When his daughters implored him to stop, Johnson simply refused. "I've raised you girls," he told them, "I've been president, and now it's my time."

One January evening in 1973, viewers of *CBS News* watched Walter Cronkite sit in somber silence, clutching a phone to his ear. It was nearly a decade after the awful weekend that followed the Kennedy assassination. That had been a grotesque and mesmerizing new experience: the whole country learning something awful and unexpected from their television sets minutes after it occurred. But over the course of ten years, so much had happened that was awful and unexpected, and almost all of it had been captured on TV. Now, when the CBS anchor clutched the phone to his ear, viewers knew the cue: something momentous had happened, most likely something bad.

"I'm talking to Tom Johnson," Cronkite told the nation, "the press secretary for Lyndon Johnson, who has reported that the thirty-sixth president of the United States died this afternoon in an ambulance plane on the way to San Antonio, where he was taken after being stricken at his ranch."

Johnson had spent his last morning on earth like so many others: talking on the telephone and touring the LBJ Ranch. After returning from an inspection of a cattle fence, he ate lunch and retired to his bedroom to take a nap. There he suffered the coronary attack that took his life. Lady Bird was at a meeting in Austin when she learned of the episode. She flew immediately to San Antonio, where she was told her husband had died. As always, she maintained her composure. "Well," she said simply, "we expected it."

Lyndon Johnson was not meant for retirement. His plan for his life was to serve as president and then go home to Texas and die, most likely in the fashion of Johnson men, before he turned sixty-five. Johnson had lived his life in a storm of warring fantasies, torn between dreams of greatness and fears of disgrace. To the end, he never quite let go of his grandest dream: of serving longer, and better, than any president save FDR. The day he died, January 22, 1973, was two days after what would have been his last day as president had he run for reelection in 1968. He was seven months short of his sixty-fifth birthday. And to the end, cruel fate never quite let go of Lyndon Johnson. The day after Johnson died, President Nixon announced to the nation that he had secured a "peace with honor" settlement with the North Vietnamese government, ending the war in Vietnam.

LADY BIRD JOHNSON was sixty years old and healthy when her husband died. She devoted many of her remaining years to work on conservation and beautification, heralding the rise of the environmental movement in the 1970s and '80s. She continued to reside at the LBJ Ranch, even after it was donated to the government as a national historic site.

She lived another thirty-four years after her husband's death. She outlived many of the people who had loomed large during the years of her husband's presidency: Jackie Kennedy, Richard Nixon, Barry Goldwater, Pat Brown, Richard Daley, George Wallace. When Walter Jenkins, who had lived a quiet life in Texas after resigning from the Johnson administration, died in 1985, she released a statement that echoed the kindness she had shown him in his moment of disgrace. "Walter was a good friend and a capable person," she said. "He is one of the dearest people I know."

Her greatest service was always to her husband. She tended the Johnson legacy as best she could and spoke frequently of how much she would have loved to talk to Lyndon about this or hear what Lyndon had to say about that. But it was only when Lady Bird emerged from the shadow of her husband's commanding personality that the country fully came to understand her remarkable contributions and gifts. In 1988, she was awarded the Congressional Gold Medal, one of the two highest civilian honors the United States bestows (the other being the Presidential Medal of Freedom), in a ceremony at the White House. Presenting her with the award on behalf of the United States Congress, President Ronald Reagan was generous and warm. "I remember one story," said Reagan, "of the time that LBJ was speaking to a group in North Carolina, and after about fifty minutes, the audience became restless. Lady Bird wrote a note on a piece of paper saying 'close soon' and slipped it to him. LBJ took it, held it up, and read it aloud to the audience. And then, after the laughter died down, he continued with his speech."

Reagan paused, taking in some laughter of his own. Then he continued: "Well, before someone hands *me* a note, I will close these remarks."

As always, Reagan's sense of timing was better than Johnson's. That sense served him well throughout his presidency. In his second term in office, the Iran-Contra scandal, in which officials in the Reagan White House were revealed to have defied an embargo and sold arms to Iran in order to fund rebels illegally in Nicaragua, shook the nation's confidence in Reagan. But the course of history, which had worked against Johnson so spectacularly at the end of his presidency, boosted Reagan at the end of his. As Reagan prepared to leave office, the Soviet bloc in Eastern Europe fractured and the Soviet Union itself began to show signs of mortal strain. It was the total victory over the Communist menace that Reagan had hoped for, envisioned, and promised since the beginning of his political career. He left office a beloved president, the first sitting president since Roosevelt to see his party win the White House for a third consecutive term. And, thanks in large part to devoted disciples in later generations who still thrill to his story, his reputation for greatness continues to grow.

That would have pleased Reagan. He carried his dream—to be

the hero—with him to the end. Shortly before leaving the White House, he wrote to Joy Hodges, the old friend who'd wangled him a screen test in his first days in Hollywood, urging Reagan never to put on his glasses again. "There will be some things of course that we will miss when we leave here," he told her, "but we are really looking forward to California and boots and saddles. I have a horse waiting for me at the ranch. I hope he's ready for a lot of riding."

But sitting atop a horse was not how Reagan would spend his final days. Nearly six years after leaving the White House, Reagan announced that he had been diagnosed with Alzheimer's disease and was retiring from public life. The man who liked nothing so much as the "heady wine" feel of the eyes of the world upon him was never seen in a formal capacity again. He died in 2004 at the age of ninety-three. His state funeral was the grandest send-off for any president since the funeral of President Kennedy four decades before.

Reagan wanted his country to believe in the story he told. Four decades before his death, in the midst of a turbulent thousand days, he had warned his country that it faced a momentous choice: "We'll preserve for our children this, the last best hope of man on earth, or we'll sentence them to take the last step into a thousand years of darkness." At the end, Reagan believed that the danger had passed, that the country had made the right choice. "I now begin the journey that will lead me into the sunset of my life," Reagan wrote at the end of his farewell letter to the country. "I know that for America there will always be a bright dawn ahead."

Leaving the stage for the last time, Reagan wanted his people to believe the same thing that, forty years earlier, Lyndon Johnson had sought so desperately to prove—that the time of trial was over, that from now on, all would be well. That was what each of them wanted, always: to tell the story of a noble hero, a story with a happy end.

Afterword

"*I know that for America there will always be a bright dawn ahead.*"
From Reagan's pen, the words look reassuring, capturing the
sunny optimism that was his specialty as president. But in the mouths
of today's politicians, where similar words often appear, they sound
hollow, at best an improbable wish, at worst an insane delusion.

Indeed, so much of Johnson's and Reagan's grand visions for the
country ring false when today's leaders call on them. Those visions
have persisted over the past half century, shaping the political debate. But neither Reagan's nor Johnson's myth has served its respective party, or its country, well.

Johnson's promises of a government-led utopia haunted his
Democratic Party for the remainder of the twentieth century—years
of trial and trauma in which the government too often failed its people. For decades, liberals clung to the story they'd embraced after
the stinging 1966 midterm defeat—the story that cast off Lyndon
Johnson, his Vietnam policy, and the hawkish side of Cold War liberalism but retained Johnson's utopian vision of government. Up
against the Reagan vision—*Believe in America, limit the government, unleash the transformative power of individuals pursuing the
American dream*—the liberal story proved a political disaster. Outside of the extraordinary post-Watergate elections of 1974 and 1976,
the Democrats failed for more than two decades to find a plausible

Courtesy Richard Nixon Library

strategy to connect with the American middle. The party surrendered the White House to the Republicans for twenty out of twenty-four years.

Finally, in 1992, a Democratic candidate, Bill Clinton, won the White House by offering a "third way," distinct from the governing visions of both right and left. Yet Clinton quickly discovered that the old myths were not easy to escape. When, early in his term, Clinton attempted to pass a program for universal health care, Republicans decried the return of Great Society overreach. The public listened. In the congressional elections halfway through Clinton's first term, the GOP ran against the president as an old-style Big Government liberal and captured both houses of Congress, a stunning rebuke that echoed the one Johnson had suffered at the midterm nearly thirty years earlier.

Clinton had much in common with his fellow southerner Johnson: a rare empathy and a genius for interpersonal politics, a host of insatiable appetites, a voluble temperament.

But in crucial ways Clinton was also like Reagan, with a keen sense for where public mood was headed and how to speak to the public's hopes and fears. And perhaps most crucially, Clinton possessed Reagan's uncanny capacity for pragmatism in matters of his own self-interest. He responded to his midterm loss by co-opting the Reagan vision, declaring "The era of Big Government is over" in his 1996 State of the Union address. That same year he signed into law his signal domestic achievement, a welfare reform law aimed at *limiting* the government safety net. When he won reelection for the presidency in the fall of that year, it was a return from the wilderness for the Democrats—Clinton was the first reelected Democratic president since FDR. But the triumph owed much to Reagan's vision, and very little to Johnson's.

Despite its long string of electoral successes, the Reagan myth had its limitations as well. These were apparent even while Reagan was still president. In office, Reagan struggled to produce a positive governing agenda that complemented his antigovernment rhetoric.

"You Ain't Seen Nothing Yet," his campaign for reelection promised, but both his political and policy advisers knew that Reagan had
no substantive domestic program in place for a second term. The
great achievement of that term would be tax reform, an effort that
lowered corporate tax rates but attacked business-friendly tax breaks
and maintained the status quo size of government. It was not the
stuff of conservative revolution.

And that was precisely the point. In the White House, Reagan's
more pragmatic aides quickly perceived that the public that had
voted for the conservative revolutionary did not really want conservative revolution. Americans liked the sound of limiting government
in theory but had little tolerance for limiting popular government
entitlements such as Social Security and Medicare—or for cutting
back on national defense. Rather than address this contradiction
and risk the president's popularity, Reagan's aides simply let it be,
puffing up the image of the president as a crusader against Big Government, an image they knew had more basis in fantasy than fact.

It was good politics for Reagan, but soon enough this fantasy
would come to haunt his Republican heirs. The first victim was his
successor as president, George H. W. Bush, a model citizen of the
Republican Party's realist wing. Looking squarely at the staggering
deficits of the Reagan years, Bush violated a campaign pledge and
struck a deal with a Democratic-controlled Congress to raise taxes
in order to put the country's fiscal affairs in order. Conservatives in
Congress promptly labeled their president a traitor to Reagan's legacy and broke with him, ensuring Bush's defeat in the next election.

The lesson was not lost on Bush's son, who wished his own presidency in the first decade of the twenty-first century to be bathed in
Reagan-like glory. George W. Bush's White House aides obsessively
mimicked Reagan's use of "optics"—eschewing messy and contradictory details in favor of simple, clear, and stirring symbols. The
most memorable product of this mimicry came in May 2003 aboard
the USS *Abraham Lincoln,* where Bush emerged in a flight suit to
proclaim the end of major combat operations in Iraq under a banner

reading "Mission Accomplished." The event would prove a lasting embarrassment: Bush's Iraq war would, in fact, last for nearly a decade longer, kill and injure thousands of Americans and tens of thousands of Iraqis, and cost nearly a trillion dollars.

The "Mission Accomplished" debacle revealed the dangers facing presidents in an age when politics are divorced from reality. In office, Bush and his powerful vice president, Dick Cheney, pursued contradictory policies—two costly wars and the creation of a massive national security surveillance state were matched with a generous tax cut for wealthy Americans, loosening of federal regulations, and the creation of a new entitlement for senior citizens. Advised that this toxic mix would bring on staggering deficits, Cheney shrugged: "Reagan proved deficits don't matter."

But while they were eager to relive Reagan's myth, Bush and Cheney lacked his pragmatic instinct to adjust in the face of shifting public mood. And they also lacked Reagan's luck. Reality intruded on the latter years of the Bush presidency: the occupation of Iraq unraveled; the federal government appeared powerless to help the citizens of New Orleans after Hurricane Katrina destroyed their city; a financial crisis devastated the American economy. By the time Bush and Cheney left office in January 2009, the Republican Party's national image was more seriously damaged than it had been at any point since Barry Goldwater's disastrous campaign of 1964.

And yet the Republicans who have come after them have doubled down on the old myth, accepting the Reagan of fantasy as a figure of historical fact. In the contemporary conservative version of history, Reagan dramatically shrank government and earned the public's everlasting affection and gratitude in return. Big Government persists after Reagan, Reagan's contemporary admirers admit, but only because liberals and Washington elites have used government programs to buy off the public's votes and used allies in the media to cloak their unpopular policies. Like the utopian liberals of the Johnson era, who headily promoted untested new programs, thinking they were finishing the work of Roosevelt, these contemporary conservatives seek to drastically shrink government in the belief that they are fulfilling the vision of Reagan and answering the public will.

The result for the Republican Party of the twenty-first century has been the same as for the Democratic Party in the sixties: disaster. Today's Reagan fantasists, with their hostility to government programs and their distaste for reality, have driven the American middle away. Their message no longer resonates with the centrist, suburban voters who were so influential in the old Reagan coalition. And it has alienated the party from the rising majority coalition of the new millennium. This new majority is younger, more diverse, and more urban than its Reagan-era predecessor, and its constituents appear more disposed to want government services and policies to aid their rise to affluence. Belief in the Reagan myth, that utopia will come from a revolutionary reinvention of government that is near at hand, has left the twenty-first-century GOP as a minority party with no obvious path out of the wilderness.

Today's Democrats have clearly benefited politically from the Republicans' problems. They have won the popular vote in five out of the last six presidential elections. But in governing, the old visions haunt them still. This springs in part from the great damage that the lingering myths of Reagan and Johnson have done to government itself. Each of the myths discredited government. Reagan's did it overtly, maintaining that government was the source of America's problems. Johnson's did it by example, making promises for government that it could not possibly fulfill. As a result, a generation of Americans has come of age with little faith in government's ability to do much of anything. Today's America faces a host of complex problems that demand strong federal action. Among them are the catastrophic potential of global climate change, the strain on the nation's finances of an aging population, and the disruptive effects on the workforce caused by the transition to a technology-based economy. But the memory of the old myths makes it nearly impossible to summon the political support for large-scale government action of any kind.

At first it seems bizarre that Reagan's and Johnson's visions should have such staying power. After all, they were the product of unique moments in time. Indeed it can seem that Johnson's and Reagan's thousand days never would have happened were it not for the coincidence of unique, utterly unpredictable events.

Who could have predicted that the greatest legislator in modern history would be thrust suddenly into the presidency and presented with the greatest legislative opportunity of any president since FDR?

Who could have predicted that a man who won the largest landslide in American history would lose his popularity and control of his presidency in just two years' time?

Who could have predicted that a middle-aged actor playing a supporting character in a troubled Hollywood film would rise, in the space of just a thousand days, to transform his country's politics for generations?

And yet, as we have seen, none of these strange coincidences was accidental—they were all tied up in one another, each one both cause and effect. And with the distance of history, we can see that they are all connected by a single strand: the tension that thrives in a nation with its eyes on an uncertain future, the promise, and the terror, of a world that is changing fast. A thousand days is not a long time, but it is more than long enough for a country's people to journey from fear to hope and back again.

It makes sense, then, that today's America, gripped once again by profound anxieties about its future, would still reach for the old myths. Reagan's and Johnson's visions were specifically designed to reassure a country that was sometimes terrified about what was coming next. The old myths, for all their flaws, offer comfort in a time of uncertainty. The problem for today's political system—and it is an existential one—is that people no longer believe those myths.

To fix its broken politics, today's America needs new stories. Or perhaps it just needs a new version of an old one. The shared vision that Johnson and Reagan discarded in the course of their thousand days—the old consensus vision of Roosevelt and Kennedy—

contained lasting wisdom that today's leaders would do well to adopt. In that worldview, politicians had to be deeply realistic and humble when making promises for the future, for they knew that the future never turns out exactly the way we think it's going to. But they also had to have the courage to tell the people that though government would never be able to solve all its people's problems, it had a sacred obligation to try.

That old vision could serve America well in an often frightening new century. The answer to our problems may come from a leader who brings such a simple message. It is a message that neither Reagan nor Johnson had much use for but that the story of both of their lives confirms: what lies ahead of us is not the certain promise of utopia, but the infinite possibilities of life itself.

Acknowledgments

In the preceding pages, I have set out to tell the story of how two iconic presidents took hold of the American imagination over a period of three years. To understand how Americans in the mid-1960s saw the world, I immersed myself in their media. Much of the texture in my story comes from television newscasts and broadcasts, Hollywood films, print and television advertising, and magazine and daily newspaper coverage from the period. I took great pleasure in the long hours I spent reading issues of *Time* and *Newsweek* from the 1960s, a golden age of newsmagazines in which writers crafted sweeping stories from a wealth of small but significant details. Those details proved a treasure trove in my research.

In focusing on a brief period in the careers of Lyndon Johnson and Ronald Reagan, two men who, between them, played a significant part in national politics for half a century, I have necessarily relied on the existing scholarship on both men's lives. Luckily, both have been blessed with fantastic biographers. My understanding of Johnson owes a great deal especially to the work of Robert Caro and to informative biographies by Robert Dallek and Doris Kearns Goodwin. Michael Beschloss's masterly study of the Johnson White House recordings first drew me into the mesmerizing mind of LBJ, and in returning to the recordings for this project, my appreciation grew for the scope and skill of Beschloss's undertaking. My work on

Reagan was illuminated by a number of biographies, most significantly those by two formidable chroniclers, Lou Cannon and Edmund Morris. My understanding of decision-making in the Vietnam War was shaped by enduring works by Stanley Karnow and David Halberstam.

In my research, I was lucky to have the help of a talented archivist, Jessica Gallagher. In spite of her training as a medievalist (or perhaps because of it), Jessica quickly took a shine to the unique personage of Lyndon Baines Johnson and became an expert on the topic. She offered vital assistance throughout the project, and her work on the chapter notes and bibliography was brilliant and heroic. Melissa Carson Thomas is a gifted researcher who provided fantastic fact-checking with remarkable thoroughness, efficiency, and good cheer.

In writing this book, I have looked to the example of two great teachers from my career in journalism. I have been fortunate to have an esteemed biographer, Jon Meacham, as a friend and wise editor for the past decade. Jon helped me find my way to this topic and offered sage advice and reassurance at crucial moments in the process. At *Newsweek,* I watched Evan Thomas turn the mess of the busy world into gripping, elegant drama for the magazine's pages each week, and from him, I learned so much about storytelling. A distinguished historian of the period I write about, Evan provided helpful advice and encouragement, and I am thankful for both.

At Random House, it is my great good fortune to have Kate Medina as an editor. Kate's wisdom and her extraordinary sense for the shape of a book, combined with her graceful, generous spirit, make her an ideal guide, protector, and champion of a writer publishing a book for the first time. Like Kate, Anna Pitoniak manages to match uncommon insight with unfailing kindness, and the combination makes her a brilliant editor. Every page of this book is better because of her. I am thankful for the talented professionals at Random House who have published this book with creativity, foresight, and style. Thanks especially to Tom Perry, Sally Marvin, London King, Leigh Marchant, Selby McRae, Robbin Schiff, and Janet Wygal.

I am grateful to Andrew Wylie, whose high standards, sharp thinking, and lively wit make him an invaluable agent and a wonderful ally. Many thanks to Sarah Chalfant, who helped bring me to Random House. Thanks as well to Diego Nunez and Jacqueline Ko.

Thanks to friends and colleagues for kindnesses large and small offered in the writing of this book. I am especially obliged to Oscie Thomas, Louisa Thomas, Julie Bosman, Ceridwen Dovey, Kate Burch and Gary Belkin, Elliott Holt, Katherine Marino, Mark Kirby and Erin Owens, Madeleine Sackler, and Rachel Ptak. Will Darman and Elizabeth Holt provided comfortable and congenial accommodations in Washington and I am grateful to them, and to Emmet Darman, for encouragement along the way. James Lawler read, pondered, and lived this book from conception to publication and I am grateful for all of his contributions and for everything else.

My mother, Kathleen Emmet, is a gifted storyteller who first introduced me to the captivating story of America in the 1960s. My late father, Richard Darman, taught me that politics can be noble and that the drama of politics can reveal deep, human truths. I am grateful to my parents for encouraging me as a writer and for introducing me to the questions posed in the 1960s, still the most important questions of all.

Notes

Prologue: Men on Horseback

ix   **"There is but one way to get the cattle out of the swamp"** Goodwin, *Lyndon Johnson,* 172.

xi   **"like a bunch of cattle caught in the swamp"** Ibid.

xi   **The previous day—Election Day** Mohr, "President Sees a Unity Mandate," *New York Times.*

xi   **"For the first time in all my life"** Goodwin, *Lyndon Johnson,* 209.

xi   **"He spent the night"** "The Presidency: A Different Man," *Time.*

xii   **"that son of a bitch"** Telephone conversation between LBJ and John Connally, November 4, 1964, Citation #6145.

xii   **As the hour grew late on Election Day** Perlstein, *Before the Storm,* 512.

xii   **"By God, we said we would get you seven-fifty"** Telephone conversation between Richard Daley and LBJ, November 4, 1964, Citation #6167.

xiii   **"May the Lord shower his blessings upon you"** Ibid.

xiii   **"Well, you oughtta be a banker, Pat"** Telephone conversation between Edmund G. Brown and LBJ, November 5, 1964, Citation #6237.

xvi   **"You've been around this business long enough"** Morris, *Dutch,* 323.

xvii   **"In the space of a single Autumn day"** "GOP '66: Back on the Map," *Newsweek.*

xix   **"We shall overcome"** Lyndon B. Johnson, "Special Message to Congress: The American Promise" (speech, Washington, DC, March 15, 1965), *Public Papers of the Presidents,* 1965, vol. I, 284.

xxi   **"It's the time of peace on Earth and good will among men"** Lyndon B. Johnson, "Remarks at the Civic Center Arena in Pittsburgh" (speech, Pittsburgh, PA, October 27, 1964), *Public Papers of the Presidents,* 1963–64, vol. II, 1479.

xxii   **"Is our world gone?"** Lyndon B. Johnson, "Inaugural Address" (speech, Washington, DC, January 20, 1965), *Public Papers of the Presidents,* 1965, vol. I, 74.

xxii   **All that has happened in our historic past** "Lyndon Johnson's Pledge," *Newsweek.*

xxiii   **"We have every right"** Ronald Reagan, "Inaugural Address" (speech, Washington, DC, January 20, 1981), *Public Papers of the Presidents,* 1981, 2.

xxiv **"has three telephones in his car"** Reston, "The Three Telephone Man in the White House," *New York Times.*

xxiv **"When you're bleeding up on that Hill"** Lawrence (Larry) O'Brien OH VI.

xxvi **"Hell . . . if I'd stayed in there much longer"** Miller, *Lyndon: An Oral Biography,* 524–25; Goodwin, *Remembering America,* 320–24.

xxviii **"Abundance or annihilation"** Lyndon B. Johnson, "Remarks at the Opening of the World's Fair" (speech, New York, April 22, 1964), *Public Papers of the Presidents, 1963–64,* vol. I, 515.

xxviii **"We'll preserve for our children this"** Ronald Reagan, "Campaign Address for Goldwater Presidential Campaign: A Time for Choosing" (speech, October 27, 1964), *Rendezvous with Destiny* Recorded Program.

xxix **"Heady wine"** Reagan, *Where's the Rest of Me?,* 28–29.

Chapter One: Stories

3   *"The president of the United States is dead"* Today, NBC, November 23, 1963.

4   **At 1:35 P.M., the network Teletypes carried a wire** Manchester, *Death of a President,* 221.

4   **"The body of John Fitzgerald Kennedy is at this moment in the White House"** Today, NBC, November 23, 1963.

6   **The department stores have taken down their Christmas decorations** Caro, *Passage of Power,* 355.

6   **"The people here . . . are like the people out on Christmas Eve,"** Today, NBC, November 23, 1963.

7   **only a single White House photographer** See Manchester, *Death of a President,* 324–26 and Caro, *Passage of Power,* 322 and 333.

7   **For a while the phones in Washington don't even work** Manchester, *Death of a President,* 254–55.

7   **On average this weekend, American households will watch 8.5 hours of television each day** Feldman and Sheatsley, "The Assassination of President Kennedy" 197, and "National Survey on Public Reactions and Behavior," 159.

7   **"we were watching you to see if you had any"** Watson, *Expanding Vista,* 215; "America's Long Vigil," *TV Guide,* January 25, 1964.

7   **"old friends . . . telling us about the tragedy until we could absorb it"** Watson, *Expanding Vista,* 216.

8   **At 8:40 that Saturday morning** Semple, *Four Days in November,* 203.

8   **To think of the things they'd been worried about** See Manchester, *Death of a President,* 6–7, for preparations for the Kennedy visit to the ranch.

9   **The Johnsons had been riding several cars behind the Kennedys** See Manchester, *Death of a President,* 155–56 and 166–67; Lady Bird Johnson, *White House Diary,* 3–7; Caro, *Passage of Power,* for accounts of Johnson during events of the assassination.

9   **"Let's get out of here"** Manchester, *Death of a President,* 163.

9   **"They've killed him"** Lady Bird Johnson, *White House Diary,* 4.

9   **At the instructions of his security detail** Manchester, *Death of a President,* 229 and Caro, *Passage of Power,* 316–17.

9   **"He's gone"** Caro, *Passage of Power,* 317.

10   **He worried that Kennedy's assassination might be the first step** Manchester, *Death of a President*, 220.

10   **at his insistence** See Caro, *Passage of Power*, 326–33.

10   **Greeted at Andrews Air Force Base** Ibid., 365.

10   **Still, when . . . he finally climbed into this own bed** Ibid., 371.

10   **Americans . . . "were all spinning around and around"** Goodwin, *Lyndon Johnson*, 172.

11   **"Hell . . . the Johnsons could strut sitting down"** Caro, *Means of Ascent*, 68.

11   **"Now the light came in from the East"** Rebekah Baines Johnson, *A Family Album*, 17; Goodwin, *Lyndon Johnson*, 21.

12   **"A United States Senator was born today!"** Caro, *Path to Power*, 3.

12   **Johnson refused to read** This story is repeated in several biographies: see Steinberg, *Sam Johnson's Boy,* and Caro, *Path to Power,* 69.

12   **"When Miss Kate excused one of her students"** Caro, ibid.

12   **In August 1934** Russell, *Lady Bird,* 15.

12   **"he told me all sorts of things that I thought were extraordinarily direct"** Goldman, *Tragedy of Lyndon Johnson,* 406–7; Goodwin, *Lyndon Johnson,* 80. Lady Bird discusses her courtship with Lyndon in oral history accounts, commenting that "he came on very strong, he was very direct and dynamic," and references his swift proposal: "I do believe before the day was over he did ask me to marry him, and I thought he was out of his mind" (Lady Bird OH IV); also see Lady Bird interview with Ruth Montgomery, Baylor University.

12   **The goal . . . was "to keep her mind completely on me"** Goodwin, *Lyndon Johnson,* 80.

13   **As a twenty-three-year-old clerk** Caro, *Means of Ascent,* 3.

13   **a margin of 87 votes** See Caro, *Means of Ascent,* 386–87. Johnson's tiny margin in the 1948 run-off prompted accusations of fraud that followed him throughout his career. In his second volume, *Means of Ascent,* published in 1990, Caro demonstrated that Johnson's campaign did in fact use unlawful means—including falsifying votes from the dead and those who did not participate in the election—to erase a 20,000 vote deficit and steal the election from Stevenson.

13   **"the right size"** Caro, *Master of the Senate,* 136; Miller, *Lyndon: An Oral Biography,* 171.

13   **"genius for studying a man"** Caro, *Master of the Senate,* 136.

14   **"FDR-LBJ, FDR-LBJ—do you get it?"** Ibid., 111.

15   **"When you and I talked last night"** Caro, *Passage of Power,* 374.

16   **The night before** Marie Fehmer OH II.

17   **"You are dealing with a very insecure, sensitive man"** Reeves, *President Kennedy,* 119. Kenneth O'Donnell OH I, 25.

17   **"a spectral presence"** Schlesinger, *Robert Kennedy,* 622.

18   **On the rare occasions** Thomas, *Robert Kennedy,* 290.

18   **"It was like the teacher walks"** Harry McPherson OH I.

18   **"He looked absolutely gross"** Ibid.

20   **"He can't even let the body get cold"** Gillon, *Kennedy Assassination,* 179; Cliff Carter OH.

21   **In the year 1961 it had been ten hours and nineteen minutes** Schlesinger, *Robert Kennedy,* 622.

22   "I need you more than you need me" Manchester, *Death of a President*, 453.

22   "Do you know he asked me to be out by *9:30*?" Ibid.

22   "First he expressed his condolences" Schlesinger, *Robert Kennedy*, 609.

23   "Where's Jackie?" Thomas, *Robert Kennedy*, 278.

23   "Why, God?" Charles Spalding, interviewed by Jean Stein, January 22, 1970, 18–19 Stein Papers, cited in Schlesinger, *Robert Kennedy*, 611.

24   "I want to talk to you" Manchester, *Death of a President*, 454.

24   "Hey sonny" Thomas, *Robert Kennedy*, 96.

24   "Son, you've got to learn to handle a gun like a man" Dallek, *Flawed Giant*, 33.

25   "Now, you don't like me, Bobby" Schlesinger, *Robert Kennedy*, 623. Thomas, *Robert Kennedy*, 278.

26   "a very very ambitious young man" Telephone conversation between Lyndon Johnson and Dean Rusk, August 17, 1964, citation #5009.

26   "I thought they'd get one of us" Schlesinger, *Robert Kennedy*, 609. Guthman, *We Band of Brothers*, 244.

26   "Without question" Thomas, *Robert Kennedy*, 283.

27   Could Johnson wait a while before moving in? Manchester, *Death of a President*, 454.

27   "Well, of course" Ibid.

28   Under Jacqueline Kennedy's instruction Ibid., 418.

28   "Morning, Mr. President" *Today*, NBC, November 23, 1963.

28   "Mr. Johnson . . . prefers to hold his appointments in the vice presidential office" Ibid.

28   "It will give the people confidence" Manchester, *Death of a President*, 454–55.

Chapter Two: Watching

32   "I want you to talk him into playing that role" Siegel, *Siegel Film*, 240.

33   Horses are like people Ibid., 241.

33   "the boss . . ." Ibid., 242.

33   "You'll steal the show" Ibid., 250.

34   Years later, Siegel would recall the announcer's words Ibid., 250–1.

34   Kennedy . . . was a Marxist with a pretty face Dallek, *Right Moment*, 38.

34   Walter Cronkite didn't help matters Perlstein, *Before the Storm*, 248.

35   A mob was forming Ibid., 247.

35   "Well, your parents will probably be happy!" Davis, *Way I See It*, 82.

36   "Lee had a theory about drinking" Siegel, *Siegel Film*, 248.

36   "An actor likes a death scene" *The Killers*, directed by Don Siegel, 1964, Criterion Collection DVD Commentary by Clu Gulager.

39   "The story begins with a closeup" Reagan, *Where's the Rest of Me?*, 3.

40   "His heroes . . . were always heroes" Cannon, *Governor Reagan*, 17.

40   "You know why I had such fun at it?" Edwards, *Early Reagan*, 64.

40   "All of this commenced to create in me a personality" Reagan, *Where's the Rest of Me?*, 38.

41   "I discovered that night" Ibid., 28–29.

41   "You were always aware when he came into a room" Cannon, *Governor Reagan*, 43. (emphasis added)

41   "I like to swim, hike and sleep" Ronald Reagan, "How to Make Yourself Important," *Photoplay*, August 1942, quoted in Cannon, *Governor Reagan*, 59.

41   "the guy who didn't get the girl" Cannon, *Ronnie and Jesse*, 29.

42   "I *always* got the girl" Ibid., 33.

42   "The Reagans' home life" Cannon, *Reagan*, 61.

42   "appears to have accepted the studio propaganda" Ibid., 62.

42   when they were with him Morris, *Dutch*, 128.

42   Reagan earned genuine critical acclaim Cannon, *Governor Reagan*, 57.

43   he was assigned to the Army Air Force's First Motion Picture Unit Ibid., 57.

43   "Ronald Reagan is having his picture taken" Nancy Reagan, *My Turn*, 126.

43   "coaxing me to take a breath" Reagan, *Where's the Rest of Me?*, 195.

43   "Don't ask Ronnie what time it is" Edwards, *Early Reagan*, 229.

43   in her petition Deaver, *Behind the Scenes*, 110; Edwards, *Early Reagan*, 355.

43   *"I couldn't stand to watch that damn 'King's Row' one more time,"* Kelley, *Nancy Reagan*, 61.

44   "Lew is the love of my life" Edwards, *Early Reagan*, 354.

44   "The trouble is" Cannon, *Governor Reagan*, 72.

44   "Ronald Reagan always received top billing" Deaver, *Nancy*, 6.

45   "My life . . . didn't really begin" Nancy Reagan, *My Turn*, 93.

45   For a wedding gift Edwards, *Early Reagan*, 431.

45   Ronnie especially treasured a birthday gift Reagan, *Where's the Rest of Me?*, 291.

45   "Jane had said publicly that she was bored" Nancy Reagan, *My Turn*, 100.

45   Edmund Morris . . . asked him to recall his mindset Morris, *Dutch*, 266.

46   "I am seen by more people in one week" Ibid., 304.

46   Many children of the baby boom See Noonan, *When Character Was King*, 80–81, for descriptions of watching Reagan on *GE Theater*.

46   by 1958, a survey would determine Morris, *Dutch*, 305.

46   the routine was punishing Morris, *Dutch*, 305; Reagan, *Where's the Rest of Me?*, 257.

47   the show was getting beaten in the ratings by *Bonanza* Nancy Reagan, *My Turn*, 129.

47   By his own account *Reagan: American Life*, 138.

47   "years . . . of relative calm" Nancy Reagan, *I Love You, Ronnie*, 75.

47   Dean Miller traveled to Yearling Row Dean Miller, *Here's Hollywood*, directed by Gene Law, 1961.

49   "Ronnie's easygoing manner is deceiving" Nancy Reagan, *My Turn*, 114.

49   Edmund Morris spoke to Brower's widow Morris, *Dutch*, 321.

49   Reagan denied Mrs. Brower's account Ibid. In *Where's the Rest of Me?* Reagan acknowledges that he received a phone call from an advertising executive at GE asking him how he would feel about limiting his speeches to a discussion of GE products, about which he writes, "I told this gentleman that if the speeches were an issue I could see no solution short of severing our relationship. . . . Twenty-four hours later the *GE Theater* was canceled. I don't know—maybe eight years was long enough." Reagan, *Where's the Rest of Me?*, 273.

49   "Like any actor" Ibid., 322; Ronald Reagan, *Sunset*, October 1961.

50   For the rest of his life Reagan, *American Life*, 138.

50   "A lot of people who went to see *The Killers*" Ibid., 381.

50   The theme of evil is there from the very beginning of the film *The Killers*, directed by Don Siegel (1964, Los Angeles, Universal).

51   "Everybody dies in it" Davis, *Way I See It*, 99.

51   "Just kiss me, you fool!" *The Killers*, directed by Don Siegel, 1964.

52   President Johnson "has been, shall we say, a little bit in the background today" CBS, November 23, 1963.

53   An FBI agent . . . had been amazed to find Reports of the President's Commission on the Assassination of President John F. Kennedy, 1964, 202.

53   "He's been shot" Tom Petit, NBC, November 24, 1963.

54   "The chase ends in a theater" Ibid.

Chapter Three: Myths

55   Black Jack Manchester, *Death of a President*, 490, 596.

57   "like a Roman Queen, a stone statue" Smith, *Grace and Power*, 455.

57   "Jacqueline Kennedy has given" "Magic Majesty of Mrs. Kennedy," *London Evening Standard*, November 25, 1963; Semple, *Four Days in November*, 485.

58   In one extravagant gesture Russell, *Lady Bird*, 211.

58   "Never before has Texas beef found a market" Russell, *Lady Bird*, 211.

58   "too flip" Ibid.

58   "totally doomed child" Manchester, *Death of a President*, 406.

58   "burned alive" Ibid.

58   "I consider that my life is over" Bradlee, *A Good Life*, 262.

59   "Is there anything *we* can do for *you*?" McCullough, *Truman*, 342.

59   "what an awful way for you to come in" Manchester, *Death of a President*, 538.

59   A black lace mantilla Graham, *Katharine Graham's Washington*, 539.

59   "of the country grieving" Bradlee, *Conversations with Kennedy*, 244.

60   "We've got to start being—not to be cold-blooded" Telephone conversation between Lyndon Johnson and Jack Brooks, November 24, 1963.

61   "It was quite clear" Shesol, *Mutual Contempt*, 120.

61   Then Adlai Stevenson, the UN ambassador, rose to read a lengthy statement Manchester, *Death of a President*, 476.

61   "a few paragraphs on how nice Lyndon Johnson was" Shesol, *Mutual Contempt*, 120.

62   "A nice little statement" Schlesinger, *Robert Kennedy*, 627.

62   "I can't sit still" Telephone conversation between Lyndon Johnson and John McCormack, November 23, 1963.

63   The assassination . . . had struck him harder than the death of his own father Alsop, *I've Seen the Best of It*, 464.

63   "the show must go on" Manchester, *Death of a President*, 470.

64   the Kennedy Administration bankrolled an expansion Karnow, *Vietnam*, 284.

65   "I am not going to lose Vietnam" Wicker, *JFK and LBJ*, 205.

65   "I wonder if you will get me a little synopsis" Beschloss, *Taking Charge*, 23.

65   "What would you think of the possibility" Sorensen, *Counselor*, 379; Manchester, *Death of a President*, 481.

66   "my heart is not in it" Schlesinger, *Journals*, 206.

66 "Yes, Mr. President" Manchester, *Death of a President*, 412.

66 "I carried *my* president" Ibid., 172.

66 "the impact of Kennedy's death was evident everywhere" Goodwin, *Lyndon Johnson*, 175.

66 "Suddenly they were outsiders" Ibid.

66 "littered with male widows" Alsop, *Best I've Seen of It*, 464.

67 "We'll never laugh again" Manchester, *Death of a President*, 506.

67 "is of a different generation" Semple, *Four Days in November*, 245.

68 Lunching with Daniel Moynihan For what became known as the "Harvard Lunch" see Manchester, *Death of a President*, 474 and Shesol, *Mutual Contempt*, 143.

68 he "could stay here forever" Smith, *Grace and Power*, 445.

68 A favorite poem Schlesinger, *A Thousand Days*, 98.

69 Except the Lord keep the city Manchester, *Death of a President*, 57.

69 "All sorts of people are remembering" Smith, *Grace and Power*, 446.

69 "one of the really beautiful places on earth" Reeves, *President Kennedy*, 654.

69 "Don't worry, Lyndon" Ibid., 119.

69 Soon there would be plans to rename "Land of Kennedy," *Time*, December 13, 1963; Manchester, *Death of a President*, 671.

70 "God lives and the Government at Washington still stands" Semple, *Four Days*, 88.

70 The next day Ibid., 306–7.

70 "a youthful Lincoln" Richard Cardinal Cushing, "Eulogy to John F. Kennedy" (speech, Boston, MA, November 24, 1963). Vital Speeches of the Day 1963, vol. 30, Issue 4, 100.

70 "the second president we've lost" Semple, *Four Days*, 90.

71 "so concerned about being President" Carson, ed., *Autobiography of Martin Luther King Jr.*, 150.

71 A memo that Sorensen prepared Reeves, *President Kennedy*, 277; Sorensen memo to Kennedy, "Notes for Congressional Session," January 17, 1962.

72 "There won't be a library" Reeves, *President Kennedy*, 654.

73 "Those brass hats have one great advantage" Thomas, *Robert Kennedy*, 217.

74 "Gradually expanding federal government" Perlstein, *Before the Storm*, 13.

76 "All this will not be finished" John F. Kennedy, "Inaugural Address" (speech, Washington, DC, January 20, 1961), *Public Papers of the Presidents*, 1961, 2.

77 "He had so little time" Schlesinger, *Thousand Days*, 1030.

77 "Everything I had ever learned" Goodwin, *Lyndon Johnson*, 178.

78 "So you liked Galbraith?" Telephone conversation between Lyndon Johnson and Ted Sorensen, November 23, 1963.

79 I who cannot fill his shoes Sorensen, *Counselor*, 382.

79 "This is a fine speech" Schlesinger, *White House Ghosts*, 148.

79 "All I have" Lyndon B. Johnson, "Speech Before Joint Session of Congress" (speech, Washington, DC, November 27, 1963), *Public Papers of the Presidents*, 1963–64, vol. I, 8.

82 "pale, somber and inscrutable" Schlesinger, *Robert Kennedy and His Times*, 628.

82 Trying to be sympathetic Sorensen, *Counselor*, 380.

82 The crowd . . . had interrupted him Beschloss, *Taking Charge*, 45; Telephone

conversation between Lyndon Johnson and Adam Clayton Powell, Jr., November 27, 1963.

82   **"We cannot bring him back"** *Jack Paar Show,* NBC, November 29, 1963.

83   **"You can't stop the living from living"** "The People: The Mood of the Land," *Time,* December 20, 1963.

83   **Holiday sales in the first week of December** Ibid.

84   **"Do you know what chair you're sitting in"** Kennedy, *Historic Conversations on Life with John F. Kennedy,* 85.

85   **Over and over he repeated** Schlesinger, *Robert Kennedy,* 588.

85   **Theodore White was in the chair at his dentist's office** White, *In Search of History,* 672-3.

85   **"without tears"** Ibid, 674.

86   **"Then Jack turned back so neatly"** Ibid., 676.

86   **"There's one thing I wanted to say"** Ibid., 678.

87   **"There will be other great presidents"** Theodore White, "Epilogue," *Life,* December 13, 1963, 159.

87   **"And all she could think"** "The Enduring Legacy of Jacqueline Kennedy," *Washington Post,* November 19, 2013.

Chapter Four: Home

89   **"we will never be quite settled"** Lady Bird Johnson, *White House Diary,* 20.

90   **Just as the assembled kinfolk were about to sit down to their dinner** See Johnson, *White House Diary,* 21; "The Presidency: Whatever You Say, Honey," *Time,* January 3, 1964; "The President: Spare Rib Summit," *Newsweek,* January 6, 1964.

90   **"I promised to give them a wonderful tour"** "The Presidency: Whatever You Say, Honey."

90   **"It'll only take a minute"** Ibid.

91   **"Mrs. Johnson's locked the door on me!"** "The President: Spare Rib Summit."

91   **"Lynda," he called to his elder daughter** Ibid.

91   **"He assumes that if there is something to be done"** Reston, "The Three Telephone Man in the White House," *New York Times,* December 7, 1963.

92   **"has done everything but cut the White House lawn"** Ibid.

92   **"I never saw a man work harder"** See Robert McNamara Special Interview OH: "I've never seen anybody work harder nor with more determination"; Ed Clark said of Johnson in 1937, "I never thought it was possible for anyone to work that hard" (Caro, *Path to Power,* 237).

92   **"Dammit, Hubert"** Caro, *Master of the Senate,* 460.

92   **Opening the door to the limousine** "Despite 'Frugality' the Budget Rises," *Newsweek,* December 16, 1963.

93   **"Could I drop by and bum a drink from you?"** Beschloss, *Taking Charge,* 80; telephone conversation between LBJ and Walter Lippmann, December 1, 1963.

93   **"Man-in-Motion Johnson"** "The President: Business and Busyness," *Time,* December 20, 1963.

93   **"two shift day"** Dallek, *Lyndon,* 151.

94   **"The LBJ phone calls"** Carpenter, *Ruffles and Flourishes,* 4-5.

94   **"Isn't that bed a little short for you?"** "The President: Home on the Range," *Newsweek*, December 30, 1963, 14.

94   **"We shall be wrong"** Walter Lippmann, "Today and Tomorrow: The Transfer of Power."

95   **"You're the *y* in Lyndon"** "The President: Home on the Range," 14.

95   **"the President used and gave away 169 pens."** "The President: Home on the Range."

95   **"Are we now being emotionally stampeded"** "Out of Control," *Newsweek*, December 23, 1963, quoting Buckley, "JFK: The Morning After," *National Review*, December 7, 1963, 17.

95   **"you're either the party of Lincoln or you ain't"** Branch, *Pillar of Fire*, 180; Telephone conversation between Lyndon Johnson and Robert Anderson, November 30, 1963.

96   **"Nobody ever has been more to me"** Telephone conversation between Lyndon Johnson and Richard Russell, November 29, 1963.

96   **"I'm not going to cavil"** Johnson, *Vantage Point*, 157–58; Branch, *Pillar of Fire*, 187.

96   **"If Dick Russell hadn't had to wear Jim Crow's collar"** Lemann, *Promised Land*, 137.

97   **"You enjoy talking about what you love"** Lady Bird Johnson, *White House Diary*, 22.

97   **"I keep reminding myself of Lyndon"** Ibid., 16.

97   **"orderly, composed and radiating her particular sort of aliveness"** Ibid., 11–12.

98   **ten different homes** Russell, *Lady Bird*, 149

98   **the Johnsons purchased a two-story colonial on Thirtieth Place** Russell, *Lady Bird*, 148; Caro, *Means of Ascent*, 228.

98   **Seized by impulse one day** Caro, *Master of the Senate*, 228.

98   **The house, modeled on a château in Normandy** For descriptions of The Elms interiors and gardens, see "Ormes and the Man," *Time*, November 17, 1961; "Summer Flowers in the Johnson Garden," *Washington Post*, July 7, 1963; and O'Brien, "France and Texas Contribute to Décor in the Johnsons' Washington Home," *New York Times*, October 31, 1961.

99   **"Every time somebody calls it a château"** "Ormes and the Man."

99   **In the living room, she placed a cherry-red chair** Ibid.

99   **"I would to God I could serve Mrs. Kennedy's comfort"** Lady Bird Johnson, *White House Diary*, 14.

100   **"When I wake up in the morning"** "The White House: Home Away from Home."

100   **"glass house"** Lady Bird Johnson, *White House Diary*, 15.

100   **"don't ever close the light out until the very last ray is gone"** Carpenter, *Ruffles and Flourishes*, 10.

100   **"I feel ... like I am suddenly onstage"** Lady Bird Johnson, *White House Diary*, 16.

100   **she also took extra courses** Russell, *Lady Bird*, 87.

100   **"My poor little girl"** Russell, *Lady Bird*, 53.

101   TJ TAYLOR ... DEALER IN EVERYTHING Ibid.

101   **As a child growing up** Ibid.

101   **"I hoped the ladies weren't in"** Ibid., 134.

102   "By God, he's gonna kill her!" Caro, *Master of the Senate,* 224.

102   One afternoon in Washington Russell, *Lady Bird,* 119.

102   He made little effort to hide either relationship Ibid. 212.

103   "Everyone felt sorry for her" Ibid., 22.

103   "like a trained hunting dog" Kennedy, *Historic Conversations,* 85.

103   "It was just like finding yourself in the middle of a whirlwind" Russell, *Lady Bird,* 93.

104   "You're seeing the best side of me" Ibid.

104   "Ours was a compelling love" Ibid., 20.

104   "It seems as if one great crescendo" Lady Bird Johnson, *White House Diary,* 27.

105   "Lynda Bird . . . was deep in conversation with him" Ibid., 28–9.

106   "That's my kind of program!" Lemann, *Promised Land,* 141.

106   "the way our economic attitudes are rooted in the poverty" Galbraith, *Affluent Society,* 2.

106   "The interesting thing about his pronouncement" Macdonald, "Our Invisible Poor," *New Yorker,* January 19, 1963.

107   "wanted to do the right thing" Reeves, *President Kennedy,* 480.

107   "I wouldn't do that" Ibid., 656.

107   "the new shopping centers on the highways" Ibid.

108   "it might be less than $10,000 a year" Ibid., 657.

108   "It's going to be a new kind of politics" Ibid.

108   "I'm still very much in favor" Lemann, *Promised Land,* 134.

109   "I thought of all the little folks" Dallek, *Lone Star Rising,* 266.

109   "we might as well face it" Caro, *Master of the Senate,* xv.

110   "personal magnetism" "Business and Labor Meet the President," *Newsweek,* December 16, 1963.

110   "puts the emphasis on all the right things" Ibid.

110   "Everyone in the country thinks he has a winner in Lyndon Johnson" "The People: The Mood of the Land," *Time,* December 20, 1963.

110   "no budget slasher" Lemann, *Promised Land,* 141.

110   "What are we going to do, Mr. President?" Telephone conversation between Lyndon Johnson and Dwight Eisenhower, December 25, 1963, #16.

111   His grandfather Sam Ealy Johnson Dallek, *Lone Star Rising,* 20.

111   "the farming people and the working people" Caro, *Path to Power,* 83.

113   "I think he is going to come around" Telephone conversation between LBJ and Katharine Graham, December 2, 1963.

113   "Let's go join them!" Sorensen, *Counselor,* 378.

115   "The time has come to organize a national assault" Schlesinger, "A Eulogy for JFK," *Saturday Evening Post,* December 14, 1963.

115   In his office, Lemann, *Promised Land,* 142.

115   "Why did you say that?" Branch, *Pillar of Fire,* 199.

115   "Johnson realized" Lemann, *Promised Land,* 142.

116   "the American in the middle" Ibid., 144; memorandum from Horace Busby to LBJ, December 30, 1963, Welfare Files, LBJL.

116   "America's real majority" Dallek, *Flawed Giant,* 62; letter from Horace Busby to LBJ, December 30, 1963, WHCF: EX/FG1.

117   "People here do not like to compare the old and the new" James Reston, "The

Mood of the Capital: Change and Continuity," *New York Times,* December 13, 1963.

118   Reston received a call from Johnson aide Bill Moyers Reston, *Deadline*, 306–7.

118   "Mr. Johnson now seems Gary Cooper as President" Ibid.

118   "hiding with her infant children in the cellar" Lady Bird Johnson, *White House Diary,* 30.

Chapter Five: B Movie

123   The policy of "staving off a direct confrontation with our enemies" Richard Bergholz, "Young GOP Refuses Party Loyalty Pledge," *Los Angeles Times,* February 16, 1964.

123   "that it doesn't give us the choice" Ibid.

124   His parents paid for thick eyeglasses Edwards, *Early Reagan,* 52.

124   "That's the mike in front of ye" Reagan, *Where's the Rest of Me?,* 49.

125   "I have visions of becoming an actor" Morris, *Dutch,* 130.

125   "I think I might be able to fix something" Ibid.

125   His children would find him looking puzzled Cannon, *Governor Reagan,* 79.

125   "My name is Ronald Reagan" Michael Reagan, *On the Outside Looking In,* 96.

125   Just before going onstage, he would remove the contact lens Nancy Reagan, *My Turn,* 244.

126   Come now let us reason together "The 36th President" *New York Times,* November 24, 1963.

127   "Our money in Bolivia" Bergholz, "Young GOP Refuses Party Loyalty Pledge."

127   "dangerously close to appeasement" Ibid.

128   "I was the Errol Flynn of the Bs" Cannon, *Role of a Lifetime,* 68.

128   Unfortunately, many Americans live on the outskirts of hope Lyndon B. Johnson, "Annual Message to the Congress on the State of the Union" (speech, Washington, DC, January 8, 1964), *Public Papers of the Presidents,* 1963–64, vol. 1, 113.

129   I got eighty-one applauses Beschloss, *Taking Charge,* 153.

129   He has out Roosevelted Roosevelt "Republicans: Fastest Guns," *Newsweek,* January 20, 1964.

129   Sarge, I'm going to announce your appointment Beschloss, *Taking Charge,* 202.

130   We are told . . . that many people lack skills "Republicans: The Poverty Issue," *Time,* January 24, 1964.

130   *Mr. Ed* will not be seen tonight "A Conversation with the President," CBS, March 15, 1964; "Transcript of Johnson's Assessment in TV Interview of his First 100 Days in Office," *New York Times,* March 16, 1964.

131   What sort of a vice president was Lyndon? Kennedy, *Historic Conversations,* 275–8.

132   Now boys, you let me finish the Kennedy program Goodwin, *Remembering America,* 271.

132   The Great Society rests on abundance Lyndon B. Johnson, "Remarks at the University of Michigan" (May 22, 1964), in *Public Papers of the Presidents of the United States: Lyndon B. Johnson, 1963–64,* vol. I, 704–7.

133   **Good morning to all you irresponsible Republicans!** Charles Mohr, "Attacks Provoke Goldwater Camp," *New York Times,* May 30, 1964.

133   **"Ronald Reagan, the youthful-looking former Hollywood actor"** Dallek, *Right Moment,* 65; Mohr, "Attacks Provoke Goldwater Camp."

133   **"I don't know, I've never played a governor before"** Cannon, *Governor Reagan,* 61.

133   **"Well, George, here we are on the late show"** Ibid., 171.

134   **"heady wine"** Reagan, *Where's the Rest of Me?,* 28–29.

134   **Two of the eight years were spent traveling** Ibid., 257.

134   **an "almost mystical ability to achieve an empathy with almost any audience"** Edwards, *Essential Ronald Reagan,* 43.

134   **On the side, Dunckel recalled, the men would stand** Dallek, *Right Moment,* 37; Earl Dunckel OH.

135   **Reagan had idolized Franklin Roosevelt** Edwards, *Early Reagan,* 149.

137   **"as inspiring as mud"** Edwards, *Early Reagan,* 301.

137   **Republican senator Joseph Ball** Cannon, *Reagan,* 91.

137   **"Mayor Humphrey"** Ibid., 91.

137   **"You have an opportunity to decide"** Dallek, *Right Moment,* 36.

138   **"the so-called Communist Party"** Cannon, *Reagan,* 87.

138   **"like the cough of a dying man"** Reagan, *Where's the Rest of Me?,* 166.

138   **"Pray as I am praying"** Morris, *Dutch,* 292.

139   **"stands athwart history"** Buckley, "Our Mission Statement," *National Review,* November 19, 1955.

139   **"a predominantly monitoring task"** Tanenhaus, *Death of Conservatism,* 52; Wills, *Confessions,* 33.

140   **"The forces of international Communism"** Tanenhaus, *Death of Conservatism,* 59.

141   **"a position that has not grown old"** Buckley, *Athwart History,* 8.

141   **infamous Wheeling address** Joseph McCarthy, "Enemies from Within" (speech, West Virginia, February 9, 1950).

141   **"rubbed shoulders with boys of all classes and races"** Perlstein, *Before the Storm,* 18.

142   **"the siren song of socialism"** Ibid., 33.

142   **I do not undertake to promote welfare** Goldwater, *Conscience of a Conservative,* 23.

142   **Either the Communists** Ibid., 123.

142   **"To many young readers"** Perlstein, *Before the Storm,* 67.

142   **"Shouldn't someone tag Mr. Kennedy's 'bold new imaginative program'"** Weinraub, "Mondale Says Reagan Note Compared Kennedy to Marx," *New York Times,* October 24, 1984; Morris, *Dutch,* 315–16, citing letter from Ronald Reagan to Richard Nixon, July 15, 1960, Richard Nixon Presidential Library.

143   **If you and I don't do this** Dallek, *Right Moment,* 250.

144   **When the loudspeakers wouldn't turn on** Buckley, *Let Us Talk of Many Things,* 458.

145   **"Government is not the solution to our problem"** Ronald Reagan, "Inaugural Address" (speech, Washington, DC, January 20, 1981), *Public Papers of the Presidents,* 1981, 1.

145   "I almost laughed them out of the house" Reagan, *American Life*, 144.

146   "I'd never given a thought to running for office" Ibid., 145.

146   "He said I would be crazy" Ibid.

146   "I was introduced to Max Arnow" Skinner, *Reagan: In His Own Hand*, 433.

146   "you can win back California" Maureen Reagan, *First Father, First Daughter*, 138.

147   "a day job, not a passion" Davis, *Way I See It*, 84.

147   "She said her stepfather was willing to raise $200,000" Michael Reagan, *On the Outside*, 96.

148   convinced that Reagan had his eye on the presidency Deaver, *Nancy*, 51.

148   "Depends on conditions" Cannon, *Reagan*, 61.

149   "It was a year and a half" Nancy Reagan, *My Turn*, 125.

149   "Money was a big issue in my family" Davis, *Way I See It*, 74.

149   "there'd be a cabinet member or other high official" Reagan, *American Life*, 137.

150   "Government contracts" Davis, *Way I See It*, 67.

150   "There's no way that I could go out now" Cannon, *Reagan*, 96.

150   "They thought I was the hottest thing around" Ibid., 65.

151   "Give me Barry" Reeves, *President Kennedy*, 656.

151   "In these last seven, sorrowful weeks" Lyndon B. Johnson, "Annual Message to Congress on the State of the Union" (speech, Washington, DC, January 8, 1964), *Public Papers of the Presidents*, 1963–64, vol I, 117.

152   "There is no mathematical way" Hughes, "The Defeating of LBJ," *Newsweek*, February 22, 1964, 17.

152   "Nelson and Happy Rockefeller couldn't have been happier" "Who Would Run Best Against LBJ," *Newsweek*, January 13, 1964.

153   "I say with confidence tonight" "Nation: Go-Day," *Time*, February 7, 1964.

155   "Out here in the West" Perlstein, *Before the Storm*, 19; Stewart Alsop, "Can Goldwater Win in 1964," *Saturday Evening Post*, August 24, 1964.

157   "There is no point in saving souls in heaven" Reagan, *Where's the Rest of Me?*, 296–97.

157   "We are going to have to forget an awful lot of bitterness" Carl Greenberg, "Goldwater Says It Would Be Party Victory," *Los Angeles Times*, June 3, 1964.

157   Reagan's advertising executive brother For a discussion of Neil Reagan and *Death Valley Days*, see Neil Reagan OH, 17–18.

158   "good, steady work" Maureen Reagan, *First Father, First Daughter*, 139.

Chapter Six: Everybody's Scared

159   "A desert state" Martin Luther King, Jr., "At the March on Washington" (1963), in *A Call to Conscience: Landmark Speeches of Martin Luther King Jr.*, edited by Clayborne Carson (New York: IPM, 2001).

159   James Chaney, a native of Meridian "Mississippi—Everybody's Scared," *Newsweek*, July 6, 1964.

161   "Mama, that's what's the matter now" Ibid.

161   At some point on June 21 For details on the events surrounding Goodman, Schwerner, and Chaney's disappearance and murder, see Cagin and Dray's thorough account, *We Are Not Afraid*.

161   "The sixty-five-year-old structure had been totally consumed" Ibid., 2.

162   "Now let's see how quick y'all can get out of Neshoba County" Ibid., 286.

162   **As Chaney drove away** Cagin and Dray have reconstructed the timeline of events using eyewitness testimony and confessions obtained by the perpetrators, 286–295.

163   "I thought you were going back to Meridian" Ibid., 292; Huie, *Three Lives for Mississippi*, 181.

163   "What do they think happened?" Telephone conversation between Lyndon Johnson and Lee White, June 23, 1964, Citation #3818.

163   "3 IN RIGHTS DRIVE REPORTED MISSING," *New York Times*, June 24, 1964.

164   "they just disappeared from the face of the earth" Ibid.

164   **Fear over the young men's fate had spread quickly** Branch, *Pillar of Fire*, 361–2.

164   "Agents of the Federal Bureau of Investigation began arriving" Claude Sitton, "3 in Rights Drive Reported Missing," *New York Times*, June 24, 1964.

165   "If they're missing" Ibid.

165   "I don't believe there's three missing" Telephone conversation between Lyndon Johnson and James Eastland, June 23, 1963, Citation #3836.

165   "That depends on the kind of men, Jim" Ibid.

165   "Apparently, what's happened" Telephone conversation between Lyndon Johnson and J. Edgar Hoover, June 23, 1964, Citation #3837.

165   "I don't like you having to see these people" Ibid.

166   "Officially, at the weekend, they were missing" "Mississippi—Everybody's Scared."

166   "they're either the party of Lincoln or they ain't" Branch, *Pillar of Fire*, 180-1.

166   "Stronger than all the armies is an idea whose time has come" Dallek, *Flawed Giant*, 119.

166   "We have now come to a time of national testing" E.W. Kentworthy, "President Signs Civil Rights Bill," *New York Times*, July 2, 1964.

166   **A Universal newsreel** "Civil Rights: President Signs Historic Bill" (California: Universal Studios Newsreel, 1964), http://www.c-spanvideo.org/program/300956-1.

169   "If he is nominated for President" Walter Lippmann, "The Goldwater Threat," *Newsweek*, July 6, 1964, 13.

169   "You can go ahead and talk about conscience" Perlstein, *Before the Storm*, 365.

169   "a shaken man" Ibid., 363.

169   "After Lyndon Johnson—the biggest faker in the United States?" Charles Mohr, "Scornful Attack: Senator Charges That President Changed Civil Rights Stand," *New York Times*, July 16, 1964.

170   **His stroke of luck, he believed, would come in a benediction from Eisenhower** Perlstein, *Before the Storm*, 357; White, *Making of the President 1964*, 110-1.

170   "the gallantry of hopelessness" Ibid., 236.

171   a "crazy-quilt collection of absurd and dangerous positions" Perlstein, *Before the Storm*, 377; White, *Making of the President 1964*, 239.

171   **NBC had 173 cameramen navigating the convention floor** "Palace Warfare," *Newsweek*, July 6, 1964.

171   "When a delegate goes to the bathroom" Ibid.

171   Eisenhower urged the delegates "Opinion: Those Outside Our Family," *Time,*
        July 24, 1964. Perlstein, *Before the Storm,* 381.

171   "leaped off their chairs" "Opinion: Those Outside Our Family," *Time,* July 24,
        1964.

171   When Rockefeller addressed the convention "The Late, Late Show," *Time,*
        June 24, 1964.

172   "violence in our streets" White, *Making of the President 1964,* 260-1.

172   Clif White, turned off the television White and Gill, *Suite 3505,* 14.

172   "a disaster for the Republican Party" "The Goldwater Nomination," *New
        York Times,* July 16, 1964.

172   "not a normal American politician" Lippmann, "The Goldwater Threat,"
        Newsweek, July 4, 1964, 13.

172   "I think the Republican Party has enough problems" Jack Raymond, "Presi-
        dent Leaves Spotlight to GOP," *New York Times,* July 12, 1964.

173   "We really won't do any campaigning until after Labor Day" Telephone con-
        versation between Lyndon Johnson and John McCormick, June 23, 1964, Ci-
        tation #3824.

173   "The Canadian Royal Mounted Police...but we've got to put this thing to-
        gether right away" Carl Albert OH II.

174   government estimates of deficit spending for fiscal 1964 "The Presidency:
        Meanwhile, Down at the Ranch," *Time,* July 24, 1964.

174   "What we really want to do with Goldwater" Telephone conversation between
        Lyndon Johnson and George Reedy, July 20, 1964, Citation #4286.

174   "swiftly spread[ing] through the capital and its environs" "The Presidency:
        Just Storing Up Energy?" *Time,* July 17, 1964.

175   "you had a whole plate of sandwiches" Marie Fehmer Chiarodo OH II.

175   On its cover the following week "Harlem: Hatred in the Streets," *Newsweek,*
        August 3, 1964.

175   "feel that most Negroes want to take jobs held by whites" Louis Harris, "The
        Backlash Issue," *Newsweek,* July 13, 1964, 27.

175   Fertile territory for resentment could also be found in the suburbs Ibid.

176   "If we aren't careful" Telephone conversation between Lyndon Johnson and
        Geroge Reedy, July 20, 1964, Citation #4286.

176   "He wants to use this as a forum" Telephone conversation between Lyndon
        Johnson and John Connally, July 23, 1964, Citation #4320.

176   "Hell, these folks have got walkie-talkies" Ibid.

176   "The white backlash itself exists" Harris, "Backlash Issue," 24.

177   "When this fellow looks at me" Telephone conversation between Lyndon
        Johnson and John Connally, July 23, 1964; Beschloss, *Taking Charge,* 468.

177   In a tense Oval Office meeting Thomas, *Robert Kennedy,* 290-1 and Shesol,
        Mutual Contempt, 186.

178   "We waited quite a while" Gillette, *Lady Bird Johnson,* 344.

178   "Stranger, when you see the Lacedaemonians" Murray Kempton, "Pure Irish,"
        New Republic, February 15, 1964.

179   "I'm sure Jack liked it" Thomas, *Robert Kennedy,* 288.

179   As a belated Christmas gift "Periscope," *Newsweek,* January 20, 1964, 10.

179   In his biography . . . Evan Thomas reveals Thomas, *Robert Kennedy,* 286-7.

179   "there is no dignity" Hamilton, *The Greek Way,* 176.

180   He referred to "the president" Thomas, *Robert Kennedy,* 291.

180   "Here I and sorrows sit" Hamilton, *The Greek Way,* 176.

180   "The worst city in the United States for rumor and gossip is Washington" Telephone conversation between Lyndon Johnson and Richard Daley, July 21, 1964, Citation #4298; Beschloss, *Taking Charge,* 463.

181   maybe he'd write a book in England Bradlee, "What's Bobby Kennedy Going to Do Now?" *Newsweek,* July 6, 1964, 25.

181   "I should think I'd be the last man" Ibid.

182   "I don't want the presidency if they do" Telephone conversation between Lyndon Johnson and Jack Connally, July 14, 1964, Citation #4224.

182   "He's got [Jackie] thinking" Telephone conversation between Lyndon Johnson and Clark Clifford, July 29, 1964.

182   wondered if the president was recording the exchange Schlesinger, *Robert Kennedy,* 661.

182   "You didn't ask me" Beschloss, *Taking Charge,* 479.

183   "I was very firm and very positive" Telephone conversation between Lyndon Johnson and Clark Clifford, July 29, 1964.

183   "Oh, I'm just so gratified" Ibid.

183   "He had communicated that decision personally" Tom Wicker, "President Bars Kennedy, Five Others, From Ticket," *New York Times,* July 31, 1964.

183   "While I'm thinking about naming him" Beschloss, *Taking Charge,* 484.

183   "When I . . . told him" Shesol, *Mutual Contempt,* 210-11

184   "a kind of stunned semi-idiot" Stewart Alsop OH.

184   "Mr. Johnson may have been seeing goblins" Evans and Novak, "Inside Report: The Johnson-Kennedy Split," *Washington Post,* August 4, 1964.

184   "I think we ought to just watch that just like hawks" Telephone conversation between Lyndon Johnson and James Rowe, Jule 31, 1964.

185   "The two destroyers would stage direct daylight runs" Karnow, *Vietnam,* 384.

185   "The entire action" Ibid., 386.

186   "Make no bones of this" Barry Goldwater, "1964 RNC Presidential Acceptance" (speech, San Francisco, CA, July 17, 1964), http://www.c-span.org/video/?4018-1/goldwater-1964-acceptance-speech.

186   "My fellow Americans" Lyndon B. Johnson, "Report on the Gulf of Tonkin Incident" (speech, Washington, DC, August 4, 1964), Miller Center Presidential Speech Archive, http://millercenter.org/president/speeches/detail/3998.

187   "the smoke was observed rising to 14,000 feet" Halberstam, *Best and the Brightest,* 414.

187   "You've taken the right steps" Telephone conversation between Lyndon Johnson and Barry Goldwater, August 4, 1964, Citation #4715.

187   "I didn't just screw Ho Chi Minh" Halberstam, *Best and the Brightest,* 414.

188   Moments before he was shot Cagin and Dray, *We Are Not Afraid,* 294. Cagin and Dray recount Schwerner's last moments using confession of his murderers and eyewitness testimony.

189   "A coronation, not a convention" "Now Johnson," *New York Times,* August 23, 1964.

189   Forty four months ago Telephone conversation between LBJ and George Reedy, August 25, 1964, Citation #6408.

190   "I'm just writing out a little statement that I'm gonna make" Ibid.

191   "I do not believe" Telephone conversation between Lyndon Johnson and Walter Jenkins, August 25, 1964

191   "I deeply feared" Johnson, *Vantage Point*, 95.

191   "I do not remember hours I ever found harder" Lady Bird Johnson, *White House Diary*, 192.

191   "To step out now would be wrong for your country" Ibid.

192   "I can't carry any of the burdens" Ibid.

192   "As I stood there warmed by the waves" Johnson, *Vantage Point*, 101.

Chapter Seven: Sacrifice

193   For a while he'd enjoyed a brief nightly reprieve "The Senior Staff Man," *Time*, October 23, 1964.

193   On this particular autumn night Al Weisel, "LBJ's Gay Sex Scandal," *Out Magazine*, December 1999.

195   One campaign advertisement "Vote for President Johnson on November 3," *Presidential Campaign Commercials 1952-2012*, Museum of the Moving Image, http://www.livingroomcandidate.org/commercials/1964.

196   In early September "Daisy Girl," September 7, 1964, *Presidential Campaign Commercials 1952-2012*, Museum of the Moving Image, http://www.livingroomcandidate.org/commercials/1964/peace-little-girl-daisy.

196   Even the parents of the little girl Mann, *Daisy Petals and Mushroom Clouds*, 64.

197   "I am not the first president to speak here" Lyndon Johnson, "Remarks in Cadillac Square, Detroit" (speech, Detroit, September 7, 1964), *Public Papers of the Presidents*, 1963–64, Vol. II, 1051.

197   "FACT," wrote Jack Valenti Memo from Jack Valenti to LBJ, September 7, 1964, WHCF: EX/PL2.

197   In a memo to the DNC Dallek, *Lyndon Johnson*, 185.

197   "Confessions of a Republican" "Confessions of a Republican," 1964, *Presidential Campaign Commercials 1952-2012*, Museum of the Moving Image, http://www.livingroomcandidate.org/commercials/1964/confessions-of-a-republican.

197   "probably the most violent advocate of peanut butter" Hayes, *Smiling Through the Apocalypse*, 393.

198   "frontlash" "Periscope," *Newsweek*, October 12, 1964, 25.

198   "this big, booming, leonine Texan" "Lyndon's Pace," *Newsweek*, October 19, 1964.

198   "He needed contact with people" Marie Fehmer Chiarodo OH III.

199   People respected Johnson's performance Horace Busby, memo to Lyndon Johnson, October 5, 1964.

199   "There was nothing in particular" Robert T. Bower, "Preliminary Report: Reactions to President Johnson's Acceptance Speech to the Democratic Convention," September 1, 1964.

200   "my vice president in charge of everything" Beschloss, *Reaching*, 54.

200   "I need you badly" Al Weisel, "LBJ's Gay Sex Scandal."

200   the Jenkinses offered up their own home "Johnson Gives Wife, 51, Gift that Helped Him to Win Her," *New York Times*, December 23, 1963.

201   **Practically all of official Washington knew him** For background on Walter Jenkins see Weisel, "LBJ's Gay Sex Scandal"; Marie Fehmer Chiarodo OH; Harry McPherson OH I; Horace Busby OH; Cartha deLoach OH.

202   **"like a nigger slave"** Caro, *Master of the Senate,* 129.

202   **"Goddamn it, Walter"** Harry McPherson OH VII.

203   **In Bill Moyers, Scotty Reston** "Underground Campaign for the Vice Presidency," *New York Times,* April 5, 1964.

204   **One week later** Beschloss, *Reaching for Glory,* 57.

205   **The next day** "12,000 Slosh Through the Rain to Get Report," *Washington Post,* September 29, 1964.

205   **"the commission analyzed every issued"** Anthony Lewis, "Warren Commission Finds Oswald Guilty and Says Assassin and Ruby Acted Alone," *New York Times,* September 28, 1964.

205   **"From Mexico City to Moscow and Minsk,"** "Report Finds No Plot from Reds," *Los Angeles Times,* September 28, 1964.

205   **In a twenty-four-page cover story on the report** "The Warren Commission Report," *Newsweek,* October 5, 1964, 32-64.

205   **"Now where is the Hudson River again?"** Thomas, *Robert Kennedy,* 297.

205   **Polls showed** Ibid., 300

205   **"Walter came over to see me this morning"** Telephone conversation between Abe Fortas and Lyndon Johnson, October 14, 1964.

206   **Fortas and Clifford soon learned** Ibid.

206   **"Does his wife know about this?"** Ibid.

207   **"I just can't *believe* this!"** Ibid.

207   **"You don't foresee that you can keep this lid on"** Ibid.

207   **"No sir"** Ibid.

208   **"Now, I don't think I have any choice"** Telephone conversation between John Connally and Lyndon Johnson, October 14, 1964.

208   **YMCA's "basement men's room** "The Senior Staff Man," *Time,* October 23, 1964.

208   **Jenkins's crime could range "from the seemingly trivial"** Henry Gemmill, "Arrest of Johnson Aide Could Bolster GOP's Election Day Chances," *Wall Street Journal,* October 16, 1964.

209   **On the phone from Washington** Beschloss, *Reaching,* 73.

209   **"nearly every family has had some problem"** Ibid., 74

210   **Early the next morning** Liz Carpenter OH IV; Beschloss, *Reaching,* 86.

210   **Her whistle-stop tour of the South** Russell, *Lady Bird,* 258.

210   **On a train dubbed the *Lady Bird Special*** Ibid., 249.

210   **A sign in the crowd** Ibid., 259.

210   **"This is a country of many viewpoints"** Ibid., 258.

211   **"I would like to do two things about Walter"** Telephone conversation between Lady Bird Johnson and LBJ, October 15, 1964, Citation #5895.

211   **"I wouldn't do anything along that line now"** Ibid.

211   **"I don't think that's *right*"** Ibid.

212   **"I don't want you to hurt him"** Ibid.

212   **"Abe approves of the job offer"** Ibid.

212   **"My poor darling"** Ibid.

212 "**My heart is aching today**" Russell, *Lady Bird,* 268, citing Personal Files 5, Lady Bird, LBJL.

213 "**If any responsible person** "The Issue of Integrity," *Christian Science Monitor,* October 17, 1964.

213 "**a bouquet of mixed fall flowers**" "The Jenkins Report," *Time,* October 30, 1964.

213 "**Walter Jenkins came to the White House**" Wallace Turner, "Miller Stresses The Jenkins Case," *New York Times,* October 21, 1964.

214 "**The really remarkable thing was the mail**" Carpenter, Oral History Interview IV.

214 "**If they don't want us**" "Communism and Corruption" *Time,* October 30, 1964.

214 "**Just think about it for a moment**" Perlstein, *Before the Storm,* 508.

214 "**The Great Society**" Lyndon B. Johnson, "Remarks in Madison Square Garden at a Rally of the Liberal Party of New York" (speech, New York, October 15, 1964), *Public Papers of the Presidents, 1963-64,* Vol. II, 1349.

215 "**I am not a prophet**" Lyndon Johnson, "Remarks in Boston at Post Office Square" (speech, Boston, MA, October 27, 1964), *Public Papers of the Presidents, 1963-64,* Vol. II, 1466.

215 "**utopian society**" Charles Mohr, "Johnson Refers to Jenkins Case," *New York Times,* October 28, 1964.

215 "**It's the time when man**" Johnson, "Remarks at the Civic Center Arena in Pittsburgh" (speech, Pittsburgh, PA, October 27, 1964), *Public Papers of the Presidents, 1963-64,* Vol. II, 1479.

217 "**I'd seen the film**" Reagan, *American Life,* 391.

219 "**I JUST WANTED YOU TO KNOW**" Dean Burch, telegram to Ronald Reagan, October 28, 1964, Box C35, Telegrams in response to "The Speech," Ronald Reagan Library.

221 "**The returns . . . read like tall tales from Texas**" "LBJ: My Thanks to All America," *Newsweek,* November 9, 1964.

221 "**Listen, I pulled you through up here**" Telephone conversation between Lyndon Johnson and Robert Kennedy, November 3, 1962, Citation #6142.

222 "**Barry Goldwater not only lost the presidential election**" James Reston, "What Goldwater Lost," *New York Times,* November 4, 1964.

222 "**The American people were not prepared**" John G. Tower OH I.

222 **Jack Valenti prepared a packet of postmortems** Memo from Jack Valenti to Lyndon Johnson, November 28, 1964, LBJL, Handwriting File, Box 4.

223 "**These are the most hopeful times**" Lyndon Johnson, "Remarks at the Lighting of the Nation's Christmas Tree," (speech, Washington, DC, December 18, 1964), *Public Papers of the Presidents, 1963-64,* Vol. II.

Chapter Eight: Valley of the Black Pig

225 **Seated inside, in a robe and pajamas** Charles Mohr, "President is Ill: Goes to Hospital With Bad Cough," *New York Times,* January 24, 1965.

225 **At a ball at the Mayflower hotel** "Hail to the Chief," *Newsweek,* February 1, 1965, 17.

225 **At his brother's grave at Arlington** Ibid.

227 Briefing the press on the president's health "National Affairs: State of the President," *Newsweek,* January 11, 1965, 17.

227 "not bourbon but Scotch" Ibid.

227 the First Lady had come back and checked herself in to the hospital, too "The Uncommon Cold," *Newsweek,* February 1, 1965, 18.

227 In the late spring of 1948 Caro, *Master of the Senate,* 618-9.

227 He told Warren Woodward Caro, *Means of Ascent,* 202.

228 "Settled in her seat" Russell, *Lady Bird,* 157.

228 "Tell him to go ahead with the blue" Caro, *Master of the Senate,* 624.

228 "everything will be all right" Ibid.

228 "I think we'll be all right in a day or two" "President Is Ill."

228 I wouldn't hesitate at all. Laurence Stern, "Johnson to Remain in Hospital for Rest," *Washington Post,* January 24, 1965.

228 "By evening . . . concern about the president's health had subsided" "President is Ill"

229 He had seen the president only moments before Ibid.

229 When reporters asked how he was feeling Charles Mohr, "Johnsons Return to White House," *New York Times,* January 26, 1965.

229 "The Lord willing and the creek don't rise" Enid Nemy, "Lady Bird Johnson, 94, Dies," *New York Times,* July 12, 2007.

230 "Last night was not a good night" Lady Bird Johnson, *White House Diary,* 232.

230 1948 kidney stone Caro, *Means of Ascent,* 194.

230 "With LBJ's history" Beschloss, *Reaching,* 168.

231 "This week's mood is not good" Ibid., 170.

231 "the grim, unacknowledged thought" Beschloss, *Reaching,* 394.

231 "Is our world gone?" Lyndon B. Johnson, "Inaugural Address" (speech, Washington, DC, January 20, 1965), *Public Papers of the Presidents,* 1965, Vol. I, 74.

231 On January 7 Johnson, "Special Message to Congress: Advancing the Nation's Health" (speech, Washington, DC, January 7, 1965), *Public Papers of the Presidents,* 1965, Vol. I.

233 April 13, the hundredth day of the new term The Johnson White House focused its legislative efforts in early 1965 on a 100-day period beginning with Johnson's State of the Union address on January 5, 1965 and ending on April 12 of that year. The choice to measure one hundred days from the State of the Union, when the new Congress came into session, rather than from when his own new term began on January 20, speaks to the primacy of the legislative branch, and the legislative calendar, in Johnson's thinking.

233 Republicans must instead offer a "constructive" alternative "Nation: Aid to Appalachia," *Time,* March 12, 1965.

233 "Republican rank-and-file enthusiasm" "Periscope," *Newsweek,* February 1, 1965, 7.

234 "shouldn't even be *cast* as governor" Shana Alexander, "My Technicolor Senator," *Life,* December 4, 1964, 30.

234 "The history that interests Mr. Johnson" Drew Pearson, "A Lesson Learned from FDR," *Washington Post,* November 24, 1964.

234 "not to make Roosevelt's error" Evans and Novak, *Lyndon B. Johnson: The Exercise of Power,* 489-90.

234   "I was just elected by the biggest popular margin" Goodwin, *Lyndon Johnson*, 216; Goldman, *Tragedy of Lyndon Johnson*, 309.

234   "I knew from the start" Goodwin, *Lyndon Johnson*, 291.

235   "With Lyndon Johnson it was the reverse" Lawrence (Larry) O'Brien OH VI.

235   "wasn't informing him on an hourly basis" Ibid.

235   "If it's really going to work" Goodwin, *Lyndon Johnson*, 226.

235   "I didn't need anything to eat" O'Brien, Interview VI.

235   "God, you should have called me" Ibid.

236   "Economic policy" "Nation: Toward the Fuller Life," *Time*, February 5, 1965.

236   "Peace on earth" Lyndon B. Johnson, "Remarks to the Winners of the Science Talent Search" (speech, Washington, DC, March 1, 1965), *Public Papers of the Presidents, 1965*, Vol. I, 223.

236   By 1992, distances on earth will have lost all meaning Ibid.

237   "an area the size of Texas" Karnow, *Vietnam*, 416.

238   Throughout 1964, a massive and well-organized Vietcong army Ibid.

238   On Christmas Eve, they took provocative action Ibid., 424.

238   "We are presently on a losing track" Ibid., 425.

238   "Both of us are now pretty well convinced" Ibid., 427.

240   "that bitch of a war" Goodwin, *Lyndon Johnson*, 251.

241   "I knew that Harry Truman" Ibid., 252-3.

241   After the November election Karnow, *Vietnam*, 418-20.

242   "Bundy . . . had resorted to a classic bureaucratic device" Ibid., 419-20.

242   "we're all going to die" Ibid., 427-8.

242   "Not only Americans" "Pleiku and Qui Nhon: Decision Points," *Newsweek*, February 22, 1965, 32.

243   The National Security Council considered a request Karnow, *Vietnam*, 431.

243   "Even as he finished" Halberstam, *Best and the Brightest*, 522.

244   "Now we're off to bombing" Telephone conversation between Lyndon Johnson and Robert McNamara, February 26, 1965, Citation #6887.

245   "How long before you should hear something?" Telephone call between Lyndon Johnson and White House Situation Room, March 2, 1965, Citation # 7008.

245   "We're going to send the Marines" Telephone conversation between Lyndon Johnson and Richard Russell, March 6, 1965, Citation #7026.

245   "a turncoat if ever there was one" Branch, *At Canaan's Edge*, 114.

246   "I don't know, Dick" Telephone conversation between Lyndon Johnson and Richard Russell, March 6, 1965, Citation #7026.

246   "There's no end to the road" Telephone conversation between Lyndon Johnson and Richard Russell, March 6, 1965, Citation #7027.

246   "I can't get out" Lady Bird Johnson, *White House Diary*, 248.

246   "Lyndon lives in a cloud of troubles" Ibid.

246   "I am counting the months" Ibid.

247   "Get him! Get him!" Goldman, *Tragedy*, 367.

247   "Negroes stood in line" "Nation: Selma, Contd." *Time*, February 5, 1965.

248   "We've gone too far now" Martin Luther King Jr., "Bridge to Freedom" (speech, Selma, AL, 1965).

249   "America didn't like what it saw" Goodwin, *Remembering America*, 319.

250   "What do you want left after you when you die?" Ibid., 323.

250   "I am glad that he is launched" Beschloss, *Reaching,* 228.

251   "There was, uniquely, no need to temper conviction" Goodwin, *Remembering America,* 327.

251   "I speak tonight" Lyndon B. Johnson, "Special Message to the Congress: The American Promise" (speech, Washington, DC, March 15, 1965), *Public Papers of the Presidents,* 1965, Vol. I, 281.

251   "Pulses quickened" "Washington D.C. Watches Selma," *Time,* March 26, 1965.

251   Rarely in any time "Special Message to the Congress."

252   This time on this issue there must be no delay Ibid.

252   Lady Bird had convened a meeting Sharon Francis OH I.

252   Their cause must be our cause too "Special Message to the Congress."

253   Johnson recalled the young Mexicans Ibid.

253   "It was terrific" Beschloss, *Reaching,* 228.

253   "The greatest speech you ever made" Goodwin, *Remembering,* 337.

253   "Your speech was beyond belief" Beschloss, *Reaching,* 243.

253   Goodwin would recall the smile Goodwin, *Remembering,* 337.

253   "Let's have a little whiskey" Ibid.

253   "Roosevelt's got eleven" Telephone conversation between Lawrence O'Brien and Lyndon Johnson, April 9, 1965, Citation #7337.

254   "Lyndon talked of the last week" Beschloss, *Reaching,* 277.

Chapter Nine: Lonely Acres

257   "He can't separate himself from it" Beschloss, *Reaching,* 280.

257   "he's never the same without you" Ibid., 389.

257   "I feel selfish" Ibid., 389.

258   In the audience Dallek, *Flawed Giant,* 200.

258   "She seemed not to realize it was meant as a souvenir" Charles Mohr, "President Signs Education Bill at His Old School," *New York Times,* April 12, 1965.

258   "No longer will older Americans be denied" John D. Morris, "President Signs Medicare Bill; Praises Truman," *New York Times,* June 31, 1965.

259   "The people of the United States love" Ibid.

259   On the same day E.W. Kentworthy, "Johnson Signs Voting Rights Bill," *New York Times,* August 7, 1965.

259   "Today is a triumph" Lyndon B. Johnson, "Remarks on the Signing of the Voting Rights Act" (speech, Washington, DC, August 6, 1965), Miller Center, http://millercenter.org/president/speeches/detail/4034.

259   He spoke in front of John Trumbull's oil painting "Johnson Signs Voting Rights Bill."

261   In July, the press reported "Johnson Predicts Vietnam Setbacks: U.S. Force to Exceed 75,000," *New York Times,* July 10, 1965.

261   "Incidents are going up" Lyndon Johnson, "The President's News Conference," (Televised News Conference, July 9, 1965), *Public Papers of the Presidents,* 1965, Vol. II, 725.

261   security officials learned of a plot "Taylor Escapes a Plot in Saigon," *New York Times,* July 20, 1965.

261   **Vietnam is a different kind of a war** "At War in Vietnam," *New York Times,* July 14, 1965.

261   **"military victory in Vietnam"** William Fulbright, "The War in Vietnam" (speech, Washington, DC, June 15, 1965), Fulbright Collection, University of Arkansas, http://scipio.uark.edu/cdm/ref/collection/Fulbright/id/762.

262   **"we have set ourselves a task"** Walter Lippmann, "The Hard Lesson," *Newsweek,* July 19, 1965.

262   **"it is essential that the President"** Ibid.

262   **Through his ambassador in Moscow** Karnow *Vietnam,* 437.

263   **At a White House reception** "Foreign Relations: While the Bullets Whiz," *Time,* March 12, 1965.

263   **"The headlines are all I read and all anybody reads"** Ibid.

264   **"The sky over Saigon is alive"** James Reston, "Saigon: The Tragic Paradox of Vietnam," *New York Times,* August 29, 1965.

264   **Shirley O'Neal** See "Crime: Summer Job," *Newsweek,* July 19, 1965; "Eighth Suspect Held in Attack on O'Neal Girl," *Los Angeles Times,* July 5, 1965; "Handcuffed Rape Suspect Shot by Policeman," *New York Times*; "4 Youths Found Guilty in Attack on O'Neal Girl," *Los Angeles Times,* October 5, 1965.

265   **"like a man in a dream"** "Girl Describes Being Raped as Father Tried in Shooting," *Tuscaloosa News,* September 23, 1965.

265   **A report showed** "Crime in the Streets," *Newsweek,* August 16, 1965, 21.

265   **The story began with the tale of one Chester E. Pierce** Ibid., 20.

265   **Suellen Evans, on her way home from summer school** Ibid.

265   **Mary Ellen Bay** Ibid.

265   **Two "pretty . . . University of Texas coeds"** Ibid.

265   **"many observers believe"** Ibid.

265   **"A malignant enemy in America's midst"** Ibid.

266   **"I've been staggered"** George Plimpton, "The Story Behind a Non-Fiction Novel," *New York Times,* January 16, 1966.

266   *Time* **reported that "resort towns"** "Youth: That Riotous Feeling," *Time,* July 16, 1965.

267   **"summer of discontent"** Fred Powledge, "Civil Rights—Another Long, Hot Summer," *New York Times,* June 13, 1965.

267   **"The fuel of unrest and injustice is still here"** Theodore Jones, "Uneasy Calm in Harlem," *New York Times,* July 17, 1965.

267   **"We're going to see to it"** "Illinois: Hot and Dry," *Time,* June 18, 1965.

268   **"this or that date is to be the time for another outbreak of violence"** Powledge, "Civil Rights."

268   **"Positive hope"** Ibid.

268   **"not just legal equity but human ability"** Lyndon Johnson, "Commencement Address at Howard University" (speech, Washington, DC, June 4, 1965), http://www.lbjlib.utexas.edu/johnson/archives.hom/speeches.hom/650604.asp

269   **"The Negro Family"** For Moynihan Report see memo from Daniel Patrick Moynihan to Bill Moyers, January 21, 1965, WHCF: EX-HU2-1; Lee Rainwater and William Yancy, *The Moynihan Report and the Politics of Controversy* (Cambridge, 1967); Patterson, *Freedom is Not Enough.*

269   **"We have been in the business"** Ibid.

270 **"The attached Memorandum is nine pages of dynamite"** Moynihan ed., *Daniel Patrick Moynihan*, 90.

270 *Time* **described a "brooding" President** "The Presidency: At the Perigree," *Time,* July 9, 1965.

271 **"stock on the gossip market"** Kenneth Crawford, "Washington: Disrobing the King," *Newsweek,* July 19, 1965.

272 **"While he had so much going for him"** Tom Wicker, "Washington: Fadeout for Super Lyndon," *New York Times,* July 7, 1965.

272 **"It is said"** Crawford, "Disrobing the King."

272 **"irrepressible longing to have every story"** Joseph Alsop, "Matter of Fact: Johnson's Achilles Heel," *Washington Post*, February 17, 1965.

272 **"To those beyond the limits"** Joseph Alsop, "Matter of Fact: The State of LBJ," *Washington Post,* July 5, 1965.

273 **"The major industry in New York this summer,"** Sorensen, *Counselor,* 408.

273 **In her notes** Ibid., 406.

273 **"tone down my references to JFK's praise of LBJ"** Ibid., 404.

274 **Most insidious** "JFK's Alter-Ego," *Newsweek,* January 27, 1964, 17**.

274 **"mawkish, tasteless"** "Remembering JFK," *Newsweek,* August 2, 1965, 46-47.

274 **"Images do not spring full-blown"** Jack Valenti, memo to LBJ, November 11, 1964, Box 4, Special Files, Handwriting File, LBJL.

274 **"Jacksonian and Rooseveltian"** Ibid.

276 **"Mr. President, You're Fun!"** "Mr. President, You're Fun!" *Time,* April 10, 1964.

276 **"He first called his dogs"** Helen Thomas OH I.

277 **"an awfully strong Kennedy man"** Telephone conversation between Lyndon Johnson and Bill Moyers, July 1, 1965, Citation #8301.

277 **"I think there's a lot can be done with just more candidness"** Ibid.

277 **"I don't want to get in a war"** Beschloss, *Taking Charge,* 403.

279 **"I hate this war"** Clifford, *Counsel to the President,* 419-20.

279 **"He said, 'Things are not going well here'"** Beschloss, *Taking Charge,* 390.

279 **"I do not find it easy to send the flower of our youth"** Lyndon B. Johnson, "The President's News Conference" (press conference, Washington, DC, July 28, 1965), *Public Papers of the Presidents,* 1965, Vol. II, 797.

280 **"monkeys in a zoo"** "New Negro Riots Erupt on Coast," *New York Times,* August 13, 1965.

281 **"tragic and shocking"** Califano, *Triumph and Tragedy,* 60.

281 **"deeply distressed"** Ibid., 61.

Chapter Ten: Like a Winner

284 **"Governor Volpe"** Speech delivered at New England convention of Federation of Republican Women, Hotel Statler Hilton, Boston, September 29, 1965, folder "RR Material (2/4)," Box C32, 1966 Campaign, Reagan, Ronald: Gubernatorial Papers, Ronald Reagan Library.

286 **"With this legislation"** Lyndon B. Johnson, "Remarks at the Signing of Bill Establishing a Department of Housing and Urban Development" (speech, Washington, DC, September 9, 1965), *Public Papers of the Presidents,* 1965, Vol. II, 986.

286 **"Admiration flows abundantly"** "The President: Greyer, Graver—and Growing," *Time,* September 3, 1965.

287 **"People just aren't going to get excited"** "The People: Not Great, but Good," *Time,* October 8, 1965.

287 **"How's your battle going out in Vietnam?"** Telephone conversation between Lyndon Johnson and Robert McNamara, November 2, 1965, Citation #9103.

288 **making millions by selling spears in Watts** "TV Riot Squad," *Newsweek,* September 11, 1965.

288 **"Our president is fond of quoting from Isaiah"** Speech delivered at New England convention of Federation of Republican Women.

290 **"the one-time motion picture star"** David B. Wilson, "Reagan Assails Welfare State," *Boston Herald,* September 30, 1965.

290 **Two months after Johnson's 1964 landslide** Cannon, *Reagan,*103.

291 **"Reagan . . . is the man"** Ibid.

291 **"Oh, my God"** Cannon, *Governor Reagan,* 133.

291 **"I almost laughed them out of the house"** Reagan, *American Life,* 144-5.

292 **"Double parking in Sacramento"** Peter Kaye, "Reagan Impresses National Press Club Members," *San Diego Union,* [date does not appear], folder "66: Press/Media (2)," Box C35, 1966 Campaign, Reagan, Ronald: Gubernatorial Papers 1966-75, Ronald Reagan Library.

292 **He would effectively *be* a candidate for governor** U.S. Borax, News Release, 4 January, 1966, folder "66 Campaign: RR (2/4)," Box C32, 1966 Campaign—Subject Files, Reagan, Ronald: Gubernatorial Papers, Ronald Reagan Library.

293 **"Oh gosh, Jack!"** Interview with Ronald Reagan, KNBC, April 10, 1965, Box C35, 1966 Press Media, Ronald Reagan Library.

293 **"I'm thinking of running"** Stuart Spencer OH.

294 **"We had heard"** Cannon, *Reagan,* 104; James Perry, "Ronald Reagan in Dazzling Performance," *National Observer,* January 10, 1966, Box C32, 1966 Campaign, Reagan, Ronald: Gubernatorial Papers, Ronald Reagan Library.

294 **"He was obsessed with one thing"** Stuart Spencer OH.

294 **"darling of the Goldwaterites and the choice of the John Birch Society"** Dallek, *Right Moment,* 111; Evans and Novak, "Sen. Kuchel Knows He Won't Run," *St. Petersburg Times,* Sept. 1, 1965.

294 **"hyphenated Republicans"** Interview with Ronald Reagan, KNBC, April 10, 1965, Ronald Reagan Gubernatorial Campaign, Box C35, 1966 Press Media, Ronald Reagan Library.

295 **"I'm sure that we all recognize"** Ronald Reagan, "Speech at Hilton Inn, San Diego," February 25, 1966, Box C30, Campaign Materials: Ronald Reagan Speeches and Statements I, Ronald Reagan Library.

295 **"I think you have to preface anything"** Lee Edwards, "Why Californians Look to Ronald Reagan," *Human Events,* February 19, 1966, 8-10, Ronald Reagan Gubernatorial Campaign Files, Box C35, 1966 Press Media, Ronald Reagan Library.

295 **"You'd have me going counter to the talks"** Ronald Reagan, News Conference, Televised on KNBC, April 10, 1965, Ronald Reagan Gubernatorial Campaign, Box C35, 1966 Press Media, Ronald Reagan Library.

296 **"I have no intention of compromising my beliefs"** Ronald Reagan, letter to

Harry Feyer, July 21, 1966, Ronald Reagan Gubernatorial Campaign, Box C35, Republican Party, Ronald Reagan Presidential Library.

296 **"Do you really want to be mayor?"** Sam Tanenhaus, "The Buckley Effect," *New York Times*, October 2, 2005.

296 **"a miracle"** Richard J. H. Johnston, "William Buckley Opens Headquarters," *New York Times*, August 31, 1965.

296 **"a ban on mid-day truck deliveries"** Richard Witkin, "William Buckley Jr. Is Reported Considering Running for Mayor," *New York Times*, June 4, 1965.

297 **"I don't think it's very pertinent"** Interview with Ronald Reagan, KNBC, April 10, 1965, Ronald Reagan Gubernatorial Campaign, Box C35, 1966 Press Media, Ronald Reagan Library.

297 **"I have received some kick-back"** Ronald Reagan, letter to Barry Goldwater, January 13, 1965, Box C29, 1966, Personal Correspondence of Barry Goldwater, Ronald Reagan Library.

298 **"Spencer Roberts does not handle any Democrats"** Lee Edwards, "Why Californians Look to Ronald Reagan."

298 **"I think he should have been briefed"** John L. Harmer, letter to Bill Roberts, July 12, 1965, Box C32, 1966 Campaign, Ronald Reagan: Gubernatorial Papers, Ronald Reagan Library.

298 **"If he can zero in on California"** Gordon C. Luce, letter to Stu Spencer, July 7, 1965, Box C32, 1966 Campaign: Ronald Reagan, Ronald Reagan Presidential Library.

298 **"I think Henry tried to say"** W. S. McBirnie letter to RR, November 30, 1965, Box C31, 1966 Campaign, Ronald Reagan: Gubernatorial Papers, Ronald Reagan Library.

299 **"Damn," he exclaimed to BASICO co-founder Stanley Plog** Reagan *Dutch*, 342.

299 **"positive direction"** W. S. McBirnie letter to Ronald Reagan, November 30, 1965, Box C31, 1966 Campaign, Ronald Reagan: Gubernatorial Papers, Ronald Reagan Library.

300 **"These are the most hopeful times"** Lyndon Johnson, "Remarks at the Lighting of the Nation's Christmas Tree," (speech, Washington, DC, December 18, 1964), *Public Papers of the Presidents*, 1963-64, Vol. II.

300 **"We must show the voters"** Dave Hope, "Reagan on Verge of Declaring," *Oakland Tribune*, December 9, 1965, Box C32, 1966 Campaign, Ronald Reagan: Gubernatorial Papers, Ronald Reagan Library.

300 **The idea of an actor named Ronald Reagan** Emmett John Hughes, "The Squandering Republicans, *Newsweek*, June 27, 1966.

300 **"Sure he's drawing the crowds"** James Phelan, "Can Reagan Win California?" *Saturday Evening Post*, June 4, 1966.

300 **"It was on the late show"** James Perry, "Ronald Reagan in a Dazzling Performance."

300 **"Ronald Reagan . . . who recently announced he was seeking"** John Voorhees, "Ulysses: Man or Myth," *Washington Post-Intelligencer,* January 11, 1965, Box C35, 1966 Campaign, Reagan, Ronald: Gubernatorial Papers 1966-75, Ronald Reagan Library.

301 **"He is assiduously playing the role"** "Play Acting Can Give Illusion of Compe-

tence," *Fresno Bee*, July 3, 1965, Box C35, 1966 Campaign, Reagan, Ronald: Gubernatorial Papers 1966-75, Ronald Reagan Library.

301   **He would tell crowds that his son** "Ronald Reagan Republican for Governor," *Los Angeles Times*, September 13, 1966.

301   **"Only a generation ago"** Ronald Reagan, "Address at the Comstock Club," August 2, 1965, 1966 Campaign: Speeches and Statements, Box C30, Ronald Reagan Library.

301   **Entries included** Campaign Resume, Ronald Reagan Gubernatorial Papers, Box C32, 1966 Campaign, Ronald Reagan Library.

302   **"So what's this empty nonsense"** "Political Ad: 'John Wayne' Reagan, 1966" *Political Advertisement*, New York, NY: NBC Universal, 1966. Accessed Wed, Sep 5, 2012 from NBC Learn: https://archives.nbclearn.com/portal/site/k-12/browse/?cuecard=4100

302   **"I'll probably be the only fellow"** "The Illustrated," *Orange County Illustrated,* May 1965, Box C35, 1966 Press Media, Ronald Reagan Presidential Library.

302   **"There are no jobs in politics"** Ronald Reagan, Letter to the Editor, *Oroville Mercury Register,* November 24, 1965, Box C32, 1965 Press Media, Ronald Reagan Library.

302   **"Roll it"** James M. Perry, "Ronald Reagan in a Dazzling Performance."

303   **California also leads in some things** "Ronald Reagan Announces for Governor," Campaign advertisement, January 4, 1966.

304   **"This is like a stage play"** Stuart Spencer OH.

304   **"She'd say something every now and then"** Ibid.

304   **"the daughter of one of the world's great neurosurgeons"** "Ronald Reagan" campaign brochure sponsored by the Orange County Reagan for Governor Committee, folder "66 Campaign: RR (4/4)," Box C32, 1966 Campaign, Reagan, Ronald: Gubernatorial Papers, Ronald Reagan Library.

304   **"Reagan Girls"** "Reagan Girls" Flyer, Box C33, Ronald Reagan Staff Interoffice Memos III, Ronald Reagan Library.

305   **mostly expunged his first marriage** Maureen Reagan, *First Father, First Daughter,* 149.

305   **"Ronald Reagan and his wife Nancy have two childen"** Ibid.

306   **"an ordinary citizen"** Reagan for Governor Committee, News Release, Noon April 19, folder "66 RR: Philosophy of Government Citizen Participation," Box C35, 1966 Campaign, Reagan, Ronald: Gubernatorial Papers 1966-75, Ronald Reagan Library.

306   **"Here's Boraxo waterless hand cleaner"** Ronald Reagan Advertisement for Boraxo, shown during *Death Valley Days*, December 27, 1964, Ronald Reagan Library.

306   **In one episode he played the nineteenth-century senator George Vest** "Tribute to the Dog," *Death Valley Days*, December 27, 1964.

307   **"I don't believe that just holding public office"** "Ronald Reagan for Governor," Campaign Advertisement 1966, http://www.youtube.com/watch?v=aHyt-l6XLAM.

307   **As the teleplay begins** "The Battle of San Francisco," *Death Valley Days,* March 18, 1965.

307   "People have been coming to this place" "Reagan Announces for Governor."

308   "You have read about the report" Reagan, *The Creative Society*, 125.

308   "That's the way you lose a mob" "The Battle of San Francisco."

308   "did more harm than anything to the Republican Party" Cannon, *Governor Reagan*, 142.

309   "We did some studies" Stuart Spencer OH.

309   **In California, actor Ronald Reagan and Mrs. Reagan arrive** "Ronald Reagan Nominated for California Governor," *Universal Newsreel*, November 8, 1966.

310   "Are you feeling all right?' Telephone conversation between Lyndon Johnson and Edmund G. "Pat" Brown, June 13, 1966, Citation #10228.

310   "President Eisenhower and [Republican Party chair] Ray Bliss" Joe Califano, letter to Ronald Reagan, June 10, 1966.

311   "You're selling everybody on the fact that you can't win!" Telephone conversation between Lyndon Johnson and Edmund G. "Pat" Brown, June 13, 1966, Citation #10228.

311   "California is the most populous state in the Union" "Political Battle for State Seen," *San Diego Union*, June 14, 1966, Box C35, 1966 Press Media II, Ronald Reagan Library.

311   "We've just got to go after him" Telephone conversation between Lyndon Johnson and Edmund G. "Pat" Brown, June 13, 1966, Citation #10228.

312   "Here in a brick house on a shaded lawn" Julius Duscha, "Ike Likes Reagan as 1968 Possibility," *Washington Post*, June 16, 1966.

312   "I've never advocated selling the Post Office" Robert Donovan, "Reagan Chides Brown in Deft Debut at National Press Club," *Los Angeles Times*, June 17, 1966.

312   "Right-winger" the columnist William S. White, "GOP Shake-up," *Washington Post,* June 21, 1966.

312   "Even a Reagan in the clothing of a right-winger" Ibid.

312   "I was unable to reach you by telephone" Richard Nixon, letter to Ronald Reagan, June 9, 1966, Box C29, 1966 Campaign: Gov. Personal Correspondence with Nixon, Richard M., Ronald Reagan Library.

313   "I won't try to write much of a letter" Ronald Reagan, letter to Richard Nixon, June 14, 1966, Box C29, 1966 Campaign: Gov. Personal Correspondence with Nixon, Richard M., Ronald Reagan Library.

313   "It has taken me all of my life" Ted Lewis, "Ronald Reagan Another Wendell Willkie," *New York Daily News*, June 17, 1966.

313   "The Great Society grows greater every day" David S. Broder, "Reagan Attacks the Great Society," *New York Times*, June 17, 1966.

Chapter Eleven: A Thousand Days

315   "While this period constitutes a thousand days" Robert Kintner, letter to Lyndon Johnson, August 18, 1966, Box 16, Confidential Files, LBJL.

315   gilded thousand days Kennedy's own thousand days actually numbered 1,037. LBJ reached one thousand days on August 17, 1966, and matched Kennedy's 1,037 on September 23, 1966. See Thomas Bailey, *Essays Diplomatic and Undiplomatic of Thomas Bailey*, 237.

316   "the Great Congress" "The Congress: The Late Great," *Time,* October 21, 1966.

316   The "B plus Congress" "The B+ Congress: Key Votes in the 89th," *New Republic*, October 22, 1966; "The Road Ahead," *The Progressive*, December 1, 1966.

316   "We prefer to call it the foot in the door Congress" Ibid.

317   "Historians in future decades" Thomas A. Bailey, "Johnson and Kennedy: The Two Thousand Days," *New York Times Magazine*, November 6, 1966.

317   *That way Kennedy would live on forever* Goodwin, *Lyndon Johnson*, 178.

319   "Disunity, frustration, suspicion" "Election 1966," *Saturday Evening Post*, November 15, 1966.

319   "You have a home, but what about interest rates?" "On Election Day," *New Republic*, November 5, 1966.

319   "we shall not rest until that war is won" Lyndon B. Johnson, "Address on the State of the Union" (speech, Washington, DC, January 8, 1964), *Public Papers of the Presidents, 1963-4*, Vol. I, 114.

320   Late that summer of 1966 "Nation: The Madman in the Tower," *Time*, August 12, 1966.

320   "Now we come here with mobs in the streets" "The Congress: New Game," *Time*, August 5, 1966.

321   "had never won anything" "The White Backlash," *Newsweek*, October 10, 1966.

321   Wallace was backing his wife, Lurleen Ibid.

322   "They're just out here for no other purpose" Telephone conversation between Richard Daley and LBJ, August 16, 1966, Citation #10614.

322   "There is a matter" "The Economy: A Call for Action," *Time*, September 9, 1966.

322   "From Vietnam . . . flows a river of woe" "Johnson and Kennedy: The Two Thousand Days."

323   "Don't pay any attention" Clifford, *Counsel to the President*, 417.

323   "should go all out, short of nuclear attack" Bill Moyers, Memorandum to Lyndon Johnson, June 9, 1966, WHCF, Box 82, PR 16, LBJL.

323   "Bomb the devil out of Haiphong Harbor!" "The Choice We Face," *The Progressive*, November 1966.

324   "For the first time now" Perlstein, *Nixonland*, 128; "Nixon, in Saigon, Bids US Bare Goals," *New York Times*, August 6, 1966.

325   "do not understand how a country" Bill Moyers, Memorandum to Lyndon Johnson, June 9, 1966, WHCF, Box 82, PR 16, LBJL.

325   It was followed by a White House reception "The White House: Three Ring Wedding," *Time*, August 5, 1966.

325   "semimonarchical event" Ibid.

325   "as proud as a man can be" "The Presidency: An Unusual Ceremony," *Time*, August 12, 1966.

325   "The wedding day will be something beautiful" "Three Ring Wedding."

327   "What do you think about the elections?" Telephone conversation between Lyndon Johnson and Richard B. Russell, June 2, 1966, Citation #10205.

328   "This is the off-year" "An Off Year Election with a Difference," *Life*, November 4, 1966.

328   "John Gardner has talked to Bill Moyers" Douglass Cater, Memorandum to Lyndon Johnson, EX/FG1, August 4, 1966.

328   **"My proposed theme"** Walt Rostow, Memorandum to Lyndon Johnson, June 6, 1966, WHCF, Box 82, PR 16, LBJL.

329   **"This stubborn, yearning man"** Tom Wicker, "Long Distance Runner," *Atlantic,* April 1966.

329   **"a dropout from the electoral college"** Jules Witcover, *Reporter,* August 11, 1966.

329   **"to lead this great country"** Ibid.

330   RFK MINUS LBJ IN 1972 . . . KENNEDY FOR PRESIDENT ANYTIME "The Bobby Phenomenon," *Newsweek,* October 24, 1966, 30-35.

330   **"We need help wherever we can get it"** Ibid., 30.

330   **"there is no Kennedy who does not feel"** "Kennedy Chemistry," *Newsweek,* October 3, 1966.

331   **By mid 1966, the Harris and Gallup polls both showed Bobby leading the president** "Bobby Phenomenon," 30.

331   **"This . . . is what every officeholder should do"** "LBJ Reaches Out to Rally His Consensus," *Life,* September 2, 1966. (emphasis added)

332   **"Instead of fifty states,"** "Across the River to Bathos," *Time,* October 14, 1966.

332   ALL HAIL TO JOHNSON "The Word From Washington," *Progressive,* December 1966.

333   **"conferring with his proconsuls"** Ibid.

333   **"I'm glad you're not standing for Prime Minister"** "The Presidency: On Top Down Under," *Time,* October 28, 1966.

333   **"I have said so often"** Lyndon Johnson, "Remarks at the Art Gallery of New South Wales" (speech, Sydney, Australia, October 22, 1966), *Public Papers of the Presidents,* 1966, Vol. II, 1251.

334   **"He went in . . . prepared to dislike Reagan"** Memo from Robert Kintner to Lyndon Johnson, June 21, 1966, CF/FG1, LBJL.

334   **In October, his face was featured on the cover of** *Time* "California: Ronald for Real," *Time,* October 7, 1966.

334   **He mocked the notion of a citizen-politician** Cannon, *Governor Reagan,* 151.

335   **"The governor's office . . . is not a movie set"** "Governor's Office," Brown Ad Transcripts, Box C32, Ronald Reagan Library.

335   **"I'm running against an actor"** Cannon, *Ronald Reagan: The Presidential Portfolio,* Vol. I, 40.

336   **"Who was it"** "California: Ronald for Real."

336   **"Reagan is anti-labor"** "Reagan for President," *New Republic,* July 2, 1966.

337   **"I had always thought"** Nancy Reagan, *My Turn,* 78.

337   **Orange County** McGirr, *Suburban Warriors,* 209.

337   **It had been a great night for Republicans** Walter Dean Burnham, "Death of the New Deal," *Commonwealth,* December 9, 1966.

338   "I AM LOOKING FORWARD TO WORKING WITH YOU" Telegram from Spiro T. Agnew to Ronald Reagan, November 9, 1966, Box C26, Personal Correspondence, Ronald Reagan Library.

338   **"In these circumstances"** "Republican Resurgence," *New York Times,* November 13, 1966.

339   "CONGRATULATIONS ON THAT GREAT VICTORY" Nelson Rockefeller, telegram

to Ronald Reagan, November 11, 1966, Box C29, 1966 Campaign: Gov. Personal Correspondence, Letters of Congratulations 2, Ronald Reagan Library.

339   **"I thought you would be interested"** Richard Nixon, letter to Ronald Reagan, November 28, 1966, Box C29, 1966 Campaign: Gov. Personal Correspondence, Letters of Congratulations 2, Ronald Reagan Library.

339   **"I think more than any other governor"** Ronald Reagan, letter to James A. Rhodes, November 21, 1966, Box C29, 1966 Campaign: Gov. Personal Correspondence, Letters of Congratulations, Ronald Reagan Library.

340   **"a distinguished physicist"** White, *Making of the President,* 35.

340   **"I've been a little disappointed"** Ronald Reagan, letter to Carl T. Curtis, November 28, 1966, Box C29, 1966 Campaign: Gov. Personal Correspondence, Letters of Congratulations 2, Ronald Reagan Library.

340   **"I think we can claim a mandate"** Ronald Reagan, letter to Edward J. Drewinski, December 8, 1966, Box C29, 1966 Campaign: Gov. Personal Correspondence, Letters of Congratulations 1, Ronald Reagan Library.

340   **"Some way"** Telephone Conversation between Richard Daley and LBJ, December 17, 1966, Citation #11145.

341   **"The mimeograph machines"** "Impact on Johnson; He May Have to Trim His Program," *New York Times,* November 13, 1966.

341   **"There was no question"** "Republican Resurgence."

341   **"In the space of a single Autumn day"** "GOP 66: Back on the Map," *Newsweek,* November 21, 1966.

341   **"The election results"** Walter Lippmann, "War and the Election," *Newsweek,* December 5, 1966.

342   **"The feeling is widespread"** "The Choice We Face," *The Progressive,* November 1966.

342   **"a fantastic mood"** Michael Harrington, "New Shape of American Politics," *Dissent,* January 1967.

342   **"If the Dixiecrat-Republican coalition"** Ibid.

342   **"young conservative"** William F. Buckley, "Election, What Did It Mean?" *National Review,* November 29, 1966.

343   **"I don't know"** Warren Weaver, "Governors Link Loss to Johnson," *New York Times*, December 16, 1966.

343   **"The Great Society is tarnished"** Telephone conversation between Richard Daley and LBJ, December 1966, Citation #11145.

344   *Look* **magazine planned to publish an excerpt** "Jackie Kennedy: Plaintiff," *Newsweek*, December 26, 1966.

345   **My dear Mrs. Kennedy** Lyndon Johnson, Letter to Jackie Kennedy, December 16, 1966, Special File on the Assassination of John F. Kennedy, Box 1, Manchester Files, LBJL.

346   **"a fraud"** Beschloss, *Taking Charge*, 16.

346   **"vicious, mean, dirty, low-down stuff** Ibid., 16.

347   *for one brief shining moment* Theodore White, "Epilogue," *Life*, December 3, 1963.

347   **"They're going to write history as they want it written"** Beschloss, *Taking Charge,* 16.

347   **she had met with the landscape architect** Sharon Francis OH I.

348 "I have so little time" James Reston, "Washington: LBJ—I Have So Little Time," *New York Times,* November 27, 1966.

Epilogue

349 "Governor Rockefeller of New York" Press Conference, National Governors Conference, 1967.

351 "Most South Carolinians" Ronald Reagan, *Reagan Talks to America,* 48.

351 His office maintained a thick file of index cards Box C39, Johnson Administration, Ronald Reagan Gubernatorial Campaign Files 1966, Ronald Reagan Library.

352 *Facing a projected 1968 budget deficit* William Conrad Gibbons, *Government and the Vietnam War,* 755.

352 *"it is increasingly clear to this reporter"* Walter Cronkite, "We Are Mired in Stalemate," CBS News, February 27, 1968.

352 "matchless boondoggle" Reagan, *Reagan Talks to America,* 52.

352 "leadership gap" Cannon, *Governor Reagan,* 260-1.

352 "There is a question abroad in the land" Reagan, *Reagan Talks to America,* 61.

353 Throughout 1967 and early 1968 For a detailed account of Johnson's deliberations on the 1968 campaign, see Dallek, *Flawed Giant,* 524-9.

354 Lyndon's "face was sagging" Johnson, *White House Diary,* 642.

354 "Remember . . . pacing and drama" Ibid., 645.

354 "With American sons in the field far away" Lyndon Johnson, "President Lyndon B. Johnson's Address to the Nation Announcing Steps To Limit the War in Vietnam and Reporting His Decision Not To Seek Reelection" (speech, Washington, DC, March 31, 1968), LBJL, http://www.lbjlib.utexas.edu/johnson/archives.hom/speeches.hom/680331.asp.

355 "those who love him must have loved him more" Johnson, *White House Diary,* 645.

355 "For those of you who are black" Robert F. Kennedy, "Statement on the Assassination of Martin Luther King Jr. (speech, Indianapolis, April 4, 1968), JFK Library, http://www.jfklibrary.org/Research/Research-Aids/Ready-Reference/RFK-Speeches/Statement-on-the-Assassination-of-Martin-Luther-King.aspx.

355 "Too horrible for words" Califano, *Triumph and Tragedy,* 297.

356 "Is he dead yet?" Ibid.

356 "I called her name and put out my hand" Johnson, *White House Diary,* 684.

356 "I hope . . . it may be said, a hundred years from now" Lyndon Johnson, "Annual Message to the Congress on the State of the Union" (speech, Washington, DC, January 14, 1969), http://www.lbjlib.utexas.edu/johnson/archives.hom/speeches.hom/690114.asp.

357 *"I seek to celebrate my glad release"* Johnson, *White House Diary,* 783.

357 "The Southerners . . . had had enough of gallant lost causes" White, *Making of the President 1968,* 241.

358 men with lunch pails Reeves, *President Kennedy,* 656-7.

360 "We have a group of elitists in Washington" Drew, *Portrait of an Election,* 116-117.

361 "I believe in states' rights" Ronald Reagan, "Speech at Neshoba County Fair"

(speech, Mississippi, August 3, 1980); Bob Herbert, "Righting Reagan's Wrongs," *New York Times*, November 13, 2007.

361 **"For those who have abandoned hope"** Ronald Reagan, "Address Accepting the Presidential Nomination at the Republican National Convention in Detroit" (speech, Detroit, July 17, 1980), *Public Papers of the Presidents*, http://www.presidency.ucsb.edu/ws/?pid=25970.

362 *In this present crisis* Ronald Reagan, "Inaugural Address" (speech, Washington, DC, January 20, 1981), *Public Papers of the Presidents*, 1981, 1.

363 **Reagan would add more debt to the nation's ledgers** Richard Darman, *Who's in Control*, 73.

364 **"The simple truth"** Ronald Reagan, "Remarks at a Fundraising Dinner Honoring Former Representative John M. Ashbrook" (speech, Ashland, OH, May 9, 1983), 1983, Vol. I, 670.

365 **"I've raised you girls"** Michael Beschloss, "In His Final Days, LBJ Agonized Over His Legacy," *Rundown*, December 4, 2012, http://www.pbs.org/newshour/rundown/2012/12/lbjs-last-interview.html

365 **"I'm talking to Tom Johnson"** Walter Cronkite, CBS Evening News, January 22, 1973, http://www.cbsnews.com/videos/walter-cronkite-announces-the-death-of-lbj/.

365 **"Well . . . we expected it."** Dallek, *Portrait of a President*, 372.

366 **most likely in the fashion of Johnson men, before he turned sixty-five** Beschloss, *Reaching for Glory*, 394.

366 **"Walter was a good friend and a capable person"** Marjorie Hunter, "Walter Wilson Jenkins, Aide to Lyndon Johnson," *New York Times*, November 26, 1985.

367 **"I remember one story"** Ronald Reagan, "Remarks on Presenting the Congressional Gold Medal to Lady Bird Johnson" (speech, Washington, DC, April 28, 1988), *Public Papers of the Presidents*, 1988, Vol. I, 528.

368 **"There will be some things of course that we will miss"** Skinner, *Life in Letters*, 126.

368 **"We'll preserve for our children this"** Ronald Reagan, "A Time for Choosing" (speech, October 27, 1964), http://www.reagan.utexas.edu/archives/reference/timechoosing.html.

Afterword

369 *"I know that for America there will always be a bright dawn"* Text of a letter written by Ronald Reagan announcing he has Alzheimer's disease, November 5, 1994, Ronald Reagan Library, http://www.reagan.utexas.edu/archives/reference/alzheimerletter.html.

371 **"The era of Big Government is over"** William J. Clinton, "Address Before a Joint Session of the Congress on the State of the Union" (speech, Washington, DC, January 23, 1996), *Public Papers of the Presidents*, http://www.presidency.ucsb.edu/ws/?pid=53091.

373 **"Reagan proved deficits don't matter"** John Cassidy, "Taxing," *New Yorker*, January 26, 2004.

Works Consulted

Oral Histories (OH)

Oral History Collection, Lyndon B. Johnson Presidential Library, Austin, TX

Bess Abell
George D. Aiken
Carl B. Albert
Stewart Alsop
George W. Ball
Hale Boggs
McGeorge Bundy
Horace Busby
Elizabeth (Liz) Carpenter
Clifton C. Carter
Douglass S. Cater
John Chancellor
Marie Fehmer Chiarodo
Clark M. Clifford
John Connally
Cartha D. DeLoach
Sharon Francis
Orville Freeman
Abe Fortas
Arthur J. Goldberg
Lady Bird Johnson
Arthur B. Krim
Godfrey McHugh
Robert S. McNamara
Harry C. McPherson, Jr.
Lawrence (Larry) O'Brien
Drew Pearson

Benjamin H. Read
George Reedy
Dean Rusk
Jewel Malechek Scott
Dorothy Territo
Helen Thomas
John G. Tower
Earl Warren
Lew Wasserman

***John F. Kennedy Oral History Collections, John F. Kennedy Presidential
Library and Museum, Boston, MA***

Sid Davis, JFK #1
Nancy Tuckerman and Pamela Turnure, JFK #1
Jack Valenti, JFK #1

***Robert F. Kennedy Oral History Collections, John F. Kennedy Presidential
Library and Museum, Boston, MA***

Joseph W. Alsop, RFK #1
Joseph W. Alsop, RFK #2
Joseph W. Alsop, RFK #3

***Ronald Reagan Gubernatorial Era Series, Bancroft Library, University
of California, Berkeley, CA***

Earl Dunckel, "Ronald Reagan and the General Electric Theater, 1954–1955"

***Powell Library Oral History Program, Governmental History Documentation
Project, University of California, Los Angeles, CA***

Neil Reagan, "Private Dimensions and Public Images: The Early Political Campaigns
of Ronald Reagan"

***Ronald Reagan Oral History, Miller Center, University of Virginia,
Charlottesville, VA***

Stuart Spencer

Manuscript Collections

Lyndon B. Johnson Presidential Library, Austin, TX

Diaries and Appointment Logs of Lyndon B. Johnson
Handwriting File
Office Files of the White House Aides

Joseph A. Califano, Jr.
Walter Jenkins
Harry C. McPherson
Bill Moyers

Office of the President Files
Social Files

Bess Abell's Subject Files
Liz Carpenter's Subject Files

Special File on the Assassination of John F. Kennedy

White House Central Files (WHCF)
Confidential File (CF)
Executive Series (EX)
Subject Files

Ronald Reagan Presidential Library, Simi Valley, CA

Reagan, Ronald: Governor's Papers, 1967–1975
1966 Campaign, Series I–V

Recorded telephone conversations are from *Presidential Recordings of Lyndon Baines Johnson*, Miller Center, University of Virginia, Charlottesville, VA, http://millercenter.org/scripps/archive/presidentialrecordings/johnson

Books

Acheson, Dean. *Among Friends: Personal Letters of Dean Acheson.* New York: Dodd, Mead, 1980.

Albert, Judith Clavir, and Stewart Edward Albert, eds. *The Sixties Papers: Documents of a Rebellious Decade.* New York: Praeger, 1984.

Alsop, Joseph. *I've Seen the Best of It: Memoirs.* Mount Jackson, VA: Axion Press, 1992.

Bailey, Thomas A. *Essays Diplomatic and Undiplomatic of Thomas A. Bailey,* eds. Alexander deConde and Armin Rappaport. New York: Appleton, 1969.

Baldrige, Letitia. *A Lady, First: My Life in the Kennedy White House and the American Embassies of Paris and Rome.* New York: Viking, 2001.

Beran, Michael Knox. *The Last Patrician: Bobby Kennedy and the End of American Aristocracy.* New York: St. Martin's Press, 1998.

Bermann, Larry. *Planning a Tragedy: The Americanization of the War in Vietnam.* New York: W. W. Norton, 1982.

Beschloss, Michael. *Reaching for Glory: Lyndon Johnson's Secret White House Tapes 1964–1965.* New York: Simon and Schuster, 2001.

————. *Taking Charge: The Johnson White House Tapes 1963–1964*. New York: Simon and Schuster, 1987.

Boyarsky, Bill. *Ronald Reagan: His Life and Rise to the Presidency*. New York: Random House, 1981.

Bradlee, Benjamin C. *Conversations with Kennedy*. New York: W. W. Norton, 1984.

————. *A Good Life: Newspapering and Other Adventures*. New York: Simon and Schuster, 1995.

Branch, Taylor. *At Canaan's Edge: America in the King Years, 1965–1968*. New York: Simon and Schuster, 2006.

————. *Pillar of Fire: America in the King Years, 1963–1965*. New York: Simon and Schuster, 1998.

Brinkley, Alan. *Liberalism and Its Discontents*. Cambridge, MA: Harvard University Press, 1998.

Bruck, Connie. *When Hollywood Had a King: The Reign of Lew Wasserman, Who Leveraged Talent into Power and Influence*. New York: Random House, 2003.

Buckley, William F., Jr. *Athwart History: Half a Century of Polemics, Animadversions, and Illuminations; A William F. Buckley, Jr., Omnibus*. New York: Encounter Books, 2010.

————. *Let Us Talk of Many Things: The Collected Speeches*. New York: Basic Books, 2008.

Busby, Horace. *The Thirty-First of March: An Intimate Portrait of Lyndon Johnson's Final Days in Office*. New York: Farrar, Straus and Giroux, 2005.

Cagin, Seth, and Philip Dray. *We Are Not Afraid: The Story of Goodman, Schwerner, and Chaney, and the Civil Rights Campaign for Mississippi*. New York: Bantam Books, 1991.

Califano, Joseph A., Jr. *The Triumph and Tragedy of Lyndon Johnson: The White House Years*. College Station: Texas A&M University Press, 2000.

Campbell, Joseph. *The Hero with a Thousand Faces*. Novato, CA: New World Library, 2008.

Cannon, Lou. *Governor Reagan: His Rise to Power*. New York: Public Affairs, 2003.

————. *President Reagan: The Role of a Lifetime*. New York: Public Affairs, 2000.

————. *Reagan*. New York: G. P. Putnam's Sons, 1982.

————. *Ronald Reagan: The Presidential Portfolio*. New York: Public Affairs, 2001.

————. *Ronnie and Jesse: A Political Odyssey*. Garden City, NY: Doubleday, 1969.

Caro, Robert A. *The Years of Lyndon Johnson: Master of the Senate*. New York: Vintage Books, 2003.

————. *The Years of Lyndon Johnson: Means of Ascent*. New York: Vintage Books, 1991.

————. *The Years of Lyndon Johnson: The Passage of Power*. New York: Vintage Books, 2013.

————. *The Years of Lyndon Johnson: The Path to Power*. New York: Vintage Books, 1990.

Carpenter, Liz. *Ruffles and Flourishes*. Garden City, NY: Doubleday, 1970.

Carson, Clayborne, ed. *The Autobiography of Martin Luther King, Jr.* New York: Warner Books, 1998.

————. *A Call to Conscience: The Landmark Speeches of Dr. Martin Luther King, Jr.* New York: IPM, 2001.

Chait, Jonathan. *The Big Con: The True Story of How Washington Got Hoodwinked and Hijacked by Crackpot Economics.* Boston: Houghton Mifflin, 2007.

Clifford, Clark, and Richard Holbrooke. *Counsel to the President: A Memoir.* New York: Random House, 1991.

Cohen, Lizabeth. *A Consumer's Republic: The Politics of Mass Consumption in Postwar America.* New York: Alfred A. Knopf, 2003.

Dallek, Matthew. *The Right Moment: Ronald Reagan's First Victory and the Decisive Turning Point in American Politics.* New York: Oxford University Press, 2004.

Dallek, Robert. *Flawed Giant: Lyndon Johnson and His Times, 1961–1973.* New York: Oxford University Press, 1998.

———. *Lone Star Rising: Lyndon Johnson and His Times, 1908–1960.* New York: Oxford University Press, 1991.

———. *Lyndon B. Johnson: Portrait of a President.* New York: Oxford University Press, 2004.

Darman, Richard Gordon. *Who's in Control?: Polar Politics and the Sensible Center.* New York: Simon and Schuster, 1996.

Davis, Deborah. *Party of the Century: The Fabulous Story of Truman Capote and His Black and White Ball.* Hoboken, NJ: John Wiley, 2006.

Davis, Patti. *The Way I See It: An Autobiography.* New York: Putnam, 1992.

Dean, Robert D. *Imperial Brotherhood: Gender and the Making of Cold War Foreign Policy.* Amherst: University of Massachusetts Press, 2001.

Deaver, Michael K. *Behind the Scenes.* New York: William Morrow, 1987.

———. *Nancy: A Portrait of My Years with Nancy Reagan.* New York: William Morrow, 2004.

Dugger, Ronnie. *The Politician: The Life and Times of Lyndon Johnson; The Drive for Power, from the Frontier to Master of the Senate.* New York: W. W. Norton, 1982.

Edwards, Anne. *Early Reagan: The Rise to Power.* Lanham, MD: Taylor Trade Publishing, 2012.

Edwards, Lee. *The Essential Ronald Reagan: A Profile in Courage, Justice, and Wisdom.* Lanham, MD: Rowman and Littlefield, 2005.

Evans, Rowland, and Robert Novak. *Lyndon B. Johnson: The Exercise of Power.* New York: New American Library, 1966.

Galbraith, John Kenneth. *The Affluent Society and Other Writings 1952–1967.* New York: Library of America, 2010.

Gallagher, Mary Barelli. *My Life with Jacqueline Kennedy.* Edited by Francis Spatz Leighton. New York: D. McKay, 1969.

Gentry, Curt. *J. Edgar Hoover: The Man and the Secrets.* New York: W. W. Norton, 1991.

Gibbons, William Conrad. *Government and the Vietnam War.* Washington: GPO, 1984.

Gillette, Michael L. *Lady Bird Johnson: An Oral History.* New York: Oxford University Press, 2012.

Gillon, Steven M. *The Kennedy Assassination—24 Hours After: Lyndon B. Johnson's Pivotal First Day as President.* New York: Basic Books, 2009.

Goldman, Eric F. *The Tragedy of Lyndon Johnson.* New York: Alfred A. Knopf, 1969.

Goldwater, Barry. *Conscience of a Conservative*. New York: MJF Books, 2007.

Goodwin, Doris Kearns. *The Fitzgeralds and the Kennedys: An American Saga*. New York: St. Martin's Press, 1991.

————. *Lyndon Johnson and the American Dream*. Norwalk, CT: Easton Press, 1983.

————. *No Ordinary Time: Franklin and Eleanor Roosevelt: The Home Front in World War II*. New York: Simon and Schuster, 1995.

Goodwin, Richard N. *Remembering America: A Voice from the Sixties*. Boston: Little, Brown, 1988.

Graham, Katharine. *Personal History*. New York: Alfred A. Knopf, 1997.

Guthman, Edwin O. *We Band of Brothers*. New York: Harper and Row, 1971.

Halberstam, David. *The Best and the Brightest*. New York: Modern Library, 2001.

————. *The Powers That Be*. Urbana: University of Illinois Press, 2000.

Hamilton, Edith. *The Greek Way*. New York: W. W. Norton, 1964.

Harrington, Michael. *The Other America: Poverty in the United States*. New York: Penguin Books, 1992.

Hayes, Harold. *Smiling Through the Apocalypse: Esquire's History of the Sixties*. New York: McCall, 1969.

Hayward, Steven F. *The Age of Reagan: The Conservative Counter Revolution, 1980–1989*. New York: Crown Forum, 2009.

Hersh, Seymour M. *The Dark Side of Camelot*. Boston: Little, Brown, 1997.

Hofstadter, Richard. *The Paranoid Style in American Politics and Other Essays*. New York: Vintage Books, 2008.

Holland, Max. *The Kennedy Assassination Tapes*. New York: Alfred A. Knopf, 2004.

Huie, William Bradford. *Three Lives for Mississippi*. Jackson: University Press of Mississippi, 2000.

Isaacson, Walter, and Evan Thomas. *The Wise Men: Six Friends and the World They Made; Acheson, Bohlen, Harriman, Kennan, Lovett, McCloy*. New York: Simon and Schuster, 1986.

Johnson, Lyndon Baines. *The Vantage Point: Perspectives of the Presidency, 1963–69*. New York: Holt, Rinehart and Winston, 1971.

Johnson, Rebekah Baines. *A Family Album*. New York: McGraw-Hill, 1965.

Johnson, Robert David. *All the Way With LBJ: The 1964 Presidential Election*. New York: Cambridge University Press, 2009.

Karnow, Stanley. *Vietnam: A History*. New York: Penguin, 1997.

Kelley, Kitty. *Nancy Reagan: The Unauthorized Biography*. New York: Simon and Schuster, 1991.

Kennedy, Jacqueline. *Historic Conversations on Life with John F. Kennedy*. Edited by Michael Beschloss and Caroline Kennedy. New York: Hyperion, 2011.

Kennedy, Robert F. *Thirteen Days: A Memoir of the Cuban Missile Crisis*. New York: W. W. Norton, 1971.

Lasky, Victor. *JFK: The Man and the Myth*. New York: Macmillan, 1963.

Lemann, Nicholas. *The Promised Land: The Great Black Migration and How It Changed America*. New York: Vintage Books, 1992.

Lerner, Max. *Ted and the Kennedy Legend: A Study in Character and Destiny*. New York: St. Martin's Press, 1980.

Lincoln, Evelyn. *My Twelve Years with John F. Kennedy*. New York: D. McKay, 1965.

Lipsitz, George. *Rainbow at Midnight: Labor and Culture in the 1940s.* Urbana: University of Illinois Press, 1994.

Manchester, William. *The Death of a President: November 20–November 25, 1963.* New York: Harper and Row, 1967.

———. *The Glory and the Dream: A Narrative History of America, 1931–1972.* Boston: Little, Brown, 1974.

Mann, Robert. *Daisy Petals and Mushroom Clouds: LBJ, Barry Goldwater, and the Ad that Changed American Politics.* Baton Rouge: Louisiana State University Press, 2011.

May, Ernest, and Phillip Zelikow, eds. *The Kennedy Tapes: Inside the White House During the Cuban Missile Crisis.* New York: W. W. Norton, 2002.

McGirr, Lisa. *Suburban Warriors: The Origins of the New American Right.* Princeton: Princeton University Press, 2001.

McCullough, David. *Truman.* New York: Simon and Schuster, 1992.

McNamara, Robert S. *Argument Without End: In Search of Answers to the Vietnam Tragedy.* New York: Public Affairs, 1999.

McPherson, Harry. *A Political Education: A Washington Memoir.* Boston: Houghton Mifflin, 1988.

Miller, Merle. *Lyndon: An Oral Biography.* New York: Putnam, 1980.

Morris, Edmund. *Dutch: A Memoir of Ronald Reagan.* New York: Random House, 1999.

Moynihan, Daniel Patrick. *A Portrait in Letters of an American Visionary.* New York: Public Affairs, 2010.

Noonan, Peggy. *When Character Was King: The Story of Ronald Reagan.* New York: Viking, 2001.

Patterson, James T. *Freedom Is Not Enough: The Moynihan Report and America's Struggle over Black Family Life; From LBJ to Obama.* New York: Basic Books, 2010.

———. *Grand Expectations: The United States 1945–1974.* New York: Oxford University Press, 1996.

Perlstein, Rick. *Before the Storm.* New York: Hill and Wang, 2001.

———. *Nixonland: The Rise of a President and the Fracturing of America.* New York: Scribner, 2008.

Posner, Gerald L. *Case Closed: Lee Harvey Oswald and the Assassination of JFK.* New York: Anchor Books, 2003.

Public Papers of the Presidents of the United States: John F. Kennedy. Washington: Government Printing Office, 1961–1963.

Public Papers of the Presidents of the United States: Lyndon B. Johnson. Washington: Government Printing Office, 1963–1969.

Public Papers of the Presidents of the United States: Ronald Reagan. Washington: Government Printing Office, 1981–1989.

Quirk, Lawrence J. *Kennedys in Hollywood.* Dallas: Taylor, 1996.

Rainwater, Lee and William Yancy. *The Moynihan Report and the Politics of Controversy.* New York: Cambridge University Press, 1967.

Reagan, Maureen. *First Father, First Daughter.* Boston: Little, Brown, 1989.

Reagan, Michael. *On the Outside Looking In.* New York: Zebra Books, 1988.

Reagan, Nancy. *I Love You, Ronnie: The Letters of Ronald Reagan to Nancy Reagan.* New York: Random House, 2000.

————. *My Turn: The Memoirs of Nancy Reagan*. New York: Random House, 1989.

Reagan, Ronald. *An American Life*. New York: Simon and Schuster, 1990.

————. *The Notes: Ronald Reagan's Private Collection of Stories and Wisdom*. Edited by Douglas Brinkley. New York: Harper, 2011.

————. *Ronald Reagan Talks to America*. Old Greenwich, CT: Devin Adair, 1983.

————. *Where's the Rest of Me? The Autobiography of Ronald Reagan*. New York: Sloan and Pearce, 1965.

Reeves, Richard. *President Kennedy: Profile of Power*. New York: Simon and Schuster, 1994.

————. *President Nixon: Alone in the White House*. New York: Simon and Schuster, 2001.

————. *President Reagan: The Triumph of Imagination*. New York: Simon and Schuster, 2005.

Regnery, Alfred. *Upstream: The Ascendance of American Conservatism*. New York: Threshold, 2008.

Renehan, Edward. *The Kennedys at War, 1937–1945*. New York: Doubleday, 2002.

Reston, James. *Deadline: A Memoir*. New York: Times Books, 1992.

Rorabaugh, W. J. *Kennedy and the Promise of the Sixties*. New York: Cambridge University Press, 2002.

Rovere, Richard Halworth. *Arrivals and Departures: A Journalist's Memoirs*. New York: Macmillan, 1976.

Russell, Jan Jarboe. *Lady Bird: A Biography of Mrs. Johnson*. New York: Scribner, 1999.

Samuel, Lawrence R. *Brought to You By: Postwar Television Advertising and the American Dream*. Austin: University of Texas Press, 2001.

Saunders, Frances Stonor. *The Cultural Cold War: The CIA and the World of Arts and Letters*. New York: New Press, 2000.

Schlafly, Phyllis. *A Choice, Not an Echo*. Alton: Pere Marquette, 1964.

Schlesinger, Arthur M., Jr. *Journals 1952–2000*. New York: Penguin, 2007.

————. *Robert Kennedy and His Times*. Boston: Houghton Mifflin, 1978.

————. *A Thousand Days: John F. Kennedy in the White House*. New York: Greenwich House, 1983.

————. *The Vital Center: The Politics of Freedom*. Cambridge, MA: Riverside Press, 1962.

Schlesinger, Robert. *White House Ghosts: Presidents and Their Speechwriters*. New York: Simon and Schuster, 2008.

Schulman, Bruce J. *Lyndon Johnson and American Liberalism: A Brief Biography with Documents*. New York: Palgrave Macmillan, 2007.

Schuparra, Kurt. *Triumph of the Right: The Rise of the California Conservative*. Armonk, NY: M. E. Sharpe, 1998.

Semple, Robert B., ed. *Four Days in November: The Original Coverage of the John F. Kennedy Assassination*. New York: St. Martin's Press, 2003.

Sheehan, Neil. *A Bright Shining Lie: John Paul Vann and America in Vietnam*. New York: Random House, 1988.

Shesol, Jeff. *Mutual Contempt: Lyndon Johnson, Robert Kennedy, and the Feud That Defined a Decade*. New York: W. W. Norton, 1997.

Siegel, Don. *A Siegel Film: An Autobiography*. Boston: Faber and Faber, 1996.

Skinner, Kiron K., ed. *Reagan: A Life in Letters*. New York: Free Press, 2003.

————. *Reagan: In His Own Hand*. New York: Free Press, 2001.

Smith, Sally Bedell. *Grace and Power: The Private World of the Kennedy White House*. New York: Random House, 2004.

Sorensen, Theodore C. *Counselor: A Life on the Edge of History*. New York: Harper, 2008.

————. *Kennedy*. New York: Harper and Row, 1965.

Steel, Ronald. *Walter Lippmann and the American Century*. New Brunswick, NJ: Transaction, 1999.

Stein, Jean. *American Journey: The Times of Robert Kennedy*. New York: Harcourt Brace, 1970.

Steinberg, Alfred. *Sam Johnson's Boy*. New York: Macmillan, 1968.

Talbot, David. *Brothers: The Hidden History of the Kennedy Years*. New York: Free Press, 2007.

Tanenhaus, Sam. *Death of Conservatism: A Movement and Its Consequences*. New York: Random House, 2010.

————. *Whittaker Chambers: A Biography*. New York: Random House, 1998.

Thomas, Evan. *Robert Kennedy: His Life*. New York: Simon and Schuster, 2000.

————. *The Very Best Men: Four Who Dared; The Early Years of the CIA*. New York: Simon and Schuster, 1995.

Valenti, Jack. *A Very Human President*. New York: W. W. Norton, 1975.

Wapshott, Nicholas. *Ronald Reagan and Margaret Thatcher: A Political Marriage*. New York: Sentinel, 2007.

Watson, Mary Ann. *The Expanding Vista: American Television in the Kennedy Years*. New York: Oxford University Press, 1990.

Whalen, Richard J. *Founding Father: The Story of Joseph P. Kennedy*. New York: New American Library, 1964.

White, Clifton F. and William J. Gill. *Suite 3505: The Story of the Draft Goldwater Movement*. New Rochelle, NY: Arlington House, 1967.

White, Theodore H. *In Search of History: A Personal Adventure*. New York: Warner Books. 1978.

————. *The Making of the President, 1964*. New York: Atheneum, 1964.

————. *The Making of the President, 1968*. New York: Atheneum, 1969.

White, William B. Smith. *The Professional: Lyndon B. Johnson*. Boston: Houghton Mifflin, 1964.

Wicker, Tom. *JFK and LBJ: The Influence of Personality on Politics*. New York: Morrow, 1968.

Wilentz, Sean. *The Age of Reagan: A History, 1974–2008*. New York: Harper, 2008.

Wills, Garry. *Confessions of a Conservative*. Garden City, NY: Doubleday, 1979.

————. *The Kennedy Imprisonment: A Meditation on Power*. Boston: Houghton Mifflin, 2002.

————. *Reagan's America: Innocents at Home*. New York: Penguin, 2000.

Young, Dwight, and Margaret Johnson, eds. *Dear First Lady: Letters to the White House*. Washington, DC: National Geographic, 2008.

Zelizer, Barbie. *Covering the Body: The Kennedy Assassination, the Media, and the Shaping of Collective Memory*. Chicago: University of Chicago Press, 1992.

Articles

"The 36th President." *New York Times,* November 24, 1963.

"12,000 Slosh Through the Rain to Get Report." *Washington Post,* September 29, 1964.

"Across the River to Bathos." *Time,* October 14, 1966.

"America's Long Vigil." *TV Guide,* January 25, 1964.

"At War in Vietnam." *New York Times,* July 14, 1965.

"Barry's War." *Newsweek,* January 27, 1964, 18.

"Brave Little Woman." *Newsweek,* February 17, 1964, 18.

"Business and Labor Meet the President." *Newsweek,* December 16, 1963, 65.

"Communism and Corruption." *Time,* October 30, 1964.

"The Congress: New Game." *Time,* August 5, 1966.

"Crime in the Streets." *Newsweek,* August 16, 1965.

"Crime: Summer Job." *Newsweek,* July 19, 1965.

"Despite 'Frugality' the Budget Rises." *Newsweek,* December 16, 1963, 21.

"The Enduring Legacy of Jacqueline Kennedy." *Washington Post,* November 19, 2013.

"Foreign Relations: While the Bullets Whiz." *Time,* March 12, 1965.

"Girl Describes Being Raped as Father Tried in Shooting." *Tuscaloosa News,* September 23, 1965.

"The Goldwater Nomination." *New York Times,* July 16, 1964.

"GOP '66: Back on the Map." *Newsweek,* November 21, 1966, 31.

"Hail to the Chief." *Newsweek,* February 1, 1965.

"Harlem: Hatred in the Streets." *Newsweek,* August 3, 1964.

"Illinois: Hot and Dry." *Time,* June 18, 1965.

"Investigations: Between Two Firsts." *Time,* February 14, 1964.

"The Issue of Integrity." *Christian Science Monitor,* October 17, 1964.

"Jackie Kennedy: Plaintiff." *Newsweek,* December 26, 1966.

"The Jenkins Report." *Time,* October 30, 1964.

"JFK's Alter-Ego." *New Republic,* January 27, 1964.

"Johnson Gives Wife, 51, Gift That Helped Him to Win Her." *New York Times,* December 23, 1963.

"Johnson Predicts Vietnam Setbacks: U.S. Force to Exceed 75,000." *New York Times,* July 10, 1965.

"Land of Kennedy." *Time,* December 13, 1963.

"The Late, Late Show." *Time,* June 24, 1964.

"LBJ: My Thanks to All America." *Newsweek,* November 9, 1964.

"Lyndon's Pace." *Newsweek,* October 19, 1964.

"Lyndon Johnson's Pledge." *Newsweek,* February 1, 1965.

"Mississippi—Everybody's Scared." *Newsweek,* July 6, 1964.

"Magic Majesty of Mrs. Kennedy." *London Evening Standard,* November 25, 1963.

"Mr. President, You're Fun!" *Life,* April 10, 1964.

"Nation: Aid to Appalachia." *Time,* March 12, 1965.

"Nation: Go-Day." *Time,* February 7, 1964.

"Nation: The Madman in the Tower." *Time,* August 12, 1966.

"Nation: Selma, Cont'd." *Time,* February 6, 1965.

"New Negro Riots Erupt on Coast." *New York Times,* August 13, 1965.

"Newsmakers." *Newsweek*, February 10, 1964, 48.

"On Election Day." *New Republic*, November 5, 1966.

"Opinion: Those Outside Our Family." *Time*, July 24, 1964.

"Ormes and the Man." *Time*, November 17, 1961.

"Out of Control." *Newsweek*, December 23, 1963.

"Palace Warfare." *Newsweek*, July 6, 1964.

"The People: The Mood of the Land." *Time*, December 20, 1963.

"Periscope." *Newsweek*, January 20, 1964; October 12, 1964; February 2, 1965.

"Pleiku and Qui Nhon: Decision Points." *Newsweek*, February 22, 1965.

"The Presidency: A Different Man." *Time*, November 4, 1964.

"The President: Business and Busyness." *Time*, December 20, 1963.

"The President: Home on the Range." *Newsweek*, December 30, 1963.

"The President: Spare Rib Summit." *Newsweek*, January 6, 1964.

"The Presidency: Just Storing Up Energy?" *Time*, July 17, 1964.

"The Presidency: Meanwhile, Down at the Ranch." *Time*, July 24, 1964.

"The Presidency: Whatever You Say, Honey." *Time*, January 3, 1964; *Newsweek*, December 28, 1964.

"Remembering JFK." *Newsweek*, August 2, 1965.

"Report Finds No Plot from Reds." *Los Angeles Times*, September 28, 1964.

"Republicans: Fastest Guns." *Newsweek*, January 20, 1964, 21.

"Republicans: The Poverty Issue." *Time*, January 24, 1964.

"Republican Resurgence." *New York Times*, November 13, 1966.

"The Senior Staff Man." *Time*, October 23, 1964.

"Summer Flowers in the Johnson Garden." *Washington Post*, July 7, 1963.

"Taylor Escapes Plot in Saigon." *New York Times*, July 20, 1965.

"TV Riot Squad." *Newsweek*, September 11, 1965.

"Vietnam: The Ritual of Decision." *Newsweek*, August 2, 1965.

"The Warren Commission Report." *Newsweek*, October 5, 1964, 32–64.

"The White Backlash." *Newsweek*, October 10, 1966.

"The White House: Home Away from Home." *Newsweek*, December 23, 1963, 16.

"The White House: Three Ring Wedding." *Time*, August 5, 1966.

"Who Would Run Best Against LBJ?" *Newsweek*, January 13, 1964.

Altschuler, Bruce E. "Lyndon Johnson and the Public Polls." *Public Opinion Quarterly*, Fall 1986.

Alsop, Joseph. "Matter of Fact: The State of LBJ." *Washington Post*, July 5, 1965.

Alsop, Stewart. "Can Goldwater Win in 1964?" *Saturday Evening Post*, August 24, 1964.

Bailey, Thomas A. "Johnson and Kennedy: The Two Thousand Days." *New York Times Magazine*, November 6, 1966.

Bergholz, Richard. "Young GOP Refuses Party Loyalty Pledge." *Los Angeles Times*, February 16, 1964.

Beschloss, Michael. "In His Final Days, LBJ Agonized over His Legacy." *Rundown*, December 4, 2012, http://www.pbs.org/newshour/rundown/2012/12/lbjs-last-interview.html

Bradlee, Ben. "What's Bobby Going to Do?—An Informal Conversation with RFK." *Newsweek*, July 6, 1964.

Buckley, William F., Jr. "JFK: The Morning After." *National Review*, December 7, 1963.

————. "Our Mission Statement." *National Review,* November 19, 1955.

Cassidy, John. "Taxing." *New Yorker,* January 26, 2004.

Crawford, Kenneth. "Washington: Disrobing the King." *Newsweek,* July 7, 1965.

Evans, Rowland, and Robert Novak. "The Jenkins Affair." *Washington Post,* August 4, 1964.

————. Inside Report: The Johnson-Kennedy Split." *Washington Post,* August 4, 1964.

Erskine, Hazel Gaudet. "The Polls: Kennedy as President." *Public Opinion Quarterly* XXVIII, 1964.

Feldman, Jacob J., and Paul B. Sheatsley. "The Assassination of President Kennedy: Preliminary Report on Public Reactions and Behavior." *Public Opinion Quarterly* XXVII, no. 2, 1964.

————. "A National Survey on Public Reactions and Behavior." In *The Kennedy Assassination and the American Public: Social Communication in Crisis.* Edited by Bradlee S. Greenberg and Edwin B. Parker. Stanford: Stanford University Press, 1965.

Gemmill, Henry. "Arrest of Johnson Aide Could Bolster GOP's Election Day Chances." *Wall Street Journal,* October 16, 1964.

Greenberg, Carl. "Goldwater Says It Would be Party Victory." *Los Angeles Times,* June 3, 1964.

Harris, Louis. "The Backlash Issue." *Newsweek,* July 13, 1964, 24.

Hill, Gladwin. "Nixon Denounces Press as Biased." *New York Times,* November 8, 1962.

Hughes, Emmet John. "The Defeating of LBJ." *Newsweek,* February 22, 1964, 17.

Hunter, Marjorie. "Walter Jenkins, Aide to Lyndon Johnson." *New York Times,* November 26, 1985.

Johnston, Richard J. H. "William Buckley Opens Headquarters." *New York Times,* August 31, 1965.

Jones, Theodore. "Uneasy Calm in Harlem." *New York Times,* July 17, 1965.

Kempton, Murray. "Pure Irish." *New Republic,* February 15, 1964.

Kentworthy, E. W. "President Signs Civil Rights Bill." *New York Times,* July 2, 1964.

————. "Johnson Signs Voting Rights Bill." *New York Times,* August 7, 1965.

Lewis, Anthony. "Warren Commission Finds Oswald Guilty and Says Assassin and Ruby Acted Alone." *New York Times,* September 28, 1964.

Lewis, Ted. "Ronald Reagan Another Wendell Willkie." *New York Daily News,* June 17, 1966.

Lippmann, Walter. "The Goldwater Threat." *Newsweek,* July 6, 1964.

————. "The Hard Lesson." *Newsweek,* July 10, 1965.

————. "Today and Tomorrow." *Washington Post,* December 3, 1963.

MacDonald, Dwight. "Our Invisible Poor." *New Yorker,* January 19, 1963.

Mohr, Charles. "Attacks Provoke Goldwater Camp." *New York Times,* May 30, 1964.

————. "Johnson Refers to Jenkins Case." *New York Times,* October 28, 1964.

————. "Johnsons Return to White House." *New York Times,* January 26, 1965.

————. "President Is Ill: Goes to Hospital with Bad Cough." *New York Times,* January 24, 1965.

————. "President Sees a Unity Mandate." *New York Times,* November 4, 1964.

————. "President Signs Education Bill at His Old School." *New York Times,* April 12, 1965.

————. "Senator Charges That President Changed Civil Rights Stand." *New York Times,* July 16, 1964.

Morris, John D. "President Signs Medicare Bill; Praises Truman." *New York Times,* July 12, 2007.

Nemy, Enid. "Lady Bird Johnson, 94, Dies." *New York Times,* July 12, 2007.

O'Brien, George. "France and Texas Contribute to Décor in the Johnsons' Washington Home." *New York Times,* October 31, 1961.

Perry, James R. "Ronald Reagan in a Dazzling Performance." *National Observer,* January 10, 1966.

Plimpton, George. "The Story Behind a Non-Fiction Novel." *New York Times,* January 16, 1966.

Raymond, Jack. "President Leaves Spotlight to GOP." *New York Times,* July 12, 1964.

Reston, James B. "The Mood of the Capital: Change and Continuity." *New York Times,* December 13, 1963.

————. "Saigon: The Tragic Paradox of Vietnam." *New York Times,* August 29, 1965.

————. "The Three Telephone Man in the White House." *New York Times,* December 7, 1963.

————. "Underground Campaign for the Vice Presidency." *New York Times,* April 5, 1964.

————. "What Goldwater Lost." *New York Times,* November 4, 1964.

Schlesinger, Arthur. "A Eulogy for JFK." *Saturday Evening Post,* December 14, 1963.

Sitton, Claude. "3 In Rights Drive Reported Missing." *New York Times,* June 24, 1964.

Stern, Laurence. "Johnson to Remain in Hospital for Rest." *Washington Post,* January 24, 1965.

Trippett, Frank. "LBJ's Lady Bird Johnson—First Lady of the Land." *Newsweek,* December 28, 1964.

Turner, Wallace. "Miller Stresses the Jenkins Case." *New York Times,* October 21, 1964.

Weinraub, Bernard. "Mondale Says Reagan Note Compared Kennedy to Marx." *New York Times,* October 24, 1984.

Weisel, Al. "LBJ's Gay Sex Scandal." *Out,* December 1999.

White, Theodore. "Epilogue." *Life,* December 6, 1963.

White, William S. "GOP Shake-Up." *Washington Post,* June 21, 1966.

Wicker, Tom. "A Hero's Burial." *New York Times,* November 26, 1963.

————. "Johnson Signs Retraining Bill with 34 Pens and a Flow of Wit." *New York Times,* December 19, 1963.

————. "President Bars Kennedy, Five Others, from Ticket." *New York Times,* July 31, 1964.

Witkin, Richard. "William Buckley Jr. Is Reported Considering Running for Mayor." *New York Times,* June 4, 1965.

Index

Johnson, Lynda (daughter of Johnson),
91, 93, 105, 226, 257, 354
Johnson, Lyndon Baines, *x*, 2, 56, *370.
See also* Great Society; *and specific
legislation*
ambition of, 14–15, 92, 119, 325, 355
approval ratings and, 325–26, 331,
352–53
Asian tour of, 332–33
Baker scandal and, 19, 207
beagles and, 100
becomes president, ix, 14–15, 56
bill-signing ceremonies, 95
birth of, 11–12
Bobby Kennedy and, 22–27, 61–62,
177–84, 205, 210, 244, 346
Bobby Kennedy assassination and,
355–56
Bobby Kennedy's presidential campaign of 1968 and, 330–31, 343,
346
Bobby Kennedy's Senate campaign
and, 204–5, 221
cabinet and, 183
campaign ads and, 195–97
centrist voters and, 116
childhood and early life of, xxix–xxx,
9–14, 111–13
Civil Rights Act and, xviii–xix, 95–96,
163–70, 188, 245, 344
civil rights leaders and, *160*, 163–66
Clinton and, 371
Congress and, 94–95
as congressional aide, under Roosevelt,
103
crime policy and, 265
daughter Luci's wedding and, 325
daughters and, 365
death of, 365–66
Democratic convention of 1964 and,
173–64, 188–92
Democratic convention of 1968 and,
356
early congressional career of, 109
early presidency and hard work of,
8–10, 14–16, 19–29, 89–94, 104–5,
110, 126, 128–32
early teaching in Texas and, 253, 258
economic policy and, 105–6, 236, 322

education policy and, xiv, 232, 258,
333
Eisenhower and, 110
Eugene McCarthy challenges, in 1968,
353–54
extramarital affairs of, 102–3
father's financial problems and,
112–13
FBI and, 65–66
fears of, 65–66, 318–19
finances of, 202
Goldwater and, 129, 156–57
Great Society and, xiv, 132, 231–44,
269–70, 277, 286, 324, 340–41, 343
health problems and anxiety of,
174–75, 225–31
homes of, in Washington, 17–18,
98–99
housing discrimination bill and,
320–31
HUD created by, 286
Humphrey chosen as VP by, 177,
180–84, 192
Humphrey's presidential campaign
and, 356
image problems and, 274–75
Jackie Kennedy and, 57–59, 87,
130–31, 273, 344–46
Jenkins scandal and, 200–215, 244
Joe Kennedy and, 84
John F. Kennedy assassination and,
xxx, 2, 52, 5–6, 8–10, 65–66, 130,
344–45, 362
John F. Kennedy funeral and, 28–29,
57–61
John F. Kennedy myth and, 61, 68,
77–78, 117–18, 272–74, 315–19, 347,
375
John F. Kennedy's cabinet and staff
and, 20–22, 61–63, 66–68, 91
labor and, 110
leadership by example and, xi
legacy of, 366–67, 375
legislative achievements of, xiv, xxiii,
77–78, 91, 94–95, 231–41, 253–54,
315–18, 375
loyalty and, 275
Manchester's *Death of a President*
and, 344–47

About the Author

JONATHAN DARMAN is a writer in New York City. He is a former correspondent for *Newsweek*, where he covered national politics, including John Kerry's presidential campaign in 2004 and Hillary Clinton's in 2008. This is his first book.